Latinos and Citizenship

Latinos and Citizenship:
The Dilemma of Belonging

Edited by
Suzanne Oboler

First published in 2006 by
PALGRAVE MACMILLAN™
175 Fifth Avenue, New York, N.Y. 10010 and
Houndmills, Basingstoke, Hampshire, England RG21 6XS.
Companies and representatives throughout the world.

PALGRAVE MACMILLAN is the global academic imprint of the Palgrave Macmillan division of St. Martin's Press, LLC and of Palgrave Macmillan Ltd. Macmillan® is a registered trademark in the United States, United Kingdom and other countries. Palgrave is a registered trademark in the European Union and other countries.

ISBN-10: 1-4039-6739-3   hardcover
ISBN-13: 978-1-4039-6739-8 hardcover
ISBN-10: 1-4039-6740-7   paperback
ISBN-13: 978-1-4039-6740-4 paperback

Library of Congress Cataloging-in-Publication Data

Oboler, Suzanne.
    Latinos and citizenship: the dilemma of belonging/Suzanne Oboler.
    p. cm.
    Includes bibliographical references and index.
    ISBN 1-4039-6739-3—ISBN 1-4039-6740-7 (alk. paper)
    1. Hispanic Americans—Politics and government. 2. Hispanic Americans—Cultural assimilation. 3. Immigrants—United States—Political activity. 4. United States—Ethnic relations. 5. Citizenship—United States. I. Title.

  E184.S75L3675 2006
  323.089'68073—dc22   2006045142

A catalogue record for this book is available from the British Library.

Design by Macmillan India Ltd.

First edition: November 2006

10 9 8 7 6 5 4 3 2 1

Printed in the United States of America.

Contents

List of Table

PART I

Introduction

CHAPTER 1

Redefining Citizenship as a Lived Experience

Suzanne Oboler

To be rooted is perhaps the most important and least recognized need of the human soul.

—*Simone Weil*

It is easier to view an individual as a non citizen than as a non-person.

—*Alexander Bickel*

The nation is, at once, imposed but also willed, from whence its strength.

—*L. Febvre*

INTRODUCTION

In recent years, the concept of citizenship has been increasingly discussed by scholars, particularly in Western nations.[1] Defined variously as a legal status, a political activity, a set of rights, and a collective identity (Bosniak, 2000a: 452) the concept has been debated with an urgency matched only by a simultaneous awareness of the unabated changes wrought by an evermore rampant globalization process on the autonomy of the nation-state throughout the world.

Perhaps nothing has led us to recognize the relevance of this discussion for the future of the US as a "national community" more poignantly than a poor African American woman's nationally televised, circle of decision-makers, or on court cases that have either reinforced or challenged one another in defining the scope of rights and beneficiaries of citizenship. The historical origin and political motive force of this selective and noninclusive process of defining the citizenry as well as the modes of participation in the national polity is, of course, race. Both the laws and the courts ultimately aimed to specify the role and implications of "race" in determining who could be a citizen, as well as in clarifying the responsibility of the state to the citizenry (Lopez, 1998; Johnson, 1998; Ngai, 2005).

Conflating the terms "citizen" and "People" in his decision in the *Dred Scott v. Sanford* case of 1857, for example, Chief Justice Roger Taney argued that the nation's Founding Fathers did not mean to include blacks when they spoke of "the People of the United States."[2] The subsequent Civil Rights Act of 1866 was specifically designed to reverse the *Dred Scott* decision (Bickel, 1975: 41–43), and was followed by the 14th Amendment, ratified in 1868, which created a *national* citizenry and established the principle of equality under the law for all people born in the US (Foner and Mahoney, 1995: 80). In adding the 14th Amendment to the Constitution, the 1868 Congress was not only acknowledging the inclusion of African Americans in the polity. It was also—and perhaps more significantly—expanding, albeit implicitly, the previous, more restricted understanding of the national community to include the idea that *all* categories of citizenship, and of rights, have to be publicly discussed in relation to all persons involved, rather than in relation to only one or another population group.

Less than two decades later, however, the *Plessy v. Ferguson* decision of 1896 effectively challenged that amendment. Ruling that "legislation is incapable of eradicating racial instincts," it established racial segregation as the law of the land for the next 60 years (Ringer, 1983).[3]

Through *Brown v. Board of Education* (Kluger, 2004), the Supreme Court ended legal segregation in 1954, thus countering the *Plessy* ruling by pointing to the ways that the psychological damage created by segregation prevented black children's access to equal opportunity. The *Brown* decision exemplified the Court's commitment at that time to what Aleinikoff (2002) has called "a powerful equality agenda" aimed at "ending the second class citizenship of Black Americans" (43). Moreover, "Mexican Americans were also recognized as a protected class. *Hernandez v. Texas,* 247 U.S. 475 (1954), appears in the same volume as *Brown*" (2002: 221, n. 41)

Still, it is important to keep in mind that

Citizenship was not a major focus of the Court in pre-Warren Court days. Birthright citizenship for African Americans and Mexican Americans was not seen as a challenge to the structures of legal discrimination and social segregation. Citizenship was understood as a status connoting state membership—a right to a passport, diplomatic protection, and (for men) the duty to serve in the armed forces. It guaranteed neither the right to vote nor entitlement to social welfare programs. (Aleinikoff, 2002: 39)

As such, it took the subsequent Civil Rights movements of the 1960s to create the various Civil Rights acts specifically aimed at enforcing the *Brown* decision, ultimately paving the way for the extension of rights and entitlements of US citizenship to racial(ized) minorities, women, and other groups.

In fact, as discussed below, the development of the Civil Rights movements of the 1960s exemplifies the extent to which the meaning of citizenship is ultimately only defined through struggle and political mobilization. Moving from the achievement of legal equality to the demand for social equality—that is, from an understanding of citizenship as an abstract concept, to that of citizenship as a lived experience—the era highlighted the need for an ongoing process of participation in a movement that continuously generates and reaffirms individuals' self-respect, and hence creates the conditions to experience belonging to a community of equals (Goodwyn, 1977; King, 1992; Evans and Boyte, 1992). From this point of view, *Brown* was the legal culmination of a process that was to reopen the national debate on the meanings of freedom, equality, and democracy as forcefully as the abolition of slavery had done in the aftermath of the Civil War almost 100 years earlier. The policies enacted in the last third of the 20th century represent, then, a new attempt to create a national community of equals—an effort grounded in the *explicit acknowledgment* of the historical role of race in shaping the political reality and social value of citizenship in the US (Chafe, 1986: 127–148; Mendel-Reyes, 1995).

Despite the gains of the Civil Rights movements of the 1960s, the notion of citizenship and the "imagined community" (Anderson, 1991) to which citizenship refers have been on the wane. Increasingly, citizenship is being conceptualized primarily in juridical terms in relation to noncitizens and (im)migrants, even while the state is strengthening its prerogatives in narrowing both the practical scope of the rights and benefits granted under this particular entitlement, and the beneficiaries, especially in relation to noncitizens. Indeed, as the essays included in this anthology suggest, the idea of citizenship in the 21st century seems more important to noncitizens than it is to those who are full citizens. For as the lived experience of Latino/as and African Americans increasingly attests, citizenship is meaningful only in the lives of those who continue to be excluded from the rights and benefits it guarantees. Moreover, as several scholars have long emphasized, the connotations of US citizenship, particularly with reference to racial(ized) minorities such as African Americans and Latino/as, are centered around issues of exclusion.

Thus, the Katrina disaster once again lays bare the extent to which underlying the unprecedented concern with the notion of "difference" in national communities is the by far more worse crisis in the very notion of community. Contrary to those who, like Samuel Huntington (2004), insist on blaming the presence of "the Other"—however that "Other" might be defined—for the social and cultural ills besetting contemporary US society, what is actually at stake is not the notion of difference itself, but rather the question of what binds people together into a self-conscious community today. As the Hurricane Katrina debacle has clearly exemplified, and as Jonas and Tactaquin (2004) aptly state, "Once the government begins to strip away the rights of the most vulnerable (Arab and Arab-American communities), the 'spillover' effect is very rapid and dangerous for all immigrants and other noncitizens— and eventually for US citizens as well."

In fact, Jonas and Tactaquin's comment lends credence to Alexander Bickel's skepticism about the concept of citizenship itself. Referring to its "thrust" as "parochial and exclusive," he argues forcefully against those who have historically upheld Justice Taney's conflation of the terms "people of the United States" and "citizens" as synonymous in the *Dred Scott* case:

> A relationship between government and the governed that turns on citizenship can always be dissolved or denied. Citizenship is a legal construct, an abstraction, a theory. No matter what the safeguards, it is at best something given, and given to some and not to others, and it can be taken away. It has always been easier, it always will be easier, to think of someone as a noncitizen, than to decide that he is a non-person. (Bickel, 1975: 53)

And yet, the extent to which this observation, basically relevant to the wealthy developed societies in the Northern hemisphere is limited—in both time and space—is daily exemplified by the plight of the stateless Palestinian people and, to use the eloquent Brechtian metaphor, the latest "harvest of sorrow": the Darfur refugees and their millions-strong kindred within and across sovereign states. Thus, it is in view of this contemporary dialectic that the relevance of citizenship as a possible restraint on globalized racism and economic pillage can be discussed.

Within this framework, the present anthology is very much a product of our times. For what is currently at stake in the US—for citizens and noncitizens alike—is the meaning and social value of citizenship. Indeed, only in this context of questioning what should or could bind people together today does the unprecedented weight of "difference" make sense. Indeed, as the Katrina tragedy again makes clear, the prevalence of the notion of "difference" itself has become a symptom of the crisis of community and indeed a contributor to this crisis. Hence, our aim is to rethink the meaning of belonging to a political community that is in the midst of easily ascertainable disintegration owing to the ongoing racism in the nation.

From the pre–Civil War era to the present, citizenship in the US cannot be understood without reference to the history of race relations and discrimination against nonwhite people that has long structured political and social relations in US society. As Renato Rosaldo (1993) has pointed out, through its exclusionary structures, US citizenship has long served as a proxy for race—historically defining inclusion and exclusion—not so much in its theoretical, legal formulations but rather in the differentiated daily-life realities and expectations of this society's members. From this perspective, we have to take seriously the idea that there has always existed a glaring difference between the letter and the spirit of the law—that is, the laws enacted by the state and often discussed as "reality" by members of white and privileged sectors of our society—and the actual lived experience of people of color, including the distinctive experiences of immigrants.

Our point of departure in this volume is thus the contemporary reemergence of racism, both in explicitly social terms, and in international relations. Suffice it to think of racial profiling posited officially as seemingly "predictable" and perhaps "necessary," to ensure "national security." At the same time, the decision to address the changing meanings of contemporary citizenship, and its corollary, the dilemma of belonging, from the specific perspective of the lived experience of Latino/as in the US, is not fortuitous. While more than 50% of the over 40 million Latino/as in the US are today US citizens, either by birth or through naturalization, this "ethnic group," which was first officially created and labeled "Hispanic" by an administrative fiat of the US Census Bureau's Office of Management and Budget in 1977 (Oboler, 1995), combines two historical minorities (Mexican Americans and Puerto Ricans, whose US citizenship dates back to the mid-19th century and early 20th century, respectively) with the growing numbers of people of Latin American descent who have arrived in the US in the post–World War II period and who live in this society as citizens or legal residents, as exiles, or as refugees. In addition, the umbrella designation of "Hispanic" (or its grassroots variation, "Latino/a") includes an unknown number of undocumented workers, whose lives are consistently disrupted by the ambiguous and changing meanings, political disputations, uses, and social implications of citizenship in US society (Hondagneu-Sotelo, 1994; Jonas and McCaughan, 1994; Perea, 1997; Chávez, 1997).

The fact that Latino/as do not share a common legal status and that they have been racialized (and hence officially homogenized) through the label "Hispanic" (Oboler, 1995) is undoubtedly an effective and time-honored method of social control. The label serves, on the one hand, to divide those so designated from others in similar positions or from potential allies in the wider society. On the other, it serves to keep control over those who have not actually been conquered through a combination of the state-organized "trickle down" strategy for the distribution of social benefits and the simultaneous stimulation of competition for scarce social resources and legitimate positions among the group members. Through this "ethnic" version of "divide" and control, then, the perpetuation of racial stereotyping and the image of ineradicable foreignness are guaranteed. Thus, to the extent that Latino/as continue to be the one population that, whether formally citizens or not, is consistently considered "alien" in their own land, they will continue to be an essential component of discussions on the changing meanings of citizenship in the US context, while also remaining central to US immigration policy and hemispheric power dynamics.

Focusing specific attention on the meaning and social value of citizenship for both the Latino/a population as a whole as well as for the specific national origin groups encompassed by this label, this volume brings together broad theoretical considerations of various aspects of the concept with discussions of historical and contemporary case studies and issues pertaining to Latino/as within contemporary debates on citizenship. The essays are grounded in the complex realities of Latino/as' historical and continuing struggles against exclusion, access to dual citizenship, multiple national allegiances, transnational political and social participation, political and social status, and regional cultural citizenship and loyalties. In so doing, the contributors seek to address broader fundamental questions about contemporary US citizenship and belonging, such as: What does it mean, in the current context of globalization and the consequent changing nature of the state, to belong to a national community of citizens? Who belongs, and how do people experience that belonging today? How do we even "know" that we belong?

While the state has various legal procedures for determining belonging, the experience of Latino/as—like that of African Americans, Native Americans, and other people of color in the US—would suggest that there is more to the sense of belonging than the formal state rules and regulations concerning birthplace, naturalization, and citizenship (Hedetoft and Hjort, 2002). Who then has the right to define the experience of belonging for those whom mainstream conceptions continue to define as "the Other" within a nation? Who determines who can and will be part of a national community, and on what grounds?

To address these questions, this anthology examines the varied ways in which the definition and social value of citizenship are being challenged and reconfigured by the different meanings attributed to citizenship by Latino/as, as well as by the social movements and transnational initiatives undertaken by Latino/a citizens and immigrants alike. For whether as second-class citizens or as noncitizens, Latino/as are engaged in constant dialogue with the changing state rules of citizenship (Coutin, 2003). Nowhere is this more visible today than in the massive, national protests of 2006, led and organized primarily by Latino/as, but also including nationals from other countries, against HR 4437, the anti-immigration legislation that specifically called for the criminalization of all undocumented immigrants and of any institution or person who came to their aid. The pro-immigrant marches and protests that swept across the major cities of the US in response to this legislation, originally proposed by Congressman Sensenbrenner, and which passed by the House of Representatives on December 16, 2005, served to confirm once again that practical issues, such as employment or wages, are not always the only, nor actual, reasons why people clamor and "stand up to be counted" (Goodwyn, 1977, King, 1992). Instead, the main mobilizing force of the 2006 demonstrations is the fact that across the country, immigrants—and indeed, most Latino/as—perceive the attempt at criminalizing immigrants as a direct attack on their very dignity and humanity. In short, as a result of their varied participation in the public sphere, and regardless of their status, Latino/as are simultaneously contributing, once again, to the reconfiguration of the meaning of belonging to a collectivity—and hence of citizenship in its broadest sense—through their struggles against ongoing exclusion and for social justice and the affirmation of human dignity.

CITIZENSHIP AND STRUGGLES FOR POLITICAL INCLUSION AND DIGNITY IN THE 20TH CENTURY

Citizenship has traditionally been understood as a designated legal status, a relationship between an individual and the nation-state that defines the terms of his or her political membership in society (Barbalet, 1988). Throughout the 20th century, there was an unprecedented expansion of citizenship to include economic and social rights. Particularly in the post–World War II period, and largely as a result of various minorities' struggles for inclusion—the best known and perhaps most successful of which are the Civil Rights movements of the 1960s and 1970s—there has been a significant expansion of political, civil, and, particularly, social rights for various sectors previously excluded from full community membership in the sense of meaningful belonging and contribution to the polity. These include African Americans, Latino/as, and other racialized populations, women, gays and lesbians, and the handicapped. While the struggles were waged by specific groups and responded to the specific and differentiated realities of their members, many of the changes inevitably benefited the entire society through the overall expansion of the scope of individual rights. This, in turn, represents a shift and expansion of both the meaning and the practical experience of citizenship in the US.

In hindsight, the changes illuminate the extent to which, prior to the civil rights era, various sectors of the US population were excluded from full and equal participation in the polity. Indeed, as Lorrin Thomas argues in her contribution to this volume, the struggles that took place in the decades prior to the beginning of the civil rights movements can be rightfully called the precursors of what was to become "a real rights revolution." Writing about Puerto Ricans' early struggles demanding that "liberal citizenship live up to its ideals of 'liberty and sovereignty,'" as one activist of the time phrased it, Thomas describes the ways that Puerto Rican activism during the 1930s sought to claim equality and rights for all Puerto Ricans, both on the island and in the mainland. Since US citizenship was granted to all Puerto Ricans in 1917, New York City's early migrants developed and articulated expectations and practices of citizenship that in effect sought to connect their rights in the local and homeland arenas. As Thomas writes, in so doing, Puerto Ricans developed a new framework during the New Deal era, grounded in the presumption of "a necessary relationship between, on the one hand, their social rights as US citizens in a local arena (New York City) and, on the other hand, their political and civic rights as US citizens in a national/international arena (Puerto Rico)." Noting that the meanings and definitions of citizenship were in flux for all Americans in the 1930s, Thomas uses historical events as concrete examples to detail the changing meanings and social value that Puerto Ricans placed on citizenship at the time. At the same time, she points to some of the issues that differentiated their struggle against discrimination and exclusion from that of African Americans. Thomas argues that although Puerto Ricans ultimately failed in their attempt to challenge the liberal idea of American citizenship, their movements testify to the seriousness of this challenge. Simultaneously, the Puerto Rican case represents an early example of the development of a "diasporic citizenship discourse"—a paradigm, that is very much present in today's discussions of transnational citizenship (Jonas, 1996; Laguerre, 1998).

Indeed, contrary to the way that much of mainstream US society lives its membership in the nation, as Thomas' article clearly suggests, Puerto Ricans, like other minorities, have long been aware that citizenship must be seen, in the words of William V. Flores, as "an active process of claiming rights, rather than the passive acquisition of an arbitrary and limited set of rights" (2003: 295-296; cf. also Goodwyn, 1977; King, 1992; Mendel-Reyes, 1995). Not surprisingly, during the Civil Rights era, for example, the various movements by Mexican Americans or Chicanos, and Puerto Ricans emphasized their respective long historical presence and the specificity of their participation as citizens in the US. In so doing, they responded to what Richard King (1992), in a different context, has called the *experience of exclusion,* which had long been a significant factor in shaping both the political and cultural legacies of their diverse communities and individual lives. At the same time, on an ideological, level, their struggles challenged their often politically orchestrated image as "eternal" foreigners in the American civic imaginary (see Rocco, this volume; Johnson, 1998). As Iris Marion Young (2000: 158) has observed, "However many generations of American citizens they can trace in their ancestry, Hispanics/Latino/as in the United States are liable to be treated as foreigners" in their homeland.

It is important in this respect to underscore the long histories of civil rights activism of both Chicano/as and Puerto Ricans, although this too has been systematically purged from the nation's historical imaginary and the national public consciousness (cf. Colón *et al.,* 1993; M. García, 1995; García and García, 1997; Rosales, 2000; Pantoja, 2002; Acuña, 2003). During the 1960s and 1970s, the specific and varied Civil Rights movements by these two Latino/a historical minorities, like those of African Americans and other groups, served to expose the ongoing racialized boundaries and implications of the legal definition and practical limitations of citizenship with respect to race, class, social status, and gender.[4]

Approaching citizenship as a complex reality, particularly in the case of Latino/as, is important for at least two reasons. In the first place, the Latino/a movements help us to understand in what way and to what extent citizenship actually constitutes the fundamental, sociopolitical expression of national belonging. Second, it compels us to look at the empirically observable implications of extending political, legal, and social rights to a variety of social groups without, however, radically altering the distribution and access to social resources. Hence, it may not be surprising that by the 1990s, as Dorothee Schneider[5] has pointed out, "there was little besides the right to vote to distinguish holders of US passports from those who held a green card" (2001, 65-66).

Nevertheless, to the extent that, as Raymond Rocco points out, citizenship today "is not solely nor even primarily a legal status, but rather a political mechanism for the control and containment of access to institutions of power and of the distribution of rights, benefits, privileges, entitlements and resources to different sectors of the population who reside within the territorial, sovereign boundaries of the nation-state," access to citizenship remains a point of major political contention.

CITIZENSHIP: PUBLIC POLICY IMPLICATIONS

Indeed, the extension of rights has also elicited different reactions at the level of both the state and the dominant social groups, which tapped into historical nativist sentiment, never entirely dormant in US society (Higham, 1955; Bennet, 1995; Brimelow, 1996; Perea, 1997; Schuck, 2000). The state's response to these practices has been as predictable as it has been varied. Particularly since the 1990s, the state has sought to slow the demise of citizenship as a critical political value by using legislation to reconstitute the distinction between citizens and noncitizens (Schneider, 2001).

Framed within a larger set of questions about race and citizenship, Nick de Genova's contribution to this volume shows the extent to which the ongoing (re)definition of immigrants' presence and (non)belonging in US society can be seen to be a result of state policies with respect to the "illegality" of migrants, particularly Mexican migrants, and violations of immigration law. In his account of the history of US immigration law since the 19th century, de Genova points to a seeming paradox: on the one hand, liberalizing immigration laws appears to have in fact concealed significantly the restrictive features of naturalization and citizenship, especially for Mexicans; on the other hand, ostensibly restrictive immigration laws, purportedly intended to deter migration, have nonetheless been instrumental in sustaining Mexican migration—but only by significantly restructuring the legal status of migrants as "undocumented" workers. Beginning in the 1960s, precisely when Mexican migration began to rise dramatically, and to this day, persistent revisions in the law have effectively foreclosed the possibilities for the great majority of Mexican immigrants to acquire a recognized legal status. Tolerated illegality in the form of "undocumented workers" has been instrumental in maintaining a climate of rightlessness. The systematically rediscoverable presence of "illegal aliens" can always be counted upon to stir public indignation at politically expedient points in time.

In fact, as de Genova suggests, and as the 2006 immigration debates attest, efforts to raise the value of the right to be in US society have historically included changes in the nation's immigration laws (Schneider, 2001; Ngai, 2005). Moreover, and particularly in the past decade, immigrants have been redefined as a "national security threat" (Jonas and Tactaquin, 2004: 70) as legislation aimed primarily at undocumented workers, but eventually also affecting all noncitizens, has been passed at both the federal and state levels. In this respect, Linda Bosniak has pointed to several measures "designed to make national citizenship status either harder to obtain, more socially significant, or both" (Bosniak, 2000b: 963). In addition to the proposed HR 4437 federal immigration bill of 2005, among the most controversial of these are federal and state measures, including the "Security and Immigration Compliance Act," signed into law in April, 2006, in the state of Georgia[6], and the state of California's Proposition 187, which Bosniak succinctly described as "a ballot initiative passed by California voters in 1994 which sought to deny health care, education, and other public services to undocumented immigrants and to require social service providers to report to law enforcement authorities any service user they suspected of having undocumented status" (2000b, 963–964, n.3).

While Proposition 187, curtailing immigrants' access to social and welfare services in 1994, was eventually ruled unconstitutional by the courts,[7] in 1996, three significant anti-immigrant laws were passed and were to shift substantially the social and political landscape for immigrants. The Illegal Immigration Reform and Immigrant

Responsibility Act (IIRIRA) served to overhaul the due process procedures with regard to immigrants, stripping the latter of their legal rights (including the right to due process) and making more crimes subject to deportation. The Anti-Terrorism and Effective Death Penalty Act (AEDPA), passed as a result of the Oklahoma bombings of 1995, although unrelated to immigrants, nevertheless criminalized them, making more crimes, ranging from petty theft to felonies, subject to deportation. It also included a clause that allowed for all noncitizen immigrants—legal residents and undocumented workers alike—who have ever broken the law to be deported retroactively from the US regardless either of the seriousness of the crime or of when the crime was committed. Finally, the Personal Responsibility and Work Opportunity Reconciliation Act (PRWORA) (commonly known as the Welfare Act) denied public services to all noncitizens, regardless of their status. As Greta Gilbertson describes in this volume, taken together, these three acts restricted most benefits for immigrants—documented and undocumented alike. In the case of the Welfare Act, for example, those benefiting from it were now required to show proof of citizenship. This act also elevated enforcement efforts and deportation procedures, and increased the responsibility of those sponsoring arriving immigrants, insisting that the Immigration and Naturalization Service (INS) had to verify the immigrants' status before they could get benefits.

In addition to redefining immigrants as a national security threat,[8] one result of the 1996 legislation was that even legal resident noncitizens felt the need to apply for naturalization to ensure that they did not lose access to their benefits. As a result, in 1997, just one year later, 1.4 million applications for US citizenship had been recorded.

In effect, the Welfare Act linked social benefits and the claiming of rights to citizenship, a point noted with some concern by scholars who believe, as Cristina Escobar explains, that immigrants' use of citizenship to secure rights ultimately devalues citizenship (Schuck, 2000; Martin, 2002: 229). Yet by situating naturalization and citizenship as a process whereby immigrants today both accommodate to and resist different forms of state power within transnational social spaces, Gilbertson takes the argument a step further. She shows that how immigrants view and articulate citizenship in the contemporary period is tied to how state power produces complex and contradictory ideas regarding the meaning and nature of membership. Moreover, she notes that an important consequence of these measures has been the fact that other nations in the Americas responded to the draconian anti-immigrant measures taken by the US state. Former President

Leonel Fernandez's call to Dominicans to become US citizens as a shield against the "vicissitudes of North American society, stemming from the end of the welfare era," is a significant case in point. Indeed, a key question that naturalization has raised for the meaning of citizenship in this era of transnational migration and globalization refers to changes in traditional notions of nationality and patriotism, love of country, loyalties, and allegiance to a single state.[9]

Perhaps not surprisingly, as Escobar points out, dual nationality has become a major issue among immigrants (see also Spiro, 2003). While Gilbertson's essay notes the relationship between the expansion of social rights and dual citizenship, Escobar grounds her research on Colombians' political incorporation, arguing that state policies in both the US and the homeland are leading immigrants to opt for naturalization as a means of retaining their ties to their homeland, even as they seek political participation in their new society (Guarnizo *et al.*, 2003). In the process, they are redefining the meaning of belonging in transnational terms, reaffirming their participation in and loyalties to both societies. Incorporation into US society thus also entails retaining multiple political identities (see Spiro, 2003). Escobar concludes that "membership in the country of origin, along with transnational connections and general embeddedness in transnational fields, is not opposed to assimilation and political participation in the US."

Indeed, contemporary immigrants' transnational practices and allegiances have ensured that Latino/as can actually live in the US and run for office back home—a point amply discussed by Alejandra Castañeda in this volume through the case of Mexico's "Rey del Tomate"—a California resident who successfully ran a campaign in Mexico from his home in the US. Castañeda argues that US citizenship, created and protected by laws that are lived and enacted by individuals, simultaneously requires migrants' presence in US society even as it constitutes an ongoing obstacle for them. Her chapter brings together three elements—law, belonging, and the formal political arena—to address Mexican migrants' practices of transnational citizenship and their relations with both Mexico and the US. Castañeda reviews the set of laws formed by the Mexican "Non-Loss of Nationality Law" as well as Mexico's Constitutional reform to Article 36, which opened the possibility for Mexican citizens to vote in Mexico's elections from their residence abroad. Similarly, she examines the 1996 welfare reform legislation, particularly as it pertains to immigration, and California's Proposition 187 of 1994. In so doing, she points to the contradictions and limitations entailed in these laws, and argues that citizenship today is constructed both by nation-states and by immigrants' transnational practices.

Whether or not this current practice of "absentee citizenship" will share the fortunes of traditional absentee landownership in terms of its impact on the home societies is an urgent issue to be explored.

LATINO/AS AND CITIZENSHIP: THE IMMIGRANTS' PERSPECTIVE

Spurred on by the actions of the US state as well as by official institutions in their respective countries of origin, US Latino/a citizens, residents, and immigrants alike have been redefining belonging with respect to the acquisition of social rights. In the process, citizenship is being defined along the lines outlined by Susan Bibler Coutin (2003) in her study of Salvadorans. While legal determinants of citizenship undoubtedly continue to be significant, as Bonnie Urciuoli and Kathleen Coll amply demonstrate in this volume, Latino/as are actively participating today in the redefinition of the meaning(s) and social value attributed to citizenship and belonging in various ways.

Noting that cultural citizenship in the US privileges the notion of *fitting in*—meaning that any form of racial/ethnic, linguistic, and (above all) class difference should fit within clearly prescribed boundaries—Urciuoli focuses on the paradoxical fact that policies of inclusiveness in contemporary institutions simultaneously mean that members must be recruited on the basis of "diversity," that is racial difference. Needless to say, this puts bilingual Latino/as from working-class backgrounds in something of a bind, for linguistic belonging in the US is not simply a matter of *whether* one speaks English, but rather *how* one speaks English.

Those Latino/as who grow up as working-class bilinguals routinely find that their accents and tendency to code-switch become lightning rods for race/class judgments, a fact that creates a bind for Latino/a students at elite liberal arts colleges. On the one hand, college diversity recruitment routinely includes working-class bilingual Latino/a students. Moreover, much of the work of enacting diversity (a form of good-college-citizen work) becomes the task of college multicultural organizations, including Latino/a organizations. On the other hand, while such identity enactment is supposed to appear cultured, it is not supposed to appear raced and classed. Hence the paradox: for such students, Spanish is key to the performance of diversity, but that performance is supposed to be tightly controlled. Any sign of Spanish leaking (so to speak) into English in an uncontrolled manner (working-class Latino/a accents, switching) may appear disorderly, yet it is exactly that "disorderliness" that provides such students with a sense of social belonging, with a sense of home away from home.

Thus, Urciuoli highlights issues of language and bilingualism to detail the paradoxes of constructing belonging, particularly among second-generation (im)migrant students who, while not necessarily US citizens, nevertheless have been raised in US society. From a different perspective, Kathleen Coll focuses on immigrant Latinas, describing grassroots leadership workshops they attended together with Chinese immigrant women. In the course of several meetings, the barriers of language and experience notwithstanding, the participants shared their lives and ultimately experienced a sense of social communion—not "in spite of their differences with one another but rather," as Coll argues, "because of a deepened understanding of both their shared and divergent interests, values, and experiences." Centering her analysis on Latinas' use of the language of *problemas, necesidades,* and *convivencia* ("problems, needs, and coexistence") in the retelling and negotiation of their experiences, Coll argues that these are in fact "new terms of citizenship." For beyond their strategic bases for building coalitions among different interest groups, these concepts point to "human relationships, subjectivity, and feelings as central to understanding contemporary US citizenship theory and practice in local communities." At the same time, Coll notes the ways in which the workshop participants drew on both North American and Latin American vernaculars of citizenship to produce new ideas about belonging, entitlement, and political engagement.

While immigrants draw on their transnational experience to develop new understandings of themselves and their needs, rights, and political engagement in their new society, this by no means suggests that they are not aware of the lack of formal political representation in their daily lives in the US. Indeed, an increasing number of workers in the labor force are *not* formal members, or citizens, in the nation-states in which they permanently reside. Thus, focusing on undocumented immigrants, Monica Varsanyi notes that while their labor is integral to the national economy, they are simultaneously excluded from full membership in their host societies. She suggests that in addition to their exclusion, their lack of status also erodes the democratic legitimacy of the community as a whole.

Varsanyi discusses this crisis from the perspective of a politically marginalized population. As members of the city's progressive labor unions, many undocumented residents of Los Angeles who cannot vote nevertheless do participate in electoral politics—whether through candidate endorsements, campaign rallies, or "get out the vote" efforts. Their political solidarity contributes to the emerging Latino/a voting bloc, and hence, indirectly, to the negotiations concerning their own social positions in US society. For instance, organized labor's recent declaration of support for immigrant workers is an important achievement for both the immigrant workers and the Latino/a community. As Varsanyi suggests, and as the 2006 immigrant marches also attest, their actions portend future reconfigurations of what it means to be a citizen during this era of globalization.

Like undocumented workers, undocumented high school and college students have also become engaged and participate in the legislative process and the claims of rights in relation to the state.[10] In her chapter, Hinda Seif provides an ethnographic description of the ways in which the presence and activism of undocumented Latino/a youth in US society have led Latino/a legislators in southeast Los Angeles to advocate on their behalf, despite their multiple disenfranchisement due to age, immigration status, class, and race in the aftermath of California's Proposition 187. She argues that youth raised and educated in the US are formally excluded from the nation and hence live on a fault line of US democracy. In so doing, she shows the extent to which undocumented youths' struggle for access to higher education reveals competing legislative narratives over the symbolic placement of the Mexican immigrant in the imagined communities of both the state of California in particular and US society in general. Moreover, their struggle also challenges assumptions about the contours of formal US legislative politics, citizenship practices, and the location of Latino/a legislative struggle. Hence, the legal right to attend public school and to ensure political representation cannot be underestimated, for both are significant struggles in the context of belonging.

REDEFINING CITIZENSHIP—THE PRESENT CONUNDRUM

While Latino/as, regardless of their status, participate—whether through the formal political arena or through grassroots initiatives and movements—in the process of redefining citizenship and belonging in the US context, the state-sponsored initiatives in this context are also of vital significance. The Latino/a experience is particularly useful in bringing to the fore some of the contradictory issues all US citizens and residents confront today. Ana Yolanda Ramos-Zayas argues that contemporary constructions of "homeland security" are actually US nation-state ideological and judicial projects that configure domestic opportunities, power inequalities, and racial formations.

The author seeks to demonstrate how political marginalization and social deprivation can be confronted by strategies to "prove" value—a "politics of worthiness" largely centered around Puerto Ricans' involvement in the US military. Nevertheless, she shows that in practice, the stigma of social and economic marginalization translates into fostering delinquency and ideologically criminalizes whole communities. The current debates on what and who is a "terrorist" are, most probably, of long-term impact since, as seen in the proposed HR 4437 legislation passed by the US House of Representatives, and the above-mentioned 2006 immigrant marches in response, the label may ultimately be applied to both undocumented immigrants and those citizens and legal residents harboring them.[11]

As Ramos-Zayas and, indeed, all the contributors to this volume suggest, granting citizenship continues to be the monopoly of the nation-state, though not without constant challenge from the members of the polity. The common thread running through these articles is the understanding that citizenship is less and less central to the quality of the community in which people live. Yet, while an alternative to liberal capitalism has not yet been found, there are today new thoughts, trends, desires, movements, and ongoing struggles aimed at winning the notion of citizenship back to the determination of the members of the society.

Hence, a key theme of this volume is the extent to which, through their lives, practices, activism and participation, Latino/a citizens, residents and immigrants—regardless of political status—are also contributing to the ongoing efforts to redefine and expand the very meaning of citizenship beyond the discussion of rights, of who has them, and who does not. Yet while the contributors suggest that we need to look deeper into the conditions under which individuals belong to a community, their essays ultimately also lend credence to the point made by Aleinikoff (2002: 193): "Citizenship is both more than a commonly held set of rights and less than a common culture. It is an important joint venture, on a defined piece of territory, to which people contribute from their particular circumstances (of faith, gender, occupation, race, region, and ethnicity)."

Indeed, as the Latino/a experience in the US demonstrates, beyond the issue of rights is the crucial issue of what it really means to "belong" and participate in building a community of equals that is grounded in social justice and human dignity. Raymond Rocco's contribution to this volume advances an alternative and original approach to the future of citizenship in a transnational context. Rethinking citizenship in a way that fully incorporates Latino/as' historical presence, and that thus fully takes into account their status and lived experience as residents or citizens, would obviate, Rocco argues, the perpetual notion that has cast them, irrespective of actual status, as "foreigners" or "outsiders" in US society. Indeed, he goes a step further in proposing the creation of a regional democratic citizenship that could move us beyond the limited and limiting perspective currently framed by our emphasis on the economic activities of global corporations. Instead, Rocco proposes incorporating Latino/as' various countries of origins in the region, thus creating a more meaningful context for looking at citizenship, one firmly grounded in the realities of Latino/as' contemporary transnational lives and practices. Ultimately, Rocco argues, regional citizenship would promote a more inclusive and democratic sense of political community in the context of the fundamental changes at the level of the economic and political interdependence that characterizes contemporary international relations.

Focusing attention on Latino/a citizenship provides an invaluable opportunity for academics, policymakers, and the society at large to broaden ideas and practices about democratic citizenship and democratic governance, nationally and regionally. Undoubtedly, the reduction of citizenship to a legal status consecrated by the sovereign state has had a profound impact on the nature of the national community—often depriving it of vitality with respect to the mode and content of collective decision-making. Legal restrictions have tended to prevail, and citizenship has become a universal tool that legitimizes public policy while its own proper content as a constitutive unit of the polity has been effectively restricted to the right to vote. Indeed, as the Latino/a experience attests, it is not citizenship per se but the lack of it that fuels political debates and conservative measures today. Thus, the experience of an encompassing national community has also pretty much been "gutted out" from our daily lives. Again, it is not the nature of the relations in the polity but the terms of access for outsiders—immigrants, the undocumented, and others—that holds center stage most often.

In this context, as this anthology suggests, Latino/as provide a collective experience that is of special value in the present. Because Latino/a citizens are often perceived and consequently treated as foreigners and because they also comprise a significant proportion of immigrants and other noncitizens, their experience is essential for understanding some of the impact of globalization not only on US society but also on the political changes under way in the Americas as a whole. Stated in different terms, today, noncitizenship is paradoxically a much more meaningful and immediate life experience in structuring perceptions of belonging than is citizenship itself.

If citizenship is to survive in US society as a socially meaningful experience in the context of globalization, such alternatives as the regional citizenship suggested by Rocco in this volume could be a step on the way. But the viability of adopting any such alternatives this will ultimately depend on the imagined community that is in the process of being articulated through much transformation and struggle and to which globalization ultimately must refer.

ACKNOWLEDGMENTS

With two exceptions (the chapters by Monica Varsanyi and Bonnie Urciuoli), the articles in the present volume were initially prepared for a conference sponsored by the journal *Latino Studies* and held at the University of Illinois at Chicago in April 2003. All were published in two special issues of *Latino Studies* (Vols. 2(1) and 2(2)) in March and July 2004, respectively. I want to take this opportunity to thank Karen Benita Biegel, the journal's managing editor, for lending her impressive organizational skills to ensure the success of our conference and for her excellent copyediting skills, which are again visible in the final version of the present manuscript. In publishing these articles in book form today, I also want to acknowledge the generous support of Stanley Fish, who, during his tenure as dean of the College of Liberal Arts and Sciences at the University of Illinois at Chicago, and together with Frances Aparicio and the Latin American and Latino Studies program at UIC, made the project of a national journal for the field of Latino Studies a viable reality. I also thank David Bull, the Palgrave (UK) publisher of the journal *Latino Studies*, for agreeing to the publication of this anthology, and, more generally, for his ongoing and steadfast support; and Gabriella Pearce, acquisitions editor at Palgrave (US), for her patience and assistance with this book project. Last but by no means least, I want to thank Anani Dzidzienyo and Elitza Bachvarova, for their thoughtful readings and many contributions to this introductory chapter, and more generally for all the support I have received from them on this project.

In presenting these essays, it is my hope that, as academics, scholars, intellectuals, activists, and students—as citizens and residents in this society—we can embark on an affirming and instructive dialogue that may help all of us to take control, collectively, of our social and political lives, of our society, and, above all, of the paths we choose to walk.

NOTES

1. This includes its definition and various (re)formulations (Marshall, 1950; Barbalet, 1988; Brubaker, 1992; Mouffe, 1992; Kymlicka and Norman, 1995; Shafer, 1998; Bosniak, 2000a; Aleinikoff and Klusmeyer, 2001; Isin and Turner, 2002); its persistence (Scobey, 2001: 11–16); its current "postnational" decline (Soysal, 1994; Jacobson, 1997; Bosniak, 2000b); its social value, policy implications, and changing interpretations in US and immigration history (Smith, 1997; Pickus, 1998; Jones Correa, 1998; Schuck, 2000; Klusmeyer and Aleinikoff, 2002; Ngai, 2005); and its relationship to multiculturalism, group rights, and cultural diversity (Kymlicka, 1995; Young, 1995; Flores and Benmayor, 1998; Joppke, 2002), globalization and belonging (Castles and Davidson, 2000; Hedetoft and Hjort, 2002), as well as to contemporary immigrants' transnational lives (Coutin, 2003; Hondagneu-Sotelo, 1994; Jonas, 1996; Laguerre, 1998; Guarnizo *et al.*, 2003).

2. Dred Scott was a freed slave who was resold into slavery in another state. Dred Scott had turned to the US courts to support his contention that insofar as he had been living in a slave-free state and had thus been a free man for two years, his subsequent capture and sale back into slavery was illegal. The Supreme Court, however, did not address the issue raised by Scott. Instead it focused on the larger question of whether those who were enslaved had the legal right to recourse to the US system of justice. Arguing that the writers of the Constitution did not intend to recognize blacks as "people" at all, much less to recognize them as citizens of the US, the majority ruling concluded that Dred Scott did not have the right to appeal to the US system of justice in the first place. Hence he was denied legal recognition of his freedom from slavery.

3. The *Plessy v. Ferguson* case challenged the constitutionality of an 1890 Louisiana law that re-established segregation of blacks and whites in the state's railroad trains. Grounded in the 14th Amendment guaranteeing citizenship to African Americans, this case was brought to the Supreme Court in Louisiana by Homer Adolph Plessy,—a man whom Richard Kluger (2004) has described as "exceedingly light-skinned," in a part of the country where the racial mixture of blacks, French, Indians, and Anglo Saxons had created "a racial *bouillabaise* unlike any other state in the union." The "separate but equal" decision thus brought to light issues of racial passing and the difficulty of disentangling racial origins. At the same time, it served to legally acknowledge the presence of blacks and simultaneously justify their segregation on the grounds that "social equality" could not be reached in the national community through what the Court referred to as "laws which conflict with the general sentiment of the community upon whom they are designed to operate." For a thought-provoking interpretation of the social implications of the Court's decisions, cf. Crenshaw (1997: 280–288).

4. There is today a growing literature on the civil rights movements of Chicanos and Puerto Ricans. Among the many recent titles, cf. Abramson, 1971; Muñoz, 2003; Rodríguez-Morazzani, 1991; Ignacio Garcia, 1997; Gutiérrez, 1998; Torres and Velazquez, 1998; Vigil, 1999; Lopez, 2003; Melendez, 2003; Mariscal, 2005.

5. In fact, as Alison Parker (2004) notes, "Only three constitutional rights—voting in elections, holding certain political offices, and the absolute ability to enter and remain in the country—are denied to noncitizens in an outright manner. Otherwise, the Constitution grants to "the people" or "persons"—not just to citizens—the rights to due process and equal protection of the law, to freedom of speech and assembly, and to freedom from arbitrary detention or cruel and unusual punishments."

6. This Act, signed by Republican Governor Sonny Perdue, is by all accounts, "one of the nation's toughest." According to a report in TIME magazine, "It includes provisions requiring residents who are seeking state social welfare benefits to prove their legal status, as well as mandating that the police check the legal status of everyone they arrest and alert federal authorities to any violations." Cf. Greg Fulton. "Is Georgia's Immigration Bill a Step Forward or Back?" TIME Magazine, internet edition. http://www.time.com/time/nation/article/0,8599,1185259,00.html. Accessed April 21, 2006.

7. Although it was ruled unconstitutional, the continued impact of Proposition 187 can be seen in its modified revival in Arizona's Proposition 200, which was voted into law during the 2004 elections.

8. Jonas and Tactaquin (2004) also note that "Other measures accompanied these three bills: militarization of the border with Mexico, curtailment of the definition of "refugee," harsher attitudes against legalization programs, and even such extreme proposals as repeal of the 14th Amendment to the Constitution, which gives citizenship to all who are born on US soil. (In the late 1990s, this last campaign was unsuccessful, but it reappeared in 2003.) Taken together, these bills created a national security regime for immigrants, stripping away their rights punitively and arbitrarily."

9. This question was the subject of a thought-provoking debate during the 1990s by Nussbaum and Cohen (1996).

10. For a complementary perspective on this subject, see Leisy Abrego's (2006) essay, " 'I can't go to college because I don't have papers': Incorporation Patterns of Latino Undocumented Youth."

11. According to *The Washington Post*, on December 16, 2005, the US House of Representatives "passed tough immigration legislation" that

> would end the "catch and release" policy for immigrants other than Mexicans who are caught entering the country illegally and then released with a court date. All illegal immigrants apprehended at the border would have to be detained, and deportation processes would be streamlined. Criminal penalties for smuggling immigrants would be stiffened, with new mandatory minimum sentences. Immigrant gang

members would be rendered inadmissible under any circumstance. Mandatory minimum sentences would be established for immigrants who reenter illegally after deportation, and local sheriffs in the 29 counties along the Mexican border would be reimbursed for detaining illegal immigrants and turning them over to federal custody.

Moreover, additional amendments were also passed by which "the nation would spend more than $2.2 billion to build five double-layer border fences in California and Arizona, totaling 698 miles at $3.2 million a mile . . . [and that] would empower local law enforcement nationwide to enforce federal immigration law and be reimbursed for their efforts" (cf. Weisman, 2005).

REFERENCES

Abramson, Michael, and The Young Lords Party. 1971. *Palante: The Young Lords Party*. New York: McGraw-Hill.
Abrego, Leisy. 2006. I can't go to college because I don't have papers: Incorporation Patterns of Latino Undocumented Youth. *Latino Studies* 4: 2.
Acuña, Rodolfo. 2003. *Occupied America: A History of Chicanos*. 5th ed. New York: Longman Press.
Aleinikoff, T. Alexander. 2002. *Semblances of Sovereignty. The Constitution, The State and American Citizenship*. Cambridge, MA: Harvard University Press.
Aleinikoff, T. Alexander, and Douglas Klusmeyer. ed.. 2001. *Citizenship Today: Global Perspectives and Practices*. Washington, DC: Carnegie Endowment for International Peace.
Anderson, Benjamin. 1991. *Imagined Communities: Reflections on the Origin and Spread of Nationalism*. London: Verso.
Barbalet, J. M. 1988. *Citizenship*. Minneapolis: University of Minnesota Press.
Bennet, David. 1995. *The Party of Fear: From Nativist Movements to the New Right in American History*. New York: Vintage.
Bickel, Alexander M. 1975. *The Morality of Consent*. New Haven and London: Yale University Press.
Bosniak, Linda. 2000a. Citizenship Denationalized. *Indiana Journal of Global Legal Studies* 7: 447—508.
———. 2000b. Universal Citizenship and the Problem Of Alienage. *Northwestern University Law Review*. 94: 963—982.
Brimelow, Peter. 1996. *Alien Nation: Common Sense about America's Immigration Disaster*. New York: Harper Press.
Brubaker, Roger. 1992. *Citizenship and Nationhood in France and Germany*. Cambridge, MA: Harvard University Press.
Castles, Stephen, and Alastair Davidson. 2000. *Citizenship and Migration: Globalization and the Politics of Belonging*. New York: Routledge.
Chafe, William H. 1986. The End of One Struggle, the Beginning of Another. In *The Civil Rights Movement in America*, ed. Charles W. Eagles, 127–148. Jackson and London: University Press of Mississippi.

Chávez, Leo. 1997. *Shadowed Lives: Undocumented Immigrants in American Society*. OH: Wadsworth Publishing.

Colón, Jesús, Edna Acosta Belén, and Virginia Sanchez Korrol. 1993. *The Way It Was and Other Writings*. Houston, TX: Arte Publico Press.

Coutin, Susan Bibler. 2003. *Legalizing Moves: Salvadoran Immigrants' Struggle for U.S. Residency*. Ann Arbor: University of Michigan Press.

Crenshaw, Kimberlé Williams. 1997. "Color Blindness, History and the Law." In *The House that Race Built: Black Americans, U.S. Terrain*, ed. Wahneema Lubiano. pp. 280–288. New York: Pantheon Books.

Croucher, Sheila L. 2004. *Globalization and Belonging: The Politics of Identity in a Changing World*. Lanham, MD: Rowman and Littlefield.

De Genova, Nick, and Ana Yolanda Ramos-Zayas, eds. 2003. Latino Racialization and the Politics of Citizenship. Special issue of the *Journal of Latin American Anthropology* 8(2).

Evans, Sara M., and Harry C. Boyte. 1992. *Free Space: The Sources of Democratic Change in America*. Chicago and London: University of Chicago Press.

Flores, William V. 2003. New Citizens, New Rights: Undocumented Immigrants and Latino Cultural Citizenship. *Latin American Perspectives* 30: 295–296.

Flores, William V., and Rina Benmayor. 1998. *Latino Cultural Citizenship; Claiming Identity, Space and Rights*. Boston, MA: Beacon Press.

Foner, Eric, and Olivia Mahoney. 1995. *America's Reconstruction: People and Politics After the Civil War*. New York: Harper Collins.

García, Alma, and Mario García. ed. 1997. *Chicana Feminist Thought: The Basic Historical Writings*. New York: Routledge.

García, Ignacio M. 1997. *Chicanismo: The Forging of a Militant Ethos Among Mexican Americans*. Arizona: University of Arizona Press.

García, Mario T. 1995. *Memories of Chicano History: The Life and Narrative of Bert Corona*. Berkeley: University of California Press.

Goodwyn, Lawrence. 1977. *The Populist Moment: A Short History of the Agrarian Revolt in America*. New York: Oxford University Press.

Guarnizo, Luis, Alejandro Portes, and William Haller. 2003. From Assimilation to Transnationalism: Determinants of Transnational Political Action among Contemporary Migrants. *American Journal of Sociology* 108: 1211–1248.

Gutiérrez, José Angel. 1998. *The Making of a Chicano Militant: Lessons from Cristal*. Madison and London: University of Wisconsin Press.

Hedetoft, Ulf, and Mette Hjort. ed. 2002. *The Postnational Self: Belonging and Identity*. Minneapolis: University of Minnesota Press.

Higham, John. 1955. *Strangers in the Land: Patterns of American Nativism, 1860–1925*. New Brunswick, NJ: Rutgers University Press.

Hondagneu-Sotelo, Pierrette. 1994. *Gendered Transitions: Mexican Experiences of Immigration*. Berkeley: University of California Press.

Huntington, Samuel P. 2004. *Who Are We: The Challenges to America's National Identity*. New York: Simon & Schuster.

Ignatieff, Michael. 2005. The Broken Contract. *The New York Times Magazine,* October 9, 8.

Isin, Engin F., and Bryan S. Turner, ed. 2002. *Handbook of Citizenship Studies.* London, Thousand Oaks, New Dehli: Sage Publications.

Jacobson, David. 1997. *Rights Across Borders: Immigration and the Decline of Citizenship.* Baltimore, MD: Johns Hopkins University Press.

Johnson, Kevin R. 1998. Citizens as Foreigners. In *The Latino Condition: A Critical Reader,* ed. Richard Delgado and Jean Stefancic, 198–201. New York: New York University Press.

Jonas, Susanne. 1996. Rethinking Immigration Policy and Citizenship in the Americas: A Regional Framework. *Social Justice* 23(3): 68–96.

Jonas, Susanne, and Cathi Tactaquin. 2004. Latino Immigrant Rights in the Shadow of the National Security State: Responses to Domestic Preemptive Strikes. *Social Justice* 31: 67–91.

Jonas, Susanne, and Edward J. McCaughan, ed. 1994. *Latin America Faces the Twenty-First Century: Reconstructing a Social Justice Agenda.* Boulder, CO: Westview Press.

Jones Correa, Michael. 1998. *In Between Two Nations: The Political Predicament of Latinos in New York City.* Ithaca, NY: Cornell University Press.

Joppke, Christian. 2002. Multicultural Citizenship. In *Handbook of Citizenship Studies,* ed. Engin F. Isin and Bryan S. Turner, 231–245. London, Thousand Oaks, New Dehli: Sage Publications.

King, Richard H. 1992. *Civil Rights and the Idea of Freedom.* New York: Oxford University Press.

Kluger, Richard. 2004. *Simple Justice: The History of Brown v. Board of Education and Black America's Struggle for Equality.* New York: Vintage.

Klusmeyer, Douglas, and Alexander T. Aleinikoff. 2002. *Citizenship Policies for an Age of Migration.* Washington, DC: Carnegie Endowment for International Peace.

Kymlicka Will. 1995. *Multicultural Citizenship: A Liberal Theory of Minority Rights.* Oxford: Oxford University Press.

Kymlicka, Will, and Wayne Norman. 1995. Return of the Citizen: A Survey of Recent Work on Citizenship Theory. In *Theorizing Citizenship,* ed. Ronald Beiner, 283–322. Albany, NY: State University of New York Press.

Laguerre, Michel S. 1998. *Diasporic Citizenship: Haitian Americans in Transnational America.* New York: St. Martin's Press.

Lopez, Ian F. Haney. 1998. *White By Law: The Legal Construction of Race.* New York: New York University Press.

———. 2003. *Racism on Trial: The Chicano Fight for Justice.* Boston, MA: Belknap/Harvard University Press.

Mariscal, George. 2005. *Brown-Eyed Children of the Sun: Lessons from the Chicano Movement, 1965–1975.* Albuquerque: University of New Mexico Press.

Marshall, T.H. 1950. *Citizenship and Social Class, and Other Essays.* Cambridge, MA: Cambridge University Press.

Martin, Susan. 2002. The Attack on Social Rights: U.S. Citizenship Devalued. In *Dual Nationality, Social Rights and Federal Citizenship in the U.S. and Europe*, ed. Randall Hansen and Patrick Weil, 215–232. New York: Berhahn Books.

Mendel-Reyes, Meta. 1995. *Reclaiming Democracy: The Sixties in Politics and Memory*. New York: Routledge.

Melendez, Miguel. 2003. *We Took the Streets: Fighting for Latino Rights With the Young Lords*. New York: St. Martin's Press.

Mouffe, Chantal. 1992. Feminism, Citizenship and Radical Democratic Politics. In *Feminists Theorize the Political*, ed. Judith Butler and Joan W. Scott, 369–384. New York and London: Routledge.

Muñoz, Carlos. 2003. *The Chicano Movement: Youth, Identity, Power*. New York: Verso.

Ngai, Mae M. 2005. *Impossible Subjects: Illegal Aliens and the Making of Modern America*. Princeton, NJ: Princeton University Press.

Nussbaum, Martha C., and Joshua Cohen. 1996. *For Love of Country: Debating the Limits of Patriotism*. Boston, MA: Beacon Press.

Oboler, Suzanne. 1995. *Ethnic Labels, Latino Lives; Identity and the Politics of (Re)Presentation in the United States*. Minneapolis: University of Minnesota Press.

Pantoja, Antonia. 2002. *Memoir of a Visionary: Antonia Pantoja*. Houston, TX: Arte Publico Press.

Parker, Alison. 2004. Inalienable rights: Can human-rights law help end U.S. mistreatment of noncitizens? *The American Prospect*, October 1. http://www.prospect.org/web/page.ww?section=root&name=ViewPrint &articleId=8556 (accessed January 2, 2006).

Perea, Juan Francisco. 1997. *Immigrants Out! The New Nativism and the Anti-Immigrant Impulse in the United States*. New York: New York University Press.

Pickus, Noah M. J. ed. 1998. *Immigration and Citizenship in the 21st Century*. London and New York: Rowman and Littlefield.

Ringer, Benjamin B. *We the People and Others: Duality and America's Treatment of Its Racial Minorities*. New York: Tavistock Publications, 1983.

Rodríguez-Morazzani, Roberto. 1991. Puerto Rican Political Generations in New York: Pioneros, Young Turks, and Radicals. *Centro Bulletin* 4(1): 102–107.

Rosaldo, Renato. 1993. *Culture and Truth: The Remaking of Social Analysis*. Boston, MA: Beacon Press.

Rosales, Francisco A. 1997. *Chicano! The History of the Mexican American Civil Rights Movement*. 2nd ed. Houston, TX: Arte Publico Press.

———. 2000. *Testimonio: A Documentary History of the Mexican-American Struggle for Civil Rights*. Houston, TX: Arte Publico Press.

Schneider, Dorothee. 2001. Naturalization and United States: Citizenship in Two Periods of Mass Migration: 1894–1930, 1965–2000. *Journal of American Ethnic History* 20: 50–82.

Schuck, Peter H. 2000. *Citizens, Strangers, and In-Betweens: Essays on Immigration and Citizenship.* Boulder, CO: Westview Press.

Scobey, David. 2001. The Specter of Citizenship. *Citizenship Studies* 5(1): 11–16.

Shafer, Gershon. 1998. *The Citizenship Debates: A Reader.* Minneapolis: University of Minnesota Press.

Smith, Rogers M. 1997. *Civic Ideals: Conflicting Visions of Citizenship in U.S. History.* New Haven, CT: Yale University Press.

Soysal, Yasemin Nuhoglu. 1994. *Limits of Citizenship: Migrants and Postnational Membership in Europe.* Chicago, IL: University of Chicago Press.

Spiro, Peter. 2003. Political Rights and Dual Citizenship. In *Rights and Duties of Dual Nationals,* ed. David A. Martin and Kay Hailbronner, 135–152. The Hague, London, New York: Kluwer Law International.

Torres, Andrés, and José E. Velazquez. 1998. *The Puerto Rican Movement: Voices from the Diaspora.* Philadelphia, PA: Temple University Press.

Weisman, Jonathan. 2005. House Votes to Toughen Laws on Immigration; One Setback for Bush: No Guest-Worker Plan. The Washington Post, December 17, A01. http://www.washingtonpost.com/wp-dyn/content/article/2005/12/16/AR2005121601814_pf.html (accessed on January 4, 2006).

Vigil, Ernesto B. 1999. *The Crusade for Justice: Chicano Militancy and the Government's War on Dissent.* Madison and London: University of Wisconsin Press.

Young, Iris Marion. 1995. Polity and Group Difference: A Critique of the Ideal of Universal Citizenship. In *Theorizing Citizenship,* ed. Ronald Beiner, 175–208. Albany: State University of New York Press.

———. 2000. Structure, Difference, and Hispanic/Latino Claims of Justice. In *Hispanics/Latinos in the United States: Ethnicity, Race, and Rights,* ed. Jorge J. Gracia and Pablo De Greiff, 147–165. New York: Routledge.

PART II

Citizenship and Struggles for Political Inclusion and Dignity in the 20th Century

CHAPTER 2

"How They Ignore Our Rights as American Citizens": Puerto Rican Migrants and the Politics of Citizenship in the New Deal Era

Lorrin Thomas

In the spring of 1936, following a spate of political violence amid Nationalist agitation in Puerto Rico, US Senator Millard Tydings proposed a bill granting the island independence from the US. Many Puerto Ricans had been pushing for independence since the US takeover in 1898, but the Tydings bill did not represent a concession to those demands. Rather, its impossibly punitive terms—involving the end of all New Deal federal assistance programs, the quick implementation of a full US tariff on Puerto Rican goods, and the withdrawal of all US government infrastructure and military within six months— advertised it as a quick fix to the political embarrassment due to Puerto Ricans' intensifying anti-American sentiment.

While a number of moderate supporters of independence were outraged by the bill, such as the popular Liberal senator Luis Muñoz Marin, who called its terms "unjust" and likened it to "highway robbery," most Nationalists—those who advocated unconditional and absolute independence for the island—supported it. In New York, the Tydings bill inspired the Puerto Rican barrio in East Harlem to "come alive" in a riot of "political upheaval," in the words of a WPA (Works Progress Administration) fieldworker. Like their counterparts in Puerto Rico, many Nationalists in the migrant community (or *colonia*) championed the Tydings bill in spite of its steep price; one supporter's letter to *La Prensa*, New York's Spanish-language daily, proclaimed, "*aunque nos muramos de hambre, independencia!*" ("even if we die of hunger, independence!"). Others pointed out that the "relief" Puerto Rico got from the US government was so miserly to begin with that losing such aid would hardly make a difference in the island's plight.

Pilar Pacheco, a Nationalist activist well known in the *colonia,* used the tumult over the Tydings proposal to expand a *La Prensa* debate about island independence to address what she saw as the failures of migrants' US citizenship, conferred on all Puerto Ricans by the 1917 Jones Act. "Each Puerto Rican is a free and sovereign citizen of the United States," she began her letter in a bitterly ironic tone,

> free and sovereign to struggle against indigence and circumstance . . . free and sovereign to chase after his bread . . . which he is denied. . . The Puerto Rican in the United States has the privilege of clearing and scrubbing plates in restaurants; of rising at five in the morning on harsh winter days to line up at the factory, at the cafeteria, at the docks with the hope of being chosen among the hundreds of foreigners who comprise the working masses of this people . . . We are absolutely free to hear how they call us "niggers," to see how they ignore our rights as American citizens . . . If this is the liberty and sovereignty that a people gives to loyal men . . . it is not strange that nationalist Puerto Ricans feel aggrieved and cry out for justice and equality and try to tear down with a valiant hand the veil of the hypocrites . . . (August 18, 1936)

In most respects, Pacheco's perspective on Puerto Ricans' US citizenship was typical of the Nationalist party line, which held that US citizenship, imposed on Puerto Ricans without their consent, signified the hypocrisies of a democratic nation that had ruled the island of Puerto Rico as an imperial power since 1898. But Pacheco went further than most Nationalists in her criticism of US citizenship, drawing attention to the specific ways in which it had failed to include Puerto Ricans in its promise of equality and justice and spinning the idea of "freedom and sovereignty" as rights held by persons as well as nations—but rights that, given the injustices of American society and the hypocrisy of its government, provided no real protection for Puerto Ricans.

Taking Pacheco's commentary as a starting point, this chapter explores Puerto Rican migrants' first focused effort at making demands of the state on the basis of their citizenship, as participants in the *colonia*'s political culture struggled, throughout the 1930s, to combine a new local rights discourse with a more long-standing emphasis on homeland politics. It analyzes how the conditions of economic hardship and the florescence of liberal politics in the US inspired this new discourse of rights among Puerto Rican migrants in the 1930s. It then traces how extreme political volatility on the island spurred a new politics of nationalism in the *colonia* that, I argue, permanently altered the fragile relationship between Democrats and Puerto Ricans in the US. Puerto Rican migrants' persistent engagement in homeland politics, combined with their increasing demands for access to equality and rights in New York, caused politicians to regard migrants as "volatile," a political liability more than a viable constituency. The actual *results* of migrants' efforts to develop and deploy a rights discourse were not auspicious, and on the eve of the massive postwar "great migration" from Puerto Rico, any measure of political empowerment continued to elude residents of the New York *colonia*.

Yet, the "end of the story" of Puerto Ricans' Depression-era political mobilization is only one reason that the story itself matters. Aside from the historically tangible results of migrants' activism—or in this case, the near absence thereof—there are the more "subterranean" dimensions to the story, wherein we see the creation of a distinct rights discourse by marginalized political actors and then its silencing. These dimensions of Puerto Ricans' experience in New York in the 1930s have real implications for a larger history of citizenship politics and rights discourses in this period in the US and need to be understood. Scholars are only just beginning to look at the politics of citizenship from the point of view of social history; this research on Puerto Rican migrants contributes a perspective on the changing meanings of citizenship for a group of newcomers to the US about whom historians know shockingly little—especially in the period before the "great migration" from Puerto Rico.[1] More illuminating than the concrete outcomes of Puerto Ricans' practice of citizenship are the expectations that they articulated along the way in the form of a diasporic citizenship discourse—that is, a way of framing citizenship that sought to connect their rights in the local and homeland arenas (Somers, 1993; Laguerre, 1998).

The 1930s was a decade when meanings and definitions of citizenship were in flux for all Americans. Roosevelt's Economic Security Act of 1935 would fundamentally redefine what Americans could expect from the state, not just in terms of a "safety net," but also in terms of a minimum basis of social equality. In the same era, as the nation's fear of a growing "fascist menace" in Europe made racial divisions at home look more dangerous, African American activists' efforts at claiming equal rights were beginning to gain some legitimacy in the eyes of national-level Democrats and were winning public support from liberals. From their vantage point in New York City, amid this seismic shift in American society, Puerto Rican migrants probably did not see themselves as participating in the early stages of what would become a real "rights revolution"; they described themselves simply as rightful claimants in a social and political arena that promised tangible benefits to all its citizens. Yet Puerto Ricans' nascent diasporic rights discourse added a distinct "public narrative"—to borrow Margaret Somers' (1993) description of how groups of actors construct their ideas of institutions, including the "nation"—to Americans' understanding of their liberal-democratic idea of citizenship, and challenged American liberalism to admit to its colonialist and imperialist contradictions. I argue here that it was because of this challenge—Puerto Rican migrants' demand that liberal American citizenship live up to its ideals of "liberty and sovereignty," as Pilar Pacheco put it—that Puerto Ricans were effectively silenced in both local and national conversations about the expansion of liberal citizenship in the 1930s.

"EL HOME RELIEF" AND A NEW RIGHTS TALK: POLITICS IN THE LOCAL ARENA

During the 1920s, as the Puerto Rican *colonia* began to expand and flourish in New York City, if migrants talked about their US citizenship at all, it was in pragmatic terms at election time. *Colonia* leaders invoked citizenship as a tool that would allow the small Puerto Rican community to imitate the political successes of earlier immigrants, who had forged alliances with local machine politicians via their voting power and reaped the rewards of garbage collection, police protection, and patronage jobs. Following in the footsteps of most other urban immigrants in the US, Puerto Rican voters sought political empowerment via the Democratic Party. Migrants overwhelmingly supported Democrats in local elections, even after a series of political scandals in 1932, when the conviction of scores of Tammany Democrats on corruption charges paved the way for an easy mayoral victory by Fiorello LaGuardia's Republican reform coalition in 1933.

But behind the veneer of unified support among Puerto Ricans for the ailing Democratic machine in New York—LaGuardia's 1933 victory marked the ascendancy of his reform coalition, which would hold power for 12 years—lay a more divisive reality: a migrant political culture fractured by class loyalties and entrenched island divisions over the question of Puerto Rico's political status. During the summer of 1934, for instance, when *La Prensa* sponsored a debate on "*el momento político y los hispanos*" ("Hispanics and the political moment"), working-class and elite community leaders squared off over questions of whether to focus Puerto Ricans' meager political capital on the "politics of here" (i.e., on local issues such as housing, discrimination, and relief) or on pursuing independence for Puerto Rico. Leaders on both sides of the class divide counted on migrants' power as voting citizens to pursue their own political agendas, despite their persistent rhetoric of "unity."

While leaders at the top levels of *colonia* political culture focused on electoral politics and questions of political representation in the early 1930s, it was the controversies over locally administered welfare programs that animated thousands of other migrants, providing a concrete focus for migrants' political energy as well as a new forum for popular discussion about the uses of citizenship in the *colonia*. In the context of such controversies, migrants began to talk about the utility of citizenship beyond voting, articulating expectations of citizenship in terms of access to social welfare and to equal treatment by political and social institutions. In the absence of a federal safety net, which was not in place until the Social Security Act of 1935, New York City had begun implementing small-scale "Home Relief" programs in the early years of the Depression, providing food and cash assistance to needy city residents. Since the inception of such programs, Puerto Ricans had reported that they were "ignored" by the city's relief administration and that local relief workers discriminated against them in the distribution of benefits. In 1932, *La Prensa* told readers that "we receive persistent and detailed complaints from destitute *hispanos* who, after speaking to relief station officials, either don't receive any aid at all or are given some indefinite date—which never actually arrives" (February 8, 1932). Many also complained that they were treated with outright disrespect and hostility. One applicant summarized his experience with the Home Relief Bureau (HRB) with biting humor: "In this land to which we have come in search of new horizons, what we have discovered is insults and the opportunity to have our character assailed at the 'Home Relief' offices" (August 20, 1934). Other Puerto Ricans who applied for Home Relief or for assistance from private charitable organizations in the city seconded the objection that those who dispensed aid often dispensed judgments about the lifestyle of their culturally foreign clients.

Such complaints inspired a group of migrants from Harlem to organize a delegation to meet with the Democratic city comptroller Frank Prial in 1933 (New York City Board of Elections, 1934). The delegation laid out its grievances against the city for its failure to administer relief justly to Puerto Ricans, and their grievances against private charitable institutions, which it also charged with "injustices" and "prejudice." The comptroller reportedly expressed surprise at these revelations and was "taken aback" that "such a situation could exist in this city"—despite the fact that the relief administration had been the object of various Harlem demonstrations for at least two years. Most likely the delegation itself viewed this reaction with some cynicism; *La Prensa*'s intrepid reporter of community news wrote scornfully about Prial's "sincerity" in an important election season (November 6, 1933). If Prial said he was surprised at Puerto Ricans' problems in obtaining relief, he offered no formal response to the delegation's complaints. Migrants continued to encounter delays and obstacles at the HRB offices in Harlem.

The city may have been ignoring them, but "needy and destitute" Puerto Ricans continued their efforts to draw attention to their plight and to assert their social rights as citizens. In April 1935, a group of Spanish speakers, most of them Puerto Rican, staged a protest outside the HRB office at 116th Street and Madison Avenue. More than 400 *colonia* members reportedly joined in the picketing, giving voice to the demands laid out in a flyer circulated by the protest organizers: that the value of relief "tickets" increase by 25%; that rents floated by the HRB be paid on time; that clothing be provided for whole families, not just children; that moving costs be included among relief benefits; and that "closed" cases be reopened. Although the *World Telegram*, the *Daily News*, and the *Times* all covered news of other protests outside HRB offices in the mid-1930s, none of them deemed the demonstration by "Spanish Harlem" residents important enough to report on. *La Prensa* reported that some 30 police officers patrolled the protest area, "perhaps worried about the occurrence of riots similar to the recent events on 125th Street." The reporter hastened to add, however, that "no altercations of any kind" had been observed at or near the protest (April 6, 1935).

One reason for the lack of attention to Puerto Ricans' protests was city officials' more acute concern about African Americans at that moment: following a series of riots in the western section of Harlem in March 1935, New Yorkers' attention was trained on the "explosive conditions" of poverty and privation that were widely blamed for the violence in Harlem.[2] Mayor LaGuardia pledged to appoint a committee of "representative citizens" to study the riot and its causes; the Mayor's Committee on Conditions in Harlem (MCCH) was to begin a series of hearings the week after Puerto Ricans' HRB protest. But that "representative" committee turned out to consist only of African Americans and white Americans, despite the fact that Puerto Ricans comprised the majority or plurality of residents on about one-quarter of Harlem's residential blocks and ranked second only to African Americans as the largest national or "ethnic" group in the neighborhood.[3]

In spite of their exclusion from the MCCH, *colonia* activists expected to participate in the discussions about conditions in Harlem. The head of one labor organization explained to the mayor:

> We have in our possession several cases of discrimination, denials of relief, deaths due to the carelessness of the officials representing the different aid societies, police terror against Spanish-speaking workers, corruption of police by using gangsters to provoke workers and especially the workers' organizations. (LaGuardia Papers, March 25, 1935)

Another *colonia* leader told the Mayor's Committee, "So that you may hear the different slights and humiliations to which the Puerto Ricans are subjected, we expect from you, that you allow this Committee, which is composed of more than 60 organizations, Spanish-speaking and in their majority Puerto Rican, to testify" (LaGuardia Papers, March 25, 1935). Yet official reports of the hearing document no testimony by Puerto Ricans.[4] After the hearings had been completed, representatives of two *colonia* organizations, the Liga Puertorriqueña e Hispana, Inc., and the Junta Liberal Puertorriqueña de Nueva York, wrote to the mayor to point out what they saw as the injustice of their exclusion from the MCCH. "We believe that excluding the Puerto Ricans from that committee was unfair if you will take in consideration the great number of unemployed Puerto Ricans not only unemployed but antagonized with so much prejudice against them," wrote Antonio Rivera (LaGuardia Papers, June 24, 1935). Isabel O'Neill, a Nationalist activist, wrote to the mayor a more pointed indictment of his treatment of Puerto Ricans:

> What is most displeasing—and . . . unwarranted—is not only the discrimination shown in the selection and . . . appointment of members to the investigating committee, but also the complete ignoration of Puerto Ricans; of them, whose interest in Harlem and the betterment thereof is a vital factor and uppermost consideration in their lives and general social welfare and being.

> It seems that we have been omitted from every civic activity that has presented itself . . . and the omission is even more flagrant in this instance, an act of political and civic indifference and unmindfulness at which we feel aggrieved . . . We feel that we are entitled to some consideration by way of recognition in civic affairs of this city and hereby seek of you the fulfillment of our just request. (LaGuardia Papers, June 24, 1935)[5]

It is not clear how LaGuardia's office decided to respond, if it responded at all, to such charges. What is clear is that Puerto Ricans' specific grievances—anything that could not be subsumed under the consideration of "Negro problems"—did not make it into the Committee's reports.

Despite the public silence, the incidents recounted above show that in fact Puerto Ricans *were* making demands—on Harlem streets and in city officials' offices—for fairness in relief distribution. And in doing so, migrants were making claims to social rights as Americans, claims that ran parallel to the incipient "rights talk" of African Americans on similar issues. By tracing in detail how Puerto Ricans were beginning to articulate their rights in the US, we open a window onto their visions of US citizenship in the absence of effective political representation. But in addition to looking *beyond* the silence, at the activism that lay behind it, we also must read *into* the official silence that met Puerto Ricans' complaints. What was it about the Puerto Rican migrant community that made New York City officials reluctant to acknowledge their claims? Certainly, African Americans were a more visible and numerically powerful constituency in city politics—a constituency becoming more important as racial politics heated up around the mid-1930s. But it was not only Puerto Ricans' relative weakness as a "minority" voting bloc that led to their marginalization in city politics. Indeed, even when the *colonia* could boast barely 20,000 residents in the mid-1920s, a few Democratic representatives had noted its political importance.[6] By 1936, it was the appearance of Puerto Rican New Yorkers' political volatility—as their focus on political tensions on the island shaped their demands of US political representatives—that drove a definitive wedge between Puerto Ricans and major party leaders, especially the Democrats.

LA SEÑORA ROOSEVELT AND THE PUERTO RICANS, 1934

Migrants' first real encounter with national-level Democrats actually involved a continuation of the local battle over anti-Puerto Rican prejudice and discrimination that they had begun waging in the late 1920s.[7] Although it did not involve explicitly political action, the community mobilization described below was nevertheless galvanized by the new "rights talk" emerging from the East Harlem *colonia* and foreshadowed a new field of tensions between Puerto Ricans and the Democratic Party. The controversy centered on a speech that Eleanor Roosevelt made following her "good-will" visit to Puerto Rico in 1934, a trip intended "to convey . . . to Puerto Rico much of the buoyant optimism Washington has exhibited in the last year" regarding the establishment of New Deal programs on the island through the Puerto Rican Emergency Relief Administration (PRERA). Publicity about the trip emphasized the warm reception she received on the island and the appreciation that the islanders expressed, both for her attention to their suffering and for the hope she imparted to them. A *Times* reporter gushed that "her mere presence, bringing new hope of that fuller life of which the President is an exponent, was a greater tonic than anything she did or said" (March 18, 1934). Puerto Rico's US-appointed Governor Winship also proclaimed that "her gracious contacts with the people have universally charmed them and brought them to love her." These grandiose accounts were not inaccurate: Puerto Ricans, both on the island and the mainland, loved Eleanor Roosevelt and her husband and believed that their New Deal for America would extend not just to its newcomers but to its island "possession" as well.

During a 1,000-plate dinner held by the Women's Trade Union League in April, Mrs. Roosevelt roused the sympathy of her audience with descriptions of the travails of Puerto Rican workers, especially the women who struggled to make a living by embroidering handkerchiefs at three cents per dozen. She then told her audience that "the colony of the islanders in New York" was "one of the worst in the city—not only for the unpleasant happenings but for diseases." She emphasized the "shockingly high" rate of tuberculosis on the island, and claimed it was "just as high in their colony here." And, underlining the growing danger of the situation, she reminded her audience that there were no immigration restrictions on Puerto Ricans entering the US.[8] Immediately, outraged *colonia* leaders called scores of meetings for "community defense" and deluged the First Lady with letters demanding that she apologize and recant. In their "violent protests" against "such an unwarranted statement against a group of law-abiding, hard-working American citizens," as one migrant wrote to the *New York Times* (April 13, 1934), migrants invoked what they perceived as their right to freedom from discrimination.

A group called the "Puerto Rico Spanish League" informed the First Lady via telegram that her pronouncements had created a hysteria about tuberculosis that threatened both the jobs and future employment prospects of Puerto Ricans working in restaurants, hotels, and private homes. Responding publicly at a dinner of social workers "interested in New York's Puerto Rican colony," she shot back sanctimoniously, "I think that the Puerto Rico Spanish League should face the fact that one never finds solutions until they confront a problem and accept the truth. If they continue to hide a condition, they will continue to have it. It is far better to bring it into the open and seek a cure."[9]

Bernardo Vega, a well-known activist and author of the telegram, followed up his communication to the First Lady with a long and eloquent letter to *La Prensa* readers, explaining why her comments had so injured residents of the *colonia* and implicitly rejecting her accusation that Puerto Ricans in New York sought to "hide their condition":

> . . . We already know how damaging such prejudice can be against any racial group in the United States.
>
> We continue to believe that a hostile atmosphere for the Puerto Rican element has been created unnecessarily, because those who do not go beyond the superficial in examining the statements of la Señora Roosevelt, will feel inclined, when they see a Puerto Rican, to shun him the way one flees from pests or the plague.(Iglesias, 1984)

There is no way to determine how many migrants actually lost their jobs or failed to land jobs in restaurants or private homes owing to public fears about their "contagion" in the spring and summer of 1934; Vega asserted that the numbers were substantial. He went on to link local conditions to the colonial condition of the island: he argued that Puerto Ricans' poor health and poor living conditions were largely attributable to the state of peonage to which they had been reduced by being displaced from the land, often at the hand of "compatriots of Mrs Delano Roosevelt" who owned most of the *latifundios* (sugar plantations) in Puerto Rico by the 1930s.[10] Migrants came to New York "fleeing the misery" of their island. "The sons of Puerto Rico who live in this city are not here by choice nor desire. We live in New York by necessity . . ." Finally, Vega wrote, "our problems cannot be solved by doing what Mrs. Roosevelt has done and portraying Puerto Ricans as a racial group afflicted with contagious diseases so that a few charitable Americans can give us alms while the rest—the majority—do nothing but insult us" (Iglesias, 1984).

Toward the end of the summer, migrants discovered that the "insult" to their *colonia* had also done concrete harm to an unexpected group: their children. Since the 1920s, several religious groups had provided funds to send several thousand Puerto Rican children, along with those of other "needy" families, to summer camps for several weeks in the summer. But this year, community leaders discovered that the casework supervisor at the Federation of Protestant

Welfare Agencies had decided that the Puerto Rican children of an East Harlem parish would not be allowed to attend the church's summer camp this year, "as we have been asked not to send any Puerto Rican children."[11]

Again from the *colonia* was swift and outrage widespread. The Liga Puertorriqueña called a mass demonstration, and Vega wrote that "practically every social, political, and religious group in El Barrio showed up for the planning meeting." The protest, held at the Park Palace, took the form of a mock tribunal in which the offending organizations were tried before a jury panel of "twenty-three delegates from various labor and religious organizations," with two attorneys as judges. The migrant activist and writer Jesús Colón acted as one of the district attorneys arguing on behalf of the Puerto Rican community. Colón and other Brooklyn community leaders also staged a mass demonstration to protest the discrimination against Puerto Rican children. The names of 24 organizations—including Democratic, communist, and labor groups, not all of them Puerto Rican or even Hispanic—crowded the bottom of the circular that advertised the demonstration (Iglesias, 1984; Colón Papers). Eleanor Roosevelt's name was not mentioned in the nine-paragraph "manifesto" included on the protest flyer, and she was not one of the "defendants" in the Park Palace mock trial, over which Bernardo Vega presided. But *colonia* members knew that the respected wife of their beloved president had rolled the first stone in what seemed like a new avalanche of discrimination against Puerto Ricans in New York.

This controversy over the First Lady's remarks remained outside of the realm of explicitly political concerns for *colonia* leaders, but it did forecast a new level of tension between Puerto Ricans and the federal government. José Giboyeaux, a migrant who worked as a carpenter for the WPA, later told an interviewer that although he had supported Roosevelt "absolutely 100%," he sympathized with the many Puerto Ricans, many of them Nationalists, who had "split from Roosevelt and from Mrs. Roosevelt over this issue." Although the controversy had nothing to do with the issue of Puerto Rican independence, protesters such as Vega framed their local rights—to freedom from defamation and discrimination—such that they were inseparable from the problem of Puerto Rico's political relationship to the US. In so doing, Vega championed a new framework for understanding Puerto Rican migrants' US citizenship, a diasporic one that presumed a necessary relationship between, on the one hand, their *social* rights as US citizens in a local arena (New York City) and, on the other hand, their *political* and *civic* rights as US citizens in a national/international arena (Puerto Rico). This interpretation of citizenship would be reflected throughout the period of nationalist fervor that erupted in the *colonia* less than two years later.

"*EL BARRIO* COMES ALIVE": DIASPORIC CITIZENSHIP RIGHTS AND NATIONALISM IN THE *COLONIA*

Whereas the Home Relief protests and the controversy with the First Lady mobilized primarily working-class migrants, the issue of Puerto Rican independence, heating up dramatically in the mid-1930s, generated a new twist in the class-inflected campaign for *colonia* "unity." After an explosion of Nationalist agitation in Puerto Rico in 1936 ignited Puerto Rican migrants in a firestorm of protest and political mobilizing over the question of independence, migrants across the class and political spectrum began to express support for Nationalist politics. But more important than this intra-*colonia* rapprochement was the pressure it generated on national-level policy: the entire *colonia* began to lean more heavily on the rhetorical promises of their American citizenship, now pushing not just for rights affecting their day-to-day survival, but for their ability to influence political outcomes on the island. The diasporic identity and focus on island issues that had earlier made Puerto Ricans seem irrelevant in US politics now—as migrants staged demonstrations in reaction to island turmoil and increasingly demanded that local representatives give them a voice in Congress on Puerto Rico's intractable "status question"—made them seem politically dangerous. Real political tension would develop between the Roosevelt administration and Puerto Rican islanders—and migrants, too—when an explosion of Nationalist-related violence on the island turned Puerto Rico into a political hot potato for the Roosevelt administration.

President Roosevelt had been beloved by Puerto Ricans on the mainland since his early public works programs seemed proof that he would make good on his campaign promises to help the poorest Americans. They admired him even more as a political leader when he began to advocate funds and leadership to begin a program of economic recovery in Puerto Rico. President Roosevelt and the First Lady had both played an active role, alongside several "brain trust" New Dealers, in the establishment of the Puerto Rican Reconstruction Administration (PRRA) in 1934; they had also lent their support to the PRRA's radical economic restructuring plan, named for its Puerto Rican Liberal author, Carlos Chardón. Puerto Ricans in New York, beginning to see some real improvements in daily life that they credited to the New Deal, had high hopes for the Roosevelts' recovery efforts in Puerto Rico as well, and some pronounced FDR "the greatest American ever born." Even against evidence that the New Deal had accomplished little in Puerto Rico in its first year—one man interviewed by reporters during Mrs. Roosevelt's 1934 visit said that he and his large family were forced to live on 50 cents a day, and pronounced that "the NRA treats us like dogs"—migrants' faith in the political good will of Roosevelt remained unshaken (*La Prensa*, March 12, 1934).

But the shooting of four young Nationalist demonstrators in October 1935 set off a chain of events that would alter the relationship of "*nuestro presidente*" to his Puerto Rican constituency. Nationalist Party leader Albizu Campos had been pushing to increase the visibility of his party, in part through Nationalists' practical and political support of the exploding labor movement; in response, federal and island officials had begun to redouble their repression of Nationalists, whom they saw as rabble-rousers aiming to use the antigovernment sentiment surrounding the strikes to build support for independence. Then, in late 1935, police killed four young Nationalists participating in a demonstration at the University of Puerto Rico at Río Piedras. Albizu and his party promised to avenge these deaths, and four months later, the police chief, Colonel Francis Riggs, was assassinated. The Nationalist Party did not publicly admit responsibility for the assassination; the police arrested two Nationalists who denied any involvement in the crime and who were then shot to death in San Juan as they allegedly tried to escape from jail. Puerto Ricans of all political stripes expressed outrage over what they saw as naked political violence committed by the government to further its agenda of public order and colonial control. Luis Muñoz Marín, the rising young leader in the Liberal Party and a staunch supporter of the Democratic administration in Washington, refused to condemn the Riggs assassination until the US government condemned the police shootings of the young Nationalists.

Suddenly, the Nationalist cause no longer looked like an extremist agenda nurtured by a small, unpopular minority. Across the island and in the New York *colonia*, sympathy for independence and its Nationalist proponents increased in inverse proportion to the declining tolerance of the US presence in Puerto Rico.[12] One East Harlem resident, who was not active in any of the Nationalist organizations but who described herself as a "Puerto Rican patriot," wrote to *La Prensa* that given the power of the US government across the world, "we must be friends of the United States, but we wish to apply the Monroe Doctrine to ourselves: Puerto Rico for the Puerto Ricans" (March 12, 1936).

In addition to the insular government's harsh reprisals against Nationalists—culminating in the charge of sedition against a number of party leaders, including Albizu—there were two far-reaching political outcomes of the events of 1935–1936. First, Senator Millard Tydings, a close friend of Riggs, proposed his punitive independence bill, which President Roosevelt and Interior Secretary Ickes had most likely helped to draft (Mathews, 1960). Tydings argued that the island's "disgraceful, corrupt, and fraudulent" elections had caused American lawmakers to "question the worth of American institutions . . . being adapted to the people of Puerto Rico and to the conditions under which they live" (US Congress, *Congressional Record*, 1936: 5925). In other words, Puerto Ricans should be granted independence because they were not worthy of the American-sponsored political system that served them under the current colonial arrangement. If Puerto Ricans voted for independence in the plebiscite outlined by the bill, they would separate from the US under the following terms: all federal assistance programs, including New Deal programs under the PRRA, would immediately cease (Tydings told the Congress that "it seems as if the more we do the worse conditions become in the island"); the full US tariff on imported goods would be imposed incrementally over four years at the rate of 25% per year; and the new government of the island would have to create its own military force and infrastructure within six months. In addition, Puerto Ricans would have six months to choose between Puerto Rican and US citizenship, and thereafter Puerto Ricans entering the US would be subject to US immigration laws, which under the Tydings bill would allow only 500 islanders a year to immigrate to the US (US Congress, *Congressional Record*, 1936: 5926; Trías Monge, 1997).

Simultaneously, Ernest Gruening, head of the PRRA, and another member of the Roosevelts' inner circle, systematically "purged" his organization of virtually all Liberal Party members (most of whom supported independence), accusing them of corruption and "anti-American" activity, although the Liberals had been New Dealers' staunchest supporters on the island. Gruening's anti-Liberal campaign eviscerated the PRRA by driving out its key leaders; ultimately, the organization was stripped of its power to such an extent that its role in the island's economic reconstruction and recovery faltered (Mathews, 1960).

In New York, the *colonia* had "come alive," politically, in the wake of these events. The Tydings bill in particular inspired agitation; it "raised all Puerto Ricans' hopes so high and then dashed them, [and] seems to have lighted the spark that revived Lower Harlem's political life," observed a WPA field worker (Spanish Book, WPA Papers). Support for the Nationalist party, which had traditionally come from the elite, now flowed from the *colonia*'s working class as well. At scores of rallies in dance halls and on the streets of Harlem, migrants of all classes lobbied for independence at a fair price (Meyer, 1989).[13]

A year later, the killing of more than 20 unarmed Nationalist demonstrators by police in Ponce, Puerto Rico, added even more intensity to the political situation (Mathews, 1960: 310–315; Iglesias, 1984: 192).[14] In the aftermath of the "Ponce massacre," when the Roosevelt Administration came to the defense of the island's governor, Blanton Winship—whom many, not just Nationalists, viewed as guilty of "gross violation of civil rights and incredible police brutality," as an ACLU memo put it—President Roosevelt, could not emerge unscathed in the eyes of his migrant constituency. A number of Puerto Ricans interviewed by WPA fieldworkers admitted, diffidently, to a newly critical view of the president. Said one, "President Roosevelt is my ideal of a great leader of peoples, politically and socially . . . I do not approve of his foreign policy, however I admit that perhaps I do not have the proper knowledge of his aims." The migrant Ramón Giboyeaux asserted simply that "Roosevelt . . . committed a tremendous error . . . over the issue of Poncho [Ponce]" (Spanish Book, WPA Papers).

Amid the fallout from this political tumult, Puerto Ricans in New York gravitated in even greater numbers to the leadership of Vito Marcantonio, East Harlem's beloved congressional representative from 1934 to 1948. With radical-left rhetoric, Marcantonio supported both the Nationalist cause in Puerto Rico and the everyday rights, particularly those relating to housing and relief, of his poor constituency in East Harlem. During the summer of 1936, while the staff of his East Harlem office continued to respond personally to virtually every request for assistance from the residents of his largely Puerto Rican district, Marcantonio flew to Puerto Rico to offer legal counsel to Albizu Campos and the seven other Nationalists who had been convicted of conspiring to overthrow the US government.

When the Tydings bill threatened to divide the *colonia*—some advocated accepting independence "even if we die of hunger," while others argued that independence on Tydings' terms would be the death of the island nation—Marcantonio countered with a bill of his own in which he emphasized the the Puerto Rican people's "right of self-determination." He proposed his bill as a real alternative to a Tydings-style independence, but also as an effort to bridge Nationalists' rhetoric of anti-imperialism with the "rights talk" stemming from the Puerto Rican diaspora's local concerns.[15] "The dignity of the American people as a freedom-loving Nation," Marcantonio declared, "demands that Puerto Rico be judged under the principle of self-determination of nations." The counter-bill that he proposed called for open immigration of Puerto Ricans to the US and a suspension of the tariff on Puerto Rican products shipped to the US. Most boldly, the bill included a "substantial indemnity" to be paid to the "long-suffering people of Puerto Rico" as partial compensation for the estimated $400 million "extracted" from the island's economy by US citizens and business interests (US Congress, *Congressional Record,* 1936: 6726). Typical of its hands-off approach to the matter of Puerto Rico's political status, Congress took no action on either of these bills, and both died after the legislative session ended.

Migrants themselves echoed these demands linking local (New York City) and island-based rights in the chants they sounded in the largest public demonstration the *barrio* had ever seen, a proindependence rally staged on the day of Marcantonio's return from Puerto Rico. The *New York Times* reported that 10,000 Puerto Ricans, "representing a score of political and social clubs in the city, paraded for three hours through the streets of lower Harlem . . . to protest the attitude and actions of `Imperialistic America' in making 'slaves' of the natives of the island" (August 30, 1936). "Free Puerto Rico," "Down with Yankee Imperialism!"; and "Puerto Ricans should not have to die of hunger for independence!" shouted protesters. One demonstrator interviewed by *La Prensa* insisted, in the language of this diasporic rights talk, that "the New Deal is for Puerto Ricans in the island and in New York!" (August 31, 1936). The combination of rising nationalist sentiment in the *colonia* and the Roosevelt administration's response to the political problems in Puerto Rico—its divestiture, more or less, from the island—had inspired a shift in the political discourse of the working-class *colonia* in particular. Where migrants formerly had focused primarily on rights to political representation in the city and rights to relief and to freedom from discrimination, as discussed in the previous sections, they now articulated demands, using anti-imperialist discourse, for a set of rights that linked local problems to the right of self-determination for Puerto Ricans.

THE SHORT-LIVED VICTORY OF OSCAR GARCÍA RIVERA

While a new concatenation of leftists and Nationalists was busy fomenting the "political upheaval" that defined the political culture of the Puerto Rican *colonia* in 1936–1937, more centrist migrant leaders focused on cementing a deal with the city's Republican Party to back a

Puerto Rican candidate for the New York State Assembly in the 1937 elections. Oscar García Rivera, a lawyer who had migrated to New York after World War I, won the race in a landslide victory that depended on an unprecedented crossover vote from Puerto Ricans in the 17th District. Whereas registered Democrats in this district typically outnumbered Republicans six to one in the 1930s, and Democratic candidates almost always defeated their Republican opponents, García Rivera beat out the three-term incumbent Meyer Alterman, with almost 60% of the vote (New York City Board of Elections, 1932–1937).[16] Even as an increasing percentage of *colonia* voters was moving further to the left, García Rivera's center-left campaign became a rallying point for migrants across the political spectrum, and he became the first Puerto Rican to win a major office in the US.

Although García Rivera's victory signified the political "unification" of the East Harlem *colonia* on voting day, the political upheaval of the mid-1930s and continuing economic depression made the long-term project of political empowerment look at least as problematic as it had seemed at the beginning of the decade. When *La Prensa* editors solicited input from readers in the spring of 1938 on the question "How can the *colonia* organize itself politically?"—mirroring its 1933 series on " *el momento político y los hispanos*"—more than half of the letters came from Democratic leaders and voters who either directly or indirectly admonished Puerto Ricans for betraying the Democratic Party, or at least suggested that it was a mistake for Puerto Ricans to turn their backs on the Democrats who had for so long provided patronage to the migrant community (Thomas, 2002). Several echoed the claim of the rising leader among Puerto Rican Democrats Dr. José Cesteros, who had issued a radio address during the November campaign invoking "our savior" Roosevelt, and proclaiming that the candidates of the state Democratic ticket "represented the poor and the suffering." José Vivaldi, president of East Harlem's New Deal Democratic Club, faulted the "professional classes" among Democrats of East Harlem for "losing control" of their traditionally Democratic district.[17] Across the river, Puerto Rican leaders in Brooklyn, who worried little about losing their district to a Republican ticket, spearheaded the organization of a nonpartisan "*gran conferencia*" of political and community groups from both boroughs in the fall in an effort to patch up political divisions and heal political wounds in the *colonia*.[18]

García Rivera's response to this partisan frenzy on the part of Democrats was to remind Hispanic voters that they should vote for candidates, not for parties. "The Puerto Rican *colonia* living here must abandon the denigrating and outdated strong-man leadership style [*encaudillamiento*] associated with the political 'Bosses,' and unite themselves efficiently to select their own [Puerto Rican] candidates, those who best bring together their multiple interests," he declared. A Republican reader seconded García Rivera's claim, arguing that the Democrats never had and never would live up to their promises to Puerto Ricans, who, "for inexplicable reasons line up in droves for the Democrats." As the 1938 elections approached, another Republican reader admonished her audience to "teach a lesson once again to those [Democrats] who deny us, after 25 years of exploitation, the right to have a representative that is genuinely ours."[19]

Several community leaders who planned to participate in the *congreso* argued that "voices of the *colonia*" should be included while it set its agenda and cited the broad range of input provided by the public's letters published in *La Prensa*'s spring debate. A number of readers had warned that political and social unity could not be realized without greater attention to the economic problems that still plagued the community. Many contributors agreed that poverty hindered community organization, but argued that it was discrimination that kept Puerto Ricans poor, and that political and social empowerment offered the only real weapons to protect "our orphaned and abandoned *Colonia*." "We must make [leaders] understand the necessity of political brotherhood in a country in which, despite having the right to vote, they consider us foreigners, . . . [because] we were the last to arrive . . . " said one contributor (August 25, 1938). The Nationalist Isabel O'Neill implored her readers, "beware, brothers, because we are ALONE" (June 23, 1938).

After winning again on the American Labor Party ticket in 1938, García Rivera lost the 1940 election—a year of Democratic landslide as FDR prepared the US for war—to a West Indian–born Harlem Democrat, Hulan Jack. It is unclear how many Puerto Ricans in the 17th District cast Democratic votes that year, and it is possible only to speculate about the motivations of *colonia* voters in this election. Evidently, the fragile "unity" of the *colonia*, its ability to line up behind a Puerto Rican candidate, foundered once again on migrants' problematic relationship to the Democratic Party, and *colonia* leaders across the political spectrum continued to disagree about which party's support promised the most payoff in future elections.[20]

In many ways, Puerto Rican migrants' rhetoric of ethnic unity and their approaches to local political empowerment had changed little in the years of political tumult and intensive activism both on the island and in the *barrio*. The same class-inflected disagreements about party affiliations and electoral strategies that had shaped the discourse in the 1933 debate on "*el momento político y los hispanos*" were trotted out again in 1938 in a similar forum on political organization in the *colonia*. Yet during this decade, Puerto Rican migrants had in fact revolutionized the role they played in both local and national politics. In local protests against unfair relief distribution and through their overwhelming support for independence in the wake of political repression of Nationalists on the island, Puerto Ricans had begun to make claims on their rights as local citizens, demanding social equality. They also defined their rights as citizens of a Puerto Rican diaspora, demanding, before a national audience that included the Democratic Party and the Roosevelt administration, the right to self-determination for their homeland. *Colonia* activists called attention to the fact that liberals' commitment to "freedom and democracy" elsewhere in the world had yet to be extended to the island of Puerto Rico. In making these claims, migrants were not just elaborating a Puerto Rican, diasporic version of a nascent New Deal "rights talk"; they were also articulating, a critique of the practice of New Deal liberalism in the local and international arenas.

Unlike the "rights talk" of African American activists, which was backed by a far-reaching urban constituency that grew steadily in numbers and in power throughout the World War II era, Puerto Ricans' political challenges would be contained: at the local level, they paid a price for their association with Marcantonio, who would within a few years be marked "red"; and agitation about island independence, never part of the American public's consciousness to begin with, was easily edged out of the headlines by the shadow of war in Europe. By the start of the "great migration" from Puerto Rico at the end of World War II, Puerto Ricans' particular version of a New Deal rights discourse had been all but erased from political memory. Amid wave after wave of media vilification of the new migrants, starting around 1947, and obsessive public discussion of New York's "Puerto Rican problem," even migrants' liberal defenders labeled them "passive" and politically "apathetic," treating them as victims rather than as collaborators with a history of political activism in the city (Thomas, 2002).

This erasure of Puerto Rican actors in 1930s politics in New York can be attributed partly to a demographic fact: Puerto Ricans lacked the numerical force, even by 1940, to sustain the attention of Democratic Party leaders.[21] But more importantly, I argue, it was because their protests against New Deal liberals' actions in Puerto Rico were so forceful, and so threatening to the newly triumphal version of late-1930s liberalism, that Puerto Ricans were erased from the larger story of the New Deal "rights revolution." In the tumultuous politics of the 1930s, Puerto Ricans were silenced—not only as historical actors, people participating in "what happened"; more importantly, they were silenced as *narrators,* people who control "that which is said to have happened" (Trouillot, 1995). Recently, historians have recovered the voices of diverse narrators who pointed to cracks in the façade of liberal citizenship on the domestic front in the 1930s: African American activists on the vanguard of the civil rights movement and labor leaders at the helm of the Congress of Industrial Organizations (CIO), historical actors waging a "rights revolution" for social, civic, and legal equality (Weiss, 1979; Cohen, 1990; Brinkley, 1995; Savage, 1999). Puerto Rican leaders of the *colonia*'s vibrant political culture have narrated—in interviews, memoirs, and other little-known sources—their particular participation in this movement. They, too, are a central part of the history of changing discourses of US citizenship, for all Americans, during the New Deal.

NOTES

1. Citizenship, studied from a theoretical and structural point of view, has become a popular topic among social and political scientists in the last decade or so. See, for instance, the work of Brubaker (1992, 1996), Smith (1997), and Ellison (1997). In the past several years, a handful of historians, anthropologists, and others have begun to investigate citizenship in terms of its meaning and practice in the everyday lives of people. See, for instance, Somers (1993), Flores and Benmayor (1997), and Arnot and Dillabough (2000). There is a paucity of academic study of Puerto Ricans' experience in the US *except* as a "problem population" studied "ad nauseum" (as historian Ruth Glasser has written) by social scientists. Only three book-length studies of Puerto Ricans in the US have been published by historians: Whalen (2000), Sanchez-Korrol (1983), and Glasser (1995). Puerto Ricans have also been entirely left out of most scholarly histories of New York City; a rare exception is Schneider (1999).
2. For general sources on the Harlem riot of 1935, see Greenberg (1991) and Fogelson and Rubenstein (1969).
3. See the population map, "Street Map Shows Distribution of Harlem's Population," accompanying the article "Idleness, Harlem's Chief Threat," reproduced by the *New York Sun* (March 23, 1935), which borrowed the map from a publication by the Welfare Council (Welfare Council, 1930). In a preliminary memo suggesting possible areas of investigation for the Mayor's Committee, Walter White, Secretary of the

NAACP, did refer to the presence of Puerto Ricans in advising that the "origin of population" in Harlem be examined along with housing, schools, health, and recreation. White proposed that the Committee address the "interrelation of various groups making up [the] Negro community of Harlem," including Puerto Ricans, West Indians, and Virgin Islanders, as well as "the effect of friction or cooperation between various groups" (LaGuardia Papers).

4. There was, moreover, only one piece of testimony (reported in *The Red H.R.B. Worker,* May 1935) that was even *about* Puerto Ricans, and it was palpably hostile. James Ford, one of black Harlem's leading Communist organizers, singled out a Puerto Rican Harlem HRB precinct administrator, Victor Suárez, as the local relief official most guilty of outright prejudice against his Negro clients. Ford alleged that Suárez had stated, "on the record," that 90% of Harlem's Negro relief recipients were "fakers." Suárez had also reportedly explained that the low level of promotions among Negro HRB employees was due to the fact that "Negroes were not educationally qualified to hold the better jobs in the Home Relief Bureau." Neither James Ford nor any of his fellow complainants framed the accusations against Suárez in terms of his identity as a Puerto Rican; nor did any of the press coverage of the issue remark on the fact that Suárez was Puerto Rican; yet the subtext of Ford's accusations suggests that the latent hostility toward Puerto Ricans in Harlem is an important part of the story (Colón Papers).

5. Since this and the above-cited letter were written on the same day (June 24, 1935), and since the membership of the two organizations overlapped (Antonio Rivera, who wrote a letter in his capacity of secretary of the Liga, was also the president of the Junta Liberal, of which Isabel O'Neill served as treasurer), it is clear that the letters together represent an organized protest against LaGuardia's exclusion of Puerto Ricans from the riot investigations.

6. Sol Bloom, a Democratic congressional representative for East Harlem in the 1920s, had actually visited Puerto Rico in a show of support for his migrant constituency in 1925. But his efforts backfired when Bloom later advised Puerto Ricans to give up their struggle for autonomy and compared *independentistas* to "children who refuse to take their medicine, and in the end will have to take what the doctor . . . gives them." A coalition of angry migrants wrote to Bloom to renounce his abuse of his constituents' support. They also informed Bloom that, since Puerto Ricans in the 19th District "hold the balance of power," they could, "at a moment's notice . . . decide the victory of a candidate" in the next election. Apparently, Bloom took this threat seriously, and in 1926 made an election-eve pledge to Puerto Ricans in his district that he would "uphold the liberal recognition of autonomous rights of small nations and groups of people" with the introduction of a House bill to allow Puerto Ricans to elect their own governor by 1928. *La Prensa* covered this issue in articles on 28 April, 1925 and 22 October, 1925, and the

New York Times mentioned Bloom's bill on Puerto Rico in an article on 15 July, 1926. Bernardo Vega also talks about the incident in his *Memoirs* (Iglesias, 1984).

7. Fears about anti–Puerto Rican prejudice galvanized the *colonia* for the first time during the summer of 1926, after a series of violent clashes between Jews and Hispanics in Harlem. In the wake of these events, a number of community defense organizations sprang up, most notably the Liga Puertorriqueña e Hispana. For more on this period of the migrant community's development, see Thomas (2002) and James (1998).

8. These events were reported in both the *New York Times* ("President's Wife Sees a New Order," 10 April, 1934) and *La Prensa,* ("Instantáneas de la Colonia" April 23, 1934).

9. The telegram was from the Liga Puertorriqueña e Hispana, whose president at the time was Bernardo Vega. *La Prensa* printed Vega's letter (April 30, 1934) and the *New York Times* covered the issue as well (April 19, 1934).

10. Indeed, there was much truth in Vega's assertion. Between the US takeover of the island in 1898 and 1935, the amount of arable land converted to sugar production had increased almost 400%, and over two thirds of this land was owned or controlled by four US sugar corporations; during approximately that time period, the value of sugar exports increased about 1000%. Moreover, although the Jones Act of 1917 included a clause that outlawed the creation of plantations larger than 500 acres, more than 65% of the island's land devoted to sugar was held by plantations of more than 500 acres (Dietz, 1986).

11. Vega claims that up to 6,000 Puerto Rican children were sent to such camps in this period (Iglesias, 1984).

12. Illustrations of the increasing popularity of Nationalist events, both leading up to and following the killing of the four Nationalists and the assassination of Riggs, include the following: "Gran Mitín Público, Pro-Presos Nacionalistas de Puerto Rico," a flyer by the Junta Nacionalista Puertorriqueña issued on 29 October, 1936 (Vando Papers); a letter from Carlos Vélez, Presidente del Partido Nacionalista de Puerto Rico, Junta de Nueva York, to Sr. Presidente y Señores Miembros de la Vanguardia Puertorriqueña, regarding a "magno Congreso Pro-Convención Constituyente de la República de Puerto Rico" dated May 16, 1936, (Colón papers); and a flyer by the Junta Nacionalista Puertorriqueña, titled "Gran Mitín de Protesta," from February 24, 1937 (Vando papers). There were also scores of letters from readers printed in *La Prensa*'s "De Nuestros Lectores" section between mid-March and late August 1936 illustrating the same trend. Although *La Prensa*'s politically moderate-to-conservative editors printed a number of letters criticizing the growing levels of radical nationalism among *colonia* members, or expressing generally moderate views on the question of the US presence in Puerto Rico, the series of readers' letters suggests a broad level of support for independence in this period.

13. Nationalist demonstrations in Harlem were becoming more frequent by 1934–1935, as leaders in the *colonia* rode the wave of popularity of Nationalists in Puerto Rico, who capitalized politically on the worsening economic situation there. *La Prensa* covered these demonstrations in a number of articles in this period (January 3, 1934; September 3, 1935; March 2, 1936).

14. Organizers of the Nationalist demonstration had been issued a permit by the town's mayor, but the island's police chief and governor revoked the permit at the last minute because they believed that the parade would end in violence. Demonstrators proceeded with the event anyway, and the local chief of police stationed 150 officers, armed with rifles and submachine guns, along the parade route. The source of the first shot was never determined, but photographs of the event reveal that the marchers, at least, were unarmed.

15. About his opponent's vision of the island's "apparent independence," Marcantonio remarked: "Instead of offering genuine independence to the people of Puerto Rico, his bill offers them an American-controlled plebiscite and a commonwealth which will be under the thumb of the American Government. The independence subsequently offered by the Tydings bill would be considerably curtailed by the menacing presence of an American naval reservation . . . At the same time the Tydings bill, with its tariff provisions, threatens to ruin the only present source of Puerto Rican income, which is the sale of their cash crops in the American market. His bill does not provide for the development of substitutes for the dominating and American-dominated sugar industry." (US Congress, *Congressional Record*, 1936: 6726).

16 The voter registration figures for the 17th Assembly District for 1932, 1933, and 1937, for example, are as follows: 1932: 17,439 Democrats; 2,864 Republicans 1933: 15,185 Democrats; 2,328 Republicans 1937: 12,464 Democrats; 2,834 Republicans García Rivera won 8,798 votes in the 1937 election, compared to 6,218 votes won by Alterman.

17. *La Prensa* covered this campaign in a number of articles, including "Los comités hispanos cerraron anoche con discursos su campaña en New York," (November 2, 1937) and "Los boricuas debemos de controlar el Distrito 17," (May 17, 1938). Despite these laments about Puerto Ricans' disorganized support for the Democratic Party, Tammany representatives lingered in the *colonia*, still, in the late 1930s, and many migrants supported them. A WPA field worker wrote a memo in May 1936 on "Puerto Rican Organizations in New York—Puerto Rican Political and Social League," describing the Puerto Rican Political and Social League, organized in January 1936, as an "independent political and social organization composed mostly of Puerto Ricans and avowedly concerned only with political affairs in the 17th Assembly District," with 265 members, men between the ages of 21 and 30. He went on to note parenthetically that "in the opinion of the Field worker, backed by

general information current in the neighborhood and by remarks of Mr. Pagan Tomei and others, this is one of the many political groups set up by Tammany political leaders in Lower Harlem to control the vote there by means of privileged patronage. The social fact of the existence of these organizations among PRs is of importance in any depiction of Puerto Rican life in Harlem" (Spanish Book, WPA Papers).

18. A number of articles in *La Prensa* discussed these trends in Brooklyn: "Debe celebrarse una asamblea para la unificación de hispanos en Brooklyn" (May 30, 1938); "Formaron ya su delegación para la gran conferencia" (August 11, 1938); and "La unión de las sociedades borinqueñas fue acordada" (August 27, 1938).

19. These positions were expressed in a series of articles and letters printed in *La Prensa,* including "Nos hace falta un líder político hispano en N.Y." (June 7, 1938); "¿Cómo puede organizarse políticamente la colonia hispana de New York?", an interview with Oscar García Rivera (June 10, 1938); Juan J. Blasini's response to "¿Cómo puede organizarse políticamente la colonia hispana de New York?" (June 11, 1938); and a letter from María Luisa Lecompte de Varona (August 6, 1938). Despite these partisan salvos, Puerto Ricans Republicans made good on their promises to promote nonpartisan unity, and participated in the "Congreso Borinqueño," along with community leaders across the political spectrum, just after the election. The victorious Republican Party members or sympathizers headlined the event, covered by *La Prensa*—Resident Commissioner Santiago Iglesias, Mayor LaGuardia, and *La Prensa* owner and editor José Comprubí, among others—but Democrats figured prominently on the program, as did representatives of workers' organizations and nonpartisan community groups. (November, 11 1938; Iglesias, 1984).

20. Historian Gerald Meyer, who has written in detail on the political history of East Harlem during the Marcantonio years, attributes Jack's victory (and García Rivera's defeat) primarily to the "coattails" effect of the presidential election, which Meyer claims brought an additional 4,000 Democratic voters to the polls in the 17th District that year (Meyer, 1989).

21. In 1940, the US Bureau of the Census counted just under 70,000 Puerto Ricans living in the US, 61,463 of those in New York City. African Americans, however, numbered over 450,000 in New York City by 1940 (US Bureau of the Census, 1963). It is important to note, of course, that historically, Puerto Ricans—like all racial minorities and other impoverished groups—have been significantly undercounted by census-takers.

REFERENCES

Arnot, Madeleine, and Joanne Dillabough. eds 2000. *Challenging Democracy: International Perspectives on Gender, Education, and Citizenship.* New York: Routledge.

Brinkley, Alan. 1995. *The End of Reform: New Deal Liberalism in Recession and War.* New York: Vintage.

Brubaker, Rogers. 1992. *Citizenship and Nationhood in France and Germany.* Cambridge, MA: Harvard University Press.

Brubaker, Rogers. 1996. *Nationalism Reframed: Nationhood and the National Question in the New Europe.* New York: Cambridge University Press.

Cohen, Lizabeth. 1990. *Making a New Deal: Industrial Workers in Chicago, 1919–1939.* New York: Cambridge University Press.

Colón, Jesús. Papers. 1915–1965. Center for Puerto Rican Studies, Hunter College.

Dietz, James. 1986. *Economic History of Puerto Rico: Institutional Change and Capitalist Development.* Princeton, NJ: Princeton University Press.

Ellison, Nick. 1997. Towards a New Social Politics: CITP and Reflexivity in Late Modernity. Sociology 31: 697–717.

Flores, William V, and Rina Benmayor. ed. 1997. *Latino Cultural Citizenship: Claiming Identity, Space, and Rights.* Boston, MA: Beacon Press.

Fogelson, Robert, and Richard Rubenstein, ed. 1969. *The Complete Report of Mayor LaGuardia's Commission on the Harlem Riot of March 19, 1935.* New York: Arno Press and the New York Times.

Glasser, Ruth. 1995. *My Music Is My Flag: Puerto Rican Musicians and Their New York Communities, 1917–1940.* Berkeley: University of California Press.

Greenberg, Cheryl Lynn. 1991. *Or Does it Explode? Black Harlem in the Great Depression.* New York: Oxford University Press.

Iglesias, César Andreu, ed. 1984. *Memoirs of Bernardo Vega: A Contribution to the History of the Puerto Rican Community in New York.* New York: Monthly Review Press.

James, Winston. 1998. *Holding Aloft the Banner of Ethiopia.* New York: Verso.

LaGuardia, Fiorello. Papers. Municipal Record and Research Center, New York City.

Laguerre, Michel. 1998. *Diasporic Citizenship: Haitians in Transnational America.* New York: St. Martin's Press.

Mathews, Thomas. 1960. *Puerto Rican Politics and the New Deal.* Gainesville: University of Florida Press.

Meyer, Gerald. 1989. *Vito Marcantonio: Radical Politician, 1902–1954.* Albany: State University of New York Press.

New York City Board of Elections. 1932–1937. *Annual Report.*

Sanchez-Korrol, Virginia. 1983. *From Colonia to Community: The History of Puerto Ricans in New York City, 1917–1948.* Westport, CT: Greenwood Press.

Savage, Barbara. 1999. *Broadcasting Freedom: Radio, War, and the Politics of Race, 1938–1948.* Chapel Hill: University of North Carolina Press.

Schneider, Eric. 1999. *Vampires, Dragons, and Egyptian Kings: Youth Gangs in Postwar New York.* Princeton, NJ: Princeton University Press.

Smith, Rogers. 1997. *Civic Ideals: Conflicting Visions of Citizenship in U.S. History.* New Haven, CT: Yale University Press.

Somers, Margaret. 1993. Citizenship and the Public Sphere: Law, Community, and Political Culture in the Transition to Democracy. *American Sociological Review* 58: 587–620.

Thomas, Lorrin. 2002. Citizens on the Margins: Puerto Rican Migrants in New York City, 1917–1960. Ph.D. dissertation. University of Pennsylvania.

Trías Monge, Jos. 1997. *Puerto Rico: The Trials of the Oldest Colony in the World.* 94–96. New Haven, CT: Yale University Press.

Trouillot, Michel-Rolphe. 1995. *Silencing the Past: Power and the Production of History.* Boston, MA: Beacon Press.

US Bureau of the Census. 1963. *U.S. Census of Population: 1960.* Washington, DC: U.S. Government Printing office.

US Congress. 1936. *Congressional Record.* Volume 80.

Vando, Erasmo. Papers. Center for Puerto Rican Studies, Hunter College.

Weiss, Richard. 1979. Ethnicity and Reform: Minorities and the Ambiance of the Depression Years. *Journal of American History* 66: 566–585.

Welfare Council of New York City. 1930. *Population in Health Areas: New York City, 1930.* New York.

Whalen, Carmen. 2000. *From Puerto Rico to Philadelphia: Puerto Rican Workers and Postwar Economies.* Philadelphia, PA: Temple University Press.

WPA Federal Writers Project. 1936. "Puerto Rican Political Alignments in New York." September. Spanish Book, WPA files, reel 269.

PART III

Citizenship: Public Policy Implications

CHAPTER 3

The Legal Production of Mexican/Migrant "Illegality"

Nicholas De Genova

Mexican migration to the US is distinguished by a seeming paradox that is seldom examined: while no other country has supplied nearly as many migrants to the US as Mexico has since 1965, virtually all major changes in US immigration law during this period have created ever more severe restrictions on the conditions of "legal" migration from Mexico. Indeed, this seeming paradox presents itself in a double sense: on the one hand, apparently liberalizing immigration laws have in fact concealed their significantly restrictive features, especially for Mexicans; on the other hand, ostensibly restrictive immigration laws intended to deter migration have nonetheless been instrumental in sustaining Mexican migration, but only by significantly restructuring migrants' legal status as "undocumented." Beginning in the 1960s—precisely when Mexican migration escalated dramatically—and ever since, persistent revisions in the law have made it virtually impossible for the great majority who would migrate from Mexico to do so in accord with the law and have thus played an instrumental role in the production of a legally vulnerable, undocumented workforce of "illegal aliens."

This chapter elaborates the historical specificity of contemporary Mexican migration to the US as it has come to be located in the legal (political) economy of the US nation-state, and thereby constituted as an object of the law, especially since 1965. More precisely, it interrogates the history of changes in US immigration law through the specific lens of how these revisions have had a distinct impact upon

Mexicans in particular. Only in light of this sociolegal history does it become possible to sustain a critical perspective that is not complicit in the naturalization of Mexican migrants' "illegality" as a mere fact of life, the presumably transparent consequence of unauthorized border crossing or some other violation of immigration law.[1] Indeed, to sustain an emphatic concern to denaturalize the reification of this distinction, I deploy quotes throughout this chapter, wherever the terms "legal" or "illegal" modify migration or migrants.

In addition to simply designating a juridical status in relation to the US nation-state and its laws of immigration, naturalization, and citizenship, migrant "illegality" signals a specifically *spatialized* sociopolitical condition. "Illegality" is lived through a palpable sense of deportability, that is the possibility of deportation, which is to say, the possibility of being removed from the space of the US nation-state. The legal production of "illegality" provides an apparatus for sustaining Mexican migrants' vulnerability and tractability as workers whose labor power, inasmuch as it is deportable, becomes an eminently disposable commodity. Deportability is decisive in the legal production of Mexican/migrant "illegality" and the militarized policing of the US–Mexico border, however, only insofar as some are deported so that most may ultimately remain (undeported)—as workers whose particular migrant status has been rendered "illegal." Thus, in the everyday life of Mexican migrants, in innumerable places throughout the US, "illegality" reproduces the practical repercussions of the physical border between the US and Mexico across which undocumented migration is constituted. In this important sense, migrant "illegality" is a spatialized social condition that is inseparable from the particular ways that Mexican migrants are likewise racialized as "illegal aliens"—as invasive violators of the law, incorrigible "foreigners" subverting the integrity of "the nation" and its sovereignty from *within* the space of the US nation-state. Thus, as a simultaneously spatialized and racialized social condition, migrant "illegality" is also a central feature of the ways that "Mexican"-ness is thereby reconfigured in *racialized* relation to the hegemonic "national" identity of "American"-ness (De Genova, 2005). Although it is beyond the scope of this chapter, it is nevertheless crucial to locate these conjunctures of race, space, and "illegality" in terms of an earlier history of the intersections of race and citizenship. That history is chiefly distinguished, on the one hand, by the broader historical formulation of white supremacy in relation to "immigration" and, on the other, by the more specific legacy of warfare and conquest in what would come to be called "the American Southwest," culminating in the Treaty of

Guadalupe Hidalgo of 1848, which occasioned the first historical deliberations in the US over questions concerning the citizenship and nationality of Mexicans.

THE "REVOLVING DOOR" AND THE MAKING OF A TRANSNATIONAL HISTORY

Originating in the shared, albeit unequal, history of invasion and war by which roughly half of Mexico's territory came to be conquered and colonized by the US nation-state, the newly established border long went virtually unregulated and movement across it went largely unhindered. During the latter decades of the 19th century, as a regional political economy took shape in what is now the US Southwest, mining, railroads, ranching, and agriculture relied extensively on the active recruitment of Mexican labor (Barrera, 1979; Acuña, 1981; Gómez-Quiñones, 1994). Mexicans were encouraged to move freely across the border, and in effect, come to work without any official authorization or documents (Samora, 1971; García, 1980; Calavita, 1992).[2]

After decades of enthusiastically recruiting Chinese migrant labor, among the very first actual US immigration laws was the Chinese Exclusion Act of 1882 (22 Stat. 58). So began an era of immigration regulation that sought to exclude whole groups even from entry into the country, solely on the basis of race or nationality. Eventually, with the passage of the Immigration Act of 1917 (Act of February 5, 1917; 39 Stat. 874), an "All-Asia Barred Zone" was instituted, prohibiting migration from all of Asia (Hing, 1993; Kim, 1994; Salyer, 1995; Ancheta, 1998; Chang, 1999).[3] In the wake of repeated restrictions against "Asiatics," Mexican migrant labor became an indispensable necessity for capital accumulation in the region. During and after the years of the Mexican Revolution and World War I, from 1910 to 1930, approximately one-tenth of Mexico's total population relocated north of the border, partly owing to social disruptions and dislocations within Mexico during this period of political upheaval, but principally driven and often directly orchestrated by labor demand in new industries and agriculture in the US (cf. Cardoso, 1980).

During this same era, a dramatically restrictive system of national-origins immigration quotas was formulated for European migration and put in place through the passage of the Quota Law of 1921 (Act of May 19, 1921; 42 Stat. 5), and then further amplified by the Immigration Act of 1924 (Act of May 26, 1924; 43 Stat. 153; also known as the Johnson–Reed Act). The 1924 law's national-origins system limited migration on the basis of a convoluted formula that made unequal numerical allotments for immigrant visas, on a country-by-country basis. In effect, this regulatory apparatus had confined migration from the entire Eastern Hemisphere to approximately 150,000 annually; within that ceiling, it had guaranteed that roughly 85% of the allotments were reserved for migrants of northwestern European origin (Higham, 1955[1988]; Reimers, 1985[1992]). Drawing upon 42 volumes (published in 1910 and 1911 by US Immigration Commissions) that compiled "findings" concerning the "racial" composition and "quality" of the US population, the 1924 Immigration Act codified the gamut of popular prejudices about greater and lesser inherent degrees of "assimilability" among variously racialized and nationally stigmatized migrant groups. *The Congressional Record* bears ample testimony to the avowed preoccupation with maintaining the "white"/"Caucasian" racial purity of "American" national identity—"an unmistakable declaration of white immigration policy" (Hutchinson, 1981: 167). Remarkably, in spite of the vociferous objections of some of the most vitriolic nativists and, more importantly, as a testament to the utter dependency of employers upon Mexican/migrant labor, particularly in the Southwest, migration from the countries of the Western Hemisphere—Mexico, foremost among them—was left absolutely unrestricted by any numerical quotas.

It is revealing that the US Border Patrol, from 1924—when it was first created—until 1940, operated under the auspices of the Department of Labor. By the late 1920s, the Border Patrol had very quickly assumed its distinctive role as a special police force for the repression of Mexican workers in the US (Mirandé, 1987; Ngai, 1999, 2004). Selective enforcement of the law—coordinated with seasonal labor demand by US employers—instituted a "revolving door" policy, whereby mass deportations would be concurrent with an overall, large-scale importation of Mexican migrant labor (Cockcroft, 1986). Although there were no *quantitative* restrictions (numerical quotas) on "legal" Mexican migration until 1965, Mexican migrants could nonetheless be conveniently denied entry into the US, or deported from it, on the basis of a selective enforcement of *qualitative* features of immigration law, beginning at least as early as the 1920s.

During this era, the regulatory and disciplinary role of deportation operated against Mexican migrants on the basis of rules and regulations governing *who* would be allowed to migrate, with *what* characteristics, and *how* they did so, as well as *how* they conducted themselves once they had already entered the country. Thus, attempted entry could be refused on the grounds of a variety of infractions: a failure upon entry to pay a required immigrant head tax and a fee for the visa itself, perceived "illiteracy," a presumed liability to become a "public charge" (owing to having no prearranged employment), or violation of prohibitions against contracted labor (owing to having prearranged employment through labor recruitment). Likewise, Mexican workers could be subsequently deported if they could not verify that they held valid work visas or could otherwise be found to have evaded inspection, or if they could be found to have become "public charges" (retroactively enabling the judgment of a prior condition of "liability"), to have violated US laws, or to have engaged in acts that could be construed as "anarchist" or "seditionist." All of these violations of the qualitative features of the law rendered deportation a crucial mechanism of labor discipline and subjugation, not only coordinated with the vicissitudes of the labor market but also for the purposes of counteracting union organizing among Mexican/migrant workers (cf. Dinwoodie, 1977; Acuña, 1981; Gómez-Quiñones, 1994).

With the advent of the Great Depression of the 1930s, however, the more plainly racist character of Mexican "illegality" and deportability became abundantly manifest. Mexican migrants and US-born Mexican citizens alike were systematically excluded from employment and economic relief, which were declared the exclusive preserve of "Americans," who were presumed to be more "deserving." These abuses culminated in the forcible mass deportation of at least 415,000 Mexican migrants as well as many of their US-citizen children and the "voluntary" repatriation of 85,000 more (Hoffman, 1974; Guerin-Gonzáles, 1994; Balderrama and Rodríguez, 1995). Notably, Mexicans were expelled with no regard to legal residence, US citizenship, or even birth in the US —simply for being "Mexicans."

In the face of the renewed labor shortages caused by US involvement in World War II, however, the US federal government, in a dramatic reversal of the mass deportations of the 1930s, initiated the mass importation that came to be known as the Bracero Program as an administrative measure to institutionalize and regiment the supply of Mexican/migrant labor for US capitalism (principally for agriculture, but also for the railroads). The "Bracero" accords were effected unceremoniously by a Special Committee on Importation of Mexican Labor (formed by the US Immigration Service, the War Manpower Commission, and the Departments of State, Labor, and Agriculture) through a bilateral agreement with Mexico. Predictably, the US Department of Agriculture was granted primary authority over the program. Ostensibly an emergency wartime measure at its inception in 1942 (Public Law 45), the program was repeatedly renewed and dramatically expanded until its termination in 1964. This legalized importation of Mexican labor meant that migrant workers, once contracted, essentially became a captive workforce under the jurisdiction of the US federal government, and thus, a guarantee to US employers of unlimited "cheap" labor. In addition to this protracted contract-labor migration, however, the Bracero Program facilitated undocumented migration at levels that far surpassed the numbers of "legal" braceros—both through the development of a migration infrastructure and through employers' encouragement of braceros to overstay the limited tenure of their contracts. Preferring the undocumented workers, employers could evade the bond and contracting fees, minimum employment periods, fixed wages and other safeguards required in employing braceros (Galarza, 1964; cf. López, 1981). Indeed, as early as 1949, US employers and labor recruiters were assisted with instantaneous legalization procedures for undocumented workers, known as "drying out wetbacks" (Calavita, 1992). Some have estimated that four undocumented migrants entered the US from Mexico for every documented bracero.[4] Early in 1954, in an affront to the Mexican government's negotiators' pleas for a fixed minimum wage for braceros, the US Congress authorized the Department of Labor to unilaterally recruit Mexican workers, and the Border Patrol itself opened the border and actively recruited undocumented migrants (Galarza, 1964; Cockcroft, 1986). This period of official "open border" soon culminated, predictably in accord with the "revolving door" strategy, in the 1954–1955 expulsion of at least 2.9 million "illegal" Mexican/migrant workers under the militarized dragnet and nativist hysteria of "Operation Wetback" (García, 1980). Thus, the Bracero years were distinguished not only by an increase in legal migration through contract labor, but also by the federal facilitation of undocumented migration and the provision of ample opportunities for legalization, simultaneously coupled with considerable repression and mass deportations.

THE VISIBILITY OF "ILLEGAL ALIENS" AND THE INVISIBILITY OF THE LAW

Owing to the critical function of deportation in the maintenance of the "revolving-door" policy, the tenuous distinction between "legal" and "illegal" migration was deployed to stigmatize and regulate Mexican/migrant workers for much of the 20th century. Originally by means of *qualitative* restrictions—such as work visa and literacy requirements, contract-labor prohibitions, or, in the case of the Bracero program, the requirement of labor contracts and the prohibition against overstaying those contracts—"illegality" has long served as a constitutive dimension of the specific racialized inscription of "Mexicans," in general, in the US (De Genova, 2005; cf. Ngai, 1999, 2004). In these respects, Mexican/migrant "illegality," per se, is not new. Indeed, this reflects something of what Cockcroft (1986) has characterized as the special character of Mexican migration to the US: Mexico has provided US capitalism with the only "foreign" migrant labor reserve so sufficiently flexible that it can neither be fully replaced nor completely excluded under any circumstances. However, the US nation-state has historically deployed a variety of different tactics to systematically create and sustain "illegality": furthermore, it has refined those tactics in ways that have ever more thoroughly constrained the social predicaments of undocumented Mexican migrants. The history of legal debate and action concerning "immigration" is, after all, precisely a *history*. This chapter is centrally concerned with the task of denaturalizing Mexican/migrant "illegality" and locating its historical specificity as an irreducibly social "fact," a real abstraction, *produced* as an effect of the practical materiality of the law. Inasmuch as I am emphatically concerned with that distinct migration which is Mexican, in contradistinction to other migrations or some presumably generic "immigrant experience," I want to insist upon the historical specificities of a similarly distinct "illegality" that has predominated for Mexican migrants in particular. These historically specific Mexican experiences within US legal regimes of migrant "illegality" certainly have meaningful analogies and substantive correlations with the sociopolitical conditions of other undocumented migrations, especially those from Latin America and the Caribbean (see, e.g., Hagan, 1994; Mahler, 1995; Coutin, 2000), as well as of other racially subordinated groups, most notably Arabs and other Muslims ensnared in the immigration dragnet of the Homeland Security State since September 11, 2001 (cf. Cole, 2003). But such comparisons will only be intellectually compelling and politically cogent if they derive their force from precise accounts of the particular intersections of historically specific migrations and complex webs of "legality" and "illegality."

The history of immigration law is nothing if not a history of rather intricate and calculated interventions.[5] This is not to imply any overarching, coherent, and unified "strategy" that has single-handedly dictated these calculations throughout that history. Nor is this history merely a functional, more or less automatic by-product of some predetermined (and thus, teleological) "logic" flowing from the presumably rigid and fixed "structure" of capitalist society. On the contrary, the intricate history of law-making is best distinguished by its constitutive restlessness and the relative incoherence of various conflicting strategies, tactics, and compromises that the US nation-state has implemented at particular historical moments, precisely to mediate the contradictions immanent in crises and struggles over the subordination of labor. Thus, US immigration laws have served as instruments to tactically supply and refine the parameters of both discipline and coercion. As such, they are always conjunctural, and never assured. In other words, immigration laws, in their effort to manage the migratory mobility of labor, are ensnared in a struggle to subordinate the intractability that is intrinsic to the constitutive role of labor within capital—what Marx described as "a protracted and more or less concealed civil war" (Marx, 1867 [1976: 412]; cf. Bonefeld, 1995; Holloway, 1995). As John Holloway suggests, "Once the categories of thought are understood as expressions not of objectified social relations but of the struggle to objectify them, then a whole storm of unpredictability blows through them. Once it is understood that money, capital, the state . . . " [and here I add, emphatically, the law] ". . . are nothing but the struggle to form, to discipline, to structure . . . 'the sheer unrest of life,' then it is clear that their development can be understood only as practice, as undetermined struggle" (Holloway, 1995: 176; cf. Pashukanis 1929 [1989]). And it is this appreciation of the law—as undetermined struggle—that I want to bring to bear upon how we might apprehend the historicity of US immigration law, especially as it has devised for its target that characteristically mobile "population" made up of Mexican/migrant labor.

Migrant "illegality" is ultimately sustained not merely as an effect of such deliberate legal interventions, but also as the ideological effect of a discursive formation encompassing broader public debate and political struggle. Social science scholarship concerning undocumented Mexican migration to the US is itself often ensnared in this same discursive formation of "illegality" (De Genova, 2002). The treatment of "illegality" as an undifferentiated, transhistorical fixture is a recurring motif in much of the scholarship on Mexican migration. Across an extensive body of multidisciplinary scholarship, one encounters a remarkable visibility of "illegal immigrants" swirling enigmatically around the stunning invisibility of the law. The material force of law, its instrumentality, its productivity of some of the most meaningful and salient parameters of sociopolitical life, and also its historicity—all of this seems strangely absent, with rather few exceptions. This entanglement within the fetishism of the law tends to be true even on the part of scholars who criticize the disciplinary character of border patrol. Yet with respect to the "illegality" of undocumented migrants, a viable critical scholarship is frankly unthinkable without an informed interrogation of immigration law. In effect, by not examining the actual operations of immigration law in generating the categories of differentiation among migrants' legal statuses, this scholarship largely takes the law for granted. By not examining those operations over the course of their enactments, enforcements, and reconfigurations, this scholarship effectively treats the law as transhistorical and thus fundamentally unchanging—thereby naturalizing a notion of what it means to transgress that law.

LEGISLATING MEXICAN "ILLEGALITY"

Prior to 1965, as already suggested, there were absolutely no *quantitative* restrictions on "legal" migration from Mexico at the level of statute, and none had ever existed. There had, literally, never before been any *numerical* quota legislated to limit migration from Mexico.[6] But while this was true for all the countries of the Western Hemisphere (excluding colonies), and so has implications for nearly all Latino groups (with Puerto Ricans as the very important exception), none of these countries has ever had numbers of migrants at all comparable with those originating from Mexico. Furthermore, the reformulation of the legal specificities of "illegality" in 1965 and thereafter, it bears repeating, transpired in the midst of an enthusiastic and virtually unrelenting *im*portation of Mexican/migrant labor (increasingly impervious even to the ebbs and flows of unemployment rates). The end of the Bracero Program in 1964 was an immediate and decisive prelude to the landmark reconfiguration of US immigration law in 1965. Indeed, anticipating unemployment pressures due to the end of the Bracero Program, the Mexican government simultaneously introduced its Border Industrialization Program, enabling US-owned, labor-intensive assembly plants (maquiladoras) to operate in a virtual free-trade zone along the US border. As a result, migration within Mexico to the border region accelerated. By 1974, one-third of the population of Mexico's border states comprised people who had already migrated from somewhere else, and a mere 3% of them were employed in the maquiladoras (Cockcroft, 1986: 109; cf. Heyman, 1991). Thus, a long-established, well-organized, deeply entrenched, increasingly diversified, and continuously rising stream of

Mexican migration to the US had already been accelerating prior to 1965, and circumstances in the region that might induce subsequent migration to the US simply continued to intensify. As a consequence of the successive changes in US immigration law since 1965, however, previously unknown *quantitative* restrictions—and specifically, the apparently uniform application of numerical quotas to historically distinct and substantially incommensurable migrations—became central to an unprecedented, expanded, and protracted production of a more rigid, categorical condition of "illegality," for Mexican/migrant workers in particular, than had ever existed previously.

An ever-growing, already significant, and potentially indispensable segment of the working class within the space of the US nation-state (both in agriculture and numerous metropolitan areas), Mexican/migrant labor is ubiquitously stigmatized as "illegal," subjected to excessive and extraordinary forms of policing, denied fundamental human rights, and thus, is consigned to an always uncertain social predicament, often with little or no recourse to any semblance of protection from the law. Since the 1960s, Mexico has furnished 7.5–8.4 million migrants ("legal" as well as undocumented) migrants who currently reside in the US (in addition to unnumbered seasonal and short-term migrants). Approximately half of them (49.3%) are estimated to have arrived only during the decade of the 1990s (Logan, 2001, 2002). By May 2002, on the basis of estimates calculated from the 2000 census, researchers have suggested that 4.7 million of the Mexican/migrant total were undocumented, of whom as many as 85% had arrived in the US only during the 1990s (Passel, 2002). No other country has supplied even comparable numbers; indeed, by 2000, Mexican migrants alone constituted nearly 28% of the total "foreign-born" population in the US. It may seem paradoxical, then, that virtually all major changes in the quantitative features of US immigration law during this period have imposed ever more severe restrictions on the conditions for "legal" migration from Mexico. Indeed, precisely because no other country has supplied comparable numbers of migrants to the US during this time period, all the repercussions of the uniform numerical restrictions introduced by these legislative revisions have weighed disproportionately upon Mexican migration in particular. This legal history, therefore, constitutes a defining aspect of the historical specificity—indeed, the effective singularity—of contemporary Mexican migration to the US.

To a great extent, the seeming enigma derives from the fact that the very character of migrant "illegality" for Mexicans (as well as for other migrants within the Western Hemisphere) was reconfigured by what was, in many respects, genuinely a watershed "liberalization" of immigration policy in 1965. The Hart–Celler Act of 1965 (Public Law 89–236; 79 Stat. 911), which entailed amendments to the Immigration and Nationality Act (INA) of 1952 (Public Law 82–414; 66 Stat. 163) was an ostensibly egalitarian legislation. This monumental overhaul of US immigration law in 1965 dismantled the US nation-state's openly racist formulation of immigration control. It dramatically reversed the explicitly racist exclusion against Asian migrations, which had been in effect and only minimally mitigated since 1917 (or, in the case of the Chinese, since 1882). Likewise, the 1965 amendments abolished the draconian system of national-origins quotas for European countries, first enacted in 1921 and amplified in 1924.

With the end of the national-origins quota system, predictably, the 1965 amendments have been typically celebrated as a liberal reform, and US immigration policy suddenly appeared to be chiefly distinguished by a broad inclusiveness. But with respect to Mexico, the outcome was distinctly and unequivocally restrictive. These same "liberal" revisions (taking effect in 1968) established for the first time in US history an annual numerical quota to restrict "legal" migration from the Western Hemisphere. Indeed, the new cap imposed for the Western Hemisphere came about as a compromise with those who sought to maintain the national-origins quota system, "traditional restrictionists, who sought to deter immigration of blacks from the West Indies and 'browns' from south of the border more generally" (Zolberg, 1990, 321). However, David Reimers (1985 [1992: 79]) notes that few expressed blatantly racist attitudes, and the restriction for the Americas was notably defended in a more apparently liberal idiom, out of a concern with "fairness" for "our traditional friends and allies in Western Europe" (quoted on page 77). Although hundreds of thousands already migrated from Mexico annually, and the number of Immigration and Naturalization Service (INS) apprehensions of "deportable alien" Mexicans was itself already 151,000 during the year prior to the enactment of the new quota, now no more than 120,000 "legal" migrants (excluding quota exemptions) would be permitted from the entirety of the Western Hemisphere. However, the annual quota for such "non-exempt" "legal" migration from the Eastern Hemisphere was higher—170,000. On the scale of the globe, no single country was sending numbers of migrants at all comparable with the level of migration from Mexico, and this has remained true, consistently, ever since. Yet, the numerical quota for all nonexempt migrants within the Western Hemisphere to migrate "legally" (i.e., the maximum quota within which Mexicans would have to operate) was restricted to a level far below actual and already documented numbers for Mexican migration.

The 1965 amendments have also been characterized as expansively liberal in their provisions for migrant family reunification. For both hemispheres, some family members would be considered "exempt" from the quota restrictions and thus could migrate without being counted against the quotas. These "quota exemptions" for family reunification were restricted to the spouses, unmarried minor children, and parents of adult US *citizens* (usually migrants, but only those who had already been naturalized). Counted within the Western Hemisphere quota (i.e., nonexempt), notably, the spouses, unmarried minor children, and parents of *permanent residents,* as well as professionals and skilled nonprofessionals with labor certifications from the Department of Labor, were variously privileged through a system of ranked preferences. The respective systems of preferences within the two quotas, however, were markedly different. For the Eastern Hemisphere, in addition to the explicit ranked preferences included under the Western Hemisphere quota for the relatives of *permanent residents,* there were also provisions for the unmarried *adult* children, married children (adult or minor), and also brothers and sisters (adult or minor) of US *citizens.* Here again, the specifications for "legal" migration from the Eastern Hemisphere were clearly different and, one might say, more liberal. Furthermore, they could be interpreted to have provided additional advantages (hence, greater incentives) for naturalized US citizenship, while those for the Western Hemisphere were considerably more circumscribed and provided no such exceptional benefits for naturalization. Thus, the unequal provisions for family reunification under the two distinct hemispheric quotas imposed generally disadvantageous limitations for Western Hemisphere migrations, and in fact, did so disproportionately to Mexican migration in particular. Likewise, although the provisions for quota-exempt family reunification were equal for both hemispheres, these exemptions privileged the kin of US citizens (usually naturalized migrants), and so also disadvantaged Mexico because of the pronounced disinclination of most Mexican migrants, historically, to naturalize as US citizens (Sánchez, 1993; Gutiérrez, 1995, 1998; González Baker *et al.,* 1998). In short, the consequences of the new numerical restrictions would weigh disproportionately, almost singularly, on migration from Mexico because of Mexico's overwhelming numerical preponderance among *all* migrations. Furthermore, the new law's more expansive and apparently liberal provisions for family unification were structured in a manner that made them less easily applicable to or accessible by Mexicans.

There is still another feature of the 1965 legislation that had an exceptionally important consequence for undocumented Mexican migrants. A preference category for legal migration within the annual quota was established for migrants from the Western Hemisphere, but not the Eastern Hemisphere, who were the parents of US-citizen minors. In other words, a legalization procedure was available to undocumented Western Hemisphere migrants who were the parents of children born in the US (hence, US citizens). In effect, a baby born in the US to an undocumented Mexican migrant served as a virtual apprenticeship for eventual legal residency. Thus, in a manner analogous to earlier "drying-out" procedures, Mexican migrants would be required to serve a term as undocumented workers but then could eventually be "legalized," contingent on bearing a child in the US.[7]

Especially following more than 20 years of enthusiastic, legal, contract-labor importation from Mexico, orchestrated by the US federal government through the Bracero Program, an already-established influx of Mexican migrants to the US was accelerating prior to 1965. With elaborate migration networks and extensive historical ties already well established, Mexicans continued to migrate, but given the severe restrictions legislated in 1965 (implemented in 1968), ever-greater numbers of Mexicans who were already migrating had no alternative but to come as undocumented workers, relegating themselves to an indefinite condition of "illegality." From 1968 onward, INS apprehensions of "deportable" Mexican nationals skyrocketed annually, leaping 40% in the first year. Although these apprehension statistics are never reliable indicators of the actual numbers of undocumented migrants, they clearly reveal a pattern of policing that was critical for the perpetuation of the "revolving door" policy: the disproportionate majority of INS apprehensions were directed at surreptitious entries along the Mexican border, and this was increasingly so. In 1973, for instance, the INS reported that Mexicans literally comprised 99% of all "deportable aliens" who had entered surreptitiously and were apprehended (cf. Cárdenas, 1975: 86). While the total number of apprehensions for all other nationalities from the rest of the world (combined) remained consistently *below* 100,000 annually, the apprehensions of Mexicans rose steadily from 151,000 in 1968 to 781,000 in 1976, when migration was, once again, still more severely restricted. These persistent enforcement practices, and the statistics they produce, have made an extraordinary contribution to the pervasive fallacy that

Mexicans account for virtually all "illegal aliens." Furthermore, this effective equation of "illegal immigration" with unauthorized border-crossing has served to continuously restage the US–Mexico border in particular as the theater of an enforcement "crisis," and thus constantly rerenders "Mexican" as as a national synonym for migrant "illegality."

Immigration law, of course, was not the only thing that was changing in 1965. It has been widely recognized that the sweeping 1965 revisions of immigration policy originated from a generalized crisis of Cold War–era liberalism, in which US imperialism's own most cherished "democratic" conceits were perpetually being challenged. Taking shape in a context of Cold War international relations imperatives, confronted not only with monumental popular struggles over racial oppression at home but also with decolonization and national liberation movements abroad, US immigration policy was redesigned in 1965 explicitly to rescind the most glaringly discriminatory features of existing law. This crisis was exacerbated by the rising combativeness, in particular, of the Black struggle for "civil rights," which is to say, the mass movement of African Americans to demand their rights of *citizenship*. The civil rights struggle was increasingly articulated as a militant repudiation of the "second-class" (ostensible) citizenship conferred upon African Americans since the adoption of the 14th Amendment following the Civil War. This intransigent movement forcefully exposed and articulately denounced the treacherous fact of racially subordinated citizenship. Furthermore, the end of the Bracero Program had been principally accomplished through the restrictionist efforts of organized labor, especially on the part of the predominantly Chicano and Filipino farmworkers' movement. Thus, the specific historical conjuncture from which the 1965 amendments emerged was deeply characterized by political crises that manifested themselves as both domestic and international insurgencies of racialized and colonized working peoples. So began a new production of an altogether new kind of "illegality" for migrations within the Western Hemisphere, with inordinately severe consequences for transnationalized Mexican labor migrants in particular—a kind of transnational fix for political crises of labor subordination (cf. De Genova, 2005).

It is particularly revealing to note here that the explicit topic of "illegal immigration" had been almost entirely absent from the legislative debate leading to the 1965 law. David Reimers calls attention to the irony that the US Congress "paid little attention to undocumented immigrants while reforming immigration policy in 1965," but that "as early as 1969"—that is, the first year after the 1965 law had taken effect—"Congress began to investigate the increase in illegal immigration along the Mexican border" (1985 [1992: 207–208]). By 1976, however, legislative debate and further revisions in the law had succeeded in producing "illegal immigration" as a whole new object within the economy of legal meanings in the US immigration regime—the explicit "problem" toward which most of the major subsequent changes in immigration policy have been at least partly directed.

In 1976, new amendments to the INA were enacted (Public Law 94—571; 90 Stat. 2703), this time within days of the national elections in the US. The 1976 revisions summarily eliminated the legalization provision described above by extending to the Western Hemisphere a system of statutory preferences for legal migration that more closely resembled what had previously been established for the Eastern Hemisphere. More importantly, the 1976 statutes imposed a fixed national quota for every individual country in the Western Hemisphere for the first time, now establishing a maximum number (excluding quota exemptions) of 20,000 legal migrants a year for every country in the world. This had an incomparably dramatic, singularly disproportionate impact on Mexico in particular.[8] Once again (and also in the liberal idiom of "'fairness"), immigration law was still more dramatically revised, restricting "legal" (nonexempt) migration from Mexico to a meager 20,000 a year.[9] Then again, after legislation in 1978 (Public Law 95–412; 92 Stat. 907) abolished the separate hemispheric quotas and established a unified worldwide maximum annual immigration quota of 290,000, the Refugee Act of 1980 (Public Law 96–212; 94 Stat. 107) further reduced that maximum global quota to 270,000 and thereby diminished the national quotas of 20,000 per country to an even smaller annual maximum of 18,200 "legal" migrants (excluding quota exemptions). In the space of less than 12 years, therefore, from July 1, 1968 (when the 1965 amendments went into effect), until the 1980 amendments became operative, US immigration law had been radically reconfigured for Mexicans. Beginning with almost unlimited possibilities for "legal" migration from Mexico (literally no numerical restrictions, tempered only by qualitative preconditions that, in practice, had often been overlooked altogether), the law had now severely restricted Mexico to an annual quota of 18,200 nonexempt "legal" migrants (while also enforcing a strict system of qualitative preferences among quota exemptions, with weighted allocations for each preference). At a time when there were (conservatively) well over a million Mexican migrants coming to work in the US each year, the overwhelming majority would have no option but to do so "illegally."

There is nothing matter-of-fact, therefore, about the "illegality" of undocumented migrants. "Illegality" (in its contemporary configuration) is the product of US immigration law—not merely in the abstract sense that without the law, nothing could be construed to be outside of the law; nor simply in the generic sense that immigration law constructs, differentiates, and ranks various categories of "aliens"; but in the more profound sense that the history of deliberate interventions beginning in 1965, that have revised and reformulated the law has entailed an active process of inclusion through illegalization (cf. Castells, 1975; Nikolinakos, 1975; Burawoy, 1976; Bach, 1978; Portes, 1978: 475; Calavita, 1982: 13, 1998; Hagan, 1994: 82; Coutin, 1996, 2000; Joppke, 1999: 26–31). Indeed, the legal production of "illegality" has made an object of Mexican migration in ways both historically unprecedented and disproportionately deleterious.

A new landmark in the history of US immigration law was achieved with the passage in 1986 of the Immigration Reform and Control Act—IRCA (Public Law 99–603; 100 Stat. 3359)—whose principal explicit preoccupation was undocumented immigration. IRCA was finally adopted as the culmination of years of recommendations (first by a special Select Commission on Immigration and Refugee Policy established by Congress in 1978 and then by a presidential cabinet-level task force in 1981) and repeated efforts over four years in the two houses of Congress to pass a variety of bills aimed at revisions in immigration policy. The 1986 amendments provided for a selective "amnesty" and adjustment of the immigration status of some undocumented migrants.[10] Once again, the law instituted a legalization procedure for those undocumented workers who had reliably (and without evident interruption) served their apprenticeships in "illegality," while intensifying the legal vulnerability of others. Indeed, IRCA foreclosed almost all options of legalization for those who did not qualify, and for all who would arrive thereafter. Furthermore, INS decisions concerning the implementation of IRCA legalization procedures contributed to the pervasive equation of "illegal alien" with "Mexican." The INS persistently battled in the courts to reserve the amnesty for those whose undocumented status began with having "entered without inspection" (i.e., surreptitious border-crossers), rather than for those who had overstayed their visas. In short, the INS seemed intent to exclude from the "amnesty" those applicants who did not match the profile of "illegality" most typical of undocumented Mexican migrants (González Baker *et al.*, 1997: 11–12). As a predictable result, whereas preimplementation estimates had figured Mexicans to comprise roughly half of the total number of undocumented migrants, Mexican migrants accounted for 70% of the total pool of legalization applicants and comprised even higher proportions in California, Illinois, and Texas, the areas of highest Mexican/migrant concentration (ibid., 13).

IRCA of 1986 also established for the first time federal sanctions against employers who knowingly hired undocumented workers. Nevertheless, it established an "affirmative defense" for all employers who could demonstrate that they had complied with the verification procedure. Simply by having filled out and kept on file a routine form attesting to the document check, without any requirement that they determine the legitimacy of documents presented in that verification process, employers would be immune from any penalty. What this meant in practice is that the employer sanctions provisions generated a flourishing industry in fraudulent documents, which merely imposed further expenses and greater legal liabilities upon the migrant workers themselves, while supplying an almost universal protection for employers (cf. US Department of Labor, 1991: 124; Chávez, 1992: 169–171; Mahler, 1995: 159–187; Cintrón, 1997: 51–60; Coutin, 2000: 49–77). Likewise, in light of the immense profitability of exploiting the legally vulnerable (hence, "cheap") labor of undocumented workers, the schedule of financial penalties imposed by IRCA simply amounted to a rather negligible operating cost for an employer found to be in violation of the law. Given that the employer sanctions would require a heightening of INS raids on workplaces, inspectors were required to give employers a three day warning prior to inspections of their hiring records to make it "pragmatically easy" for employers to comply with the letter of the law (Calavita, 1992: 169). Furthermore, to avoid fines associated with these sanctions, employers would typically fire or temporarily discharge workers known to be undocumented prior to a raid. Thus, these provisions have primarily served to introduce greater instability into the labor-market experiences of undocumented migrants and have thereby instituted an internal "revolving door." What are ostensibly "employer sanctions," then, have actually functioned to aggravate the migrants' vulnerability and have imposed new penalties upon the undocumented workers themselves.

The Immigration Act of 1990 (Public Law 101-649; 104 Stat. 4978) was not primarily directed at undocumented migration, but it did nonetheless introduce new regulations that increased the stakes of "illegality." Specifically, this legislation expanded the grounds for the deportation of undocumented migrants, introduced new punitive sanctions, and curtailed due process rights in deportation proceedings.

Among other stipulations,[11] the 1990 legislation also created a special visa program that sought, in the name of "diversity," to encourage more migration from countries that had been sending relatively low numbers of migrants (clearly not Mexico!). In addition, the 1990 legislation restricted jurisdiction over the naturalization of migrants petitioning to become US citizens, rescinding a practice (in place since 1795) permitting the courts to award citizenship, and now confining this authority exclusively to the federal office of the attorney general.

THE CAPRICE OF SOVEREIGNTY AND THE TYRANNY OF THE RULE OF LAW

When undocumented migrants are criminalized under the sign of the "illegal alien," theirs is an "illegality" that does not involve a crime against anyone; rather, migrant "illegality" stands only for a transgression against the sovereign authority of the nation-state. With respect to the politics of immigration and naturalization, notably, sovereignty (as instantiated in the unbridled authoritarianism of border policing, detention, deportation, and so forth) assumes a pronouncedly absolutist character (cf. Dunn, 1996; Simon 1998). Such an absolutist exercise of state power relies decisively, of course, upon a notion of "democratic" consent, whereby the state enshrouds itself with the political fiction of "the social contract" to authorize itself to act on behalf of its sovereign citizens, or at least "the majority." In the US, this circular logic of sovereignty conveniently evades the racialized history of the law of citizenship, just as this species of majoritarianism sidesteps altogether the laborious history that has produced a "majority" racialized as "white." The racialized figure of Mexican/migrant "illegality," therefore, can be instructively juxtaposed with what is, in effect, the racialized character of the law and the "democratic" state itself. Inasmuch as the political culture of US liberalism already posits and requires "the rule of law" as a figure for "the nation," the instrumental role of the law in producing and upholding the categories of racialization reveals something fundamental about the glorified figures of "American" sovereignty and "national culture" that are invariably conjoined in the dominant discourses of "immigration control."

"Illegality" has been historically rendered to be so effectively inseparable from their migrant experience that some Mexicans even defiantly celebrate their "illegal" identity. However, the considerable legalization provisions of the 1986 amnesty afforded Mexican migrants a rare opportunity to "straighten out" or "fix" (*arreglar*) their status that few who were eligible opted to disregard. The immigration status of "legal permanent resident" vastly facilitated many of the transnational migrant aspirations that had been hampered or curtailed by the onerous risks and cumbersome inconveniences of undocumented border crossing. By 1990, however, 75.6% of all "legal" Mexican migrants in the state of Illinois, for instance, notably remained noncitizens (Paral, 1997: 8). In other words, the rush to become "legal" migrants did not translate into an eagerness to become US citizens. By the mid-1990s, especially amid the political climate of heightened nativism and anti-immigrant racism that was widely associated with the passage of California's vindictive ballot initiative, Proposition 187, Mexican migrants began to seriously consider the prospect of naturalizing as US citizens in much greater proportions than ever before.

As the veritable culmination of such anti-immigrant campaigns, the Illegal Immigration Reform and Immigrant Responsibility Act (IIRIRA) of 1996 (Public Law 104–208; 110 Stat. 3009), quite simply, was the most punitive legislation to date concerning undocumented migration (cf. Fragomen, 1997: 438). It included extensive provisions for criminalizing, apprehending, detaining, fining, deporting, and also imprisoning a wide array of "infractions" and significantly broadened and elaborated the *qualitative* scope of the law's production of "illegality" for undocumented migrants and others associated with them. It also barred undocumented migrants from receiving a variety of social security benefits and federal student financial aid. In fact, this so-called immigration reform (signed September 30, 1996) was heralded by extensive anti-immigrant stipulations in both the Anti-Terrorism and Effective Death Penalty Act—(AEDPA) (Public Law 104–132, 110 Stat. 1214; signed into law on April 24, 1996), and the so-called Welfare Reform, passed as the Personal Responsibility and Work Opportunity Reconciliation Act (PRWORA) (Public Law 104–193, 110 Stat. 2105; signed August 22, 1996). The AEDPA entailed an "unprecedented restriction of the constitutional rights and judicial resources traditionally afforded to legal resident aliens" (Solbakken, 1997: 1382). The "Welfare Reform" enacted dramatically more stringent and prolonged restrictions on the eligibility of the great majority of "legal" immigrants for virtually all benefits available under federal law and also authorized states to similarly restrict benefits programs. Without belaboring the extensive details of these acts, which did not otherwise introduce new *quantitative* restrictions, it will suffice to say that their expansive provisions (concerned primarily with enforcement and penalties for undocumented presence) were truly unprecedented in the severity with which they broadened the purview and intensified the ramifications of the legal production of migrant "illegality." By restricting access to public services and social welfare benefits, these legislations especially targeted undocumented migrant women (and their children), who had come to be equated with Mexican/Latino long-term settlement, families, reproduction, and thus, the dramatic growth of a "minority group" (Coutin and Chock, 1995; Chock, 1996; Roberts, 1997). Given the already well-entrenched practices that focus enforcement against undocumented migration disproportionately upon Mexican migrants in particular, there can be little doubt that these acts, at least prior to September 11, 2001, nonetheless weighed inordinately upon Mexicans as a group. Indeed, the language of the 1996 legislation, with regard to enforcement, was replete with references to "the border," a telltale signal that could only portend a further disciplining of Mexican migrants.[12]

THE BORDER SPECTACLE

Mexican migration has been rendered synonymous with the US nation-state's purported "loss of control" of its borders and has supplied the preeminent pretext for what has in fact been a continuous intensification of increasingly militarized control (Heyman, 1991, 1999; Kearney, 1991; Dunn, 1996; Andreas, 1998, 2000; cf. Chávez, 2001; Nevins, 2002; Durand and Massey, 2003). And it is precisely "the border" that provides the exemplary theater for staging the spectacle of "the illegal alien" that the law produces. Indeed, "illegality" looks most like a positive transgression—and can thereby be equated with the behavior of Mexican migrants rather than the instrumental action of immigration law—precisely when it is subjected to policing at the US–Mexico border. The law's elusiveness and its relative invisibility in producing "illegality" requires this spectacle of "enforcement" at the border, precisely because it renders a racialized Mexican/migrant "illegality" visible and lends it the commonsensical air of a "natural" fact.

The operation of the "revolving door" at the border that is necessary to sustain the "illegality" effect always combines an increasingly militarized spectacle of apprehensions, detentions, and deportations—as well as increasingly perilous and sometimes deadly circumstances required to evade detection—with the banality of a virtually permanent importation of undocumented migrant labor.[13] This seeming paradox is commonly evoked in many Mexican (especially male) migrants' border-crossing narratives, in which stories of great hardship are often followed by accounts of quite easy passage (Davis, 1990; Kearney, 1991; Chávez, 1992; Martínez, 1994; De Genova, in press). Indeed, US immigration enforcement efforts throughout the 20th century targeted the US–Mexico border disproportionately, sustaining a zone of relatively high tolerance within the interior (Chávez, 1992; Delgado, 1993). The legal production of Mexican/migrant "illegality" requires the spectacle of enforcement at the US–Mexico border for the spatialized difference between the nation-states of the US and Mexico to be enduringly inscribed upon Mexican migrants in their spatialized (and racialized) status as "illegal aliens." The vectors of race and space, likewise, are both crucial in the constitution of Mexican migrants' class specificity. It is not at all uncommon, therefore, for Mexican migrants to conclude their border-crossing narratives, tellingly, with remarks about low wages. These narratives of the adventures, mishaps, and genuine calamities of border crossing seem to be almost inevitably punctuated with accounts of life in the US that are singularly distinguished by arduous travail and abundant exploitation (Kearney, 1991; Martínez, 1994; De Genova, 2005; cf. Mahler, 1995).

The "enforcement" spectacle at the border, however, is not the only way that Mexican/migrant "illegality" generates and sustains a kind of border spectacle in everyday life. The "illegality" effect of protracted vulnerability has to be recreated more often than simply on the occasion of crossing the border. Indeed, the 1986 legislation that included the institution (at the federal level) of "employer sanctions" was tantamount to an extension of the "revolving door" to the internal labor market of each workplace where undocumented migrant workers were employed. The policing of public spaces outside the workplace likewise serves to discipline Mexican/migrant workers by surveilling their "illegality," and exacerbating their ever-present sense of vulnerability (Chávez, 1992; Rouse, 1992; Heyman, 1998; De Genova, 2005; cf. Mahler, 1995; Coutin, 2000). The "illegalities" of everyday life are often, literally, instantiated by the lack of various forms of state-issued documentation that sanction one's place within or outside the strictures of the law (Hagan, 1994; Mahler, 1995; Cintrón, 1997; Coutin, 2000). The lack of a driver's license, for instance, has typically been presumed by police in much of the US, at least through the 1990s, to automatically indicate a Latino's more generally undocumented condition (cf. Mahler, 1995).[14] Indeed, without driver's licenses or automobile insurance cards, undocumented migrants can be readily compelled to pay hundreds of dollars in bribes as a consequence of pervasive and casual police corruption and abuse, on the basis of the cynical presumption that those who are legally vulnerable are therefore easily exploitable. In effect, there is virtually no way for undocumented migrants not to be always already culpable of some kind of legal infraction. Their vulnerabiliy ultimately intensifies their subjection to quotidian forms of intimidation and harassment. And it is precisely such forms of everyday "illegality" that confront many undocumented Latino migrants with quite everyday forms of surveillance and repression. There are also those "illegalities," furthermore, that more generally pertain to the heightened policing directed at the bodies, movements, and spaces of the poor, especially those racialized as nonwhite. Inasmuch as any confrontation with the scrutiny of legal authorities is already tempered by the discipline imposed by their susceptibility for deportation, such mundane forms of harassment likewise serve to relentlessly reinforce undocumented Mexican and other Latino migrants' characteristic vulnerability as a highly exploitable workforce.

Yet the disciplinary operation of an apparatus for the everyday production of migrant "illegality" is never simply reducible to a presumed quest to achieve the putative goal of deportation. It is *deportability,* and not deportation per se, that has historically rendered Mexican labor as a distinctly disposable commodity. Here, I am emphasizing what have been the real *effects* of this history of revisions in US immigration law. Without engaging in the unwitting apologetics of presumptively characterizing the law's consequences as "unintended" or "unanticipated," and without busying ourselves with conspiratorial guessing games about good or bad "intentions," the challenge of critical inquiry and meaningful social analysis commands that one ask: What indeed do these policies *produce?* Although their argument is insufficiently concerned with the instrumental role of the law in the production of "illegality," Douglas Massey (2002: 41, 45) and his research associates have understandably nominated the post-1965 period as "the era of undocumented migration" and even have characterized the effective operation of US immigration policy toward Mexico as "a de facto guest-worker program". There of course has never been sufficient funding for US immigration authorities to evacuate the country of undocumented migrants by means of deportation, nor even for the Border Patrol to "hold the line." The Border Patrol has never been equipped to actually keep the undocumented out. At least until the events of September 11, 2001, the very existence of the enforcement branches of the now-defunct INS (and the Border Patrol, in particular) were always premised upon the persistence of undocumented migration and a continued presence of migrants whose undocumented legal status has long been equated with the disposable (deportable), ultimately "temporary" character of the commodity that is their labor power. In its real effects, then, and regardless of competing political agendas or stated aims, the true social role of much of US immigration law enforcement (and the Border Patrol, in particular) has historically been to maintain and superintend the operation of the border as a "revolving door" simultaneously implicated in importation as much as (in fact, far more than) deportation (Cockcroft, 1986). Sustaining the border's viability as a filter for the unequal transfer of value (Kearney, 1998; cf. Andreas, 2000: 29–50), such enforcement rituals also perform the spectacle that fetishizes migrant "illegality" as a seemingly objective "thing in itself."

With the advent of the antiterrorism state, the politics of immigration and border enforcement in the US have been profoundly reconfigured under the aegis of a remarkably parochial US nationalism and an unbridled nativism, above all manifest in the complete absorption of the INS into the new Department of Homeland Security (as of March 1, 2003). Nevertheless, this same sociopolitical moment within the US has been distinguished by a deadly eruption of genuinely global imperialist ambition. Thus, it should hardly come as a surprise that on January 7, 2004, the Bush administration proposed a new scheme for the expressly temporary regularization of undocumented migrant workers' "illegal" status and for the expansion of a Bracero-style migrant labor contracting system orchestrated directly by the US state. Such a "legalization" plan aspires only for a more congenial formula by which to sustain the permanent availability of disposable (and still deportable) migrant labor, but under conditions of dramatically enhanced ("legal") regimentation and control. Like all previous forms of migrant "legalization," and indeed, in accord with the larger history of the law's productions and revisions of "illegality" itself, such an immigration "reform" can be forged only through an array of political struggles that are truly transnational in scale and that ultimately have as their stakes the subordination—and insubordination—of labor.

NOTES

1. The category "migrant" should not be confused with the more precise term "migratory"; rather, "migrant" is intended here to serve as a category of analysis that disrupts the implicit teleology of the more conventional term "immigrant," which is posited always from the standpoint of the "immigrant-receiving" US nation-state (cf. De Genova, 2005: 56–94).

2. It is instructive to recall, however, that it was US whites who were the original " illegal aliens" whose undocumented incursions into Mexican national territory had supplied the prelude to the war (cf. Acuña, 1981: 3–5; Vélez-Ibáñez, 1996: 57–62).

3. Owing to their colonized status following the US occupation after the Spanish–American War in 1898, Filipinos were designated US "nationals" and so were a notable exception to the all-Asian exclusion.

4. Approximately 4.8 million contracts were issued to Mexican workers for employment as braceros over the course of the program's 22 years, and during that same period there were more than 5 million apprehensions of undocumented Mexican migrants (Samora, 1971; cf. López, 1981). Both figures include redundancies and are thus not indicative of absolute numbers, but reveal nonetheless a more general complementarity between contracted and undocumented flows.

5. Beyond legislation, the history of immigration and citizenship law also commands a consideration of judicial cases and administrative decisions affecting the policies regulating admission and deportation, as well as access to employment, housing, and education and eligibility for various social-welfare benefits (cf. Lee, 1999). My discussion, however, is concerned with the more narrowly legislative history affecting "illegality" for Mexican migration, inasmuch as this subject itself has been sorely neglected, if not misrepresented altogether.

6. Here I refer to the absence of any prior *statutory* quotas legislated to restrict "legal" migration from Mexico, in contradistinction to numerical restrictions imposed unofficially at the local level when US consulates in Mexico were sometimes directed to limit the number of migrant visas they issued (cf. Ngai, 1999, 2004).

7. This particular "drying-out" procedure was ultimately available only to the undocumented parents of babies born in the US between July 1, 1968, and December 31, 1976, owing to the elimination of this clause by the 1976 amendments to the INA.

8. In a contemporaneous law review, Bonaparte (1975) plainly identifies the adverse effects in store for Mexican migrants and links them to the amply evident and overt bias against Mexican migration in the transcripts of the legislative deliberations. Chock (1991) provides a compelling discussion of the ideological rhetoric of legislative debate and the discursive production of an "illegal alien crisis" during the 1975 congressional debates that eventually led to the 1976 legislation.

9. Mexico was immediately flooded with 60,000 applicants for 20,000 slots, and the excess demand became more severe every year thereafter.

10. Undocumented agricultural workers could adjust their status to temporary resident simply by proving that they had worked in perishable agriculture for at least 90 days during that prior year alone, and could apply for permanent resident status after a year or two, depending on how long they had been employed in agriculture. Otherwise, those who could establish that they had resided continuously in the US since before

January 1, 1982, were eligible for temporary resident status, and after a period of 18 months, would be eligible to apply for permanent resident status.

11. The 1990 law increased the global annual quota for nonexempt migration and also significantly restructured the preference system.

12. In strict legal terms, "the border" is constituted not simply by the territorial perimeter of the physical space of the nation-state, but also by entry points internal to the territory, e.g., airports (Bosniak, 1996: 594, n.95). The Immigration Act of 1996 specified, however, that the increased number of Border Patrol agents and support personnel would be deployed "along the border in proportion to the level of illegal *crossing*" (Title I, Section 101[c]; emphasis added).

13. See Heyman's discussion of "the voluntary-departure complex" (1995: 266–267).

14. Prior to September 11, 2001, only four states issued driver's licenses to any state resident who could pass the driving test, regardless of their legal status (*New York Times*, August 4, 2001). As of October 2003, however, anti-immigration lobbies, such as the Federation for American Immigration Reform, could contend that 24 states did not explicitly require legal residence for migrants to apply for a license. By signing the Emergency Supplemental Appropriations Act for Defense, the Global War on Terror, and Tsunami Relief into law on May 11, 2005, the U.S. president also enacted the REAL ID Act, which included in its extensive anti-immigrant provisions that driver's license and state ID card applicants must prove that they are either U.S. citizens or lawfully present in the United States.

Acknowledgments

While I am, of course, solely responsible for any errors or misinterpretations, I gratefully acknowledge the contribution of Kalman Resnick's many years of practical and engaged knowledge of immigration law to the legal analysis presented here. Appreciation is also due to Mike Kearney, María Lugones, Mahmood Mamdani, Mae Ngai, Suzanne Oboler, Josh Price, Chris Wright, and the Red Line Working Group—Bill Bissell, Manu Goswami, and Gary Wilder—as well as the anonymous reviewers for *Latino Studies*, for their various insights.

References

Acuña, Rodolfo. 1981. *Occupied America: A History of Chicanos.* 2nd ed. New York: Harper & Row.

Ancheta, Angelo N. 1998. *Race, Rights, and the Asian American Experience.* New Brunswick, NJ: Rutgers University Press.

Andreas, Peter. 1998. The U.S. Immigration Control Offensive: Constructing an Image of Order on the Southwest Border. In *Crossings: Mexican Immigration in Interdisciplinary Perspectives*, ed. Marcelo M. Suárez-Orozco, 343–356. Cambridge, MA: Harvard University Press.

———. 2000. *Border Games: Policing the U.S.–Mexico Divide*. Ithaca, NY: Cornell University Press.

Bach, Robert L. 1978. Mexican Immigration and the American State. *International Migration Review* 12(4): 536–558.

Balderrama, Francisco E., and Raymond Rodríguez. 1995. *Decade of Betrayal: Mexican Repatriation in the 1930s*. Albuquerque: University of New Mexico Press.

Barrera, Mario. 1979. *Race and Class in the Southwest: A Theory of Racial Inequality*. Notre Dame, IN: University of Notre Dame Press.

Bonaparte, Ronald. 1975. The Rodino Bill: An Example of Prejudice towards Mexican Immigration to the United States. *Chicano Law Review* 2: 40–50.

Bonefeld, Werner. 1995. Capital as Subject and the Existence of Labour. In *Emancipating Marx: Open Marxism 3*, ed. Werner Bonefeld, Richard Gunn, John Holloway, and Kosmos Psychopedis, 182–212. East Haven, CT: Pluto Press.

Bosniak, Linda S. 1996. Opposing Prop. 187: Undocumented Immigrants and the National Imagination. *Connecticut Law Review* 28(3): 555–619.

Burawoy, Michael. 1976. The Functions and Reproduction of Migrant Labor: Comparative Material from Southern Africa and the United States. *American Journal of Sociology* 81(5): 1050–1087.

Calavita, Kitty. 1982. *California's "Employer Sanctions": The Case of the Disappearing Law*. Research Report Series, Number 39. Center for U.S.–Mexican Studies, University of California, San Diego.

———. 1992. *Inside the State: The Bracero Program, Immigration, and the I.N.S.* New York: Routledge.

———. 1998. Immigration, Law, and Marginalization in a Global Economy: Notes from Spain. *Law and Society Review* 32(3): 529–566.

Cárdenas, Gilberto. 1975. United States Immigration Policy toward Mexico: An Historical Perspective. *Chicano Law Review* 2: 66–89.

Cardoso, Lawrence. 1980. *Mexican Emigration to the United States, 1897–1931*. Tucson: University of Arizona Press.

Castells, Manuel. 1975. Immigrant Workers and Class Struggles in Advanced Capitalism: The Western European Experience. *Politics and Society* 5: 33–66.

Chang, Robert S. 1999. *Disoriented: Asian Americans, Law, and the Nation-State*. New York: NYU Press.

Chávez, Leo R. 1992. *Shadowed Lives: Undocumented Immigrants in American Society*. Ft. Worth, TX: Harcourt, Brace, and Jovanovich.

———. 2001. *Covering Immigration: Popular Images and the Politics of the Nation*. Berkeley: University of California Press.

Chock, Phyllis Pease. 1991. "Illegal Aliens" and "Opportunity": Myth-Making in Congressional Testimony. *American Ethnologist* 18(2): 279–294.
———— 1996. No New Women: Gender, "Alien," and "Citizen" in the Congressional Debate on Immigration. *PoLAR: Political and Legal Anthropology Review* 19(1): 1–9.

Cintrón, Ralph. 1997. *Angels' Town: Chero Ways, Gang Life, and Rhetorics of the Everyday*. Boston, MA: Beacon Press.

Cockcroft, James D. 1986. *Outlaws in the Promised Land: Mexican Immigrant Workers and America's Future*. New York: Grove Press.

Cole, David. 2003. *Enemy Aliens: Double Standards and Constitutional Freedoms in the War on Terrorism*. New York: The New Press.

Coutin, Susan Bibler. 1996. Differences within Accounts of US Immigration Law. *PoLAR: Political and Legal Anthropology Review* 19(1): 11–20.
————. 2000. *Legalizing Moves: Salvadoran Immigrants' Struggle for U.S. Residency*. Ann Arbor: University of Michigan Press.

Coutin, Susan Bibler, and Phyllis Pease Chock. 1995. "Your Friend, the Illegal": Definition and Paradox in Newspaper Accounts of U.S. Immigration Reform. *Identities* 2(1–2): 123–148.

Davis, Marilyn P. 1990. *Mexican Voices/American Dreams: An Oral History of Mexican Immigration to the United States*. New York: Henry Holt.

De Genova, Nicholas. 1998. Race, Space, and the Reinvention of Latin America in Mexican Chicago. *Latin American Perspectives* 25(5): 91–120.
———— 2002. Migrant "Illegality" and Deportability in Everyday Life. *Annual Review of Anthropology* 31: 419–447.
————. 2005. *Working the Boundaries: Race, Space, and "Illegality" in Mexican Chicago*. Durham, NC: Duke University Press.

Delgado, Héctor L. 1993. *New Immigrants, Old Unions: Organizing Undocumented Workers in Los Angeles*. Philadelphia, PA: Temple University Press.

Dinwoodie, D.H. 1977. Deportation: The Immigration Service and the Chicano Labor Movement in the 1930s. *New Mexico Historical Review* 52(3): 193 206.

Dunn, Timothy J. 1996. *The Militarization of the U.S.–Mexico Border 1978–1992: Low-Intensity Conflict Doctrine Comes Home*. Austin, TX: Center for Mexican American Studies Books/University of Texas Press.

Durand, Jorge, and Douglas S Massey. 2003. The Costs of Contradiction: US Border Policy 1986–2000. *Latino Studies* 1(2): 235–252.

Fragomen, Austin T., Jr. 1997. The Illegal Immigration Reform and Immigrant Responsibility Act of 1996: An Overview. *International Migration Review* 31(2): 438–460.

Galarza, Ernesto. 1964. *Merchants of Labor: The Mexican Bracero Story*. Santa Barbara, CA: McNally and Loftin.

García, Juan Ramon. 1980. *Operation Wetback: The Mass Deportation of Mexican Undocumented Workers in 1954*. Westport, CT: Greenwood Press.

Gómez-Quiñones, Juan. 1994. *Mexican American Labor, 1790–1990.* Albuquerque: University of New Mexico Press.

González Baker, Susan. 1997. The "Amnesty" Aftermath: Current Policy Issues Stemming from the Legalization Programs of the 1986 Immigration Reform and Control Act. *International Migration Review* 31(1): 5–27.

González Baker, Susan, Frank D. Bean, Augustín Escobar Latapi, and Sidney Weintraub. 1998. U.S. Immigration Policies and Trends: The Growing Importance of Migration from Mexico. In *Crossings: Mexican Immigration in Interdisciplinary Perspectives,* ed. Marcelo M. Suárez-Orozco, 79–105. Cambridge, MA: Harvard University Press.

Guerin-Gonzales, Camille. 1994. *Mexican Workers and American Dreams: Immigration, Repatriation, and California Farm Labor 1900–1939.* New Brunswick, NJ: Rutgers University Press.

Gutiérrez, David G. 1995. *Walls and Mirrors: Mexican Americans, Mexican Immigrants, and the Politics of Ethnicity.* Berkeley: University of California Press.

———. 1998. Ethnic Mexicans and the Transformation of "American" Social Space: Reflections on Recent History. In *Crossings: Mexican Immigration in Interdisciplinary Perspectives,* ed. Marcelo M. Suárez-Orozco, 309–335. Cambridge, MA: Harvard University Press.

Hagan, Jacqueline Maria. 1994. *Deciding to be Legal: A Maya Community in Houston.* Philadelphia, PA: Temple University Press.

Heyman, Josiah McC. 1991. *Life and Labor on the Border: Working People of Northeastern Sonora, Mexico, 1886–1986.* Tucson: University of Arizona Press.

———. 1995. Putting Power in the Anthropology of Bureaucracy: The Immigration and Naturalization Service at the Mexico-United States Border. *Current Anthropology* 36(2):261–87.

———. 1998. State Effects on Labor: The INS and Undocumented Immigrants at the Mexico–United States Border. *Critique of Anthropology* 18(2): 157–180.

———. 1999. State Escalation of Force: A Vietnam/U.S.–Mexico Border Analogy. In *States and Illegal Practices,* ed. Josiah McC. Heyman, 285–314. New York: Berg.

Higham, John. 1955[1988]. *Strangers in the Land: Patterns of American Nativism, 1865–1925.* New Brunswick, NJ: Rutgers University Press.

Hing, Bill Ong. 1993. *Making and Remaking Asian America Through Immigration Policy, 1850–1990.* Stanford, CA: Stanford University Press.

Hoffman, Abraham. 1974. *Unwanted Mexican Americans in the Great Depression: Repatriation Pressures 1926–1939.* Tucson: University of Arizona Press.

Holloway, John. 1995. From Scream of Refusal to Scream of Power: The Centrality of Work. In *Emancipating Marx: Open Marxism 3,* ed. Werner Bonefeld, Richard Gunn, John Holloway, and Kosmos Psychopedis, 155–181. East Haven, CT: Pluto Press.

Hutchinson, Edward P. 1981. *Legislative History of American Immigration Policy, 1798–1965.* Philadelphia: University of Pennsylvania Press.

Joppke, Christian. 1999. *Immigration and the Nation-State: The United States, Germany, and Great Britain.* New York: Oxford University Press.

Kearney, Michael. 1991. Borders and Boundaries of States and Self at the End of Empire. *Journal of Historical Sociology* 4(1): 52–74.

———. 1998. Peasants in the Fields of Value: Revisiting Rural Class Differentiation in Transnational Perspective. Unpublished mansucript. Department of Anthropology, University of California at Riverside.

Kim, Hyung-chan. 1994. *A Legal History of Asian Americans, 1790–1990.* Westport, CT: Greenwood Press.

Lee, Erika. 1999. Immigrants and Immigration Law: A State of the Field Assessment. *Journal of American Ethnic History* 18(4): 85–114.

Logan, John R. 2001. The New Latinos: Who They Are, Where They Are. Press Conference Advisory. Lewis Mumford Center for Comparative Urban and Regional Research, State University of New York at Albany.

———. 2002. Hispanic Populations and Their Residential Patterns in the Metropolis. Press Conference Advisory. Lewis Mumford Center for Comparative Urban and Regional Research at the State University of New York at Albany.

López, Gerald P. 1981. Undocumented Mexican Migration: In Search of a Just Immigration Law and Policy. *UCLA Law Review* 28(4): 615–714.

Mahler, Sarah J. 1995. *American Dreaming: Immigrant Life on the Margins.* Princeton, NJ: Princeton University Press.

Martínez, Oscar J. 1994. *Border People: Life and Society in the U.S.–Mexico Borderlands.* Tucson: University of Arizona Press.

Marx, Karl. 1867[1976]. *Capital: A Critique of Political Economy.* Vol. 1. New York: Penguin Books.

Massey, Douglas S., Jorge Durand, and Nolan J. Malone. 2002. *Beyond Smoke and Mirrors: Mexican Immigration in an Era of Economic Integration.* New York: Russell Sage Foundation.

Mirandé, Alfredo. 1987. *Gringo Justice.* Notre Dame, IN: University of Notre Dame Press.

Nevins, Joseph. 2002. *Operation Gatekeeper: The Rise of the "Illegal Alien" and the Making of the U.S.–Mexico Boundary.* New York: Routledge.

Ngai, Mae M. 1999. The Architecture of Race in American Immigration Law: A Reexamination of the Immigration Act of 1924. *Journal of American History* 86(1): 67–92.

———. 2004. *Impossible Subjects: Illegal Aliens and the Making of Modern America.* Princeton, NJ: Princeton University Press.

Nikolinakos, Marios. 1975. Notes Towards a General Theory of Migration in Late Capitalism. *Race and Class* 17: 5–18.

Paral, Rob. 1997. *Public Aid and Illinois Immigrants: Serving Non-Citizens in the Welfare Reform Era: A Latino Institute Report.* Chicago: Illinois Immigrant Policy Project.

Passel, Jeffrey S. 2002. New Estimates of the Undocumented Population in the United States. *Migration Information Source,* May 22.. Washington, DC: Migration Policy Institute.

Pashukanis, Evgeny B. 1929[1989]. *Law and Marxism: A General Theory Towards a Critique of the Fundamental Juridical Concepts.* Worcester, UK: Pluto Publishing.

Portes, Alejandro. 1978. Toward a Structural Analysis of Illegal (Undocumented) Immigration. *International Migration Review* 12(4): 469–484.

Reimers, David M. 1985[1992]. *Still the Golden Door: The Third World Comes to America.* 2nd ed. New York: Columbia University Press.

Roberts, Dorothy E. 1997. Who May Give Birth to Citizens? Reproduction, Eugenics, and Immigration. In *Immigrants Out! The New Nativism and the Anti-Immigrant Impulse in the United States,* ed. Juan F. Perea, 205–219. New York: New York University Press.

Rouse, Roger. 1992. Making Sense of Settlement: Class Transformation, Cultural Struggle, and Transnationalism among Mexican Migrants in the United States. In *Towards a Transnational Perspective on Migration,* ed. Nina Glick Schiller *et al.,* 25–52. New York: Annals of the New York Academy of Sciences, 645.

Salyer, Lucy E. 1995. *Laws Harsh as Tigers: Chinese Immigrants and the Shaping of Modern Immigration Law.* Chapel Hill: University of North Carolina Press.

Samora, Julian. 1971. *Los Mojados: The Wetback Story.* Notre Dame, IN: University of Notre Dame Press.

Sánchez, George J. 1993. *Becoming Mexican American: Ethnicity, Culture, and Identity in Chicano Los Angeles 1900–1945.* New York: Oxford University Press.

Simon, Jonathan. 1998. Refugees in a Carceral Age: The Rebirth of Immigration Prisons in the United States, 1976–1992. *Public Culture* 10(3): 577–606.

Solbakken, Lisa C. 1997. The Anti-Terrorism and Effective Death Penalty Act: Anti-Immigration Legislation Veiled in Anti-Terrorism Pretext. *Brooklyn Law Review* 63: 1381–1410.

U.S. Department of Labor. 1991. *Employer Sanctions and U.S. Labor Markets: Final Report.* Washington, DC: Division of Immigration Policy and Research, U.S. Department of Labor.

Vélez-Ibáñez, Carlos G. 1996. *Border Visions: Mexican Cultures of the Southwest United States.* Tucson: University of Arizona Press.

Zolberg, Aristide R. 1990. Reforming the Back Door: The Immigration Reform and Control Act of 1986 in Historical Perspective. In *Immigration Reconsidered: History, Sociology, Politics,* ed. Virginia Yans-McLaughlin, 315–339. New York: Oxford University Press.

CHAPTER 4

Regulating Transnational Citizens in the Post-1996 Welfare Reform Era: Dominican Immigrants in New York City

Greta A. Gilbertson

Research on transnationalism[1] poses a formidable challenge to traditional views on citizenship and membership (Joppke, 1999). It documents the complex linkages between sending and receiving communities and tells how immigrants retain and cultivate ties to the country of origin (Glick Schiller *et al.*, 1992; Guarnizo, 1997; Smith, 1998; Itzigsohn *et al.*, 1999; Levitt, 2001). Studies of transnationalism emphasize the importance of memberships and allegiances as well as the social and institutional ties that immigrants bring from sending nation-states. The growth of transnational ties, including the increase in dual nationality, challenges many of the assumptions that underlie assimilation and citizenship paradigms (see Faist, 2000; Kivisto, 2001), particularly the idea that when immigrants become legal citizens of the host society, they realign their emotional and psychological attachments from the sending to the host country.

Another less-explored challenge to traditional views on US citizenship, and one that I focus on in this chapter, is the recent retrenchment of the welfare state and the rise of restrictionist sentiment. In 1996, the US enacted a series of anti-immigration legislative measures, including the "Illegal Immigration Reform and Immigrant Responsibility Act" (IIRIRA), the "Anti-terrorism and Effective Death Penalty Act" (AEDPA)[2], and the "Personal Responsibility and Work Opportunity Reconciliation Act" (PRWORA, or the "Welfare

Act"). Embedded in these laws are provisions that place restrictions on most welfare benefits to immigrants, elevate enforcement efforts and removal procedures, and increase the responsibility of immigrant sponsors (Singer, 1999, 2002).

The Welfare Act was the most significant change in welfare policy over the past several decades (Bean and Stevens, 2003). The legislation made sweeping changes to the structure of and access to public benefits for both citizens and noncitizen members of the US; however, immigrants were the most adversely affected at the outset. The Welfare Act required recipients of means-tested public assistance to be US citizens and broadened restrictions on public benefits for undocumented immigrants. The Immigration and Naturalization Service (INS) was also required to verify immigrants' status before they could receive benefits.

The Welfare Act created a wave of alarm within immigrant communities, even though by the late 1990s many of the original provisions had been modified and some benefits had been restored (Hagan *et al.*, 2003). By scaling back the rights of legal permanent residents, PRWORA made "partial membership" less attractive and encouraged noncitizen residents to naturalize or lose access to welfare benefits. These laws contributed to the large increase in the numbers of immigrants converting their status from legal permanent resident to citizen. In 1997 alone, 1.4 million applications for naturalization were filed with the INS, representing a threefold increase in the number of applications filed in 1994 (INS, 1997).

The Welfare Act reflected concern about the growth of a noncitizen immigrant population and their utilization of "state goods" (see Borjas, 1990; Borjas and Hilton, 1996) and was tied to a renewal of a national debate over the meaning of social and political participation of immigrants (Schneider, 2001).[3] It invoked notions of deserving citizenship by reinforcing the linkage between work and entitlement (Katz, 2001; Schneider, 2001) and portrayed immigrants as undeserving of citizenship.

Since the Welfare Act restricted the social rights of noncitizen immigrants, it highlighted the strong linkage between citizenship and the claiming of rights. Conceptions of "deservingness" linked to welfare reform have always been steeped in traditional gender ideology and have been highly racialized (Peterson, 2002). The Welfare Act demonstrates the state's gendered construction of the immigrant population, particularly that of immigrant women as welfare burdens and unfit mothers (Collins, 1999). By restricting access to social citizenship rights, state actions implicitly endorse views of masculine citizenship, based on constructions of immigrants as economic actors and citizens as productive workers. In this process, immigrant women, like black women, are seen as unfit citizens. Thus, immigrant women as unfit citizens. Thus, immigrant women are located outside the moral community of deserving membership (Collins, 1999).

Conventional writing on citizenship focuses on its legal and political aspects and overlooks how the state produces citizens. Drawing on interviews and observations of Dominican immigrants in New York City, I focus on how immigrants talk about citizenship, especially about its informal and cultural content. How immigrants articulate citizenship reflects the cultural practices and beliefs produced by negotiating the contested relations with the state (Ong, 1996). It also reveals how immigrants occupy the categories "immigrant" and "citizen." Immigrants draw on sets of ideas or discourses in their thinking and talking about citizenship. These discourses represent immigrants in specific ways and they have real effects that are apparent in the responses people make to them. Immigrants do not straightforwardly reproduce these representations but contest and transform them (Skeggs, 1997).

POLICY AND CITIZENSHIP CONTEXT: DOMINICAN IMMIGRANTS

Dominicans are an important group to study because the anti-immigrant legislation in the 1990s, especially the Welfare Act, had particularly strong effects on them. Dominicans are one of the largest and most residentially concentrated immigrant groups in New York City: in the year 2000, an estimated 571,000 Dominicans lived in New York State, with the overwhelming majority residing in New York City. Dominicans are one of the city's most impoverished groups, with high rates of female headship and welfare usage (Hernández, 2002; Alba and Nee, 2003). Because most Dominican aid recipients are women, Dominican women and their children are most likely to be adversely affected by cutbacks in federal aid.

Beginning in the mid-1990s, naturalization rates among eligible immigrants began to rise; many agree that anti-immigrant legislation accounts for much of this increase (Fix et al., 2003). Although rates of naturalization had declined previously —the share of legal immigrants who had naturalized fell from 64% in 1970 to 39% in 1996— by 2002, 49% of all legal immigrants had naturalized (Fix et al., 2003). The INS reports that the numbers of people naturalized in 1996 and 1997 were the highest on record, peaking at over one million in 1996, the year the Welfare Act and other restrictionist legislations were enacted. The applications for naturalization nationwide were even higher during the same period (1.3 million and 1.4 million, respectively).

Trends were similar among the Dominican population. Prior to the mid-1990s, Dominicans, like other Latin American immigrants, had relatively low rates of naturalization (see Jones-Correa, 1998).[4] This was partly due to the proximity of the origin and sending countries, the relative ease and low cost of transportation, and the growth and elaboration of multiple forms of transnational ties between the US and the Dominican Republic (Grasmuck and Pessar, 1991; Graham, 1997; Guarnizo, 1997; Itzigsohn *et al.*, 1999; Levitt, 2001). In 1996, though, more than 27,000 Dominicans naturalized, almost tripling the number of Dominicans who naturalized in the previous year (INS, 1997). The overwhelming majority (19,000) of Dominican immigrants who naturalized in 1996 were residing in New York City.

Several factors other than anti-immigrant legislation contributed to the rise in naturalization rates in the late 1990s. These include the large cohort of legalization recipients (from the 1986 Immigration and Reform and Control Act [IRCA]) who were eligible to naturalize beginning in 1994; and the INS's 1992 Green Card Replacement Program, which required permanent residents to replace their green cards but simultaneously encouraged them to become citizens. Other national- and local-level initiatives also encouraged immigrants to naturalize. Citizenship USA was a large-scale federal publicity project implemented in 1996 to facilitate the process of naturalization, particularly among those who received amnesty under the 1986 IRCA program (Schneider, 2001).[5]

Low rates of naturalization also reflect the nature of the US citizenship regime (Aleinikoff, 1998), particularly the expansion of rights and entitlements for noncitizen resident aliens. Before the Welfare Act, almost all of the rights associated with American citizenship were available to resident aliens (Schneider, 2001). Indeed, more immigrants were choosing to be partial citizen members, limiting their citizenship to social and economic participation (Schneider, 2001). The naturalization process in the US and its requirement that immigrants speak English, played a part in discouraging naturalization, particularly among first-generation immigrants (Immigration Policy Project, 1996; Fix *et al.*, 2003).

In the case of the Dominican Republic, sending-state initiatives and local responses to anti-immigrant legislation encouraged formal, legal membership in the US. The local community responded to anti-immigrant legislation by encouraging immigrants to naturalize (see Singer and Gilbertson, 2003). Many local responses to the Welfare Act emphasized the importance of citizenship as a means to claim certain social rights. In New York City, the mayor's office established a citizenship assistance program (Citizenship NYC) for immigrants; the city restricted the services of Citizenship NYC to only those immigrants who would lose access to federally funded benefits. Local media stressed the importance of naturalization in the face of anti-immigrant legislation. Dual nationality was enacted in 1994; this legislation encouraged many Dominican immigrants who were fearful of losing their origin-country citizenship to naturalize.

THE CASTILLO FAMILY

The interviews and observations used in this study were culled from data collected from an extended family group, the Castillo family,[6] including intensive interviews and participant observation during a period of three years, 1995–1998. During the three-year period, each member of the family was interviewed at least once (all interviews were conducted in Spanish and were taped and transcribed by the author), but numerous informal conversations with the various family members, in both the US and the Dominican Republic, constitute the basis for the analysis (Gilbertson and Singer, 2003). This chapter is based on further analysis of the existing interview data and is supplemented by continued observation and interaction with a substantial number of the Castillo family members and by additional taped interviews conducted in 2002–2003 with ten Dominican immigrants.

I select an ethnographic approach because it allows me to capture immigrants' views and cultural interpretations of citizenship and membership. The Castillo family was chosen because of its large size, both in terms of generations and numbers of family members, its concentration in New York City, and its cohesiveness, which facilitated the gathering of information from all family members. Most of the adult members residing in the US were legal permanent residents and, because they had been living in the US for at least five years, were eligible to become citizens.

The Castillo family (excluding spouses) spans five generations and includes 65 members, 52 of whom principally reside in the US. The Castillos originate from the city of Mao, a small city located in the northwestern region of the Dominican Republic. The migration history of the Castillos is characterized by the chain migration of legal immigrants sponsored by family members. The first immigrant left the Dominican Republic in 1969. By 1997, 52 of the 65 family members were in the US, all of them as legal permanent residents or citizens of the US. The family consists primarily of three cohorts: eight children of the matriarch (first cohort), the 27 children of this group (second cohort), and the 29 children of this group (third cohort), 17 of whom are US-born citizens.

The first cohort includes both active transnationals (individuals who live in both the Dominican Republic and the US) and sojourners (those who are at or near retirement age and whose principal residence is in the US), but who anticipate permanent return migration or active transnationalism. The second cohort refers to the children of the first cohort. They include sojourners, settled migrants and recent arrivals. As they have formed their own families, the second cohort has moved either into separate nuclear family households or into extended family households; some members of the second cohort have moved outside the New York metropolitan area in search of better living conditions. The sojourners of the second cohort, like those of the first, do not anticipate permanent settlement in the US for the most part, the settled migrants plan to remain permanently in the US, while the recent arrivals have been in the US for the least time and arrived at later ages.

The settlement of both the first and second cohorts is characterized by labor market incorporation into low-paying manufacturing or service jobs, intensive interaction with nuclear and extended family members, the maintenance of strong ties to the Dominican Republic, and residence in working-class, Spanish-speaking neighborhoods. Both groups have managed their settlement through "patchworking" survival strategies involving coresidence and income pooling, the use of different forms of public assistance, and maintaining binational connections, by spending extended periods of time in the Dominican Republic. Unlike the second cohort, many members of the first sibling cohort, including the active transnationals, own a home in the Dominican Republic and anticipate living there at some point in time or currently live in both the US and the Dominican Republic.

In the remainder of this chapter, I use findings from interviews and ethnographic fieldwork to explore three themes: welfare reform and dependency; dual nationality, the notion of rights, and the criminalization of immigrants; and return migration.

DEPENDENT CITIZENSHIP, WELFARE, AND RETURN

In this next section, I focus on how several of the Castillo family members talk about citizenship with attention to state constructions of deserving membership. I find that immigrants attempt to distance themselves from dependent citizenship, while simultaneously recognizing it as a controlling structure through which they can position themselves as different, a concept that Skeggs (1997) refers to as a "structuring absence." By drawing on state discourses of citizenship, immigrants distance themselves from groups associated with poverty and dependency, reinforcing distinctions between deserving and non-deserving members.

Zena[7] is single, no longer active in the paid labor force, and no longer maintains her own apartment in New York City. She lives in Mao for part of the year because she cannot afford to live in New York City on a year-round basis and does not want to live on a full-time basis in the household of her adult children. Zena retired after working for over 20 years and collects social security and a supplemental security income (SSI). Becoming a US citizen allows Zena to continue living in *both* the Dominican Republic and New York by securing her SSI benefits and allowing her to remain there without having to re-enter the US on a regular basis to maintain her legal permanent residency.

For Zena, being a US citizen secures her income and makes travel back and forth easier:

> Well, I always said to my daughter in-law, I'm going to become a citizen but I never made the effort . . . But now with the problem of the checks . . . I know with Social Security I won't have a problem but because they're giving me a supplemental security check [SSI], I got scared. If they take that check away, I'm not going to have anything to live on. How am I going to maintain myself in my old age? So, I came back from the DR with the objective of getting citizenship, not only because of the problem of the checks, but there are problems with everything, now you've got to become a citizen if you want to live in this country. (April, 1997)

Within this context, we can see how some immigrants position themselves relative to a discourse of dependent citizenship. Zena insisted that she deserves her old-age benefits—social security and SSI—because she was employed for 19 years, paid taxes, and during this time, while she was raising three children, she did not receive any government assistance. Zena says:

> I started working immediately when I arrived here; when I brought my children I put them in school but I didn't need food stamps [*cupones*], or welfare, or Medicaid, nothing. I thank God . . . Another thing, here they make it too easy on people, in this country, you know why? I brought my children here, but in that time there wasn't so much welfare. And someone who brought someone else, they had to wait five years before applying for any kind of aid. Now, they don't have to wait five years, they're here a year, a year and a half and they're on welfare. What's going on with that? That's why the system here is now so strict . . . (April, 1997)

Notions of dependency and entitlement are constructed around gendered visions of work and family life. In her discussions of the reasons for some of the legislative changes, Zena defines nondeserving immigrants as those who have taken advantage of the welfare state; they are implicitly women and mothers, but more importantly, those who refuse to work in the paid labor force. Zena speaks as a single mother of children who had the right to look to the state for assistance but did not, unlike many immigrant women today who are on welfare after "a year and a half." Compared with her contemporaries, who, in her view, would be on welfare today, she "started working immediately when I arrived here." Zena's statement reflects a prevailing American sentiment: the widespread belief that most welfare recipients (i.e., women) would rather sit at home and collect benefits than work hard to support themselves and their children (Gilens, cited by Katz, 2001: 321). This explains the backlashes against immigrants, or why "the system here is now so strict."

Daniel, now in his early 60s, arrived in the US in his 20s. He has a stable home in New York and has worked in a plastics factory in Manhattan for over 20 years. Daniel naturalized in 1998. He owns land in the Dominican Republic and hopes to build a home and retire there. In the following passage, Daniel talks about why he decided to naturalize:

> I'm going to tell you . . . from my own experience. *Because I can't put myself in a position of someone who hasn't worked here.* I have to put myself in the situation of someone who has always worked here. I think what made me go ahead and become a citizen is the changing laws that we're seeing right now with migration; because I was going to become a citizen when I retired, it's one way of going back to my country . . . It's one of the things that focuses you, *having had work, having worked for many years.* I can say now I'm sixty-two years old, God willing I'm going to retire and I can go back to my country to enjoy my pension. (April, 1997)

Here Daniel talks about becoming a US citizen as a way of returning to the Dominican Republic when he retires. Moreover, as a result of his continuous work history, he positions himself as a deserving citizen. His having worked constitutes his citizenship rather than the naturalization itself. In the following quotation, Daniel makes more explicit the connection between deserving or productive citizenship and work:

> With all of the changes, they are definitely realizing that the country is full of [*saturado de*] immigrants. Immigrants have created a lot of

problems here . . . Not everyone, I'm generalizing because I'm an
immigrant and we don't all cause problems, there are thousands that
come here and spend their entire lives working and paying taxes but
there are others who come to live off of welfare [*ayuda*], that don't
work and that cause problems, as a result, the laws have changed,
forget it, that's the reality. It's a way to put a stop to the migration . . .
I've always said that the government should give priority to professionals, not to people who don't know how to do anything. (April,
1997)

Some immigrants are more tentative when distinguishing between
deserving and nondeserving members, but still use the issue of welfare as a means to conceptualize their views of membership. Mariana,
who naturalized in 1998, said that she believes that the state is
punishing immigrants who are entitled to assistance on the basis of
need. When asked whether the change in laws had influenced her
decision to naturalize, she said:

Yes, a little. Although I've never been on welfare [*cogido ayuda*] in this
country. Thank God that I haven't needed it, since I've never needed
it I've never tried to get it. But I think about my brothers, they're
Hispanics that need help to live, one because he can't work, another
because he has a physical deformity that doesn't allow him to work, his
family is poor and they can't help him. (May, 1997)

In one sense I think so but in another I think that it's a way of discriminating against us, like they're obligating us, that is how I see it, as
if we're being obligated, that is how I understand it . . . In the case that
I might need I would ask for it but I wouldn't like it. I came to this
country not to look for a handout or to ask for help [*no a pedir*], but
to be with my family. (May, 1997)

In this passage, Mariana says that she believes the state is coercing
immigrants to naturalize: "I think it's a way of discriminating
against us." Mariana resists state constructions of immigrants as
undeserving citizens when she refers to her brothers, who cannot
work, and to herself, who would only reluctantly look to the state
for assistance. Mariana's statement that she came to the US " not
to look for a handout . . . but to be with my family" reflects a relational view of membership that is at odds with state constructions
of immigrants as economic actors and of citizens as productive
workers.

Pablo has lived in New York for over 20 years, works in a plastics
factory alongside his brother Daniel, is married, and has three

children. In 1997, Pablo said that he was planning to naturalize. Like his brother Daniel, Pablo anticipates permanent return migration with occasional re-entry, rather than a sojourning pattern. Like his sister Mariana, Pablo resists state constructions of immigrants as undeserving and emphasizes how the state is punishing immigrants. When asked whether he thought that the laws were discriminating against immigrants, he said:

> Partly yes and partly no. I think becoming a citizen helps the immigrant. I'm not sure if you heard the story of an immigrant who killed himself because his benefits were cut off . . . I think that if he had been a citizen, he wouldn't have killed himself. I think for old people the laws are very . . . bad. Many old people they have lived their lives here, they're sick, they don't have family, maybe whatever family they have lives far away. (April, 1997)

This story is a cautionary tale and one that resonates very strongly among immigrants, constructing and articulating their desire to return to/retire in their home countries. It reflects the belief that the state is discriminating against some groups of deserving yet dependent (i.e., aged) individuals.

Other immigrants said that they were reluctant to naturalize because of the allegations that they were naturalizing for benefits. When anti-immigrant legislation and state efforts to encourage immigrants to naturalize resulted in large numbers of immigrants naturalizing in the late 1990s in the US, immigrants were accused of naturalizing for instrumental reasons, that is, as a means to ensure access to welfare benefits, thus violating notions of what constitutes a worthy reason for becoming a citizen.

Jaime is a second-generation member of the Castillo family. He was 37 years old at the time of interview and he had resided in the US for seven years. Jaime embraces responsible citizenship by distancing himself from the idea of dependent citizenship but he does so through the act of *not* naturalizing. He said:

> People are becoming citizens for the benefits; I don't want to do that. When I become a citizen it's because I'm ready, but most people are doing it for the benefits, but not me. I don't think I'm quite ready to become a citizen, and it won't be until I'm in the right frame of mind, perhaps in the summer I'll do it. Or, I won't become a citizen out of convenience, but I'll become a citizen because I want to be a citizen. (May, 1997)

When asked why he wanted to become a citizen, he said:

Well because from what I've read you're more legal here. And, when you go to Santo Domingo on vacation, you can stay four or six months, if you're not a resident, they start to ask a lot of questions when you come back . . . They won't say anything to you if you're a citizen. And to have a "status" in this country. But not for the benefits, I think that would make me feel poorer [*me siento más pobre*], I can't do it. Listen, I have two kids here, and I don't get food stamps [*cupones*] nor welfare, no. I support them. In Santo Domingo, they didn't teach me to ask [a pedir]. I can work. I hope to God that I'll always be given the opportunity to work, so that I won't have to look to welfare. (May, 1997)

Jaime's response reflects various concerns, such as the greater protections (rights) of citizens and the greater ease of travel. "But not for the benefits" indicates Jaime's concern that becoming a citizen will be construed by others as instrumentally motivated. By not becoming a US citizen, Jaime rejects state constructions of immigrants as dependent citizens; yet Jaime positions himself relative to these ideas.

I suggest that some immigrants' rejection of naturalization, particularly in the contemporary context, is a means for them to distance themselves from notions of dependent citizenship and to affirm allegiance to dominant discourses of good citizenship. By naturalizing, but also by not naturalizing, immigrants are situated and situate themselves in a broader sense, through state constructions of citizenship.

DUAL NATIONALITIES, CITIZENSHIP, AND RIGHTS

Dual nationality was enacted in the Dominican Republic in 1994, when a constitutional reform allowed Dominicans who had become citizens of other countries to retain their rights as Dominican nationals (Graham, 1997). The reform highlighted the strong linkage between citizenship and the claiming of rights. The linking of social benefits to US citizenship was also underscored when in a televised speech, Leonel Fernández, then president of the Dominican Republic, encouraged Dominicans abroad to naturalize and assured them that they would not lose any of their rights as Dominican citizens. In his speech, Fernández called for Dominicans to become US citizens in response to "the vicissitudes of North American society stemming from the end of the welfare era" (cited in Graham, 1997).

Immigrants' views of US citizenship reflect a rights discourse linked to dual membership. Many immigrants talk about dual membership as a set of rights bestowed by the state both in the US and in the Dominican Republic. Thus, citizenship becomes a way to make claims on several states. For example, Daniel says:

> When you become a [U.S.] citizen, it's not that you can't go to your country, but you couldn't do certain things because you're a foreigner. But by law now, if you're an American citizen, you don't lose your rights as a Dominican citizen, including when you move back and to bring a car [*llevar una mudanza*]. That was the fear that many Dominicans had, that if you become a citizen, you can't move back down there or bring a car down there . . . That's natural because any migrant from any country goes back to their country some day. Of a thousand people perhaps twenty never go back to their country. (April, 1997)

Here Daniel invokes the idea that return is natural and inevitable. He represents citizenship as a means of claims-making in several places. Moreover, citizenship is defined relationally: becoming a US citizen means not losing your rights as a Dominican citizen.

Pablo engages a discourse of rights in his discussion of US and Dominican citizenship. He talks about Dominican identity in terms of legal rights and equal treatment:

> If I become a citizen, I would still feel Dominican because I am Dominican too, because there is dual nationality [*doble ciudadanía*], or here, I am American but when I go back there I am Dominican and I have my rights there, our country now has dual nationality, which means that one is American but when you arrive there you're Dominican, the same as anyone who has not been here. That helps a lot . . . Dual nationality is very good, you don't lose your rights, because you are Dominican in a legal sense, and in terms of how you feel, because you are always going to be Dominican in this sense. (April, 1997)

Pablo reluctantly identifies himself as American, but only in a narrow, legal sense:

> Yes. With regard to identity, I suppose that I would have to say that I am American, like if I were to go back to my country, there I'm a Dominican because there I could use my Dominican documents as a result of dual nationality. But here I would have to do this as well . . . (April, 1997)

In other words, he is Dominican "there" because "I could use my Dominican documents." Likewise he says, "I would have to say that

I am American" if he were to become a citizen. In the next passage, though, he uses a primordial discourse to argue for identity based on allegiance and feeling (" that's inside you . . . perhaps there are people whose feelings change") rather than one based on legal criteria.

> I'm going to tell you something, for example, to be legally married and to say, I'm not married, well you are married because you're legally married. But I'm not married in the sense that I don't feel married. It's almost the same when I tell someone that I'm Dominican, even though legally I'm American, so I think that one could say they're Dominican because that's inside you [*uno lleva eso adentro*] perhaps there are people who[se] feelings change, I've heard of that, but the day I become a citizen, I'll be the same, the only thing that will change is that I'm going to be more secure, I'm going to vote. (April, 1997)

Other first-generation immigrants also refer to a primordial discourse of origins or roots in their discussion of citizenship. This discourse is linked to the political milieu that classifies immigrants as racial and ethnic minorities; the racial labeling of immigrants by the American political context shapes immigrant and citizenship identities (Joppke, 1999). Thus, for some immigrants, the imagined community of Americans is based on "racialized" and "nativist" assumptions of citizens as white and native-born, rather than on the notion of citizenship as rights. Zena, in discussing how she identifies herself now that she has become a US citizen, said:

> I would say that one has to adapt and say, "I am American." But to say that I am an American citizen . . . to say that I am an American – no. Because American, American, that is someone who is born here, who is from this country. I would say to anyone that I am an American citizen. (May, 1997)

Isabel, who naturalized in 1997, has lived in the US for over 20 years and anticipates retiring in the Dominican Republic to be with her husband. She said:

> Well, I would have to be sincere and say that I am an American citizen. But my origins, I cannot deny them, because I have a physical appearance, I have an accent that I can't erase. So really I am Dominican, but an American citizen. (May, 1997)

The concept of rights takes on heightened importance in the discourses that construct dual nationality and the Welfare Act; both highlight the strong linkage between citizenship and the claiming of rights. Whereas immigrants were positioned as undeserving recipients of the social rights of US citizenship in the late 1990s, many immigrants were also concerned about losing rights associated with Dominican citizenship (Itzigsohn *et al.*, 1999). Dual nationality provided a language that allowed immigrants to reclaim rights as well as their identities as Dominicans while becoming/being formal citizens of the US. This construction of membership rejects binary constructions of "affective" citizenship based on loyalty and allegiance to a single nation-state. In a transnational context, these rights were linked to travel and return/relocation, but were fundamentally tied to notions of identity.

CITIZENSHIP, CRIMINALIZATION, AND CONTROL

Overt forms of coercive state control are linked to the Welfare Act, and also to other recent laws. The AEDPA, or the "Anti-Terrorist Act," for example, resulted in the detention of supposedly criminal immigrants upon re-entry into the US after travel abroad. Stories of long-time US residents being detained upon re-entry into the US criminalized the immigrant population and heightened immigrants' sense of vulnerability to the arbitrary actions of state officials.

As a result of these new laws, the importance of formal membership became evident to many immigrants in the late 1990s. These laws created a variety of concerns. Zena says:

> Before when you were here with a tourist visa, you lived with fear [*un sobresalto*] you were scared, the INS [*inmigración*] could come to the factory, they could deport me . . . that's a fear that you walk around with. Let's say you get your residency, ok? You're calm [*tranquilo*] now, right? But now comes the problem of citizenship. Now your residency isn't worth anything. Now it's a new law. People are not becoming citizens not so much for the benefits [*por los cheques*] I think, its because your residency isn't worth as much and will be worth less over time. Don't you see how things are now? You petition a family member and you have to wait ten years, for them to get papers and to enter this country. And now you have to have a huge amount of money in the bank, a job earning I'm not sure how much and you have to be a citizen too. Look, when I brought my kid here I submitted an 'affidavit' for $300 and I was able to bring him. (May, 1997)

Here Zena describes the relentless pursuit of the immigrant by the state, even as the immigrant makes the transition from being undocumented to legal permanent resident to citizen: "Now it's a new law."

Isabel and Mariana are each married and share homes in New York with their husbands and some of their adult children. Like their sisters, they spend time in both New York City and the Dominican Republic; in New York City both are active in helping to care for several of their grandchildren. Both of their husbands have serious health problems, spend at least several months a year in the Dominican Republic, and anticipate retiring permanently to the Dominican Republic. For Isabel and Mariana, as for many of the first and second cohorts, being US citizens was attractive because it would reduce the risk that they could lose their legal permanent residency as a result of being away from the country for too long. Mariana emphasized that being a citizen would allow her and her husband to remain in their home country without fear:

> Well, because now you go and you have problems when you spend six or seven months in the Dominican Republic. And another is that the health of my husband is not very good now . . . We think that we're going back to our country, and if you're not a citizen, you can't be coming and going every minute, because when you have family here, you're going to have to be coming back, but you can't be coming back every three months, every four months. This is one of the reasons. (April, 1997)

In a world where travel supplements settlement, formal citizenship becomes a means to place-making. It helps immigrants forge and sustain networks of social relations that extend beyond the boundaries of the national society. Having a US passport facilitates re-entry without consideration of length of absence, whereas in the US, legal permanent residency is contingent on continuous residence, renewal, and more intensive monitoring by the state. Citizenship is performed at the border, enabling immigrants to move back and forth with greater ease.

Among the Castillos, state controls had a greater impact on men than on women, as men were more likely to have had legal problems that might disqualify them from attaining US citizenship. In addition, men were less likely to embrace naturalization as they eventually planned to return permanently to the Dominican Republic. Women, on the other hand, were more likely to either move back and forth, owing in part to their stronger ties to children and grandchildren, or remain in the US. They naturalized as a way to consolidate settlement in the US (see Singer and Gilbertson, 2003).

Also, owing to their unwillingness or inability to comply with the requirements of the naturalization process in the context of recent anti-immigrant legislation, men were more reluctant to naturalize. The process of becoming a US citizen required that immigrants submit to varying types of testing procedures, open their lives and pasts to state surveillance, and renounce old country allegiances. For example, 38-year-old Leonel, who has resided in the US for over 20 years, resented having to naturalize but said that he had to owing to a prior drug conviction. He was afraid that he could be restricted from re-entering the US after going abroad. Leonel was advised by several lawyers to neither leave the country nor apply to naturalize.

Pablo, a member of the first cohort of the Castillo family, said that he wanted to naturalize. He said that becoming a citizen would help him to avoid possible problems when re-entering the country, owing to a conviction for welfare fraud.

> If I travel now, for example, the way the laws are now, I could have problems when I return from there. They could check in the computer, and I could have problems. It's not that I'm afraid, because I have all the receipts, but it would be a hassle, I'd have to go to court, etc. I was going to go back, but now I'm not because of this, not until I resolve this problem. This is one of the reasons for me becoming a citizen, and for many immigrants who are here. If I were a US citizen, I could go back to the Dominican Republic without fear, and even if there was a problem, they couldn't deport me because I'm a citizen. This is one of the main reasons for becoming a citizen. (April, 1997)

Yet as of 2003, neither Leonel nor Pablo has naturalized, but both have visited to the Dominican Republic and re-entered the US.

Hugo, a first-generation immigrant who arrived in the US when he was 23 years old, has lived in the US for 15 years and became a citizen in 1999. Hugo works as a parking attendant; he is married and has two children. Hugo has attempted unsuccessfully to permanently relocate to Mao several times over the past decade; he owns a home and a small business that his brother attends to when he is in the US. Several years ago, Hugo was arrested for stealing long-distance telephone numbers. He escaped prosecution and shortly after was able to naturalize. Here he talks about the increasing criminalization of immigrants by the state:

> The problem is that before you had to be careful because you were illegal, but now everybody, including people who are legal here, have to be careful because the police will give you a ticket for just about anything, and you never know, if they give you one they can check your record and they start looking into things, even if you have your papers.

Because now the problem is with deportation, everybody is afraid. (February, 2003)

Restrictions imposed by the state prompt men to imagine return as a way to escape the state. Hugo says:

> Another thing is that the situation here has changed. Before the laws were less rigid, for example, you could go to a park, stay out all night at a park drinking a beer, and the police would see you and even say "hello." Now it's different, you can't go to a park, stay out, drink a beer without the police wanting to know what's going on . . . The freedom that you once had here is gone, and they've made it so that you just end up staying at home, that's one of the things that makes you think that I've got to go back to my country. (February, 2003)

Return migration is seen as a way to resist criminalization. It is also related to gendered notions of the imagined community in the Dominican Republic. Men's dissatisfaction with gender relations is evident in Hugo's use of an emancipatory discourse. Like the Mexican migrants in Rouse's (1992) study, Hugo laments the work routines and complains of diminished authority and mobility in the US:

> Yes, usually, the woman doesn't want to go back. The Dominican man here is a man of the home [*hombre casero*], he goes from home to work. A man in Santo Domingo is a free man, there he is . . . with people, talking, the way of living there is that you go places, drink a beer at a "car wash," go to a party here, you have access to everything. Here in New York, the man goes from home to work, his wife has him to herself, no one has access to him. (February, 2003)

Return is often discussed in the literature and by immigrant men as a form of liberation from low-paying, low-status work and the emasculating and racialized experiences of settlement (Pessar, 1986; Rouse, 1992; Gold, 2003). Indeed, return migration has often been constructed around the notion of resistance or as a rejection of ways of living in the US. In this way, it may be seen as a rejection or devaluation of "good citizenshipness." Return migration or imagined return, though, also involves its own forms of discipline and is not simply a release from constraints or controls. Immigrant men talk at great length about the requisites of successful return. Emerson, who is married and has three children, has been in the US for 12 years, but travels back to the Dominican Republic regularly to work on the farm that he and his siblings inherited from his recently deceased father.

Emerson and his wife have built a home in Mao and plan on returning permanently in the next five years. Emerson says:

> For you to go back you have to plan, if you don't plan and then you
> see all the negatives about your country it is difficult . . . to adapt. You
> have to have your mind ready, more than the money, your mind. If you
> don't you will get discouraged, the electricity, everything's expensive,
> if you can come back, because it is more comfortable here . . . I would
> say that before going definitively, I am going to prepare the ground, to
> see what I can do, what's going to happen, what I am going to live on,
> what are the possibilities (*entradas*) if you plan . . . and always have
> something extra in case something goes wrong . . . the businesses are
> unstable there. (March, 2003)

Return depends on the translatability of certain kinds of knowledge, skills, capital, and discipline acquired in the US into successful
business ventures. I argue that these constructions of successful
return are a product of gendered notions of transnational citizenship.
They are based on notions of a productive citizenship, particularly the
idea of working hard, being financially responsible and self-reliant,
and sacrificing for the sake of economic gain. The dream of freedom
and leisure, which is strongly linked to the construction of Dominican
masculinity in the context of return migration, is based on the privileged access returning men have to resources and public space.
Return, in this sense, is a form of masculine citizenship, based in part
on the reclaiming of patriarchal privileges that facilitate the pursuit of
economic and social interests with less interference from the state,
employers, women, or family.

CONCLUSION: THE REGULATION OF TRANSNATIONAL CITIZENS

In this chapter, I have discussed how immigrants understand ideas of
membership and belonging in the context of anti-immigrant legislation
by drawing on interviews and observations of Dominican immigrants.
How immigrants view and articulate citizenship in the contemporary
period is tied to how state power produces complex and contradictory
ideas regarding the meaning and nature of membership. I argue that
immigrants resist and embrace various aspects of state constructions of
citizenship.

Part of the experience of contemporary citizenship acquisition
was immigrants' insertion in a gendered, racialized, and national
space where they were constructed as undeserving recipients of both

citizenship and the rights of citizenship. The fact that most Dominicans are phenotypically nonwhite, and moreover, are considered "black" contributes to their positioning through discourse in such a way that they are ideologically blackened (Ong, 1996) like native-born blacks. Thus, part of the racialized and gendered process of becoming American involves distancing the self from groups associated with poverty and dependency by making distinctions between deserving and nondeserving members. These distinctions valorize masculine notions of citizenship based on paid labor and self-sufficiency and denigrate women as unfit mothers and dependent citizens. In this respect, the apparently universalistic criteria for the basis of full citizenship are not gender neutral.

State control was also evident as immigrants were not only made into undeserving citizens but were also criminalized. Ironically, new forms of state control may intensify some immigrants' desire to escape the state. Facilitated by transnational structures and discourses, including dual nationality, US citizenship may be used to undermine state control by facilitating immigrants' moving outside the sight/site of the state while at the same time guaranteeing rights associated with legal membership in the US. In this sense, legal membership is a form of resistance to state constructions of citizenship.

Paradoxically, although rights are seen as a way to protect the individual against the state, the accumulation of such rights can strengthen the state by drawing the individuals into new arenas of state regulation. Thus, while US citizenship may facilitate return migration, it enmeshes immigrants in the state as well. State control must be seen as part of the production of citizenship; it is a disciplining production, one that immigrants both conform to and resist. Thus, immigrants can subvert some forms of state power through US citizenship, while they are at the same time regulated by it.

NOTES

1. I would like to thank Jackie Hagan and Rodolfo Soriano-Nuñez for their generous assistance.
2. IIRIRA of 1996 included provisions to bolster control of US borders, established measures to remove criminal and other deportable aliens, and provided for increased protection for legal workers through worksite enforcement. It also placed added restriction on benefits for immigrants, including making the long-required affidavit of support legally binding. The AEDPA of 1996 provided for expedited procedures for the removal of alien "terrorists" and provided for changes in criminal alien procedures, such as authorizing state and local law-enforcement officials to

arrest and detain certain illegal aliens, and providing access to certain confidential immigration and naturalization files through court order (INS, 1997).

3. Concerns over immigrants and the use of welfare benefits were seen several years earlier in California, the state with the largest immigrant population. When Proposition 187 called for the end of various government services and assistance to both undocumented immigrants and legal permanent residents.

4. In an analysis conducted by the INS, 46% of the 1977 entry cohort of immigrants from all countries had naturalized by 1995. The same cohort of Dominicans had a naturalization rate of 28.6% (INS, 1997).

5. Although the program was also meant to reduce enormous backlogs in naturalization processing and eventually came under attack when some members of Congress charged that it was designed for the purpose of gaining more voters for the 1996 election, it was originally conceived as a way to encourage naturalization. According to the then commissioner of immigration, Doris Meissner, the US had " been too passive in the promotion of citizenship" and it had "never been very aggressive in encouraging resident aliens to naturalize." A major naturalization initiative was promoted in the fiscal year 1995 under Meissner's leadership and it included promoting or publicizing naturalization (including the use of flyers and buttons and other campaign-style media) and streamlining the naturalization process (http://www.doi.gov/oig/cusarpt/cusaimp.pdf).

6. This is the real surname of one of the subfamilies.

7. All first names are pseudonyms.

REFERENCES

Alba, Richard, and Victor Nee. 2003. *Remaking the American Mainstream: Assimilation and Contemporary Immigration.* Cambridge: Harvard University Press.

Aleinikoff, Alexander. 1998. *Between Principles and Politics: The Direction of U.S. Citizenship Policy.* Washington, DC: International Migration Program, Carnegie Endowment for International Peace.

Bean, Frank, and Gillian Stevens. 2003. *America's Newcomers and the Dynamics of Diversity.* New York: Russell Sage Foundation.

Borjas, George. 1990. *Friends or Strangers: The Impact of Immigrants on the U.S. Economy.* New York: Basic Books.

Borjas, George, and Lynette Hilton. 1996. Immigration and the Welfare State: Immigrant Participation in Means-Tested Entitlement Programs. *Quarterly Journal of Economics* (May): 576–604.

Collins, Patricia Hill. 1999. Producing the Mothers of the Nation, Race, Class and Contemporary US Population Policies. In *Women, Citizenship and Difference,* ed. Nira Yuval-Davis and Prina Werbner, 118–129. London and New York: Zed Books.

Faist, Thomas. 2000. Transnationalization in International Migration: Implications for the Study of Citizenship and Culture. *Ethnic and Racial Studies* 23: 189–222.

Fix, Micheal, Jeffrey Passal, and Kenneth Sucher. 2003. Trends in Naturalization. http://www.urban.org/url.cfm?ID=310847.

Gilbertson, Greta, and Audrey Singer. 2003. The Emergence of Protective Citizenship in the USA: Naturalization among Dominican Immigrants in the Post-1996 Welfare Reform Era. *Ethnic and Racial Studies* 26: 25–51.

Glick Schiller, Nina, Linda Basch, and Cristina Szanton Blanc. 1992. *Towards a Transnational Perspective on Migration: Race, Class, Ethnicity and Nationalism Reconsidered.* New York: New York Academy of Sciences.

Gold, Steve. 2003. Israeli and Russian Jews: Gendered Perspectives in Settlement and Migration. In *Gender and U.S. Migration: Contemporary Trends,* ed. Pierrette Hondagneu-Sotelo, 127–147. Berkeley: University of California Press.

Graham, Pamela. 1997. Reimagining the Nation and Defining the District: Dominican Migration and Transnational Politics. In *Caribbean Circuits: New Directions in the Study of Caribbean Migration,* ed. Patricia Pessar. New York: Center for Migration Studies.

Grasmuck, Sherri, and Patricia Pessar. 1991. *Between Two Islands: Dominican International Migration.* Berkeley: University of California Press.

Guarnizo, Luis. 1997. The Emergence of a Transnational Social Formation and the Mirage of Return Migration among Dominican Transmigrants. *Identities* 4: 281–322.

Hagan, Jacqueline, Nestor Rodriguez, Randy Capps, and Nika Kabira. 2003. Effects of Recent Welfare and Immigration Reforms on Immigrants' Access to Health Care. *International Migration Review* 37(2).

Hernández, Ramona. 2002. *The Mobility of Workers under Advanced Capitalism: Dominican Migration to the United States.* New York: Columbia University Press.

Immigration Policy News: The State-Local Report. 1996. *Immigration Policy Project: State and Local Coalitions on Immigration,* vol. 3, no. 3. November. www.ncsl.org/statefed/sl9611.htm.

Itzigsohn, Jose, Carlos Dore Cabral, Esther Hernandez Medina, and Obed Vazquez. 1999. Mapping Dominican Transnationalism: Narrow and Broad Transnational Practices. *Ethnic and Racial Studies* 22: 216–240.

Jones-Correa, Michael. 1998. *Between Two Nations: The Political Predicament of Latinos in New York City.* Ithaca, NY: Cornell University Press.

Joppke, Christian. 1999. How Immigration is Changing Citizenship: A Comparative View. *Ethnic and Racial Studies* 22: 629–652.

Katz, Micheal B. 2001. *The Price of Citizenship: Redefining the American Welfare State.* New York: Henry Holt.

Kivisto, Peter. 2001. Theorizing Transnational Immigration: A Critical Review of Current Efforts. *Ethnic and Racial Studies* 24: 549–577.

Levitt, Peggy. 2001. *The Transnational Villagers.* Berkeley and Los Angeles: University of California Press.

Ong, Aihwa. 1996. Cultural Citizenship as Subject Making: Immigrants Negotiate Racial and Cultural Boundaries in the United States. *Current Anthropology* 37: 737–762.

Pessar, Patricia. 1986. The Role of Gender in Dominican Settlement in the U.S. In *Women and Change in Latin America,* ed. June Nash and Helen Safa, 273–294. South Hadley, MA: Bergen and Harvey.

Peterson, Janice. 2002. Feminist Perspectives on TANF Reauthorization: An Introduction to Key Issues. Briefing Paper # E511, Institute for Women's Policy Research, Washington, DC, February.

Rouse, Roger. 1992. Making Sense of Settlement: Class Transformation, Cultural Struggle, and Transnationalism among Mexican Migrants in the United States. *Annals of the New York Academy of Sciences* 645: 25–52.

Schneider, Dorothee. 2001. Naturalization and United States Citizenship in Two Periods of Mass Migration: 1894–1930, 1965–2000. *Journal of American Ethnic History* 20: 51–82.

Singer, Audrey. 1999. U.S. Citizenship Applications at All-Time High. *Population Today,* October.

———. 2002. Immigrants, Welfare Reform and the Coming Reauthorization Vote. *Migration Information Source: Fresh Thought, Authoritative Data, Global Reach.* The Migration Policy Institute.

Singer, Audrey, and Greta Gilbertson. 2003. The Blue Passport: Gender and the Social Process of Naturalization among Dominican Immigrants in New York City. In *Gender and U.S. Migration: Contemporary Trends,* ed. Pierrette Hondagneu-Sotelo, 359–378. Berkeley: University of California Press.

Skeggs, Beverley. 1997. *Formations of Class and Gender: Becoming Respectable.* London: Sage.

Smith, Robert. 1998. Transnational Localities: Community, Technology and the Politics of Membership within the Context of Mexico and U.S. Migration. In *Transnationalism From Below,* ed. Michael Peter Smith and Luis Guarnizo, 196–240. New Brunswick, NJ: Transaction Publishers.

US Immigration and Naturalization Service. 1997. *Statistical Yearbook of the Immigration and Naturalization Service, 1996.* Washington, DC: US Government Printing Office.

CHAPTER 5

Dual Citizenship and Political Participation: Migrants in the Interplay of United States and Colombian Politics

Cristina Escobar

As part of a more general phenomenon of globalization and migration, an increasing number of Latin American countries have recently ruled in favor of allowing their nationals to naturalize abroad without losing their citizen status. This enactment of dual citizenship, particularly during the 1990s, has taken place at a time when the US, in its efforts to reduce immigration, has restricted rights and privileges to citizens, indirectly pressuring migrants to naturalize. The combined effect of these two policies has been an increase in the number of dual citizens.

The growth in dual citizenship has created controversies within both the policy world and academia over its political significance. While some consider that dual citizenship represents a threat to the integrity, unity, and security of the US, others see it as a vehicle of further integration. Since dual citizenship is a growing worldwide phenomenon, policymakers and politicians in the US share the concerns of many other countries regarding its benefits or problems.

In this chapter, I deal first with naturalization among Colombians since the 1990s to understand the interplay between the US's interest in controlling immigration and the interest of the increasing number of Colombian immigrants in retaining links with their original state, where they cannot find peace, security, or work. Migrants' interest in carving a place in their new country, while retaining links to the other, deal with and are influenced by the policies of both countries simultaneously. I argue that within this context, naturalization can no longer be understood as a unidirectional phenomenon leading to the definitive incorporation of migrants into the polity of the receiving nation and to the final detachment of these migrants from previous loyalties and links to their home countries.

Second, I analyze political incorporation and participation among dual Colombian American nationals in the US. I argue that dual nationality and the links that Colombians maintain with their home country are not necessarily detrimental to their interest and participation in the US. On the contrary, Colombian transnational organizations have played a positive role by contributing to the political engagement of migrants in the US. I also argue that naturalization, even in those cases that have resulted from the pressures imposed by restrictive US immigrant policies, does not necessarily preclude migrants' interest in political participation in the US.

I base my analysis on research conducted at the national, regional, and local levels. I conducted interviews with leaders of the Colombian community and state officials and carried out research in state archives. I interviewed 30 regional and local leaders (in the area of New York City and northern New Jersey) as well as 35 Colombian immigrants in Northbrook, NJ, and 37 people in the town of La Esperanza, in the Colombian coffee region, where most of these immigrants come from. Both in Northbrook and in La Esperanza, I used the snowball technique.[1] In order to get more diversity within the samples, I started simultaneous snowballs from diverse points.

I will start by addressing the general debate on dual citizenship. Next, I will analyze naturalization among Colombians within the context of Colombian dual citizenship legislation and US immigration policy. Following this analysis, I will discuss the effects of dual citizenship and political transnationalism on the political participation of Colombians in the US.

THE DUAL CITIZENSHIP DEBATE

The debate on dual citizenship has emerged from the disagreement between conventional views, which accept single membership of individuals to states as the norm and see dual citizenship as posing insuperable problems and critical dangers to nations, versus views that address the new reality of the contemporary world (in which an increasing number of individuals are becoming dual citizens) and consider that dual citizenship may even offer advantages.

To begin, I would like to underline the various dimensions of citizenship. The first dimension is the legal status of nationality (Bauböck,

2001) or "formal citizenship" (Brubaker, 1992). A product of the territorial consolidation of nation-states, it refers to the formal membership of individuals and their subjection to state power, independent of the rights to which they are entitled. A second dimension of citizenship, called "democratic citizenship" (Bauböck, 2001) or "substantial citizenship" (Brubaker, 1992), refers to the rights and obligations of citizens as participants in the political community. Some authors still distinguish a third dimension of citizenship, which includes the actual "*practices* of participating that sustain a democratic regime" (Bauböck, 2001: 5). All three dimensions of citizenship, which are based on the assumption of single membership, are challenged by dual citizenship. However, the discussion has focused predominantly on the formal conflicts that arise from having rights and obligations in two countries as well as on the willingness and ability of dual citizens to actually practice their citizen rights in both countries without jeopardizing democracy in either of them.

Questions raised by dual citizenship with respect to diplomatic protection and military conscription, and which in theory seem to be irreconcilable, in practice can be —and have been in many cases— resolved by bilateral agreements and international law (Legomsky, 2003; Martin, 2003: 15). More acute have been the debates concerning loyalty, voting rights, and instrumentality (Schuck, 1998; Aleinikoff and Klusmeyer, 2002; Hansen and Weil, 2002; Martin, 2003; Spiro, 2003). These debates have been particularly important in the US, where the renunciation of other nationalities included in the naturalization oath is not enforced and where an increasing number of Latin American immigrants come from countries that have changed their laws to allow dual citizenship. There are at least ten Latin American countries (six of which adopted their new laws after 1990) and ten Caribbean Basin countries that recognize dual nationality (Jones-Correa, 2003). Colombia has been a pioneer in Latin America not only by allowing its nationals to retain their nationality (1991), as many other countries have done, but also by extending the franchise and creating a special electoral jurisdiction for nonresident nationals and reserving a seat in the lower house for their representation. Although other countries such as Argentina, Brazil, Peru, the Dominican Republic, and Mexico have also extended the franchise to nationals abroad,[2] no country other than Colombia has created specific congressional representation.[3]

Implicit in this debate are different approaches to migrants' incorporation into their host societies. The traditional assimilation perspective, developed as a result of the experience of European migration at the turn of the 20th century, assumes that migrants will acculturate (strip-ping themselves of their original culture and adopting the culture of the host society), integrate into the host societies' social and economic insti-tutions, intermarry, identify with and participate in the civic life of the new society (Gordon, 1964). The political corollary of this position is that as immigrants assimilate, they abandon their previous loyalties and allegiances and adhere to the new society. Naturalization is the last formal step. Contemporary assimilation arguments have tamed and enriched the original assimilation paradigm by acknowledging that assimilation might represent not a straight line but a bumpy line (Alba and Nee, 1999), that there is no single, homogenous assimilation process but rather different routes to it (Zhou, 1999), and that assimi-lation might not always represent a pursued goal but rather a conse-quence of practical steps taken by immigrants in their daily struggles (Alba and Nee, 2003). Advocates of the assimilation perspective to nat-uralization argue that despite the increase in dual citizenship, the longer immigrants stay and the more acculturated they become, the less attach-ment they will have to their home country and the less salient that country's citizenship will become. Naturalization is seen as a mechanism for immigrants to reinforce "their civic and material attachment to the United States" (DeSipio, 2000: 8). This assimilationist position coin-cides with the traditional model of citizenship, formalized in the Huge Convention of 1930, which says that the world is divided into well-defined, sovereign, national political units and that individuals identify with and are citizens of a single national state (Pickus, 1998: 108–109; Martin, 2003: 4).

Advocates of the transnational perspective on migration argue that even though migrants cross international borders, settle, and establish relations in a new state, they do not necessarily lose their social and political connections with their home country but instead "maintain ongoing social connections with the polity from which they originat-ed" (Guarnizo *et al.*, 2003). The transnational perspective addresses the reality of contemporary migration as fundamentally different from previous migration not just because of the existence of migrants' ties with their country of origin, which have always existed, but because of "the high intensity of exchanges, the new modes of transacting, and the multiplication of activities that require cross-border travel and contacts on a sustained basis" (Portes *et al.*, 1999: 219). In its broader definition, transnationalism refers to the whole set of political, economic, cultural, and social networks and institutions that connect migrants' home and host countries and influence not only the lives of those who settle in the host country and of those who move back and forth but also the lives of those who never move (Levitt and Waters, 2003). A more specific definition of transnationality refers to what has been found to be a minority of individuals (5–10% of the migrant population) who live across borders and are directly engaged in transnational practices (Portes *et al.*, 2002; Guarnizo *et al.*, 2003). From either one of these transnational perspectives, political adaptation to the new country does not necessarily preclude political involvement in the country of origin. Proponents of a new model of citizenship, more in agreement with the transnational perspective, see dual nationality as a natural consequence of the changing nature of the migration process in an era of globalization. They claim that in the contemporary world, exclusive state allegiances are no longer necessary because conflict has given place to a more stable international arena and because the states, which have lost power in the context of a globalized world, are in no position to demand this exclusive allegiance (Spiro, 1997). Contrary to those who view this development with alarm, these proponents of a new model of citizenship consider that "the needed level of loyalty or commitment to a democratic polity of which one is a member is certainly possible in the modern world even if one holds two or more nationalities" (Martin, 2003: 12). Moreover, they argue that the increase in dual citizenship, which should be not only tolerated by the receiving countries but embraced as well, will result in the acceptance of a model of citizenship that accommodates multiple political identities (Spiro, 1997, 2003: 136).

The distance between assimilation and transnational theoretical approaches to migration is narrowing. Scholars now accept that immigrants, even those from the turn of the 20th century who inspired assimilation theory, did not easily abandon relations with their countries of origin (Kasinitz *et al.*, 2003: 100). Transnationalists are also explaining that immigrants' active connections and links to their countries of origin are not diametrically opposed to assimilation (Levitt, 2001). However, concerns remain in the political and policy worlds, even though international law and bilateral agreements are resolving in practice many of the conflicts that the normative discussion on dual citizenship had conceived as insuperable. In the case of the US, concerns center on the potential dangers that dual citizenship poses for democracy and national unity and are part of more general arguments against immigration, multiculturalism, and what is considered to be a degradation of citizenship (Geyer, 1996; Miller, 1998; Pickus, 1998; Renshon, 2001).

This study of Colombian dual citizenship supports the argument that membership in the country of origin, along with transnational connections and general embeddedness in transnational fields, is not opposed to assimilation and political participation in the US. Even though some Colombians might assimilate and naturalize, many have naturalized and politicized in the US while keeping their membership, culture, and network connections with Colombia. This form of transnational assimilation among contemporary migrant groups subscribes to the more general trend that is undermining the clear-cut transnationalism/assimilation dichotomy.

The simultaneous membership of migrants in the political communities of the country of residence and the country of origin forces us to look beyond the level of migrants and to address the question of the role of the states involved. Contemporary migration—numerically significant and deeply embedded in transnational fields because technology allows migrants to keep close ties with their countries of origin[4]—is creating an interplay between the politics of the sending and receiving countries. The relation between a sending state and its citizens abroad influences the relation that these migrants maintain with their receiving state. As this chapter illustrates with the Colombian case, dual citizenship legislation in the sending countries increases the naturalization of migrants in the receiving country. The contrary is also true, that is, the policies of receiving states regarding immigrants influences the policies of sending states and their nonresident citizens. Efforts by the US to restrict legal residents' access to social rights, such as the welfare reform legislation of 1996, can become an important reason for the sending countries to enact dual citizenship or dual nationality laws, as in the case of Brazil and Mexico (Fitzgerald, 2000; Levitt, 2002). We cannot continue to address citizenship policies while ignoring this interdependency between the polities of sending and receiving states created by the migrant population.

NATURALIZATION: WHY AND HOW TO BECOME A CITIZEN OF THE US

Latinos have, in general, exhibited low rates of naturalization, and scholars have tried to explain why. DeSipio (1996), from a traditional assimilationist perspective, has suggested that low rates of naturalization are not related to Latinos' low levels of attachment to the US but to the existence of bureaucratic and sociodemographic barriers to naturalization. Jones-Correa (1998), on the contrary, attributes the low levels of naturalization to the attachment that migrants maintain with their home country; he later argues that dual citizenship has, in fact, been an incentive to naturalization (Jones-Correa, 2003). My study of Colombian dual citizenship not only supports Jones-Correa's thesis that dual citizenship has been an incentive to naturalization but also shows that transnational activism has played an important role as an agent of Colombian migrants' naturalization and politicization in the US.

ASSURING DUAL MEMBERSHIP

Colombian migration began in the wake of World War II as a small stream, which continued during the late 1960s and 1970s. Migration increased in the 1980s as a result of the economic and political difficulties affecting the country. Most of the early migrants included middle- and working class immigrants pursuing economic improvement. Many of these people settled in New York and Los Angeles. Migration has increased significantly in the last few years as the crisis in Colombia has deepened. This latest wave includes more middle- to upper-middle-class migrants escaping the political and economic crisis, and many of these people have settled in South Florida (Collier and Gamarra, 2001; Guarnizo et al., 2003). According to the 2000 census, there are half a million Colombians in the US; however, the 1997 census of the Colombian consulates, which does not include the 300,000 or more Colombians who have migrated in the last five years, estimated this population at 1.4 million.

Colombian migrants' dual nationality campaign was definitely influenced by the desire of Colombian immigrants to participate in politics in the US. As I traced the events that culminated in the enactment of Colombian dual nationality in the new 1991 Constitution, I found that the interest of Colombian immigrant leaders in US politics was a critical concern for those involved in the campaign. The problem and the dilemma faced by many Colombian leaders—generally long-time residents—was that they could not get involved in US politics unless they renounced their Colombian citizenship. This interest in participating in US politics is present in the initial documents of the campaign.[5] The interest in expanding political rights for Colombian nationals abroad was a subsequent development in the campaign.

The initiative behind the dual nationality campaign came from members of the Colombian American National Coalition (CANCO), a nongovernmental and nonpolitical organization of Colombian leaders created in Miami in 1986 to promote the interests of the Colombian community in the US and to encourage its political participation in both Colombia and the US. The idea of dual nationality became part of CANCO's agenda, which by 1988 had opened chapters in Chicago,

Washington, and New York, after its president and leader spent a year at the Congressional Hispanic Caucus Institute in Washington. The campaign for dual nationality was soon adopted by leaders of the Colombian community, especially by leaders of the newly created chapter of the Colombian Liberal Party in Queens. Even though these and other political leaders broadened the campaign of dual nationality to include the extension of political rights to Colombian nonresidents, this subsequent dimension of the campaign should not obscure the fact that dual citizenship was pursued as an opening to political participation in the US.

Following Colombia's enactment of dual citizenship in 1991,[6] Colombians' rate of naturalization[7] in the US, which had fluctuated around 0.5 from 1989 to 1992, increased to 0.87 in 1993 and to 1.03 in 1994, the years immediately after dual citizenship became law in Colombia (1992) (see table 1). The problem with the quantitative data on Latin Americans' naturalization has been that simultaneously with the enactment of dual citizenship in many of these countries during the 1990s, other factors also increased naturalization. (These included the introduction by the INS of the Green Card Replacement program, the five-year waiting period for the large pool of potential naturalization applicants that resulted from the Immigration Reform and Control Act (IRCA) in 1986, and the welfare reform legislation of 1996.) However, the early enactment of dual citizenship in Colombia in 1991 allows us to attribute the increase in naturalization

Table 5.1 Ratio of naturalization of Colombian immigrants in the US (1989–2001)

Year	Total naturalized	Residents 7 years before	Naturalization ratio
1989	4,741	8,608	0.50
1990	5,713	9,658	0.59
1991	5,619	11,020	0.50
1992	6,451	11,982	0.53
1993	9,998	11,408	0.87
1994	12,075	11,700	1.03
1995	12,355	10,332	1.19
1996	27,483	15,214	1.8
1997	11,645	24,189	0.48
1998	7,024	19,702	0.35
1999	13,168	13,201	0.99
2000	14,018	12,819	1.09
2001	10,872	10,847	0.99

Source: Immigration and Naturalization Service (1989–2001) Yearbooks.

between 1993 and 1995 mostly to the dual nationality laws and not to the increase in the number of potential citizens that resulted from IRCA legalization.[8]

My interviews with Colombian leaders in the New York–New Jersey metropolitan area not only confirm the statement that dual nationality promoted naturalization but also make evident the role played by dual nationality campaign activists in naturalization. Following the enactment of the dual citizenship law in Colombia, there was a considerable increase in applications for nationalization, and many of the local leaders who had been engaged in the campaign started programs to promote naturalization, helping people to obtain and fill out the forms and prepare for the exams. The Centro Cívico Colombiano, one of the oldest Colombian organizations in Queens, developed a volunteer program, meeting every third Sunday over a period of several years, to help people in the naturalization process. Some activists created the Latin American Integration Center (LAIC) in 1991, a nongovernmental organization interested in promoting citizen education and participation. Other organizations, such as the Charitas in Queens, the Hispanic American Alliance in Englewood, and Colombianos en Acción in Paterson, and leaders in Elizabeth, Hackensack, and other New Jersey towns, also started programs in these years (Personal interviews, New York and New Jersey, 2000–2002).

Thus, aside from the indirect effect that the enactment of the Colombian law had on naturalization, the dual nationality campaign also had a direct influence in reducing the bureaucratic barriers and facilitating the process. According to DeSipio, "Historically, the high rates of naturalization have needed an outside trigger," including political machines, national activism, or events of political activity, such as wars, that call into question migrants' attachment to the US. He attributes the low level of naturalization among Latinos to the fact that their leaders "have largely failed to promote naturalization or to assist immigrants interested in pursuing US citizenship" (1996: 152, 165). The Colombian experience suggests that dual citizenship can actually become one of these "triggers," even though the idea is not the abdication of previous loyalties but the guarantee of their preservation. Furthermore, nationally organized activism, such as that carried out by the Colombian leaders in the dual nationality campaign, is an example of Latino community efforts to promote naturalization, which DeSipio sees as having been, for the most part, absent from Latino communities.

In Northbrook, the group of interviewees who mentioned the law of dual nationality as a main factor contributing to their decision to naturalize were immigrants who had been in the US for a long time (some since the late 1960s and 1970s and others since the 1980s) but had remained legal residents to avoid losing their Colombian citizenship. For this group of migrants, most of whom naturalized in 1993 and 1994, dual citizenship eliminated the last barrier they faced before integrating more fully into US society. Some mentioned having gone to Queens to receive training from one of the Colombian organizations that had been set up to prepare people for the citizenship exam. Many in this town also remember the campaign for naturalization carried out by a Cuban American politician who was interested in increasing his Latino constituency. While enactment of dual citizenship convinced them to become citizens, the presence of this politician, as well as the activism of Colombian leaders in Queens, facilitated the process.

The following are some examples of people who naturalized in 1993–1994: Armando arrived in Northbrook in the late 1970s. He was able to bring with him his wife, Beatriz, as well as their children a few years later. One of his elder sons obtained citizenship through his job and was able to obtain resident status for them in the late 1980s. Armando and Beatriz did not naturalize until 1993. Carmen migrated one year after her husband in the late 1970s. They raised their two children in Northbrook and obtained resident status through Carmen's husband's work in the local hospital. Carmen wanted to naturalize but her husband did not. They naturalized after the dual citizenship legislation. Daniel and Emilia came to the US illegally in the early 1980s, obtained residency by false marriages, and then remarried. They did not naturalize until the dual citizenship legislation was passed.

In sum, dual citizenship has become an incentive for migrants to naturalize, and nationally based activism associated with dual citizenship has helped eliminate the practical and bureaucratic difficulties associated with naturalization. As the case of Northbrook shows, not only are national leaders interested in increasing naturalization of their fellow nationals, US political leaders in search of the Latino vote are too. This relation between dual citizenship and naturalization should not be seen as operating in only one direction. The interest in participation within the US was also a major factor behind the initial campaign for Colombian dual nationality. In other cases, the main promoter of dual nationality has been the state; once again though, the interest here has not been to disconnect people from the home country but to guarantee their links to both. Naturalization cannot be understood solely as a result of immigrants' increasing attachment to their country of residency and their dissociation from their home country. Naturalization can also be the product of migrants' interest in becoming active citizens in their host country (what Gordon [1964] calls "civic assimilation") while remaining attached to their country of origin.

RESPONDING TO RESTRICTIONS OF US RESIDENT RIGHTS

Aside from the influence of Colombian dual nationality laws, migrants have also naturalized as a response to the restrictions on family reunification and access to social rights imposed by US immigrant legislation on those with resident status. Responding to the same interest of remaining within the US and gaining access to citizen rights without losing the attachment to their home country, Colombian migrants have acquired US citizenship as an immigration and transnational strategy. One of the most common reasons for naturalization, according to leaders in the New York metropolitan area and my Northbrook interviewees, was the need to either legalize or bring relatives. This is particularly true for the group of migrants who arrived in the 1980s (many illegally, via the Bahamas and, after 1982, Mexico), or for others who overstayed their visas and obtained their legal residency through the 1986 amnesty, through arranged marriages, or by other means.

Many of those who did not nationalize until after the enactment of dual citizenship were migrants who either had come when immigration visas were available and when reunification with relatives was possible within a reasonable time for those with resident status, or had come later but had been able to bring or legalize their relatives by other means. They were, so to speak, more "free" to decide about their naturalization. On the contrary, many of those who achieved resident status in the late 1980s and early 1990s had not yet been able to bring or legalize relatives, as legislation had made citizenship status almost a requirement for family reunification. These migrants were responding to immigrant restrictions in the US.

The INS statistics show that after the steady increase in the rate of naturalization in 1993–1995, a second and even greater increase in the rate of naturalization took place in 1996, when the rate rose to 1.8 (the decrease in the rate in the following three years is the result of the backlog in the processing of applications). This increase can be explained in large part by the increase in the pool of applicants created by the amnesty offered by the aforementioned IRCA in 1986. The group of interviewees belonging to this large cohort of immigrants who gained their resident status through IRCA in the years 1989–1991 filed their applications for naturalization right after the mandatory five-year waiting time. Aside from the fact that dual citizenship facilitated their decision, most wanted to petition for their relatives to immigrate to the US (some of whom were still living in Colombia but many of whom were already living illegally in the US). Much more than the previous group, this more recent cohort of residents needed their citizenship to reunite or legalize their families.

Fernando and Gabriela immigrated illegally in the mid-1980s. Fernando was able to legalize through the IRCA. He obtained his papers and applied as soon as he could to become a citizen so that he could legalize his wife, Gabriela, and daughter. His wife has now filed an application to become a citizen.

Along with the need to bring or legalize relatives, the immigration reforms of 1996[9] are another important variable contributing to the subsequent increase in naturalization. Even though these reforms' influence on naturalization is not easily identifiable in the INS statistics because it coincided with the increased naturalization resulting from IRCA, leaders in the region consider them to be perhaps the most important motivating force behind naturalization. More than the welfare reform legislation—the fear of losing welfare privileges was not the main concern for most of my interviewees—it was the antiterrorist law and the fear of being potentially deportable that made people react. Residency, said one interviewee, "does not guarantee our stay here." Indirectly, however, the welfare reform legislation had an impact on their naturalization because of the campaigns by the New Jersey state government to encourage and facilitate naturalization and to avoid future expenses. Financed by the state government, institutions in the nearby towns offered free processing of petitions. The possibility of retaining their Colombian citizenship made the decision easier for this cohort of migrants. who nationalized after being legalized by IRCA or as a reaction to the welfare or antiterrorist legislation of 1996. It was, in the words of an interviewee, "the whipped cream" of the process. Naturalization in these cases was a combined response to the policies of the US toward its immigrants and Colombian legislation regarding nonresident nationals. This process contrasts with the Mexican and the Brazilian cases, where dual citizenship was enacted in direct response to US policies.

The use of citizenship as an immigrant strategy is relevant to the debate over the value of citizenship that has resurfaced recently within the context of the welfare reform legislation of 1996. Analysts have been concerned that migrants are naturalizing for "wrong" or "selfish" reasons (Schuck, 1998: 154). Immigrants are becoming citizens to secure social rights, and this "does not exalt citizenship, it devalues it" (Martin, 2002: 229). Aside from the fact that there is no social or political consensus regarding what are or should be the legitimate motives for naturalization (Schuck, 1998: 154), it would be very difficult to prove that previous generations of immigrants (including all those naturalized by the political machines at the turn of the 20th century) did in fact naturalize for the "right" reasons. Using the same logic, we should also add to the list of policies devaluing citizenship the family reunification policies that favor citizens over residents and that have propelled residents to naturalize.

The problem with the devaluation of citizenship argument is that it assumes that the instrumental motivation for naturalization necessarily undermines the possibility of migrants' civic and political engagement. In terms of the three dimensions of citizenship mentioned earlier, critics doubt that entitlement to citizenship rights would really result in democratic participation or, using Bauböck's words again in "the *practices* of participating that sustain a democratic regime (2001: 5)." The circumstances that motivate people to naturalize are complex, particularly if migrants' lives are influenced by the laws of both their country of origin and their country of residence. These motivations, as the following quotation shows, can and do coexist along with interest in incorporation and political participation. An interviewee who became a resident through IRCA and a citizen after a five-year wait in order to legalize his family responds in this way to my question about what led him to become a citizen of the US:

> Well, first of all there is dual citizenship, because in spite of everything, we are from Colombia . . . And here, well, we are already established and we need to be citizens to have the right to vote, to social benefits—that we never use but one never knows what will happen tomorrow . . . We have the right to vote and with it, to the extent that we work together and show some strength as a race we will be able to obtain political power; they are going to have to take us into account. There is discrimination in social services because some things are for citizens and others for residents; for example, parents can be requested only by citizens not by residents . . . But what made me decide to become a citizen is that I like this country, I feel fine here and if we are here it is better to have the opportunity . . . I think what made our decision easier was the dual citizenship [my translation].

Besides their interest in naturalization as an immigrant strategy, for bringing relatives, or preventing deportation, my interviewees also valued US citizenship as a resourceful mechanism for their transnational life. As mentioned above, becoming a US citizen is not an option that reflects less attachment to Colombia. The acquisition of citizenship becomes a transnational strategy—a way to spend more time in Colombia when they need or want to, without having to return to the US every six months, as they must if they have only resident status.

The case of Mercedes, the only US citizen among my interviewees in La Esperanza, is an example of citizenship as a transnational strategy. She migrated in the 1980s, attained residency status, and then became a citizen. Her main interest in becoming a citizen was the possibility of spending more time in Colombia with her mother without being restricted to only six months at a time. She went back to live in La Esperanza in 1994 to take care of her mother, who died in 1996. She may return to the US.

The idea of using citizen status as a transnational strategy—which is not exclusive to Colombians, as the cases presented in a study of naturalization among a Dominican family show (Gilbertson and Singer, 2003: 37–38)—was prevalent at the beginning of the 1990s among Colombians. The political and economic crisis in Colombia since the mid-1990s has caused people to reduce their trips home, to abandon investment projects, and even to give up their dreams of returning and retiring in the home country. Since the late 1990s, many people have stopped investing their money in properties or business in Colombia and have instead become homeowners in the US. Colombians in Northbrook are also retiring in Florida. In spite of the reduction of trips and the low probabilities people see today of fulfilling their dream of return, they still like to emphasize the advantages offered by citizen status, which allows them to stay in Colombia as long as they want and would enable them to have their social security check mailed there if, assuming that the situation improves, they retire in their home country. In fact, Dominican immigrant retirees, unable or unwilling to maintain permanent residency in the US, have found citizenship amore useful strategy for their transnational lives (Gilbertson and Singer, 2003: 37–38). Thus, contrary to the idea that people who do not reside permanently in the US would not be interested in acquiring citizenship, the truth is that this status, for practical reasons, is more desirable than residency status.

Roberto is another example of those who benefit from citizenship for transnational purposes. He obtained resident status while serving in the military in the late 1970s and later brought all his siblings and his parents to the US. He is a divorcee, has two children who were born and live in the US, and has a business that helps migrants to send remittances and process legal documents. He has properties and investments in Colombia, travels there once or twice a year, and does not spend as much time there as he wishes because he cannot abandon his business in Northbrook. He plans to develop his business enough to be able to travel for longer periods of time to Colombia each year and eventually retire there.

Roberto belongs to a group of transnational entrepreneurs who comprise a minority within the Colombian migrant population, especially in comparison with other Latin American immigrant groups (Portes *et al.*, 2002). As the example shows, these transnational entrepreneurs are well established in the US and have found an alternative path of assimilation that does not include the severing of their ties to the home country, but, on the contrary, the productive use of these ties. Even though this form of transnationalism is expected to grow, it may not in Colombia, at least in the short term.

Another small but interesting group of transnational migrants, or "transmigrants," are the parents, mostly mothers, of migrants. This group of transnationals has grown as people living in the US have progressively opted to bring their parents every year instead of traveling to Colombia. Aside from the reduction of costs (instead of tickets to Colombia for the whole family, they buy one or two from Colombia to the US), many of my interviewees mentioned that they hesitate to travel to Colombia, given the deteriorating situationand the insecurity they face there. This move could also be associated with the fact that migrants are investing less in Colombia and more in the US and are increasingly abandoning the dream of return. Thus, the deterioration of the political and economic situation in Colombia, which has resulted in fewer vacation trips and less investment, has reduced the pull of transnational migrants among the migrant population while increasing in inverse proportion the transnationality of their parents.

Jorge, a 73-year-old man I interviewed in La Esperanza, is a clear example of this transnational group. In 1971, he traveled to the US, worked for 20 months, and returned. By the early 1980s, his son had migrated to help the family economically. Other sons and a daughter followed him. Six of his eight children now live in the US. Jorge and Catalina, his wife, traveled back to the US in the late 1980s to visit for a few months and have continued to travel. They obtained resident status through one of their naturalized children several years ago. Although they travel frequently, they do not like to stay longer than six months at a time and do not want to move to the US permanently because they do not like the winter, they do not know the language, and they always depend on their children to get around. Their children do not want them to work. Jorge and Catalina requested a special permit to stay in Colombia for the past two years and plan to go back to the US as soon as it expires. Jorge might file to obtain citizenship although Catalina is scared of taking the exam. He is entitled to use Medicaid and has used it while in the US. He wants to become a citizen so they can stay in Colombia as long as they want and then enter the US easily. He also wants the benefits associated with citizenship.

As the previous case shows, some migrants have filed petitions to give their parents resident status. This status has the advantage of letting their parents go back and forth more easily than with regular visas and reduces the hazards of their having to travel to the US Embassy in Bogota in order to request or renew tourist visas. The downside of the resident status is the mandatory six months they have to spend in the US, and this is part of the incentive to apply for citizenship. Other incentives to pursue citizen status are the same ones as for their sons and daughters: first, to be able to bring relatives to the US, in this case other children who cannot be petitioned under the family preference system by their brothers and sisters in the US. Second, as in the case of Jorge and Catalina, an interest in the benefits that the welfare reform legislation and the antiterrorist laws denied to residents. Among this elderly group, naturalization is clearly a transnational strategy that has become more appealing as a result of the increasing limitations that resident status presents.

Does the use of citizenship as an immigrant and transnational strategy constitute a danger to US democracy? Is the growing dual citizen population endangering the core of this country? I do not think so. For many of the migrants who have recently acquired US citizenship, this move may have been the means to resolve family situations or avoid losing privileges and not, as critics would suggest, a way to express their noble and unselfish interest in becoming part of the nation to follow and defend the principles of its constitution. Independent of this initial motive (which, in any case, we cannot be sure was the force motivating the millions of immigrants who naturalized previously), these migrants, even if deeply embedded in transnational fields, are an active part of the US. They may keep close economic, political, and cultural connections to their home countries and may not want to lose their formal membership there, but they are also part of the host society, and there is no reason not to welcome their incorporation. On the contrary, as Spiro (1997) has warned, denying them citizenship poses serious costs for society, which would have to deal with an increasing number of territorial residents excluded from rights and political participation. Political incorporation might take time as migrants consolidate their economies and their families, as is usually the case for immigrants, but their dual citizenship status and their link to the home countries are not a hindrance to participation, as I explain in the following section.

POLITICAL PARTICIPATION

Concern about political participation seems to be at the center of the debate concerning dual citizenship. Civil and political rights of the home country to a great extent become dormant in the host country, and possible contradictions, such as diplomatic protection or military service, can be resolved by international or bilateral agreements (Legomsky, 2003; Martin, 2003). Political rights, however, can be active simultaneously (Bauböck, 2001; Martin, 2003). The main concerns regarding dual citizens' political participation include, first, the idea that a democracy cannot "afford to have large numbers of citizens with shallow national and civic attachment" (Renshon, 2001: 43) and who do not have to live the consequences of their vote; second, the fear that dual nationals might vote for the interest of the home country or, in the worst case, "be merely puppets of a distant government" (Martin, 2003: 13); and third, the belief that dual nationals cannot engage properly in politics not only because they have divided loyalties but also because they have the practical problem of having to divide energies and dedication (Schuck, 1998: 163).

When I designed my project, I was expecting to find very low levels of participation and interest in US politics on the part of the increasing number of dual citizens or soon-to-be dual citizens, both because of the low levels of political participation attributed to Latinos in general (DeSipio, 1996) and because of the high degree of disengagement and abstention that characterizes Colombian politics. Contrary to these expectations, and in contradiction to the assumption that dual citizenship and the strong ties with the home country limit political engagement in the host country, I found in most of my interviewees both a genuine appreciation of the political system of the US, which they particularly contrast with the political system of their home country, and an interest in participation.

DUAL CITIZENSHIP AND THE INITIAL STEPS OF COLOMBIANS IN US POLITICS

In Northbrook, the members of the older cohort, part of which naturalized following the enactment of the Colombian dual citizenship law, were more politically involved than the recent cohort. This seems to reflect the general pattern, found not only among Latinos but also among other groups, that the longer people stay, the more stable they are, and the better their economic situation, the greater their interest in political participation (DeSipio, 1996: 64, 91). However, in contrast to the traditional assimilationist perspective that predicts that "higher levels of acculturation diminish the likelihood of transnational attitudes," I found that the same group that is very interested in participation in the US is also very involved in transnational civic activities. My research in Northbrook validates the transnational argument and the conclusions reached by Guarnizo *et al.* (2003) from their survey on Colombians, Dominicans, and Salvadorians. They found that the length of residence in the US and the acquisition of US citizenship do not reduce interest or involvement in home country politics, but, on the contrary, increase it. Assimilation and transnational involvement are not, therefore, excluding practices. In my small sample of interviews it is precisely the older cohort, many of whom naturalized after the enactment of Colombian dual citizenship, that are the ones most involved in transnational organization and political participation. A more general rule, found also in the survey by Guarnizo *et al.* (2003), is that people who are more politically active in Colombia are generally also very active in the US. I found immigrants with previous political experience eager to participate even beyond just their vote, although they were limited either by their resident status or by their inability to speak English.

My interviews with regional leaders also showed that their involvement in politics in the US is not inversely proportional to their interest in Colombian politics. On the contrary, local leaders in Queens and in New Jersey towns such as Dover, Elizabeth, Englewood, Hackensack, Jersey City, Morristown, Paterson, and Union City play a double role as promoters of organization and political participation in Colombia and the US. Aside from providing immigrants with information and networking, supporting development projects, organizing collections to help victims of disasters in Colombia, or contributing to the organization of civic and cultural events, these leaders promote participation in Colombian elections, in some cases even campaigning for specific candidates to the Colombian Congress or presidency. At the same time, and in spite of the fact that the majority do not run as candidates themselves for local offices, these leaders have carved a niche in the political life of the US municipalities where they live and promote political participation. Some of them, particularly those in New Jersey towns, work not only with Colombian immigrants but with other Latino immigrants as well. They support, directly or indirectly, candidates in local and regional campaigns and play a political role.

I did find specialization among the political leaders running for offices, though. Aside from the failing campaign of a local New Jersey leader (who held an elected position as a county councilman but also ventured as a candidate in the Colombian election), most leaders play in either one of the two political arenas. Those who participate in US politics as candidates have developed the knowledge and skills required in this camp, whereas those involved in Colombian politics are generally leaders who had learned the ropes of Colombian politics before migrating. This specialization of the candidates does not make them uninterested or disengaged in the politics of the country in which they are not participating as candidates. Moreover, both types of Colombian leaders have been united in their support for campaigns that have required lobbying the US government—in particular, the certification which for various years the US government gave to Colombia and other Latin American countries (depending on the effectiveness of their anti-drug trafficking efforts) and the request to give Colombian migrants arriving in the US Temporary Protective Status (TPS).

In comparison with other Latino groups such as Dominicans, Colombian leaders in general have not been very successful in achieving elected office. Only a small number have made the move to candidacies (owing to lack of language fluency, experience, and resources) and they cannot always count on the unified support of the Colombian community. In New York, the efforts to bring a candidate to the assembly in 1998, 2000, and 2002 and to the city council in 1999 failed. In New Jersey, Colombian politicians have been more successful. Besides a councilman from Bergen County (who has held this position for many years), two Colombians were elected in 2003, one as a councilman in Bound Brook (Somerset County) and another as mayor of Dover (Morris County). Even though these are significant achievements, and many Colombians have supported the candidates, their electoral success did not depend on the Colombian community. Although it is beyond the scope of this chapter, it is possible to offer various explanations for the difficulties Colombians face in consolidating a significant political force.

First is the Colombian immigrant community's low level of cohesiveness which has been found to be related to the higher levels of education, more urban origin, and spatial dispersion of Colombians with respect to other Latin American communities (Guarnizo *et al.*, 2003). Guarnizo *et al.* (1999) also attribute this lack of cohesiveness to the distrust that the drug trade has created among Colombians. Very rarely, however, did my interviewees mention this as a cause of community fragmentation. They explained it instead as a result of what they called the "immature," "individualistic," "conflictive," or "apathetic" nature of Colombians. These general impressions may be related to a second factor that can help explain Colombians' difficulties in consolidating a political force: the institutional political environment—the extremely personalistic Colombian political system[10]—in which Colombians have been politicized at home.

Aside from the retention of nationality laws that have allowed immigrants to naturalize in the US and gain political rights, many Latin American countries, including Colombia, have also extended the political franchise to their nationals abroad. Some analysts consider that the right to vote should be restricted to the country of residency (Martin, 2003: 14). Others think that these rights should be restricted not to the first but to the second migrant generation (Bauböck, 2003: 714), and still others think that they should not be restricted at all (Spiro, 2003). Migrants' political participation in their home countries has generally been low (Spiro, 2003: 141), and Colombians have been particularly slow in taking advantage of their nonresident voting rights (Jones-Correa, 1998: 25–27; Guarnizo, 2001: 234). The low levels of participation may be related in part to the disaffection of Colombians with the political system of their home country (Guarnizo *et al.*, 2003) and also to the characteristics of the Colombian political and electoral systems mentioned above.[11] It is evident, however, that migrants do have an agenda in relation to remittances, commerce, communications, mechanisms of political participation, et cetera, that could not be put forward in state legislation unless migrants are granted political rights in their countries of origin.

TRANSNATIONAL ORGANIZATIONS: A VEHICLE OF POLITICAL ENGAGEMENT

Aside from supporting the argument that political engagement and participation in the host and home countries are not necessarily excluding practices, I found that transnational organizations have contributed to migrants' integration into US politics.

Three events have reinvigorated the organization of Colombians in the US. The first was the more active role taken by the Colombian state in promoting the development and organization of their nationals abroad with Decree 690 of 1994. Even though the new constitutions have extended important privileges to Colombians abroad, the state had remained relatively passive, dealing mostly with the problem of the increasing number of Colombians in foreign jails. The new decree allowed the consulates to play a more active role not only as "protectors" of the Colombian community, as the previous legislation defined them, but also as "promoters" of their organization. The New York Consulate has been particularly active in this respect. During President Ernesto Samper's administration, when this decree was issued, the Colombian state took an active role in organizing the Colombian leadership to lobby the US Congress for recertification (Guarnizo *et al.*, 1999). More recently, the increasing migration of Colombians—10% of the population now lives abroad—along with the importance of remittances in recent years (remittances now constitute the second-largest source of foreign exchange) has made the state eager to play a more important role and to design mechanisms to reach its emigrant population. The second event that contributed to the organization of Colombians in the US was the earthquake in the Colombian coffee region in 1996. Local organizations became revitalized and new ones emerged with the aim of collecting and sending contributions to the victims of the disaster. Many of these organizations persisted even after the immediate demand for resources subsided. The third event was the political campaigns developed by candidates for the one lower house seat reserved for Colombians abroad, which, although provided for the Constitution since 1991 was not legally attainable until the year 2000. Despite the fragmentation of parties, the consequent proliferation of candidates, and the general apathy of Colombians toward electoral participation, the elections infused the Colombian community with a new organizational dynamic. They provided the background to the first convention of Colombian associations in the US in Atlanta in May 2001. Although the National Colombian American Organization (NACAO) and its regional chapters have suffered greatly from political manipulation and divisiveness, nevertheless, it has managed to create and revitalize links at the national, regional, and local levels.

Even though the main events associated with the new organizational dynamic of Colombians in the US have originated in Colombia, the people involved are working not only to improve the relations of Colombians with their country of origin but also to make the immigrant community a political actor in the US. Aside from the coordinated efforts of Colombian organizations in support of the TPS for Colombians and the lobbying in favor of the renovation of the Andean Trade Preferential Act (ATPA), the communication networks that have developed among Colombian organizations have also served to support the campaigns of Colombian leaders running for local offices.

The lobbying and the orientation of voters and migrant organizations in favor of the interest of their home country have given rise to concerns that dual nationals could become "traitors" or "puppets" of foreign governments. However, there are two aspects that we should take into account. First, as has already been explained, not only dual citizens but any citizen can favor the interest of a foreign country, so dual nationality should not be criticized on these terms (Martin, 2003: 13). Second, the existence of a powerful lobby in favor of the interest of another country is not new in the US. It is precisely the models of the Jewish American and the Cuban American communities that have inspired Colombian leaders to play a more active role in US politics.

At the local level, the hometown association *Esperanza por Colombia* has also contributed to civic engagement and political participation of Colombians in Northbrook. This organization was formed more than 20 years ago with the aim of contributing to the hometown. Its 15–20 regular members are, for the most part, either well-established US citizens or residents, like those of many other transnational organizations. Their main activities have been the collection of resources through parties, raffles, and dinners in which most of the migrants from La Esperanza and other Colombian towns and cities participate in order to send equipment (fire trucks, ambulances, wheelchairs) and monetary contributions to hospitals, schools, nursing homes, churches, and individuals in special need. *Esperanza por Colombia* was very active in organizing relief efforts for the victims of the 1996 earthquake, as were many other Colombian organizations. It is part of the network of Colombian American organizations of New Jersey, has participated in the two national conventions of NACAO, and has been active in the campaign for TPS. In spite of its orientation toward Colombia, *Esperanza por Colombia* has also contributed to immigrants' integration into their host society. It has organized cultural events and supported community sports for various years.

In contrast to the more dispersed and anonymous migration of Colombian immigrants to bigger cities, the town-to-town migration from La Esperanza to Northbrook has maintained active networks and facilitated immigrant organization. The argument that the negative Colombian-trafficker stereotype has contributed to community fragmentation does not hold true in Northbrook, where the social networks of La Esperanza have been transferred. Moreover, the interest in fighting Colombians' bad reputation has even contributed to community organization. On one of the few times when a Colombian in town was found with cocaine, a judicial attorney warned people to be careful because "Colombians were taking over Northbrook." Colombian leaders organized a protest and forced the attorney to retract his statement in a public press conference. Even though many Colombians are buying their houses in the surrounding areas and are following the pattern of dispersion that leaders of other municipalities and academics consider detrimental to community cohesiveness, the establishment of businesses in town, along with the dense networking brought from home, has helped to maintain community cohesiveness.

Esperanza por Colombia has been defined by its members as an active civic, rather than political, organization. However, it has indirectly played a political role for its leaders, who have become recognized by the town's politicians and bureaucrats as unofficial representatives of the Colombian community. Not in the name of the organization but in their own names, its members have also supported political candidates, contributed to political campaigns, and have encouraged people to register and vote in the US. They have not launched themselves as local candidates but have great expectations for the political role that the second generation, having the language skills, the knowledge, and the education, could play in the future. Without causing migrants to lose connection to or interest in their hometown, this transnational organization has become a mechanism of public engagement for Colombians in Northbrook.

The experience of both the national and the local organizations supports the thesis that transnational activities do not decrease migrants' political engagement in their country of residence but, on the contrary, can contribute to it.

CONCLUSION

The analysis of Colombian migrants' naturalization after the enactment of the dual nationality legislation in their home country shows that people do not necessarily naturalize as a result of the abandonment of previous loyalties. They might choose to naturalize precisely when they are sure that they can keep their formal connection to their country of origin. Ties with the countries of origin, then, are not an impediment to adaptation and assimilation into the host society. Moreover, transnational organizations, such as the ones involved in the campaign for dual citizenship, can play a critical role in promoting the naturalization and political engagement that some analysts say are lacking within the Latino community. Assimilation and transnationalism appear then not as excluding but as complementary practices.

Aside from laws of dual citizenship that facilitated and promoted naturalization among Colombians, the pursuit of citizen status has also been the result of immigrant and transnational strategies oriented to family reunification, prevention of deportation, and access to federal and state resources that US legislation has progressively made exclusive to citizens. While it would be easy to condemn this practice as instrumental, we should not assume that migrants cannot be at the same time interested in political participation. Many of them are. And even if they are not initially interested, naturalization becomes a form of forced inclusion that nonetheless opens the doors to participation. In this case, the problem is not the naturalization of these immigrants, but, in Jones-Correa's words, that "the United States has intimidated its non-citizens to naturalize, but it has not figured out how to encourage them to register and vote" (Jones-Correa, 2002: 244). Even with difficulties and low coverage, Colombian leaders and organizations, including the transnational ones, are playing that important role within the Colombian community. The findings from this study of Colombian dual nationals' political participation show that the fears of disloyalty, instrumentality, and devaluation of US citizenship are unfounded. Dual or multiple political membership emerges as the best solution for those increasing numbers of migrants who have connections (familial, religious, political, or economic), interests, investments, and agendas in two countries.

Just as migration and transnationality have been found to be gendered processes (Simon and Brettell, 1985; Grasmuck and Pessar, 1991; Hondagneu-Sotelo, 1994; Pessar, 1999), naturalization and dual citizenship are also experienced differently by gender. My findings suggest several possible avenues for future research, including gender differences in transnational politics and transnational organizations, the role of gender in family decisions concerning naturalization, and its use as immigrant and transnational strategies. Migration and transnationality of the elderly, rarely the focus of migration studies, deserves attention as well. A comparative study would reveal some of the characteristics and particularities of these groups of migrants. A

critical topic for future studies is dual citizenship and political participation among the second generation.

Increasing migration of people who, instead of shedding their
culture and severing their ties with their countries of origin, are keeping and reconstituting those ties is creating a political dynamic in which
both the countries of origin and the countries of residence are becoming mutually influential. Given this interconnection of countries
through their dual nationals, and these migrants' political incorporation in both the sending and the receiving countries, citizenship cannot
expected to remain unchanged. . Dual citizenship and transnational
politics are not endangering but transforming citizenship in the US.

NOTES

1. The names of the towns as well as of the interviewees have been changed
to ensure confidentiality.
2. For more on political rights of nonresident nationals in Latin America,
see Calderón, 2003.
3. Portugal and France are other countries that have reserved exclusive par-
liamentary seats for nonresidents (Spiro, 2003: 1138).
4. For a discussion of transnationalism see Portes *et al.* (1999).
5. CANCO documents, manuscripts, 2/17/88, 3/3/88, 4/13/08, and
5/13/88.
6. After some initial defeats, the campaign for dual citizenship was finally
successful, owing to, among other things, the Constitutional Assembly
in Colombia in 1991. The new 1991 Constitution included the dual citizenship provision, as well as others allowing Colombians abroad to elect
not only a president, as they had been doing since 1961, and congress
men (regulated 1997), but also their own representative to the House
(regulated in 2001).
7. Jones-Correa calculates the rate of naturalization by dividing the number of immigrants of a sending country naturalizing in the US in a given
year by the number of immigrants arriving from the sending country
seven years earlier (2003: 321).
8. In 1989, the first cohort of 1,639 Colombians was given residency (30%
of the total immigrants admitted in 1989) and this number increased to
14,311 (59% of total residents) in 1990 (INS Statistical Yearbooks).
9. Congress approved three major immigration laws in 1996. The Personal
Responsibility and Work Opportunity Reconciliation Act (PRWORA)
reduced the level of benefits received by legal immigrants. The Illegal
Immigration Reforms and Immigrant Responsibility Act (IIRIRA) was
designed to reduce immigration by increasing border patrols and by
introducing a pilot telephone verification program for employers to
verify the status of future employees. This law also increased the level of
income required of immigrant sponsors in order to ensure that future

immigrants would not be dependent on welfare. The Anti-terrorism and Effective Death Penalty Act (AEDPA), a response to the 1993 World Trade Center bombing, made it easier to detain without bail foreigners convicted of crimes committed in the US and to deport them after they had served their sentences (Martin and Midgley, 1999).

10. For more on the Colombian political system, see Pizarro (2002) and Shugart *et al.* (2001).

11. This system explains to a large extent the low turnout and dispersion of votes among the migrant community in the Colombian congressional elections of 1998 (the first time that nonresident Colombians were allowed to cast their votes and when a New Jersey doctor participated as a second candidate in a victorious Senate list) and the multiplication of personal candidacies, seven in the New York–New Jersey area alone, for the election of the first representative of Colombians abroad in the lower house in 2002.

ACKNOWLEDGMENTS

I would like to thank the International Migration Program of the Social Science Research Council, the Program of Latin American Studies at Princeton University, and the Center for Migration and Development at Princeton University for their generous support. Thanks also to all the participants in the workshop organized by *Latino Studies* in preparation for this special volume, and to the anonymous reviewers for their insightful comments. Special thanks to the leaders of *Esperanza por Colombia* and to all my interviewees for their patience and collaboration. Finally, I would like to thank Arturo Sánchez in Queens and Liliana Peláez and Luis Alberto Pava in Colombia for inviting me into networks and neighborhoods.

REFERENCES

Alba, Richard, and Victor Nee. 1999. Rethinking Assimilation Theory for a New Era of Immigration. In *The Handbook of International Migration,* ed. Charles Hirschman, Philip Kasinitz, and Josh Dewind. New York: Russell Sage Foundation.

———. 2003. Remaking the American Dream: Assimilation and Contemporary Immigration. In *The Handbook of International Migration,* ed. Charles Hirschman, Philip Kasinitz, and Josh Dewind. Cambridge, MA: Harvard University Press.

Aleinikoff, Alexander, and Douglas Klusmeyer. 2002. *Citizenship Policies for an Age of Migration.* Washington DC: Carnegie Endowment for International Peace/Migration Policy Institute.

Bauböck, Rainer. 2001. Towards a Political Theory of Migrant Transnationalism. Working Paper Series. Center for Migration and Development, Princeton University.

————. 2003. Towards a Political Theory of Migrant Transnationalism. *International Migration Review* 37 (2): 700–723.

Brubaker, Roger. 1992. *Citizenship and Nationhood in France and Germany.* Cambridge, MA: Harvard University Press.

Calderón Chelius, Leticia, ed. 2003. *Votar en la Distancia: La extensión de los derechos políticos a los migrantes, experiencias comparadas.* México D. F: Instituto Mora.

Collier, Michael W., and Eduardo Gamarra. 2001. The Colombian Diaspora in South Florida: A Report of the Colombian Studies Institute's Colombian Diaspora Project. Working Papers. Latin American and Caribbean Center, Florida International University, Miami, Florida.

DeSipio, Louis. 1996. *Counting on the Latino Vote: Latinos as a New Electorate.* Charlottesville, VA: University of Virginia Press.

DeSipio, Louis. 2000. Adaptation or a New Immigrant Reality? An Agnostic View of "Transnationalism" among Latin American Immigrants. Paper presented at a Roundatable at Princeton University, Princeton, New Jersey.

Fitzgerald, David. 2000. *Negotiating Extra-Territorial Citizenship.* Monograph 2. San Diego Center for Comparative and Immigration Studies.

Geyer, Georgie Anne. 1996. *Americans No More.* New York: Atlantic Monthly Press.

Gilbertson, Greta, and Audrey Singer. 2003 The Emergence of Protective Citizenship in USA: Naturalization Among Dominican Immigrants in the Post-1996 Welfare Reform Era. *Ethnic and Racial Studies* 26: 25–51.

Gordon, Milton M. 1964. *Assimilation in American Life: The Role of Race, Religion, and National Origins.* New York: Oxford University Press.

Grasmuck, Sherri, and Patricia Pessar. 1991. *Between Two Islands.* Berkeley, CA: University of California Press.

Guarnizo, Luis. 2001. On the Political Participation of Transnational Migrants: Old Practices and New Trends. In *E Pluribus Unum?*, ed. Gary Gerstle and John Mollenkopf, 213–263. New York: Russel Sage Foundation.

Guarnizo, Luis, Alejandro Portes, and William Haller. 2003. From Assimilation to Transnationalism: Determinants of Transnational Political Action among Contemporary Migrants. *American Journal of Sociology* 108: 1211–1248.

Guarnizo, Luis, Arturo Sánchez, and Elizabeth M. Roach. 1999. Mistrust, Fragmented Solidarity and Transnational Migration. *Ethnic and Racial Studies* (Special Issue) 22: 367–393.

Hansen, Randall, and Patrick Weil. 2002. Dual Citizenship in a Changed World: Immigration, Gender and Social Rights. In *Dual Nationality, Social Rights and Federal Citizenship in the US and Europe,* ed. Randall Hansen and Patrick Weil, 1–15. New York: Berhahn Books.

Hondagneu-Sotelo, Pierrette. 1994. *Gendered Transitions.* Berkeley, CA: University of California Press.

Immigration and Naturalization Service (INS). 1989–2001. *Statistical Yearbook of the Immigration and Naturalization Service.* Washington: Government Printing Office.

Jones-Correa, Michael. 1998. *In Between Two Nations: The Political Predicament of Latinos in New York City.* Ithaca, NY: Cornell University Press.

————. 2002. Seeking Shelter: Citizenship and the Divergence of Social Rights and Citizenship in the US. In *Dual Nationality, Social Rights and Federal Citizenship in the US and Europe,* ed. Randall Hansen and Patrick Weil, 233–263. New York: Berhahn Books.

————. 2003. Under Two Flags: Dual Nationality in Latin America and Its Consequences for Naturalization in the United States. In *Rights and Duties of Dual Nationals,* ed. David A. Martin and Kay Hailbronner, 303–333. The Hague, London, New York: Kluwer Law International.

Kasinitz, Philip, Mary Waters, John Mollenkopf, and Marih Anil. 2003. Transnationalism and the Children of Immigrants in Contemporaty New York. In *The Changing Face of Home,* ed. Peggy Levitt and Mary Waters. New York: Russell Sage Foundation.

Legomsky, Stephen. 2003. Dual Nationality and Military Service: Strategy Number Two. In *Rights and Duties of Dual Nationals,* ed. David A. Martin and Kay Hailbronner, 79–134. The Hague, London, New York: Kluwer Law International.

Levitt, Peggy. 2001. *The Transnational Villagers.* Berkeley, CA: University of California Press.

————. 2002. Variations in Transnational Belonging: Lessons from Brazil and the Dominican Republic. In *Dual Nationality, Social Rights and Federal Citizenship in the US and Europe: The Reinvention of Citizenship,* ed. Randall Hansen and Patrick Weil. New York: Berghahn Books.

Levitt, Peggy, and Mary C. Waters, ed. 2003. Introduction. In *The Changing Face of Home: The Transnational Lives of the Second Generation.* New York: Rusell Sage Foundation.

Martin, David A. 2003. Introduction: The Trend toward Dual Nationality. In *Rights and Duties of Dual Nationals,* ed. David A. Martin and Kay Hailbronner, 3–18. The Hague, London, New York: Kluwer Law International.

Martin, Philip, and Elizabeth Midgley. 1999. Immigration to the United States. *Population Bulletin* 51: 2.

Martin, Susan. 2002. The Attack on Social Rights: US Citizenship Devalued. In *Dual Nationality, Social Rights and Federal Citizenship in the US and Europe,* ed. Randall Hansen and Patrick Weil, 215–232. New York: Berhahn Books.

Miller, John J. 1998. *The Unmaking of Americans: How Multiculturalism has Undermined the Assimilation Ethic.* New York: Free Press.

Pessar, Patricia. 1999. Engendering Migration Studies: The Case of New Immigrants in the United States. *American Behavioral Scientists* 42: 577–600.

Pickus, Noah. 1998. *Immigration and Citizenship in the 21st Century.* Lanham, MD: Rowman and Littlefield.

Pizarro, Eduardo. 2002. La atomización partidista en Colombia: el fenómeno de las micro-empresas electorales. Working Paper # 292. The Helen Kellogg Institute for International Studies, University of Notre Dame, IN.

Portes, Alejandro, Luis E. Guarnizo, and Patricia Landolt. 1999. Introduction: Pitfalls and Promise of an Emergent Research Field. *Ethnic and Racial Studies*. (Special Issue) 22: 217–237.

Portes, Alejandro, William Haller, and Luis Guarnizo. 2002. Transnational Entrepreneurs: The Emergence and Determinants of a Novel Form of Immigrant Adaptation. *American Sociological Review* 67: 278–298.

Renshon, Stanley. 2001. *Dual Citizenship and American National Identity.* Washington, DC: Center for Immigration Studies.

Schuck, Peter. 1998. Plural Citizenships. In *Immigration and Citizenship,* ed. Noah M. J. Pickus, 107–139. Boston, MA: Rowman and Littlefield.

Shugart, Mathew S., Erika Moreno, and Luis Fajardo. 2001. Deepening Democracy by Renovating Political Practices: The Struggle for Electoral Reform in Colombia. Revision of a paper originally prepared for the conference "Democracy, Human Rights, and Peace in Colombia," Kellogg Institute, Notre Dame University, Notre Dame, INMarch 26–27.

Simon, Rita, and Caroline Brettell, ed. 1985. *International Migration: The Female Experience.* Totowa, NJ: Rowan and Allenheld.

Spiro, Peter. 1997. Dual Nationality and the Meaning of Citizenship. *Emory Law Journal* 46: 1411–1485.

———. 2003. Political Rights and Dual Citizenship. In *Rights and Duties of Dual Nationals,* ed. David A. Martin and Kay Hailbronner, 135–152. The Hague, London, New York: Kluwer Law International.

Zhou, Min. 1999. Segmented Assimilation. In *The Handbook of International Migration,* ed. Charles Hirschman, Philip Kasinitz, and Josh Dewind. New York: Russell Sage Foundation.

CHAPTER 6

Roads to Citizenship: Mexican Migrants in the United States

Alejandra Castañeda

This chapter explores Mexican migrants' practices of citizenship, and the ways in which migrants engage in battles over the meanings and limits of citizenship within a transnational and translocal setting.[1] It addresses these issues by bringing together three elements at the heart of migrants' experience of citizenship: law, belonging, and the formal political arena.[2] The articulation of experiences of transnational migration provides a framework for understanding how a culture of citizenship is shaped. "Culture of citizenship" refers to the social practices and understandings of membership in a given community—at either the national or local level—in the arenas in which citizenship is negotiated and constituted. In this sense, belonging, law, and politics are inextricably related to one another.

To study the connection between law and citizenship, I review a group of laws that come from two different state formations, that of Mexico and of the US. I introduce the set of laws formed by the 1996 Mexican Non-loss of Nationality Law and the constitutional reform to Article 36 that opened the possibility for the vote abroad. In addition, I present the 1996 US immigration law, the 1996 welfare reform legislation (specifically those aspects that pertain to immigration), and California's 1994 Proposition 187. All of these affect migrants' political situation and everyday lives and play a central role in the constitution of migrant citizenship. My aim is to understand the meanings of these laws, while also reviewing the sociopolitical context that produced them. As Laura Nader (2002) explains, law is not neutral, and while seemingly on the side of the powerful, law is an evolving, dynamic phenomenon. Thus, I seek to comprehend the hegemonic forces that underlie each of these legal texts, as well as how the interaction between them shapes migrants' citizenship.

Legal texts are embedded with cultural meanings, values, and social practices that breathe life into the law. When citizenship is defined in the legal realm, with its consequent categorization of people, it appears not only as a political space where power struggles take place to determine inclusions and exclusions, but also as a space where resistance and contestation emerge. Thus, laws have to be seen as moving texts and as privileged ethnographic sites where the nation-state can be seen at work. The laws presented here describe the space where Mexican migrants and nation-states meet each other, and where the meaning and value of the nation is always invoked. This is a racialized space with many restrictions and open or undisclosed labeling (Oboler, 2002)—aspects that delineate Mexican migrants' citizenship.

To explore the connection between citizenship, law, and politics, I describe the story of the Tomato King, a migrant from Zacatecas who entered the formal political arena and, in so doing, set in motion the legal framework established by the Mexican Congress in 1996. I also review the axis of citizenship, law, and belonging through the analysis of three stories of migrants from Aguililla, Michoacán, the transnational social space they inhabit, and their interactions with the legal corpus that affects them.

CITIZENSHIP AND MIGRATION: PERSPECTIVES

This chapter takes legal definitions of citizenship and nationality as cultural practices, thus merging legal and cultural frameworks. I trace the language and interests of nation-states and individuals, because the language of the state—via its laws—and of people—via their stories and practices—appear at the heart of definitions of citizenship (Levitt, 2001; De Genova, 2002; Coutin, 2003).

Citizenship is most commonly assumed to be a legal status defined within the framework of the nation-state. However, citizenship also refers to belonging to a community, imagined or otherwise. Formed and protected by laws lived and enacted by individuals, citizenship both forbids and necessitates migrants. How do migrants enact citizenship and impact the nation-states they inhabit? Rather than accepting migrants as marginal actors confronting the nation-state, I argue that citizenship is constructed by nation-states and by migrants' transnational practices and embodiment of the law. In those instances where the nation-state and people converge, citizenship is performed, contested, and reformulated, thus shaping migrants' culture of citizenship.

Migrants construct a transnational social space shaped by their relationships with state institutions, particularly judicial ones (Hondagneu-Sotelo, 1994; Gilbertson and Singer, 2000). Moreover, the legal frameworks that surround the relation between Mexican migrants, Mexico, and the US enact the processes of institutionalization and conceptualization of citizenship, which are also marked by cultural practices and understandings of membership in an imagined community (Fitzgerald, 2000; Levitt, 2001). Holston and Appadurai (1999) argue that just as citizenship is the category through which nation-states have sought to define membership, it also appears as "that identity which subordinates and coordinates all other identities"– gender, religion, ethnicity, region, and class. Thus, this space appears strongly constituted by memory and identity practices, as well as by senses of belonging that give content to Mexican migrants' citizenship (Nájera-Ramírez, 1994).

According to Rosaldo (1994), citizenship is centrally defined by the right to be different (in terms of race, ethnicity, gender, or native language) and the right to belong, in a participatory democratic sense, within a nation-state. By celebrating "the right to be different and to belong," Rosaldo's notion of cultural citizenship addresses directly the lack of a de facto meaningful citizenship, where the principle of equality fails to be applied to all areas of social life (Rosaldo, 1994: 402). Rosaldo, together with Flores and Benmayor (1997), in turn reclaim equality in name (if not in practice) for subjects of nation-states, as well as the marker of *difference*. They argue that citizenship is not only the possession of a paper; it also implicates subjects taking action and claiming space in accordance with their cultural practices. It is about being visible, being heard, and belonging (Rosaldo, 1997: 37).

The history and stories of Mexican migrants in the US illustrate how belonging is encoded in citizenship. As migrants create a transnational citizenship marked by translocal and transnational practices within a scenario of contrasting political cultures, legal notions of citizenship are articulated with practices of belonging (Goldring, 1998; Rivera-Salgado, 2000). Because migrants—different but equal—are political actors, regardless of the possession or nonpossession of papers that establish legal residency, citizenship, or nationality, their citizenship can be viewed as a political strategy, a perspective that emphasizes its character as a historical construct rather than a universal essence. Migrants struggle to be recognized as full members of the nation, and not just as market citizens—that is, as economically productive members of the polity—(Goldring, 1998). Theirs is a "citizenship from below," in which they establish what they consider to be their rights and fight for them on the basis of their own situated cultural practices (Dagnino, 1998). Migrants' practices of belonging, of connectedness to the nation and their communities, are their best arguments for their claims to citizenship.

CITIZENSHIP, POLITICS, AND LAW

A perfect example of the ambiguities and contradictions Mexican migrants face when they turn into political actors is the story of Andrés Bermúdez—better known as the Tomato King. A migrant from Jerez, Zacatecas, and an agribusiness owner in northern California, Bermúdez began his life as a migrant in 1973, received US residency in 1982, and became a US citizen in the early 1990s (Sullivan, 2001). Once he learned English, "he became an intermediary between bosses and his *Jereziano paisanos.* He later started his own business" (Cano, 2001). Being a broker and a middleman provided Bermúdez with an arena for developing leadership skills.

Supported by the governor of Zacatecas, Ricardo Monreal, in 2001, Bermúdez became a political candidate for the municipality of Jerez. As a result of his candidacy, Jerez turned into the center of a dispute over who could or could not participate in Mexican politics. The unique electoral process that the municipality experienced reverberated both nationally as well as in certain areas of the US. The uniqueness of this election for the municipal presidency derived from the fact that two of the candidates were migrants.

The Tomato King's candidacy, representing the Partido de la Revolucion Democratica (PRD), stirred the most controversy. Bermúdez's success in the business world and the support he received from the Frente Cívico Zacatecano in northern California made him an attractive candidate. Perhaps what Governor Monreal had in mind when he invited the Tomato King to run was a gesture toward Zacatecan migrants, in order to demonstrate that he was serious when he proposed recognizing migrants' political rights during his campaign for governor (Goldring, 1998). However, behind this gesture there was no true intention of seeing Bermúdez elected (Martínez Ortega, 2002). Nobody explained this to the Tomato King, who really believed that he was the candidate and that he could win. He gained the support of Zacatecas City PRD mayor and allied himself with a sector of the PRD in Jerez (Cano, 2001). With these alliances, the money he brought to the campaign, and his own charisma, Bermúdez won on July 1, 2001, becoming one of the first migrants to win elected office.

During his campaign the Tomato King used his own resources in community projects, such as fixing 600 km of roads, installing street-lights and building sports facilities (Martínez Ortega, 2002). As the journalist Arturo Cano put it, "Andrés Bermúdez, The Tomato King as he likes to be called, is one of two candidates who left as *mojados* and came back with his pockets full with green bills to conquer power." This image of the returning migrant plays into the negative discourse of critics of the right to vote for Mexicans living outside the country. They express suspicion toward migrants returning from the US, arguing that they now share US values. Contrary to this per-spective, I consider that Andrés Bermúdez conducted a political cam-paign that very much reproduced old paternalistic ways. Through his gifts, parties, and constructions, all of which were meant to show people that he could bring investment and a better life to Jerez, the Tomato King was indeed, in an indirect manner, buying support. In so doing, he was reproducing a familiar way of practicing politics in Mexico.

While the need for and presence of migrants at the local level is evident, resentment is also visible. Some people in Jerez challenge the idea that migrants have the right to participate in local politics. They consider that migrants lack knowledge of the problems that the municipality or the community currently confronts (Sullivan, 2001). From this perspective, the right to be a citizen in order to participate in politics is based on knowledge. Others disagree, especially those who take into consideration migrants' participation in the local econ-omy. Likewise, some Jerezianos recognize that migrants do indeed have knowledge of their community, taking as proof their decision to migrate (Sullivan, 2001). Moreover, migrants communicate with their families, and today they can follow news about Jerez and the Jerezianos in the US on Jerez's website (http://www.jerez.com). Migrants continue to invest in their community through remittances and local projects usually organized through hometown associations. In this sense, their experience, exchanges, and investments—their practices of citizenship—earn them the right to be considered citizens.

As a result of Bermúdez's electoral victory, the Partido Revolu-cionario Institucional (PRI) questioned and officially presented a legal complaint against Bermúdez's eligibility as a candidate for

Jerez's municipal presidency. The objection was based on the fact that Bermúdez was a US citizen and therefore could not run for election. The Zacatecan PRI was asking, indeed, almost demanding, that the Tomato King renounce his US citizenship. According to the PRI representative in the Zacatecan Electoral Institute, "The election of the ex-bracero, better known as The Tomato King, is unconstitutional, because he had held US citizenship since the 1980s" (Amador Sánchez, 2001a). The PRI supported their argument using the new 1996 Nationality Law. For them, it was Bermúdez's dual nationality that made him ineligible (Amador Sánchez, 2001b). The PRI's reading of the nationality and electoral law illustrates the complicated relationship between migrants and their nation and hometown.

Bermúdez presented evidence of his Mexican nationality by showing his birth certificate, his electoral identification card—which, in order to be issued, requires residency verification—and a letter from the Mexican Consulate acknowledging Bermúdez's request to recover his nationality in accordance with the 1996 Nationality Law. Despite these proofs, the PRI argued that he was not a Mexican in the full sense of the term. Nationality was the contested terrain; and here a battle of belonging was being fought.

While the PRI's argument against Bermúdez's candidacy took a legal approach, behind the rhetoric were the contradictions that stand between the people that stay and those who leave. For many, especially in political circles, migrants are untrustworthy and less Mexican because the US has tainted them. For the families that stay, migrants have proven their belonging to the nation; they are symbols of endurance, the absent, who are both needed and missed.

On September 6, 2001, the Federal Electoral Tribunal overturned Andrés Bermúdez's triumph.[3] The reversal of Bermúdez's victory was based on *residency* rather than *nationality,* or, in more general terms, citizenship. As a matter of fact, the Tribunal stated, "The nationality of the Tomato King was not in question, *he is Mexican"* (Ochoa and Amador Sánchez, 2001). However, because Bermúdez registered his California address as his permanent residence, he could not be a candidate as he was not a permanent resident of Jerez. The electoral controversy made the Mexican political system face issues of inclusion and exclusion. More importantly, the Tomato King's participation in the elections provoked a debate on belonging, membership, and ultimately, on citizenship. To be there or to be absent appears as the factor that determines a person's belonging to a political community. Regardless of the fact that again and again, through their political activism, identity, and memory practices, as well as through their investment—their remittances—migrants have demonstrated their interest in Mexico, they are still excluded from full membership in the imagined community.

MIXED MESSAGES: THE MEXICAN CONSTITUTIONAL AMENDMENTS

The Tomato King's story sets up a politics of citizenship that very concretely addresses the Mexican legal system, which in 1996 approved two amendments to the Constitution related to political rights of Mexicans abroad. On August 22, 1996, the Mexican Congress passed a political reform that included a change to Article 36, which opened the possibility for Mexicans abroad to vote. That same year, on December 3, Congress approved a constitutional reform allowing for nonloss of nationality.

Prior to the reform, the Constitution stated that Mexican nationality would be lost when another nationality was adopted. The new version indicates that no one who is Mexican by birth can be deprived of his or her nationality and of the rights Mexican nationals hold. It is important to note that Mexican and US laws have a fundamentally different formula for determining and establishing citizenship.[4] Whereas in the US, a person born or naturalized within the boundaries of its territory and sovereignty is considered a citizen with full rights, according to the Mexican constitution, nationality and citizenship are two distinct attributes. A person is born a national and becomes a citizen at the age of 18. What this means is that while Mexican nationality establishes membership in the nation, it primarily ensures economic rights. In contrast, the status of citizenship mainly refers to political rights, such as voting and running for election. Moreover, a national who holds another nationality cannot exercise full citizenship rights. This means that political rights are constrained. Thus, regardless of the 1996 change to the nationality law, the distinction between these two categories remained. This distinction acquires prominence when the debate turns to political rights.

In keeping with the sublimated language of nation-states, which formulates power relations and economic ties in terms of identity and cultural ties, the presidential initiative claimed that one of the main reasons for the nationality amendment was the boundedness that Mexican migrants sustain with respect to their roots, culture, values, and national traditions.[5] Certainly, for many migrants their rootedness has been their symbolic daily bread, but it is a "bread" sustained and recreated through their quotidian praxis and their interaction with the US and Mexican nation-states. In this sense, the law recognizes an already existing practice—migrants' attachment to their roots—that would continue regardless of the legal change.

The nationality law was intended to enable Mexicans living abroad—particularly in the US—to defend their social, political, and economic rights by clearing the obstacle contained in the previous version of the law that mandated loss of Mexican nationality when acquiring another. The creation of this law meant a revision and a modification of Articles 30, 32, and 37 of the Mexican Constitution. The new rendition of Article 32, which refers to the legal characteristics of Mexican nationals, adds regulations for Mexicans who hold another nationality to avoid dual nationality conflicts. The consequences of these restrictions are far reaching, as they forbid dual nationals from participating in any elected office and performing a series of electoral functions or any functions related to national security and sovereignty. The restrictions for dual nationals have been acquiring more relevance as they clearly conflict with citizenship rights, especially with the issue of migrant political candidacies. Furthermore, these changes demonstrate that nationality is not a category with a simple definition, and that laws valorize people's membership in the nation differently, thereby creating unequal forms of national citizenship.

Despite the restrictions contained in Article 32, the nationality law carried a strong symbolic value, as it allowed those migrants who had lost their Mexican nationality when they acquired US citizenship to recover part of their identity and their sense of belonging. An important aspect to underscore is that under the previous law, those taking another citizenship had to send a formal letter renunciating their Mexican nationality addressed to the Mexican Foreign Ministry. This meant that a legal act, an act of authority, a performative act, sanctioned the separation from the nation, thereby establishing migrants' new political and cultural subjectivity. When María Sánchez, a 47-year-old home care provider from the border town of Tecate, Baja California, became a US citizen in 1985, she had mixed feelings. She was proud of her new standing and yet, at the same time, experienced a sense of loss. "I did not feel I was a traitor by becoming American, but I was leaving a part of my life" (Associated Press, 2003). For many Mexicans, renouncing their Mexican nationality was a hard decision, a difficult and emotionally complex step.

One of the characteristics of Mexican nationality refers to economic attributes, that is, to the right to hold property on Mexican territory, to work, and to invest without the restrictions placed on foreigners. By way of appealing to migrants' roots, as expressed in the presidential initiative, the government was looking to entice Mexicans living abroad to invest in their home states or hometowns. It comes as no surprise that from its inception the nationality law included secondary laws and bureaucratic mechanisms for its implementation. The fact that the Non-Loss of Nationality Law is now implemented reflects its true intention: Mexicans abroad are useful to the nation as an economic force. Whereas this particular law appears as a benefit for migrants, as a door that has been opened, it seems that the intention behind its approval was literally to capitalize on migrants' economic attributes.

While the Mexican Embassy originally estimated that 3 million naturalized [US citizens] would reclaim Mexican nationality, less than 70,000 applications were received by the March 20, 2003, deadline established by the law. However, the mere possibility of such an enormous number of dual nationals opened the doors to anti-Mexican sentiments in the US and a debate over the meaning of US nationality. Some opinions in the US emphasize the fact that dual citizenship breaks the oath that naturalized citizens take for US citizenship. Even though dual citizenship is de facto recognized in the US in many cases, when it comes to Mexicans holding dual nationality, the flexibility disappears.[6]

One important point to underscore here is that migrants also appear in Mexican discourse as a threat to Mexico. A sector of the country's political class has argued against the passing of these laws under the premise that they threaten the sovereignty of the nation. The important issue for them is not the loss of rights by those who live abroad; instead they argue that the focus should be on protecting the rights of those who "live inside." The rationale is that if migrants were allowed to vote, they could decide the result of elections. According to this perspective, when migrants settle in the US they become more susceptible to US interests and would thereby participate in Mexican politics in accordance with those interests (Carpizo, 1998). This position is founded on two revealing assumptions. First, it rests on the notion of a nation that is bounded—that there is an "inside" enclosed in some seamless way that should always be preserved from threats. Second, it relies on a value system that distinguishes between Mexicans living "abroad" and Mexicans living "inside" Mexico, where the former cannot hold full citizenship rights because they might harm those of the citizens who have remained pure by always living in Mexico.

When in 1996 the Mexican Congress approved a new version of Article 36 of the Constitution, it left unfinished the political reform that would allow citizens living abroad to vote in the 2000 elections. The amendment was introduced "to grant the suffrage to those Mexicans living abroad, thus providing an extension of the political membership and, therefore, of their citizenship" (Martínez, 2001: 4). The modified version of the Article maintained that the right to vote out of the district, including outside the country, could be exercised (for the year 2000) once Congress determined the legal reforms needed to make it possible (Comisión de especialistas, 1998: 2). Once the obligation to vote within the limits of a particular electoral district was eliminated, the possibility for the vote abroad was opened.

At first glance, the new version of Article 36 seemed to be friendly to Mexicans living abroad, but it included legal prerequisites that prevented the vote abroad. A Specialists Commission appointed by Congress to study the vote abroad delivered its final report to the Federal Electoral Institute on November 12, 1998. In its concluding statements, the commission found the vote abroad to be viable and introduced several options for its implementation. Perhaps most significantly, the commission did not find any clause within the nationality law that established the possession of another nationality as an obstacle to Mexican citizenship.[7] That is, people who had acquired another nationality could exercise most of their citizenship rights, particularly their right to vote (Comisión de especialistas, 1998).

Despite the divergent paths taken by the Non-Loss of Nationality Law and the reform to Article 36, their mere existence makes evident the fact that there are millions of Mexicans living in the US who are disenfranchised and excluded from exercising political citizenship in the nation-state they inhabit. The new nationality law opened one of the doors that had been closed. This positive step notwithstanding, the aspect of political rights remained trapped by political obstacles, legal clauses, as well as by the lack of secondary laws to implement the reform to Article 36. This has left Mexicans living abroad as de facto second-class citizens with their political rights curtailed.

The two 1996 constitutional amendments directly address the issue of citizenship and allow for a better understanding of who is considered a member of the nation-state, who is excluded from this membership, and how this membership can be practiced. Ironically, these laws demonstrate the fragility of the space called Mexico while they attempt to reenforce the structure of the Mexican nation-state, which is challenged by the fact that nearly 10 million Mexicans live in the US. The legal and political systems have responded to these challenges by reframing the terms of membership to the nation.

CITIZENSHIP, US IMMIGRATION LAW, AND BELONGING

In 1994, California voters approved Proposition 187, which banned illegal aliens from the use of basic public services. This initiative "emerged from the suburbs of Los Angeles and Orange County in 1993 as the 'Save Our State' campaign"—S.O.S.—a campaign used by then governor Pete Wilson as part of his reelection agenda (McDonnell, 1999). Through its tabloid style, the Proposition 187 campaign enhanced xenophobic attitudes not only in California but also, more generally, throughout the US, thereby galvanizing latent anti-immigrant feelings, particularly against Mexicans. According to Alejandra Marchevsky, the success of Proposition 187 rested on "its ability to closely link crime and immigration in the public imagination," thereby constructing anyone who came across the border without documents—especially from the south—as an invader and a criminal, undeserving of basic human civil rights (Marchevsky, 1996: 13). The arguments in favor of Proposition 187 stated that "welfare, medical and educational benefits are the magnets that draw *these illegal aliens* across our borders" (Arguments, California Legislature Record 1007). Proposition 187's language successfully contributed to "othering" migrants, representing them not as people, but as aliens, creatures far from human dignity.

Proposition 187 included provisions preventing illegal immigrants from attending public schools and receiving social services and subsidized health care. Likewise, it penalized the manufacture and use of false documents to conceal undocumented immigrant status. It also required that law enforcement authorities, school administrators, and medical workers turn in suspected illegal immigrants to federal and state authorities. Bringing law enforcement down to the level of public service workers produces a policing social environment where the racial "other" becomes the necessary object of suspicion. "Is it the way you speak? The sound of your last name? The shade of your skin?" These were some of the questions posed in the arguments against the proposition, which looked to use suspicion as a tool for the enactment of the law but failed to define the basis for such suspicion.

The arguments in favor of and against the initiative show how migrants are imagined and portrayed, and the very material consequences of such images (Chavez, 2001; Zavella, 2002). The main arguments in favor of the proposition rested on claims of how illegal immigration cost "an estimated five billion dollars a year" (McDonnell, 1999). For those who were feeling the effects of reductions in Medicaid or the strain in the educational system, these arguments were compelling. Because migrants are always seen as a cost rather than as producers of value, they represent the ideal scapegoat.

Opinions in favor of and against Proposition 187 both took as their point of departure a similar notion of immigrants: they are illegal, they are a problem; they are alien to this country and cannot become a part of it. The opinions against Proposition 187 did not escape the discourse of viewing immigration as a problem and immigrants as a source of expenses covered by taxpayers' money. They advocated in favor of reinforcing the border and focused on how the initiative would end up costing the state of California 10 billion dollars on account of the loss of federal funds. As Calavita (1996) argues in her study on the symbolism of Proposition 187, this initiative portrayed a "new politics" of immigration based on "balanced-budget-conservatism."

In his work on popular images of immigration and the politics of the nation, Chávez (2001) explains that "following the assumption central to Proposition 187, that social services—not jobs—[were] the magnet drawing undocumented immigrants to the United States," the US Congress responded to the legacy of California's Proposition 187 accordingly. Thus, while Proposition 187 was trapped in the courts and was never fully enacted, the ideology behind it, the negative feelings, the proposed policies, started to make their way up to Congress. In August 1996, Congress passed a welfare reform legislation—the Personal Responsibility and Work Opportunity Reconciliation Act (PRWO-RA)—that imposed new restrictions on aid to documented migrants. Moreover, in September of the same year, Congress approved the Illegal Immigration Reform and Immigrant Responsibility Act (IIRIRA), which made illegal immigrants ineligible for most nonemergency public aid. In summary, in 1996 the US Congress transformed immigration law (Legomsky, 1997). Both laws can be seen as the legacy of California's Proposition 187.

The August 1996 welfare reform legislation, signed into law by President Clinton, mainly took food stamps, funding for disability payments, and Medicaid health coverage away from documented and undocumented migrants. This legislation ended a long-standing assistance program for poor families with children. "The law was expected to save the government $54 billion over the following six years, with about half of those savings, or $24 billion, to come from restricting legal immigrants' use of food-stamps, Supplemental Security Income, and aid for low-income elderly, the blind, and the disabled" (Chavez, 2001: 193). By 1997, some of these provisions had been partially restored, in particular eligibility for documented migrants to receive disability payments and Medicaid health coverage. In 1998, Congress restored federal food stamp eligibility to needy documented migrants—namely children, the elderly, and disabled—who had been dropped from the program. Despite these changes a significant number of adults between ages 18 and 64 remained uncovered (McDonnell, 1998).

While the welfare reform legislation primarily restricted residents' rights, IIRIRA's main provisions focused on the issue of illegal immigration. It enforced policing of the border with more agents, physical barriers, and surveillance tools. Under IIRIRA the conditions for deportation changed. A migrant is now required to have good moral character, and hardship to the alien himself no longer serves as an acceptable basis for allowing a judge to stop a deportation. Migrants can be deported without a hearing and they have to demonstrate continuous presence—extended from seven to ten years—before being able to appeal a deportation decision (Legomsky, 1997).

As a consequence of immigration laws such as IIRIRA, undocumented migrants are physically separated from the rest of the population by ongoing informal judging that pushes people to accept any kind of job situation. Continuous surveillance, through the 1996 immigration law, is now the responsibility of the civilian population. This legislation, for example, requires employers to check for the legality of the papers presented by workers, or requires teachers, doctors, and nurses to request papers documenting legal presence. These expectations and obligations placed on civil society provoke a naturalization of the categories of alien immigrant, illegal worker, or illegal immigrant (Coutin, 1996). By limiting immigrants' rights, the law is enabling the existence, the very construction of the category that it seeks to ban: the illegal alien. It is the law that produces *difference* (Coutin, 1996: 11; De Genova, 2002).

Since IIRIRA's policies create a more direct connection between migration and criminalization, they impose harsher conditions on migrants' lives. With provisions that established civil penalties for illegal entries, and the authorization to fingerprint illegal aliens, IIRIRA aimed at hindering migrants' later possibilities for becoming legal residents or citizens. In this sense, migrants move between categories; they can go from being workers, fathers, and mothers, to becoming criminals. A line is crossed for migrants and they acquire a new subjectivity with far reaching ramifications for their daily lives.

IIRIRA also contained provisions that expanded the notion of "aggravated felony" and conviction for residents. These legal changes affected noncitizens who had some criminal record, making them vulnerable to deportation regardless of circumstances. As Chávez explains, "Waivers of deportation for aggravated felonies are no longer possible, and this class of felonies has been greatly expanded" (2001: 193). According to Stephen Legomsky, the Anti–Drug Abuse Act of 1988 introduced the category of *aggravated felony*. Legomsky explains that this notion "has become one of the most amended terms in the Immigration and Nationality Act" (1997: 13). The different amendments to the Immigration and Nationality Act (INA) have, in certain cases, extended the term of aggravated felony "to such crimes as minor drug possession, turnstile-jumping and graffiti-making— even if these crimes occurred years ago" (Legomsky, 1997: 13).

Moreover, while before IIRIRA residents were treated with the same eyes under the law that ruled US citizens, after IIRIRA the meaning of legal categories such as "conviction" and "aggravated felony" was expanded, making residents more vulnerable. The impact that changes to the meaning of categories have for noncitizens is very real, as it can have material consequences such as deportation or a severe reduction of their options to defend themselves. A key issue here is the retroactive nature of the criminalizing threats of deportation. Indeed, words have power, and legal categories not only proliferate in their meaning, they also threaten migrants' everyday life. In this sense, every detail of the law, every new provision, can transform a person from a minor offender into a major criminal, thus performing a change in their political subjectivity and preventing them from becoming US citizens.

In the US, objections to the presence of immigrants derive mostly from objections to cultural attributes such as race, religion, or language (Zolberg, 2000). These reservations often later translate into laws, as in the case of Proposition 187, or the "English only" initiatives that are moving through different states. Behind laws such as IIRIRA or Proposition 187 lies the perception that the established national ways are jeopardized by immigration in general. Even though these laws are phrased as practical responses to the economic problems posed by the presence of migrants, in fact they are mostly concerned with the political and cultural impact migrants have in the overall dynamic of life in the US.

An analysis of the language of US immigration law reveals an ideology where the nation-state appears to be menaced, its integrity threatened. "Protect the border" is the resulting policy. To protect the border from the southern invasion is the ever more racialized policy. The discourse produced by IIRIRA, the welfare reform legislation, and Proposition 187 is nothing less than a portrait of the institutional power they contain and project and the fear of the unwanted but so-needed "other." The solutions immigration laws propose—restricting, enforcing, deporting, apprehending—approach migrants as a negative aspect of US life. However, because they appear as texts, laws sometimes seem to remain at that level. Mexican migrants' lives demonstrate the opposite. Laws become material, real, when migrants experience them (Zavella, 1997; Martínez, 2002; Coutin, 2003). As De Genova explains, migrant illegality is "produced as an effect of the law, but it is also sustained as an effect of a discursive formation" (2002: 431). In migrants' lives, state institutions and legal discourses are a constant and spectral presence that delineate the contours of their citizenship.

CITIZENSHIP, BELONGING, AND LAW

From a state-down approach, citizenship becomes a question of rights and duties, of issues of inclusion and exclusion. However, such a perspective elides the interconnection between citizenship and identity that influences different senses of belonging within communities. As Mexican migrants have to deal with two nation-states, through their everyday practices they bring together the legal realm implicated in the idea of citizenship with the aspect of belonging to a particular political and cultural community. Migrants inhabit a transnational social space built by memory and identity-formation practices, family ties, and commodity exchanges that provide content to their culture of citizenship.

As a businessman, a *comerciante*, José trades commodities but through his trades he enacts more than an economic exchange. José—born in Aguililla, Michoacán —has been in California for 14 years and now lives in San José. After moving from Redwood City, José and his wife, Mercedes, opened a clothing store located in a Mexican neighborhood in San José. Things in the store are somewhat overcrowded. It looks like a *tienda de pueblo* (a kind of general store), just like those in Aguililla. Being in the store is like being in Mexico; a sort of transportation back home takes place by way of the power of the objects.

The commodities exchanged in the store point to various aspects of Mexican migrants' life. They are markers of difference, as José has observed throughout his years as a *comerciante:* "Mexican businesses only work because of our own race. The gringos don't buy here; they go to other stores. They come in and leave. They don't like it. We sell clothes that the Mexicans like. It's another style" (Interview, San Jose, April 1999). Just as these objects are markers of difference, of a racialized style, by the same token they are markers of commonality. The store turns into a place—a locale—where nostalgia is as much a commodity as a builder of identity. As a place for *reunion,* for economic and social exchanges, the store creates and recreates familiar images, material memory practices through which a sense of belonging, of citizenship, is also constructed. Migrants' commodity exchange appears as a practice that engulfs a myriad of social relations and contributes to the existence of a place called home characterized by its transnational linkages. Through their multilayered exchanges, migrants create a place for belonging, a place to establish citizenship.

Moreover, José's store is a place where *raza*—the race—acquires a connotation of solidarity. *Raza* is as much about difference as it is about shared identity. José's testimony points to the relevance of race and how it is already a part of his language, and of the way he conceives of himself in relation to "others." José's experience and understanding of race has more of an ethnic undertone. His story shows how ethnic enclaves are produced and reproduced in very material ways. As Comaroff (1996) explains, the making of a concrete ethnic identity occurs in everyday life and it has its origins in relations of inequality. Moreover, while José came to the US with a notion of who he was as a Mexican and a Michoacano, this social construction, this identity, changes as different conditions and social relations are established as a consequence of his migrant experience.

As Mexicans cross the border they are bound to face conditions of inequality that place them in the position of contestation. One of the forms that this contestation takes is the construction of an identity *vis-á-vis the others;* an identity that draws force from the nation, the town, tradition, nostalgia, memory, and place. Aguilillans' commodity exchanges, like those that take place in José's store, appear as a practice that engulfs a myriad of social relations and contributes to the existence of a place called home and a citizenship characterized by its transnational linkages.

Like José, María is part of Aguililla's transnational social space as a business woman, although she does not own a store. Instead, María trades goods between Redwood City and Aguililla. A working-class migrant woman in her early 30s, María is one of seven daughters from a poor Aguilillan family. She has been part of the migrant circuit since she was 18 years old, and through her multiple trips she has constructed a social network that extends from Aguililla to Redwood City. During that time, she raised three daughters and one son, all of them born in the US.

María and her husband, Ramón, decided to return to Aguililla for two primary reasons, one legal, the other parental. As parents, they were worried that their son Hilario would go down the wrong path. They decided to return to Aguililla—*"para que no se desperdiciara"* ("so that he would not go to waste," i.e., become a gang member). The legal reason was their concern over getting into trouble with the law as a result of the raucous behavior of María's husband. Because they were applying for US residency, any difficulty with the law would jeopardize their efforts to legalize their situation. María decided to play it safe and came back to Aguililla.

Like many migrants, María is well acquainted with US immigration law and has first-hand experience with the problems to which she is exposed in the US. A relationship of familiarity is established with these laws inasmuch as she knows the ones that affect her more directly. María and her family have realized the concrete impact immigration laws have on their lives. This knowledge enables her to maneuver through them. In this sense, María's experience of US immigration laws is mainly strategic, especially in relation to the needs of her family. Her familiarity with those laws that impact her everyday life include knowing that if an applicant for US residency or citizenship has a criminal record then the doors to a "legal" life are closed. This is one of IIRIRA's provisions, which has a harsher section on deportation. It is important to recall the fact that the meaning of aggravated felony and conviction have expanded through the years, making it more difficult for people who have had minor problems with the law to straighten out their legal situation. Thus María wants to be careful and avoids any problems with the law.

In the life of somebody such as María, who has traditionally moved back and forth between Mexico and the US, laws such as IIRIRA constrain her mobility and economic options, thus damaging the quality of her life. Likewise, IIRIRA also affects María's interest in acquiring US residency and later citizenship, which for her means mobility without risks and represents a strategy to protect the integrity of her family.

Lucha's experiences offer a harsher example of how laws impact migrants' lives. A 34-year-old migrant from Aguililla who lives in Redwood City, Lucha crossed the border from Mexico to the US as an undocumented migrant.

My daughter was two years old, I held her close to my chest. We swam to the ocean; it felt like the water was pulling us. It's very dangerous, like the time when a woman was yelling but we never knew what happened [to her]. I think she died . . . That time we made it out of the water, the bullets zoomed very close. We ran again . . . we went back to Tijuana . . . We tried again with the same coyote, this time we made it . . . We were hiding in the hills, and the migra would pass by on horse very close. The migra caught about six of the people who came with us . . . After that, I said we are not returning, because I saw that we suffered and my children almost drowned. (Interview, San Jose, March 1999.)

We are not returning. Lucha's decisive words are a response to a concrete and negative experience she and her family had when they crossed the border. The tightening of the border in the past years with laws such IIRIRA has made it even more difficult for the new wave of migrants. Lucha's relation with immigration laws derives from her very real experience of the materiality of the border between Mexico and the US. When Lucha's working-class family finally made it past the border patrol, a different route for their life was opened. Return to Mexico was not an option for Lucha, from the beginning of her migrant experience.

María's and Lucha's stories portray the more pragmatic side of the relation between migrants and the laws affecting them. In their lives, laws have indeed been hard texts, material realities, which they interpret and inhabit. By placing migrants in a situation where they have to negotiate their sense of cultural inadequacy and mobility, their experiences of migration set in motion the connections between citizenship, law, and belonging. Likewise, their stories show the paradoxical nature of immigration law, as it fails to hinder not only the influx but also the settlement of migrants in the US, two of its central goals.

Regardless of the particular nature of their activities, all migrants are immersed in the process of cultural and commodity exchange. And, as we saw with José, as migrants engage the network of exchanges and travel between various social conditions and relationships, the ways in which they identify themselves also change. For migrants such as José, Lucha, and María, the experience of migration is a challenge. Once they become involved in this process, they begin to negotiate their situated cultural practices, and their legal and cultural citizenship. Moreover, many Mexican migrants have a strong sense of territoriality and of belonging to a larger community— expressed through the remittances they send and the memories they sustain—which exceeds the limits established by the laws of nation-states. Their transnational social practices contest the borders of the state as well as notions of citizenship.

MIGRANT CITIZENSHIP

Through their citizenship practices migrants address the nation-state within the language of the law and the language of identity. As users of the law, as the life of the law (Nader, 2002), migrants' practices engage the nation-state in a culture of citizenship where rights and belonging have to go beyond uninational visions of citizenship. The stories introduced in this chapter touch upon ideas of democracy and identity, of who can be included in or excluded from a community. As nation-states produce laws to deal with the existence of migrants, a conflictive relation emerges. Through their political practices, Mexican migrants are weaving a culture of citizenship that continuously demands attention and responses from the two nation-states they inhabit. In the US, migrants are viewed as a labor force while at the same time they are kept out of the political community. Moreover, Mexican migrants, who have been historically disenfranchised and denied political existence, are calling upon the Mexican state and insisting on their rooted and grounded identities to claim political agency and thus challenge constraining definitions of citizenship.

In speaking of a culture of politics, of meanings and practices entangled in power struggles, the actions of Mexican migrants in the US have indeed impacted the Mexican political scenario with the appearance of new laws, and with political campaigns that take place in the US. Migrants' lobbying, protests, and debates have permeated the Mexican political sphere, and have echoed in the letter of the law through the 1996 constitutional changes and the later initiatives presented in Mexico's Congress. In this sense, migrants' emergence as transnational political actors has added a new dimension to Mexico's political culture.

Mexican migrants living in the US are practitioners of a substantive citizenship that acquires content through their daily practices and their interactions with the power structures of the nation-state. Even though migrants seem to be at a disadvantage in confronting either of the two nation-states they cross, they do have a voice and their own ways of expressing their agendas. Through transnational practices of belonging, such as those of José, or the more openly political ones, such as those of the Tomato King, migrants contribute to a larger redefinition of citizenship while at the same time partaking of a traditional notion of citizenship as bearers of political rights.

Regardless of the fact that migrants are already political actors that impact Mexico's contemporary politics, they nevertheless still seem to be at the edge of being considered full citizens. The status of their residence and social acceptance in the US is constantly shifting.

Migrants' acquisition of US citizenship, despite the new laws, makes them vulnerable to political vacillation in Mexico. Notwithstanding the 1996 legal reforms in Mexico, conservative notions of nation and citizenship continue to exist. Bermúdez's ordeal is symbolic of this. The arguments used against him could be used against anyone and continue to place migrants outside the political community. However, through their grounded practices of citizenship—political and of belonging—migrants push the language of the law, opening up legal definitions of citizenship. With their constant translocal and transnational exchanges and political activism, migrants attest to the fact that they are the life of the law.

NOTES

1. This chapter is based on my dissertation research supported by the Social Science Research Council Migration Program, the Center for US–Mexican Studies at UCSD, UC MEXUS, the University of California Santa Cruz Chicano/ Latino Research Center, CONACyT and the Fulbright-García Robles program (Castañeda, 2003).
2. The material presented here stems from multisited ethnographic research conducted in México City at the Instituto Federal Electoral, and in the Aguililla, Michoacán-Redwood City, California, migrant circuit. I also reviewed the legal framework that Mexican migrants encounter in their everyday lives, conducted media research and followed the migrant binational campaign for political rights.
3. See Tribunal Federal Electoral. Juicio de Revisión Constitucional Electoral. Expediented: SUP-JRC-170/2001. México.
4. See Article 34, *Constitución Política Mexicana*. See 14th Amendment of the *US Constitution*.
5. My translation. Docto. 201/LIV/96[I.P.O.] Año III, Dictamen H. Cámara de Diputdos 9 de Diciembre de 1996.
6. Critics of dual nationality fail to recognize that the majority of dual nationals are US-born children of Mexican parents.
7. Comisión de especialistas, 110.

REFERENCES

Amador Sánchez, Angel. 2001a. Impugna PRI al Rey del Tomate. *El Universal*, Wednesday, September 5.

Amador Sánchez, Angel. 2001b. Presenta el Rey del Tomate prueba de Nacionalidad. *El Universal*, Thursday, September 6.

1994. Arguments in favor of Proposition 187. California Legislature Record 1007.

Associated Press. 2003. US Mexicans Gain Dual Citizenship. *New York Times*, March 20.

Calavita, Kitty. 1996. The New Politics of Immigration: "Balance-Budget Conservatism" and the Symbolism of Proposition 187. *Social Problems* 43: 284–305.

Cano, Arturo. 2001. Los migrantes regresan a votary . . . ser votados. *La Jornada,* Mexico, Sunday, June 24.

Carpizo, Jorge. 1998. El Peligro del Voto de los Mexicanos en el Extranjero. *Nexos,* Mexico, July 11–12.

Castañeda, Alejandra. 2003. The Politics of Citizenship. Mexican Migrants in the United States. Ph.D. diss., University of California, Santa Cruz.

Chávez, Leo R. 2001. *Covering Immigration. Popular Images and the Politics of the Nation.* Berkeley, London, and Los Angeles: University of California Press.

Comaroff, John. 1996. The Politics of Difference in a World of Power. In *The Politics of Difference: Ethnic Preferences in a World of Power,* ed. Edwin Wilmsen and Patrick McAllister. Chicago: University of Chicago Press.

Coutin, Susan. 1996. Differences within Accounts of US Immigration Law. *Political and Legal Anthropology Review* 19.

———. 2003. *Legalizing Moves. Salvadorian Immigrants' Struggle for US Residency.* Ann Arbor: University of Michigan Press.

Dagnino, Evelina. 1998. Culture, Citizenship, and Democracy: Changing Discourses and Practices of the Latin American Left. In *Cultures of Politics Politics of Cultures. Re-visioning Latin American Social Movements,* ed. Sonia Alvarez, Evelina Dagnino, and Arturo Escobar. Boulder, CO: Westview Press.

De Genova, Nicholas P. 2002. Migrant "Illegality" and Deportability in Everyday Life. *Annual Review of Anthropology* 31: 419–447.

Fitzgerald, David. 2000. Negotiating Extra-Territorial Citizenship. Mexican Transnational Migration and the Transnational Politics of Community. Monograph 2, Center for Comparative and Immigration Studies, University of California San Diego.

Flores, William, and Rina Benmayor. 1997. *Latino Cultural Citizenship. Claiming Identity, Space, and Rights.* Boston, MA: Beacon Press.

Gilbertson, Greta, and Audrey Singer. 2000. Naturalization under Changing Conditions of Membership: Dominican Immigrants in New York City. In *Immigration Research for a New Century. Multidisciplinary Perspectives,* ed. Nancy Foner, Ruben G. Rumbaut, and Steven J Gold. New York: Russell Sage Foundation.

Goldring, Luin. 1998. From Market Membership to Transnational Citizenship: The Changing Politization of Transnational Social Spaces. *L'Ordinaire Latino Americain,* November–December.

Holston, James, and Arjun Appadurai. 1999. Introduction: Cities and Citizenship. In *Cities and Citizenship,* ed. James Holston. Durham and London: Duke University Press.

Hondagneu-Sotelo, Pierrette. 1994. *Gendered Transitions. Mexican Experiences of Immigration.* Berkeley andLos Angeles: University of California Press.

Legomsky, Stephen H. 1997. Non-Citizens and the Rule of Law: The 1996 Immigration Reforms. *Research Perspectives on Migration* 1 (4): 12–14.

Levitt, Peggy. 2001. *The Transnational Villagers.* Berkeley and Los Angeles: University of California Press.

Marchevsky, Alejandra. 1996. The Empire Strikes Back: Globalization, Nationalism and California's Proposition 187. *Critical Sense. A Journal of Political and Cultural Theory* 4.

Martínez, Jesús. 2002. La Lucha por el Voto Migrante. In *La dimension Política de la Migración Mexicana,* ed. Leticia Calderón Chelius and Jesús Martínez Saldaña. Mexico: Inst. Inv. Dr Jose María Luis Mora, Colección Contemporánea Sociología.

Martínez, Nayamín. 2001. El voto de los Mexicanos en el extranjero. Inconclusa extensión de la ciudadanía mexicana. Paper presented at the Round Table Ciudadanías Excluidas/ Excluded Citizenships: Indigenous and Migrants in Mexico, Center for US–Mexican Studies, San Diego, February 16.

Martínez Ortega, Araceli. 2002. Monreal no quería que ganara la alcaldía: Bermúdez. *El Universal,* Tuesday, February 12. Estados, 70.

McDonnell, Patrick. 1998. Food stamp eligibility to be restored for 250,000. *Los Angeles Times,* Friday, June 5.

———. 1999. Davis won't appeal Prop. 187 Ruling, Ending Court Battles. *Los Angeles Times,* July 29.

Nader, Laura. 2002. *The Life of the Law. Anthropological Projects.* Berkeley: University of California Press.

Nájera-Ramírez, Olga. 1994. Engendering Nationalism: Identity Discourse and the Mexican Charro. *Anthropological Quarterly* 67.

Oboler, Suzanne. 2002. The Politics of Labeling: Latina/o Cultural Identities of Self and Others. In *Transnational Latina/o Communities. Politics, Processes, and Cultures,* ed. Carlos Vélez-Ibáñez and Anna Sampaio. Lanham, MD: Rowman and Littlefield.

Ochoa, Jorge Octavio, and Angel Amador Sánchez. 2001. Anulan el triunfo en Zacatecas del Rey del Tomate. El aspirante perredista no pudo acreditar la residencia de un año que se requiere en contiendas electorales. *El Universal,* Friday, September 7.

Reporte Final Comisión de Especialistas que estudia las modalidades del voto de los mexicanos residentes en el extranjero. 1998. IFE, November 12, 2.

Rivera-Salgado, Gaspar. 2000. Transnational Political Strategies: The Case of Mexican Indigenous Migrants. In *Immigration Research for a New Century. Multidisciplinary Perspectives,* ed. Nancy Foner, Ruben G. Rumbaut, and Steven J. Gold. New York: Rusell Sage Foundation.

Rosaldo, Renato. 1994. Cultural Citizenship and Education Democracy. *Cultural Anthropology* 9.

———. 1997. Cultural Citizenship, Inequality and Multiculturalism. In *Latino Cultural Citizenship: Claiming, Identity, Space, and Rights,* ed. William Flores and Rina Benmayor. Boston, MA: Beacon Press.

Sullivan, Kevin. 2001. Mexico Reverses Triumphant Return of Tomato King. *The Washington Post*, September 11.

Zavella, Pat. 1997. The Tables are Turned. In *Immigrants Out! The New Nativism and the Anti-Immigrant Impulse in the United States*, ed. Juan F. Perea. New York and London: New York University Press.

Zavella, Pat. 2002. Engendering Transnationalism in Food Processing: Peripheral Vision on Both Sides of the US–Mexican Border. In *Transnational Latina/o Communities. Politics, Processes, and Cultures*, ed. Carlos Vélez-Ibáñez and Anna Sampaio. Lanham, MD: Rowman & Littlefield.

Zolberg, Aristide R. 2000. The Politics of Immigration Policy: An Externalist Perspective. In *Immigration Research for a New Century. Multidisciplinary Perspectives*, ed. Nancy Foner, Rubén G. Rumbaut, and Steven J. Gold. New York: Russell Sage Foundation.

PART IV

Latino/as and Citizenship: The Immigrants' Perspective

Boundaries, Language, and the Self: Issues Faced by Puerto Ricans and Other Latino/a College Students

Bonnie Urciuoli

INTRODUCTION: THE MULTICULTURAL COLLEGE STUDENT AND THE CONTRADICTIONS THEREIN

Let's say you are a bright student from a working-class, Spanish-speaking Caribbean or Central American family, growing up and graduating from a public school in New York. You are offered a healthy financial aid package by an elite liberal arts college, which you accept, becoming a "multicultural"—specifically, Latino/a—student. What does this mean in terms of who you are at this school? How is your identity marked, especially in terms of language?

In the past two decades, "multicultural" has become the routine referent for racially marked students and faculty in US higher education, and the routine racial classification system has become African American/black, Latino/a, Asian/Asian American/Pacific Islander, Native American, and Caucasian/white. This classification is so institutionally naturalized that universities routinely deploy the acronym ALANA (African American/Latino/a/Asian American/Native American) as a cover term for nonwhite students, hyphenating it with "Coalition," "Studies," "Student Center," "Student Affairs," and so forth. Although the specific terms came into being through federal legislation, the effect of this classification has been to make

"Latino/a" (like the other three referents) a seemingly natural subset of "multicultural." At the same time, because they are classifications of students and faculty, these terms are used in ways that presuppose a peculiarly middle-class construction of person—not surprisingly, since college education is central to class mobility. In administrative and student-life discourses, multicultural students become a special case of the regular student-citizen; certain objectified qualities are layered onto them, so that language and culture become multicultural traits that one *has*. The resultant construction is scalable. The *U.S. News and World Report* (2006) college rankings website now provides a "diversity index" along with its listings of "America's top colleges."[1]

How does this institutionally formatted identity square with the ways in which students grow up Latino/a in the US? Identities are complexly woven from specific experiences of family and neighborhood, national origin, racial and class location, linguistic routines, and knowledge. None of these experiences fall into neat categories. Growing up Latino/a involves some experience, often a lot, of racial exclusion, especially when one's family comes from the Caribbean or Central America. US Latino/as' linguistic experience is saturated with racial and class perceptions (see Mendoza-Denton, 1999, for research overview): bilingual behaviors such as code-switching and accents, which tend to be judged as Spanish[2] "interference" with English, are especially racialized. New York working-class Spanish speakers, especially Puerto Ricans, experience this routinely. Most of the Latino/a students in this study are New Yorkers. Language matters to them because when they get to college and join Latino/a student organizations, many of them take up the charge to "educate the public" about "their culture." This construction of culture involves carefully framed cultural performance and products—dance, music, food, academic presentations, and language—presented in ways that are as racially unmarked as possible; Spanish language as cultural performance is ideally framed and performed as an entity separate from English.

RACE, LANGUAGE, AND MARKEDNESS

The published work on New York Spanish-English speech situations focuses mainly on Puerto Rican bilinguals, now one of several Latino/a groups in New York. Without generalizing about formal or performance details, one can say that these studies demonstrate key dynamics in the linguistic and social experience of urban, working-class, Spanish-speaking populations as viewed from the intersection of language, family, race, and class. Zentella (1997) charts the inextricable connections between specific linguistic form and function and the ordinary routines of life in working-class families and neighborhood networks among East Harlem Puerto Ricans "growing up bilingual." My own work in Manhattan's Lower East Side and the Bronx (Urciuoli, 1996) outlines ways in which experiences of linguistic prejudice map onto the structures of race and class, particularly with respect to perceptions of "Spanish accents." Although bilingual and code-switching communicative competences involve intricate understandings of linguistic form and social function, people whose speech is marked by these features are painfully aware that insofar as this experience marks their speech, such markers are likely to be interpreted as signs of poverty, poor education, and low intelligence, all routinely associated with "being Spanish." In the neighborhoods where the fieldwork cited here was conducted, "being Spanish" carried powerful race and class overtones, which, while not part of official constructions of Latina/o, still appear to leak into them in Latino/a students' experience. In the interviews excerpted later in this study, I am struck by how much all the New York students' experience fit the Puerto Rican pattern.

It could hardly be otherwise: prejudices faced by US Latino/as are continually reinforced by judgments generated in public discourses. Judgments of what sounds like "normal" English are generated over a range of public discourses; cumulatively and performatively, they marginalize all nondominant varieties marked by race or class (Lippi-Green, 1997). The marginalization of working-class, Spanish-marked English is, in terms of cultural dynamics, of a piece with the marginalization of African –American–marked varieties of English. The issue is that of markedness: the construction of a "white public space" of language depends on the continued interpretation of certain language forms as *not* "fitting in," so that the ongoing markedness of certain forms continually regenerates the unmarkedness—the normativeness of the whole (Trechter and Bucholtz, 2001). That markedness is strongly internalized by most of those whose language is marked, such that "good English" becomes definable in large part by what "we" ("we poor people" or "we Spanish people") do not speak (Urciuoli, 1996). Hill (1998) introduces another dimension of markedness by showing that developers, restauranteurs, greeting-card makers, or entertainers can anglicize Spanish, phonologically and grammatically disordering it on street names, menus, cards, skits (on the pretext that they are just selling something, or it is just a joke), but people who are socially vulnerable and whose English is marked by Spanish are perceived as threats to the national order. Accents and code-switching are taken as signs of "broken English," of deficiency, laziness, and bad faith. Zentella (1995) makes this point strongly in her discussion of Chiquitafication: working-class Spanish speakers or Spanish-English bilinguals are routinely typified in public media and politicians' rhetoric as an unruly, alingual horde. The disorder theme is endemic in public discourses about immigrants, as Chock (1991) and others have shown.

Despite shifts in nomenclature, there has been considerable continuity in race-marking throughout US history. The structural dynamics that have generated US racial formation (Omi and Winant, 1986) have, semiotically, been interpreted in terms of origins and belonging. Thus, the defining polarity of race-marking has been: white is to non-white as unmarked/belonging is to marked/not belonging (Williams, 1989). Nonwhite has taken various colors but has been most consistently and intransigently typified as black, that is, as slave-descended (starting with the three-fifths clause in the Constitution). Not belonging has variously taken the form of slaves who are property rather than people (so that slave descendants are assumed to have no place as people), of unwanted native inhabitants of land acquired through expansion or conquest, of expendable immigrant labor (from Ireland, Eastern or Southern Europe, or Asia), or of inhabitants of conquered Spanish-speaking territories. As racial formations have hardened into social facts, physiology and region of origin have become significant markers of racial classification and exclusion. This process can be seen as a kind of semiotic sliding scale between two poles: the pole of maximum racialization, in which others interpret one's origin as a sign of being naturally unworthy of national belonging, and the pole of maximum ethnicization, in which people manage their marking, so to speak, into signs of belonging (Urciuoli, 1996).

From about 1965 to the present (and possibly ending with the present, at least rhetorically), we have been in an era of what might be called origins accounting; for at least the first part of that era, the dominant term of reference was "racial minority." The categories under which the accounting took place were federally mandated under Title VII (1964 Civil Rights Act), which prohibits discrimination by race, sex, or religion. The first race categories were black and white; the current set (black, white, Hispanic, Asian/Pacific Islander, Native American) was established in 1978 by order of the Office of Management and Budget. In the 1980s, the cover terms started shifting, as the terms race and minority were increasingly replaced by multiculturalism. Christopher Newfield and Avery T. Gordon (1996: 76) trace the earliest emergence of multiculturalism in the 1970s to the "grassroots attempt at community based racial reconstruction through . . . the neighborhood public school"; it became prominent in the 1980s in connection with humanities programs at select universities, coming to be associated by the 1990s with reform of "racial inequalities within existing institutions." Multiculturalism thus became the institutional hypernym for black, white, Hispanic, Asian/Pacific Islander, and Native American. In the 1990s, the term *diversity* became partly synonymous with *multicultural,* but could also include gender and ability classifications. Throughout this time, each of these labels took on increasingly sharp reality as a type of person. That sense had always been there in some way: US culture has always been oriented toward "the individual" (Schneider, 1968). Most Americans do not see origin categories (race or ethnicity) as historical formations. The specific variation on this theme that emerged by 1990 (to pick an arbitrary date) was the idea of "the multicultural person": thus, institutions began using the term *multicultural student* to refer to someone who is black, Hispanic, Asian, Native American. As I have argued elsewhere (Urciuoli, 1999), these categories came to represent a point of contestation between the accounting and administrative fields of college life, forms of academic production, and the establishment of student identities. To summarize, what has changed is the organization and rhetoric of origin categories; what remains is a contrast between the unmarked dominant public space and those who are marked and whose job it is to unmark themselves.

Students recruited by small, mostly white, schools for their "multicultural" qualities find themselves in a complex situation. As they are well aware, elite liberal arts schools have a strong investment in showing "good multicultural numbers" (a perception verified by admissions officers). So their presence at the school is part of the school's presentation, even part of its exchange value, in a Marxian sense. Moreover, many of them are invited to join, and are happy to join, student organizations that take up the task of "educating the public" about their culture, as I said earlier; in effect, they are demonstrating national belonging. These organizations also offer students, particularly young women, strong social relationships and the opportunity to forge important, long-term friendships. These friendships are often a piece of home, as it were, a place for students in a strongly (if often silently) differentiated racial atmosphere to relax with people like themselves. Being able to talk to and talk like others similar to themselves is very important. But that form of talk, outside such loci of sociality, can be a problem for these students. It can be judged (by teachers or other students) as incorrect English or Spanish. If being able to speak Spanish is part of one's cultural performance, and if that

same Spanish might be judged problematic, there is a double bind—
a triple bind, if one adds the problem that if one stops talking like
that, one no longer fits in with one's friends. Students are faced with
a sort of shell game, a sleight-of-hand version of symbolic capital.
This is exacerbated by the fact that they are not attending just any
college, but a nationally ranked liberal arts school, and are situated
within a "highly differentiated" stratum of higher education whose
graduates are well-positioned for post-college-entry positions into US
society (Perrucci and Wysong, 1999: 196).

What does it mean to form and enact a Latino/a culture, or to
be Latino/a? That question needs to be addressed in context: what
institutional situation, whose practices, and to what end? That
community can be imagined (Anderson, 1991) and cultural traditions invented (Hobsbawm and Ranger, 1983) is not exactly news.
What is being imagined and invented here (more accurately, conceptualized and structured) is not a national identity but a form of
belonging to a nation at a critical juncture in a person's life and in
a particular institution whose ends are education, class mobility, and
particular forms of socialization. A great deal of symbolic capital is
on the line in this imagining. In some ways, the question "What's
Latino/a?" in this context is comparable to the question raised by
Suzanne Oboler (1995), "What's Hispanic?" Both are heavily
framed by a federally mandated category (see above) and both
assume markedness with respect to a general unmarked polity. The
racialized construction of Hispanic that Oboler examines is about
the imposition, by agencies of the dominant US society, of a generic notion of Hispanic onto Latin Americans, in essence saying,
"Here are all the ways in which you are different." The construction
of Latino/a as it actively engages people self-identifying as Latino/a
is in large part a response to that racialization, an unmarking
cultural project that stresses national origin distinctions, defining
practices, and cultural contributions. But insofar as it is about a
shared identity, and therefore about specifying, foregrounding, and
performing the elements that showcase that sense of sharedness, it
is a response to an imposed construction, therefore, there always is
Sisyphus's stone of racialized elements to deal with. And here the
issue of language enters the picture.

To demonstrate the points laid out above, we need to look at the
following: Who is at the school? What is the multicultural organizational structure and how do students participate? What comparisons,
connections, and disjunctions are there between multicultural and
international students, the two groups routinely combined as

"diverse"? How is "culture" handled in college literature and in the organizations, and what role does language play? What kind of linguistic marking do students face, and what contradictions does it leave them with?

SOME BASIC DEMOGRAPHY

Since 1995 I have been studying what it means to be Latino/a at a small liberal arts college. One limitation of this study is demographic: students' origins are organized by their self-reported identity as black, Latino/a, Asian, Native American, or white, with no further systematic breakdown. So I have no further specific information about national or regional background among Latino/a students. I only know the specific backgrounds of the students I have interviewed, who comprisean even smaller proportion of the already small number of Latino/as at this school. Over the duration of this study, the proportion of self-reported Latino/a students has been about 3–4%, which in real numbers is about 50–70 at any given time. Many of those students do not actively participate in "multicultural" organizations. The active membership in the Latino/a organization might be half that number; there were perhaps 20 students at the few meetings I attended, though officers tell me that more tend to show up for party events. Active membership is predominantly female. Members tell me that girls do more organization work anyway and that boys are more likely to find their loci of sociality on sports teams and in fraternities. The active members tend to include a high proportion of New Yorkers. Until the mid-1990s, most of the members were Puerto Rican and Dominican students ; since then the demographic shifts in the New York Latino/a population (with more immigration from Central and South America) have been reflected in the group's makeup. Of the six students quoted in this article, all are female: five are from New York (one Ecuadoran, one Ecuadoran-Cuban, two Puerto Ricans, and one Dominican) and the sixth (Ecuadoran) is from Florida. Most of the New York Latino/a students seem to be from working-class backgrounds, or so interviews would indicate; the school gives no statistics on students' class background. Many New York Latino/a students, including the students quoted here, came in under the auspices of what I refer to here as the "summer program" for aiding economically disadvantaged students, a high proportion of whom are students of color (the white students in the program are often employees' children and athletic recruits).[3] The students interviewed here formed strong friendships during their pre-first year summer program, friendships that carried over to the Latino/a organization member-ship. By contrast, the general student population is predominantly (some of them *very*) upper-middle class and very northeastern, and most are not from large cities. Current *U.S. News and World Report* website statistics give the school's demographics as about 1750 cur-rent total full time (slightly more than half female, slightly less than half male). Twelve percent are counted as multicultural, that is, as US citizens self-reporting on their application form as African American (4%), Latino/a/Hispanic (4%), and Asian American (4%). Three per-cent are international, in the US on student visas; no racial categories are provided for this group. Eighty-five percent are US citizens or per-manent residents, self-identified as white (as are many international students, including white Canadians, Europeans, and British).

JOINING UP

A quick glance at the application form used by the participants in this study[4] reveals some of the key elements that figure into the construc-tion of the good college recruit. The form begins with a request for organized personal information: name, address, phone, e-mail, first language if other than English, parents' names, addresses, occupa-tion, employers, colleges (if any), and siblings. None of this figures directly into the linear assessment, but a glance at the applicant's address and his or her parents' occupation and college education (if any) suggests the applicant's class location. The next section requests optional information, which most applicants fill out: Social Security number, place of birth, citizenship (US, US permanent resident, other country), and then this sentence (which selects for multicultural students):

> How would you describe your ethnic/racial heritage? If it is not indi-cated here, please help us recognize and appreciate your heritage by using the space provided by 'other.'
> African American or Black_____
> American Indian or Alaskan Native_____
> Asian, Asian American, or Pacific Islander (including Indian subconti-nent) _____
> Hispanic or Latino/a _____
> Mixed Racial Heritage (describe) _____
> White or Caucasian American _____
> Other (describe) _____
> Parents' country of birth: Mother _____ Father _____

The next sections ask for details of education, academic distinctions, special talents, and "activities and interests" including "student government, publications, debate, school clubs and organizations, art, dance, drama, music, athletics, community service, volunteer work, religious activities, work experience." Next come directions for the personal essay and expository prose sample, then a request form for grades reports and a teacher's evaluations. The physical context in which origin questions are asked is significant. Origin information is specified as optional on the form but most applicants provide it. It is located between information about the applicant's class location and individual achievements that are scaled. So origin information becomes juxtaposed with the student's "story" of achievement. Also juxtaposed is information about parents' college experience and occupation, country of birth (if other than the US), and applicant's first language (if other than English).

Readers of admissions files look for indicators that might offset low board scores and reasonable but not high grades. They talk about applicants' work ethic, signs of effort to overcome difficult personal circumstances, and potential for contributions to or leadership in the college community. "Community" figures heavily in these discourses: applicants are routinely assessed by admissions officers in terms of their potential as community members. The successful applicant is the person who will be a "solid citizen" (*solid* often turns up in admissions assessments) or a "leader." Assessments of an applicant's academic potential are generally framed by this larger notion of a school citizen, and not the other way around. The successful multicultural applicant then becomes a special case (origin-marked) of the general (origin-unmarked) school-citizen model applicant. For both types of applicants, all documented aspects of a person must reinforce the idea of a useful, productive, contributing individual.

This is a tricky process when racial and class marking are conflated in people's general perception. Most of the Latino/a, black, and Asian American students that I have interviewed noted that most white students and a lot of faculty assume (erroneously) that the summer program specifically funds students of color. The common conflation of multicultural and summer program students reinforces an equation of racial/class marking and educational deficiency. In the construction of "diversity" numbers on the *U.S. News and World Report* website, colleges routinely put together "multicultural" and "international students." But international students are sought for their academic potential ("applications from superior students from other countries are encouraged"), and some degree of financial aid is available for them.

Once multicultural students are admitted, they receive membership invitations from their respective multicultural organizations (nongroup members may also join). There is also an international student organization. There is some membership crossover between the African American/Latino/a club and the Latino/a club, and between the Asian/Asian American club and the international student club. Otherwise there is little club membership crossover. In college literature, the function of the multicultural organizations is described in terms of promoting "the campus community's understanding and appreciation of the diversity of cultures and heritages." Phrases employed include "to broaden the awareness and appreciation of Black and Latin cultures," "help preserve the cultural identities of Black and Latin students," "promote Asian culture," and "enriching the multicultural life of the community." By contrast, the functions of the international student club are described more simply as sponsoring "cultural programs and social events." Thus, multicultural clubs are more explicitly identified with the charge of preserving their members' cultural heritage (with culture mapped onto black, Latino/a, or Asian) and educating for the general public, than are international student clubs. Moreover, while multicultural and international students represent opposite poles of class, both groups are modeled as "diverse" and as possessing "culture" in ways that assume parallel possession of defining traits such as language. But language as a defining trait for multicultural students is marked in ways that it is not for international students.

Learning to Participate

Students learn these categories as they become part of the school, and a good part of their student life is about creating a fit between their selves and their cultural identity. They work with the student-life office and its programming and entertainment budget. The organizations themselves are administered through the student affairs office. In an interview in her senior year, Patricia, a veteran officer, describes the process of reframing identity as ongoing and synergetic, combining sociality and good citizenship. Over her four years, "Latino/a" took on cultural content through activities channeled along club networks. The cultural content revolves around performance, celebration, or commemoration of historical events, and fun stuff such as food, dancing, and music, with language forming an important dimension of identity performance. It is eminently consumable and subject to being organized, and thus, a vehicle for demonstrating one's worth in US society. The organizing process is especially important for young women, many of whom were desirable recruits because of their high school history as "student leaders," a role they continued to fulfill in college. Patricia describes her organizational history:

> Well at the beginning, my first year, the class of 1997 [who were in their third year at the time] had a lot of Latino students, so they were pretty much in charge. I started helping them out, like little things. Like my first year they had the first Latino conference, so I helped them out with the whole thing, decorating, . . . handing out flyers, whatever, stuff like that. My spring semester, first year, I became the historian. Pretty much that was just going to all the activities we had. Because I had been very involved, I was going to all the activities of the organization, but I was still taking more of a passive role, because I was still learning, supposedly, how everything was working, I was just taking pictures of the events. And then my sophomore year I was more active, I became the treasurer. And the way that we scheduled activities was to try to have lectures, at least one lecture per year, parties definitely, because I don't see having a Latino year without a party, because the music is very important in our culture. We have a lot of more intimate events among the members, like pajama nights, movie nights, let's decorate the office, workshops like having you coming to the meetings and talk. That's pretty much us. We try to have one major event per semester. The first semester, during the fall semester, is Hispanic Celebration month, they use the term *Hispanic* because it's like a national holiday or celebration. And then during the spring semester we try to have Carnival, and that we do with [the Black and Latino organization], and it includes pretty much a party, dancing, workshops, and food. My junior year was really tough because the class of 1997 left and the class of 1998 was only two people and they were gone too, they were away. So I was pretty much it.[5]

She then describes how the first years have taken charge and how the cultural activities have pulled in a wider audience:

> And now the first years this year– I sat in on an E-board [Executive Board] meeting, like last week and what impressed me the most was that most of the people involved in [the Latino organization] are not Hispanics, the first years, they're African American . . . And I think it has a lot to do with the people on the E-board that are Hispanic, that are Latinos? They have reached out to every community, the white community, the African American—[the Black and Latin, and the Latino organizations] are tighter now than they were before. So that's been really good.

I asked if there was more white participation than there used to be, and she replied:

> Definitely. It's a combination of the two. It's more Hispanic—Latino—the members are more involved with it, I don't see a lot of Latino students not participating. They might not go to the meetings all the time, they might not be on the E-board but they go to the activities, and in the Carnival, there were a lot of white students. I was just like, "Ah!" We've been trying to get white students since I came here and now it happened. So it's really changed.

I met Patricia when she started in 1995; she graduated in 1999. In our first interview, eight weeks into her first semester (fall, 1995), she was still learning the terms. She had come from Ecuador to the Bronx when she was 13. As a New York high school student, she defined herself as "Hispanic" or as "Spanish people." She encountered the term "Latino" in documents, especially when applying for scholarships, but did not use it to self-identify until she got to college. There, as the interview suggests, it took on specific meaning in the context of the Latino/a club and its activities. It became a cultural definition, the culture having been processed through the organization's affiliations and activities and through the friendships winding through that organizational activity. The critical point here is that the Latinidad she worked out is institutionally contextualized and does not readily transfer "as is" out of that context.

Patricia's college cultural identity is very much an ordered construction of Latinidad. It presupposes that each trait that defines one's identity makes a positive contribution to one's individual and community persona. It also fits in more generally with how "good students" are recruited and with what is expected of the student-citizen, so it is interesting to see how multiculturalism figures into college recruitment. The application and recruitment process is about selecting students who will fit into the school as "good citizens" of the college community. Good recruits are achievers, but achieving only good grades is not considered good enough for the community. Ideal recruits must also be "student-citizens" and "leaders in the classroom and community", terms that are routine in admissions and student-life administrative discourses. These terms connote self-control, the importance of linearity in task and time management, a focus on individualism, the importance of setting goals, the importance of achievement and advancement, and the capacity to successfully move others to action—all qualities that the ideal US citizen should have. David Schneider (1968) argues that culture is organized around core symbols, with "the individual" being one core symbol in US culture. Building on Schneider's argument I would say that "the class-mobile individual" is another core national symbol, particularly with the expansion of the middle class in the 1950s. Because college is now central to the process of class mobility, the ideal college student—crystallized in the way potential students are seen as part of an imagined college community—enters into this core-symbol configuration. The ideal student is both a well-ordered individual achiever and a productive community member. The idealized multicultural student at an elite college has a neatly laminated set of traits that can frame or enhance, but never interfere with, the ideal US citizen qualities. A potential student's language and culture should fit into the idealized "multicultural student" configuration.

LINGUISTIC MARKING

Unfortunately, in actual life, this lamination does not work out so neatly, because the same multicultural students who are supposed to "have" language –and culture in a way structurally parallel to what international students "have" in fact have different experiences of language and race. In the US, there has long been a dominant ideology that foreign languages belong outside the borders; foreign languages that are native to any group within the US are highly suspect. Hence the initiatives at state and national levels for official English legislation. So multicultural students who are US natives and native speakers of Spanish are prone to racialization, particularly if their English is seen as marked by their Spanish. Furthermore, any multicultural student, especially anyone black, growing up with a nonstandard variety of English, may find themselves linguistically race-marked. International students may have linguistic issues as students in the US but their prior experience has been outside the US and does not match that of multicultural students. The mass of students— and faculty –at the college, who grew up white and middle –class, have never experienced linguistic (or other) race-marking and do not think about what it means. People who do not experience race-marking have little idea how much they take a benign social atmosphere for granted (as race-marked people cannot) and how easy it is to impose judgment. Those who experience race-marking are more sensitive to negative reactions and judgments. Michael Silverstein (1987) argues that in the ideologically monoglot US, institutional assessments have cast nonstandard English elements as impurities or accretions that can be shed through discipline and hard work. While the form of this ideology, with its emphasis on an individual work ethic, is peculiarly American, the sense of nonstandard elements as impure is not. Bilingual Latino/a students have found both their English and their Spanish criticized.

Some years ago, a few Latina students (all of whom became active in the Latino/a organization) were "diagnosed" with "language interference" by someone untrained in linguistic pathology or learning disorders. Students' problems with writing and understanding material were said to be "caused" by Spanish, and the students' advisor was told that they needed less Spanish and more English. This stance seems to have run its course; a colleague currently involved in the students' program tells me she notices less "diagnosis" of "cause" and more focus on writing issues as practical problems for students to solve. But for the students thus diagnosed, the experience constituted an introduction to college that they did not soon forget. Celia (New York-born in an Ecuadoran-Cuban family) summarized her experience in a 1995 interview:

> last year I would have said that I think they think that all of us don't know how to speak English properly and can't write and all of these negative things . . . but now I mean, not that I don't care but it's more of thing like I'm Latina but that's nice but I'm also a human being and I'm also an American citizen . . . I think for some people on this campus, they do say "Yes they're all this way" . . . It could have just been that I just didn't have a good English teacher in high school and didn't learn how to write properly or didn't learn how to do something. But [that professor] automatically associated it with language which then is culture.

Note her recognition of the race-marked lamination of language and culture. She elaborates:

> The only thing that bothered me is automatically it was assumed that just because my writing wasn't very good it had to be because I'm Latina and because my first language is Spanish which is not true. It could just mean that I didn't learn the proper way to write an essay or something or that day I was just like whatever about the paper. It could've been so many other things.

Ely (New York-born in a Puerto Rican family) describes her experience (1995 interview):

> Yes, at one point, when I was a first year, or before I even got here I was constantly being nagged about how my writing skills are very low and I should do something about it. I understand it was true, and it was just associated with being Latina and how you speak Spanish and you think in Spanish which is false because the first language I learned was English. And all my life I've taken English in school, so there was no reason for me to think in Spanish. If that's what I was thinking, that's what I was taught to think to begin with. So this specific person used to write on my papers that I had to see [the individual] because I didn't speak proper English or I didn't write proper English because I was too busy thinking in Spanish.

Rosa (Puerto Rican-born, raised in New York) described a similar experience (1995 interview):

> "Yeah. Like 'When you write, do you think in Spanish or in English?' and I'm like, well, if I'm writing in English I would have to be thinking in English. What I'm thinking is what I'm writing. So yeah, I had the same problem."

Ely adds:

> A lot of us did. And now professors just ask me now, not "Is it that you think in English" but more "Did you come from a public school?" Then they try to see the root of the problem, maybe, "How much English did you take in high school or junior high school? Did you take grammar?" and the questions and answers are there. I'm like, "Well, not as much, I only took one year of grammar in elementary school and I don't remember most of it." So people who are trying to help me would ask questions like that, they won't automatically assume that they know what the problem is.

Keeping English and Spanish strictly partitioned is seen as evidence of a person's self-control and capacity for self-improvement, which are evidence of acting like a middle-class American. So, in effect, when these three students were "diagnosed" for interference, their language partitioning was being monitored.

What these students experienced is a specific manifestation of a more general feeling that a lot of Spanish-speaking Latino/a students have about fitting in linguistically at school. Ana, who grew up in the

Bronx in a Dominican family, compares attitudes she has encountered at college with people's attitudes back in the Bronx (1995 interview):

> Ana ("A" henceforth): And also there are racial differences sometimes, like in what we do, how we talk, especially like us, with me I think it's a lot the way I talk. There's nothing wrong with the way I talk but I find it harder, still, to speak English here? Not harder but I guess I'm so aware of it that sometimes I say words wrong.

Bonnie Urciuoli ("BU" henceforth): You hear yourself—

> A: Wrong! Because I guess I could kind of see the difference so much between my accent and other people, and that kind of stops me from talking a lot.

Ana also talks about how she has internalized these judgments:

> A: Well, sometimes I think that people judge me but sometimes maybe I think it's myself—that I'm so aware that I speak differently that sometimes I kind of say to myself, "They're judging me." And they're not. So sometimes—I just have to get over it. I just have to get over it and— But sometimes it's difficult because I just can'tyou grow up, you're home, they're like, "You should learn English"; it's better you're practicing more because you speak better. But I'm just saying, what is better? . . . How can I change the way I talk? I can't. I can't. I mean, this is just my accent, I can't change it and why should I want to change it? I guess it would be easier if—I don't know, I guess because of the way I talk, it's kind of hard for me to say words? And I don't know why it has to do with that? But I guess if I didn't have so much trouble saying the words maybe I wouldn't think myself that I speak a little wrong.
> BU: Interesting. Do you think of this in terms of writing? Is it something you're aware of when you're writing?
> A: It sometimes pisses me off when I kind of want to say something and I don't know how to say it and how to write it? And I'm like maybe if I was always brought up speaking English it would be easier for me. And I get so frustrated because I'm like—sometimes my vocabulary is like fffff—it just stinks! And I'm like, God, I'm not going to do well in this paper.

The language issues these students face are not limited to their English. Here, I asked Ana if she had run into comparable issues in a Spanish class:

> A: Yeah, because especially Latin American countries, they all have different, what is it, dialects? So it's especially—even in the Dominican Republic, within the country, they're like, "Oh, you're from the *campo,*

because you speak with the 'ai,' " or whatever, whatever. And I'm just like, people are so prejudiced against each other for that.

BU: You speak with a what?

A: It's like with the "ai" and you forget the "s," or you know in Spain "*para*," you say "*pa*." And a lot of the words are just like cut off and totally . . . When you get like with Puerto Ricans and different type of people from different countries, like Guatemala and whatever, they all judge each other: "Oh, you speak kind of too fast or too this or too that." Or you forget this or you forget that. And nothing's ever proper if you're speaking to a Latin American, . . . you always think that if they're different they're wrong. Or either you're putting yourself as wrong.

BU: When you use Spanish at home it's just like part of the environment, you know, you're talking to your family, whatever, whatever, or you mix English, whatever. When you come here, when you use Spanish, are you conscious of different things about how you use Spanish here?

A: I think if it's with people who are Hispanic, I kind of speak the same way. But then if I'm speaking—even if I'm speaking with someone that's Hispanic and I see the people around me, sometimes I'm kind of aware of that, because people kind of get upset when you're speaking another language and you're around. But I guess in class it's also different because there's also like students who are white and you're Hispanic so it's like there's so much difference the way you talk. So then you're kind of saying—you're kind of thinking, which is the right way? And there's some that come from Spain and they talk differently also. And then you're kind of like, you know, how do I speak? And then even if you live in the Bronx, your Spanish is kind of different, it's never like supposedly the right Spanish. So even . . . even in the Spanish class where we Latinos know more Spanish, you kind of feel a little uncomfortable sometimes.

Ely relates her experience of linguistic prejudice in Spanish class, but with a little payback:

Well, I've been taking Spanish since my first year. And my first Spanish class was horrible, my professor was a visiting professor from Spain and he actually criticized us [a fellow student and herself] for speaking like that, because he was saying that it was unfair to the rest of the students, they don't understand a word you're saying and we're like we understand that but why are they in a 200-level class? And then we kept arguing about that the whole semester, because, "Oh you speak too fast, you don't speak clear," and so the white students were getting really annoyed because, "Oh you know they speak too fast." So we had to modify our speech to accommodate them. But when it comes to their language, their Spanish, it's very slow, and—you know I even tried to tutor one girl but—I think . . . There's a huge difference, and it not only has to do with the accent but intonation also, like where you see the highs and the lows, and then we hear the white students, well at least the ones that haven't gone to a Latin American country for a semester, and we're like, why is this person speaking like this? And it sounds funny and it's rude and it's bad and it's harsh but—[Laughter].

The experiences these students have been describing concern correctness judgments by classroom authorities. But there is another linguistic issue that Latino/a students experience, and that is peer judgment. At this school, most Spanish-English bilinguals are New Yorkers for whom code-switching is the norm. This has become something of a litmus test for Latina/o students. Julia, who grew up English-dominant in an Ecuadoran family in Florida, describes her perception and experience of this (1995 interview).

Let me just tell you my story and we can go from there. In [the Latino club], when I was president, I think the most ignorant, apathetic, stupid, ooh just jerked my cheeks—this guy—he made me feel like, "You aren't—you can't be with us because your Spanish isn't good enough. You don't know the music we're talking about. You don't know how to dance merengue and salsa." And so yeah, he made me feel like definitely I couldn't belong to that group. But when you're with your girl friends it doesn't really matter . . . I really never think about it, but when I do go to like the salsa and merengue parties, then I think about it. Because I know, like I'll say *"Hola, ¿cómo estás?", "Muy bien, y tú, ¿cómo estás?"* and they see that I don't have an—that I have a good accent in Spanish. And they'll want to keep talking to me in Spanish. and they use all those slang words and all these little sayings, and I'm like *"¿Qué? ¿Perdón?* What?" And then I'm like, "Oh God, they're not going to think I'm Latin now because I don't understand what they're saying." So that's really the only time when I'm aware of how I should act or what I should do. But other than that, I never think about it.

A similar assessment was provided by one of my colleagues, a Spanish professor whose mother's family is from Puerto Rico and father's family is from Spain, and who grew up in California. She said that when she first came to the college, her *puertorriqueñidad,* so to speak, was tested by students listening to see whether she sounded like a New York bilingual, which, she said, she did not. And that was an issue.

MULTICULTURALISM AND LANGUAGE: THE NATURE OF THE CONTRADICTION

I close by reiterating the two key dynamics of race-marking: privilege and protection. The more race-marked one is, the less voice one has in defining what is culturally real, and the less protected one is from the consequences of race-marking. Students' imagining of Latino/a identity and their invention of its defining traditions are reconstructions, within the frame of good US citizenship, of a more pervasive and pernicious construction that Oboler has analyzed and documented as "Hispanic" and that has been generated since the 1800s from privileged and protected social, economic, and legislative loci. It includes the pejorative constructions of language varieties, English or Spanish, as outlined by the young women I interviewed. The irony that should be really obvious is that those most prone to being race-marked—those less in a position to be heard and more in a position to be hurt—are the ones doing the work of changing the dominant perspective.

Club membership, and the deployment of Spanish therein, is as much about being a good US citizen as it is as about sociality. But whether Spanish, English, or both, what sounds most social, most like home (especially if home is New York), is also most subject to "official" criticism. Language becomes Janus-faced, meaning one thing to students sharing it and another to those assessing them. When language features importantly in cultural performance, especially when framed by music, it is most likely to be taken by non-members as "part of culture" without other baggage. At the same time, for Latino/a students, language –as –part –of –culture means that the shared in-group language is a key part of the sociality of the group itself, and is the language that is most problematically marked. As I said earlier, while not all these students are Puerto Rican, their experience of English and Spanish does fit that of Puerto Rican bilinguals.

The legitimacy of a foreign language lies in its capacity to emblematize national identity *outside* the US; within the US foreign languages are always problematic. The linguistic legitimacy available to foreign students is not available to native speakers of languages other than English within the US. Moreover, all languages, including Spanish, gain legitimacy when their orderliness can be assessed in classroom performance and measured against a standardized text. Only then is a language allowed "real-world utility." When students are told that their Spanish does not have the real-world utility that would give it foreign language legitimacy, they are in effect being told that they are departing from a measurable order. To that extent and in that way, they are race-marked. The very linguistic practices on which they build a sense of Latinidad—practices that should be culturally validating—become racial markers.

ACKNOWLEDGMENTS

Thanks to Susan Mason for personal insight and background information, and thanks especially to the students who took part in this study.

NOTES

1. *U.S. News and World Report* (2006) explains the Diversity Index as follows: College bound students who believe that studying with people of different backgrounds is a key part of the university experience will want to consider student-body diversity when choosing a school. To identify colleges where students are most likely to encounter undergraduates of different racial or ethnic groups, *U.S. News* factors in the total proportion of minority students—leaving out international students—and the mix of groups. The data are drawn from each institution's 2000–2001 student body. The groups forming the basis for our calculations are American Indians and Alaskan Natives (Native Americans), Asian Americans and Pacific Islanders, African Americans who are non-Hispanic, whites who are non-Hispanic, and Hispanics. Our formula produces a diversity index that ranges from 0.0 to 1.0. The closer a school's number is to 1.0, the more diverse the student population. This methodology was created by Philip Meyer and Shawn McIntosh and published in 1992 in the International Journal of Public Opinion Research (U.S. News and World Report 2006).

2. When I did fieldwork in 1988, "being Spanish" was a frequently heard referent to having Latino/a family background, and I heard New York Puerto Rican and Dominican students using it in the mid-1990s. I do not know if it is still used.

3. According to the school's catalog, the summer program is "designed to provide a wide range of services to qualified applicants who, because of educational and economic circumstances, would otherwise be unable to attend college. These services include a summer session in preparation for matriculation at the College, counseling and tutoring."

4. Starting with the class of 2005, applicants use the common application form (a standard form used by a large number of elite colleges and universities) as well as a supplement asking for information and materials specific to this college.

5. When Patricia says "like when you came to talk," she refers to the occasion on which I had come to a meeting to present my research project and recruit interviewees.

REFERENCES

Anderson, Benedict. 1991. *Imagined Communities: Reflections on the Origin and Spread of Nationalism*. Rev. ed. London and New York: Verso.

Chock, Phyllis Pease. 1991. "Illegal Aliens" and "Opportunity": Myth-Making in Congressional Testimony. *American Ethnologist* 18: 279–294.

Hill, Jane. 1998. Language, Race and White Public Space. *American Anthropologist* 100: 680–689.

Hobsbawm, Eric, and Terence Ranger. 1983. *The Invention of Tradition*. New York: Cambridge University Press.

Lippi-Green, Rosina. 1997. *English with An Accent: Language, Ideology and Discrimination in the United States*. London: Routledge.

Mendoza-Denton, Norma. 1999. Sociolinguistics and Linguistic Anthropology of U.S. Latinos. *Annual Review of Anthropology* 28: 375–395.

Newfield, C., and A.T. Gordon. 1996. Multiculturalism's unfinished business. In *Mapping Multiculturalism*, ed. A. Gordon and C. Newfield,76–115. Minneapolis: University of Minnesota.

Oboler, Suzanne. 1995. *Ethnic Labels, Latino Lives: Identity and the Politics of (Re)Presentation in the United States*. Minneapolis: University of Minnesota.

Omi, Michael, and Howard Winant. 1986. *Racial Formation in the U.S. from the 1960s to the 1980s*. New York and London: Routledge and Kegan Paul.

Perrucci, Robert, and Earl Wysong. 1999. *The New Class Society*. New York: Rowman and Littlefield.

Schneider, David. 1968[1980]. *American Kinship: A Cultural Account*. 2nd ed. Chicago: University of Chicago, Press.

Silverstein, Michael. 1987. Monoglot "Standard" in America: Standardization and Metaphors of Linguistic Hegemony. Working Papers and Proceedings of the Center for Psychosocial Studies #13, Center for Psychosocial Studies, Chicago, IL.

Trechter, Sara, and Mary Bucholtz. 2001. White Noise: Bringing Language into Whiteness Studies. *Journal of Linguistic Anthropology* 11(1): 3–21.

Urciuoli, Bonnie. 1996. *Exposing Prejudice*. Boulder: Westview Press.

———. 1999. Producing Multiculturalism in Higher Education: Who's Producing What for Whom? *International Journal of Qualitative Studies in Education* 123: 287–298.

U.S. News and World Report. 2006. America's Best Colleges 2006. Methodology:Campus Diversity. Electronic document. http://www.usnews.com/usnews/edu/college/rankings/about/diversity_brief.php (accessed on April 4, 2006).

Williams, Brackette. 1989. A Class Act: Anthropology and the Race to Nation across Ethnic Terrain. *Annual Reviews of Anthropology* 18: 401–444.

Zentella, Ana Celia. 1995. The "Chiquitafication" of U.S. Latinos and Their Languages, Or Why We Need an Anthropolitical Linguistics. SALSA III: Proceedings of the Third Annual Symposium About Language and Society, Department of Linguistics, University of Texas at Austin, 1–18.

Zentella, Ana Celia. 1997. *Growing Up Bilingual*. Oxford, New York: Blackwell.

CHAPTER 8

Necesidades y Problemas: Immigrant Latina Vernaculars of Belonging, Coalition, and Citizenship in San Francisco, California

Kathleen Coll

On an unusually fogless Saturday morning in the late spring of 1996, a van loaded with seven women and small children circled a busy block in San Francisco's Chinatown, failing to find a coveted on-street parking spot. The neighborhood was bustling already at 9 a.m. with Chinese American families arriving from outer city districts and suburbs for their weekly grocery shopping or extended family visits. The van finally double-parked in front of the enormous concrete cube of a 1970s-era public housing complex. The passengers alighted and the sound of their Spanish conversations soon joined the English and Cantonese already heard at high volume on the street. Arriving late after a cross-town trip from the Latino Mission District, the women moved quickly inside the complex to the housing project's community meeting room, dropping their children in an older multipurpose room where childcare was provided. More than a dozen other women were already there, sitting around a U-shaped table with headphones on, trying hard to help volunteer interpreters figure out how to broadcast Cantonese and Spanish translations to the appropriate participants. The sponsoring community organizations' staff welcomed everyone and asked the late arrivals to introduce themselves to the group. Thus began a summer-long workshop series on cross-cultural immigrant women's organizing, as well as my own introduction to the workshop participants as their volunteer vanpool driver, Spanish–English interpreter, and anthropologist.

This essay is based on the reflections and analyses of the ten Latina[1] immigrant grassroots members of *Mujeres Unidas y Activas,* the community organization that cosponsored this leadership-development program with the Chinese Progressive Association (CPA). It presents one rendition of a partial story of complex multiethnic, multilingual, and often faltering struggles to connect across ethnic and linguistic lines.[2] The focus of this essay is on how these participants related their experiences of sustained and substantive dialogue with their Chinese immigrant counterparts in the workshops to their own growing sense of belonging and entitlement in the US. It reflects points of resonance among the participants' individual reflections on their experiences together, as well as what they reported that this *convivencia,* or sharing of time and experiences, meant to them and to their sense of their own position and rights in the US.

COMMUNITY LEADERSHIP DEVELOPMENT AND NEW IDEAS OF CITIZENSHIP

Mujeres Unidas y Activas (*"Mujeres Unidas"*) is a grassroots women's organization that was founded in 1990 in San Francisco's Mission District (Moore, 1995). By 1996, *Mujeres Unidas* had over 200 Latin American immigrant members, principally from Mexico and Central America.[3] Participants from the organization in the leadership workshops ranged in age from the early 20s to late 40s, and had arrived anywhere from 1 to 20 years prior to their participation in these workshops. All had children and most worked at least part-time outside the home, in restaurants, hotels, garment factories, and, in one case, in her family's own small business. Participants were required to have been active participants in *Mujeres Unidas* for more than six months in order to participate, and they received a small stipend. The CPA had a large and active membership base, particularly in the areas of housing, immigrant labor, and youth organizing. As an organization it was almost two decades older than *Mujeres Unidas,* but CPA members hoped that the collaborative workshops would help develop its core of immigrant women leaders, as well as attract new women members.[4]

Few of the participants spoke any English, so the weekly, daylong workshops were carried out through simultaneous translation (Spanish, English, and Cantonese) via headphones during the three months of workshops and the following two months of the joint campaign. All of the organizers, participants, and presenters were Chinese and Latin American immigrant women except for one Chinese American male staff member, two US-born Latina staff, and myself, a US-born white volunteer. The initial plan was to alternate weekly meetings —one week in the Latino Mission District and the next in Chinatown—but the housing project's meeting space proved congenial, and the group ended up meeting only twice in the Mission that summer.

In interviews following the completion of the workshops, participants from *Mujeres Unidas* spoke of the difficulties raised by the multilingual and cross-cultural nature of the workshops, and of the powerful influence of this process on their ideas about their position and rights in the US. From these interviews emerged a sense of shared citizenship—not "in spite of" their differences with one another, but rather because of a deepened understanding of both their shared and divergent interests, values, and experiences and "a politics which recognizes rather than represses difference" (Young, 1990: 10).

Understood as new terms of citizenship, *convivencia, problemas,* and *necesidades* were more than strategic bases for building coalition among different interest groups. These concepts broaden the domain of political belonging and entitlement from strictly institutional, political, and economic realms to include the importance of human relationships, subjectivity, and feelings. This essay argues that these women's contributions are central to understanding contemporary US citizenship theory and practice in local communities. Although none of these women were US citizens, and only two were eligible for naturalization, the ways in which they spoke about their sense of belonging and exclusion were grassroots expressions of "cultural citizenship" rooted in gendered experiences of encounters with difference in urban US life (Benmayor *et al.,* 1992; Pratt, 1993; Rosaldo, 1994; Flores and Benmayor, 1997).

Women expressed complex ideas about identity, coalition, and community mobilization arising from their experiences with the women they usually referred to in the third person as *las chinas.* They emphasized the importance of *convivencia,* or getting to know one another by spending time, talking, and doing things together, as well as learning more about their shared collective concerns and experiences. In particular, *Mujeres Unidas* members spoke about shared *problemas* (problems), *necesidades* (needs), and the knowledge they had acquired about the role of race and immigration in US history. This time spent together and the heightened awareness of shared historical and contemporary experiences led women to describe "interconnected histories that interact and mutually shape one another," offering a new version of the collective national story as constituted in and between, rather than alongside, "excluded and marginalized histories" (Rosaldo, 1996: 1041).

Citizenship and immigration status continue to be primary legal and political referents in US citizenship studies in North America and Europe since World War II, which have focused largely on formal definitions and expressions of citizenship, such as how the state defines and assigns certain rights to various citizen-subjects (Marshall, 1964). However, toward the end of the 20th century, the combined effects of economic and political globalization, devolution of industrial welfare states, and postcolonial civil/human rights and feminist movements led to more processual and practice-oriented approaches to understanding citizenship (Brubaker, 1989; Taylor, 1989; Turner, 1990, 1993; Somers, 1993). Some political philosophers, sociologists, and anthropologists sought out new ideas about citizenship based on the experiences of those historically excluded from either formal or substantive "first-class" status. The subject positions theorized in this literature include women (Barbalet, 1988; Pateman, 1989; Orloff, 1993, 1996; Walby, 1994; Yuval-Davis and Anthias, 1994; Lister, 1997), people of color and diasporic communities (Hall and Held, 1990; Dagnino, 1994; Rosaldo, 1994; Ong, 1996; Flores and Benmayor, 1997; De Genova and Ramos-Zayas, 2003), lesbians and gays (Herrell, 1996; Berlant, 1997; Bell and Binnie, 2000), and transnational migrants (Brubaker, 1989; Shklar, 1991; Mouffe, 1992; Soysal, 1994; Clarke, 1996; Bhabha, 1998; Yuval-Davis, 1999; Goldring, 2001). In some cases, renewed academic concern with citizenship focused on liberal defenses of inclusion (Kymlicka, 2001), while others promised more radical challenges to global political economic systems of inequality (Lowe, 1996: 33).

As this burgeoning literature reveals, citizenship is about more than the bundle of rights and obligations to which newly arrived or emergent citizen groups hope to gain full access. Narrow legal-juridical definitions obscure the multiplicity of ways in which many people, including Latino/as of diverse nationalities and immigration statuses, act to claim their rights as entitled political subjects in the US. This essay offers an ethnographic consideration of forms and practices of citizenship articulated by immigrant Latina grassroots activists involved in a community project in California in the 1990s. This is not intended as a "view from the margins," but rather as a recentering of thinking about citizenship based on the experiences and analyses of noncitizen women deeply concerned with issues of political, social, and cultural membership in US society. In addition to individuals' relationships to nation-states, such an approach to citizenship includes issues of tensions and difference within and between local communities, social movements, religious groups, workplaces, households, and intimate relationships.

XENOPHOBIA AND 1990S CALIFORNIA

The cross-cultural women's leadership-training project I observed in 1996 occurred in the midst of a powerful backlash against years of efforts by immigrants and people of color in California to claim full civil and political status as well as public benefits of social citizenship (Marshall, 1950; Hall and Held, 1990). The 1990s were characterized by dismantling of welfare states and tightened immigrant controls in the north along with structural adjustment policies that shrank worker and peasant economic opportunity as well as governmental services in the south. Global social and structural tensions played out in what were particularly virulent anti-immigrant and anti-Latino terms in California. Anti-immigrant political forces gained momentum when voters passed three statewide ballot initiatives aimed at marginalizing immigrants and people of color in the state. Proposition 187, the "Save Our State Initiative" passed in 1994, blamed and punished undocumented immigrants for the state's economic and political problems. By blocking access to public health, education, and social services for "suspected" undocumented immigrants, Proposition 187 supporters argued, the proposition could stem the tide of Latin American immigration altogether.[5] In one "Letter to the Editor" in *The New York Times,* the campaign media director for Proposition 187 promoted the proposition's agenda on the national stage, declaring California on the verge of a *reconquista* from the south.

> Proposition 187 is . . . a logical step toward saving California from economic ruin. Illegal aliens collect welfare payments through post office boxes in San Ysidro, just a 15-minute walk from Mexico. They receive free medical care and flood schools with non-English speaking students. By flooding the state with 2 million illegal aliens to date, and increasing that figure each of the following 10 years, Mexicans in California would number 15 million to 20 million by 2004. During those 10 years about 5 million to 8 million Californians would have emigrated to other states. If these trends continued, a Mexico-controlled California could vote to establish Spanish as the sole language of California, 10 million more English-speaking Californians could flee, and there could be a statewide vote to leave the Union and annex California to Mexico. (Hayes, 1994)

Proposition 187 was enjoined by the courts and never took effect, but it did set the political tone for the rest of the decade, when additional regressive ballot initiatives were passed and enforced at the state level. At the same time, national welfare and immigration "reforms" sought further to exclude poor people and immigrants from basic entitlements at the national level. This amplified the immigrants' usual anxieties about claiming rights and services, while additional anti-immigrant ballot initiatives were also passed and enforced. In 1996, supporters of Proposition 209 challenged the social, educational, and economic claims for equity of Latinos, African Americans, Native Americans, and Pacific Islanders, including many immigrants. Proposition 209 eliminated state governmental affirmative-action programs and overturned affirmative action at the University of California, the country's largest public university system.[6] In 1998, Silicon Valley entrepreneur Ron Unz, with no previous interest or experience in educational issues, bankrolled the successful Proposition 227 that eliminated bilingual education in many public school districts.

According to the women I worked with in this research, the impact of these measures on immigrant lives and subjectivity was profound. In the words of one *Mujeres Unidas* member, "It is a psychological war against immigrants."[7] Community groups were among the few forums in which many felt safe speaking out about the political climate. The 63% of Latino voters in California who opposed Proposition 227 recognized the attacks on bilingual education as more than a civil disagreement over how to best educate immigrant children. Proposition 227 was really "about re-institutionalizing discrimination and legalizing the deprivation of knowledge and educational opportunity. This proposition sanctions the rejection of Latino culture and our language in society and in the public schools" (Andrade, 1998).[8] These various California ballot initiatives and campaigns were widely perceived as direct attacks on Latino, immigrant, and nonwhite cultural, political, and social citizenship.

CONVIVIENDO EN EL BARRIO CHINO: THE IMMIGRANT WOMEN'S LEADERSHIP PROJECT

It was in this highly fraught and tense context that *Mujeres Unidas* and the CPA initiated a joint project to build the leadership skills of rank-and-file immigrant women members of their respective organizations.[9] The focus on the working-class, cross-racial concerns of immigrant women and on the centrality of collective political struggle signaled the uniquely ambitious character of this project. The two community groups hoped to develop women's organizational and political skills and to carry out joint community outreach and educational campaigns on topics the participants identified as personal and community priorities. This group of women wanted to understand the welfare and immigration reform legislation that was being considered in Congress that summer. They hoped to learn to both explain the new policies to other affected community members and also to mitigate as much as possible the local impact by gaining commitments of support from local officials and service providers.

The main point of the leadership training was to facilitate exchange between immigrant women across the significant divides of language, culture, age, immigration status, economic position, and educational backgrounds. In the spirit of coalition-building for direct, joint political action around issues of shared concern, the participants had already spent time prior to the start of the summer workshops considering themes such as domestic and youth violence, education, and housing. They had agreed that they wanted the sessions to help them understand pending federal immigration and welfare reform legislation.

Each week's session covered a particular topic or issue related to the facts of the immigration and welfare reform legislation and community mobilization. One week the activities and discussion focused on getting to know one another, with each woman designing, drawing, and presenting a graphic representation of herself, her nationality, her family, and her immigration experience with the group. Local school-district officials and service agency staff people were invited to speak about their work. Labor organizers and community educators led sessions on the basics of grassroots organizing and how welfare and immigration "reform" legislation worked its way through local, state and federal levels of government. One week a community agency's psychologist led a discussion on "self-esteem" and what it meant for the participants to have, develop, or project a positive sense of themselves. In another session, a community educator offered a full-day workshop covering topics such as American ethnic/immigration/racial history from conquest, annexation of Mexico, slavery, 19th- and 20th-century immigration waves, and the African American civil rights movement. These sessions on self-esteem, immigration, and civil rights history stood out in women's later reflections on their experiences in the workshops.

NECESIDADES: DIGNITY, COALITION, AND CITIZENSHIP

The experience of working together in these workshops taught women about immigration history, legislation, and one another's families and life stories. Many women cited this new knowledge and experience as prompting them to strengthen their claims for social belonging and membership in the US. They based these claims on the notion that marginalization, organization, and activism for inclusion are experiences shared by many current US citizens or their ancestors. *Mujeres Unidas* members cited the process of struggle for citizenship rights itself as the basis for claims for their rightful place in US society. They spoke of the importance of learning about US immigration history as well as getting to know women whom they had previously deemed totally different from themselves in reformulating their sense of their position and rights in this country.

Caridad Ríos was a 40-year-old native of Lake Chapala in Jalisco, Mexico, who had lived in the US for more than 20 years at the time of the leadership training. She had worked as a unionized hotel room cleaner and in the garment industry in San Francisco during most of these years and had three children whom she was raising alone. Reflecting on her experiences after the final workshop of the summer, Caridad said that she had been impressed by how much the two groups of women had in common. She volunteered that prior to this experience, she had had little contact with Chinese people, and had ridiculed their language when she heard it. After the workshops, she instead focuses on what they have in common.[10]

> One knows that, well, we have almost the same needs and worries. They also have children, work a lot, and want the best for their children, like us. They are mothers with families, as are we. Like us, they are hardworking and honest people.

Caridad's emphasis on the women's shared *necesidades* (needs) was a significant and common theme throughout the narratives of the Latina participants. These needs included quality education, health care, and housing for their children and themselves, as well as equality of opportunity for their own economic survival and a political voice for themselves, their families, and other community members. The discourse of *necesidades*, instrumental support, and public services also reflected Latin American popular discourses about citizenship and human dignity (Díaz-Barriga, 1996, 2000). Although Caridad had not participated in organizing in Mexico, she came to the US with a consciousness of the traditions of Mexican urban popular movements' demands of the state for basic social and infrastructural services such as pavements, water, and electricity. These are among the most common and powerful of grassroots expressions of citizenship and constitute political arenas in which women play prominent roles.[11] None of the women I interviewed reported participating in such urban movements themselves in their countries of origin. However, they apparently agreed with the idea that there is a significant relationship between self-respect, having one's dignity recognized by others, both privately and publicly, and state accountability for providing basic human services to all people living under its authority.

In the US, where basic state-provided infrastructure such as water and pavements is more ubiquitous than in Latin America, the citizenship discourse of *necesidades* includes access to public assistance programs, quality public education, decent housing, and, perhaps most importantly, wage labor under fair conditions. While Latina needs-based formulations of citizenship contrast with North American rights-based citizenship in significant ways, the women I interviewed employed both discourses of citizenship to affirm their expectation of social benefits as supranational entitlements, as human rights. Latinas' insertion of their expectations of state-funded housing, health care, and education into North American discussions about individual rights and individual obligations was a powerful political move. It was especially significant at a moment when the US government was exponentially accelerating the devolution of welfare provisions, not just for immigrants, but for all citizens.

These issues were reflected in women's public practice as well as in the workshops and our interviews. During the months following the summer workshops, I drove and interpreted for delegations of participants during visits to local officials and service providers, including members of the county board of supervisors and the head of the county human services office. They began these meetings by telling the officials about what they had learned about one another in the leadership training, focusing especially on their common needs and problems. Participants from both groups told officials their concerns about the content of the new federal welfare and immigration reform policies and how they would affect immigrants on the ground in San Francisco. They emphasized why it was important to divert other local or state monies to cover federal cuts that would disproportionately affect already vulnerable immigrant families, immigrant elders, and battered women in San Francisco.

During these visits, both *Mujeres Unidas* and CPA members provided the officials with concrete stories from each of their communities. They offered personal testimonials about how public services help immigrant families, including US-born children, and rationales for how such support strengthens the whole local community. They said that as

Chinese and Latina immigrant parents, workers, and community members, they needed not only instrumental public support from the state, but also dignified and humane treatment.

While several *Mujeres Unidas* members joked among themselves after one such meeting that they felt quite comfortable in the Human Services building, having spent so much time there in waiting rooms over the years, they also stated how remarkable it was to be received with respect at the chief administrator's office, as well as at various supervisors' offices in City Hall. Officials could not promise these delegations that services would not be cut, but they were attentive, respectful, and engaged with the political actors before them. These particular elected officials and service providers were themselves African American, Asian, or Latina women, with the exception of one gay white male official. They also included first- and second-generation immigrants who could speak either Spanish or Cantonese. The question at stake concerning public resources and services was evidently urgent, material, and far more than symbolic. However, the demands for instrumental supports were bound up with interrelated issues of dignity and respect underlying group members' formulation of the rights due to them as community members.

Despite this fairly unified public performance of citizenship, participants also internally discussed and debated the issues at hand. At many points in the workshop, participants talked over how they might best organize their communities in the face of imminent cuts in health care, housing, and welfare supports to immigrant families entailed by 1996 federal legislation. Conversations over lunch and in the car en route to and from meetings revealed diverse views about using public services and what constitutes a "worthy" citizen-subject. These issues sometimes became explicit points of contention among *Mujeres Unidas'* membership, though they were not shared with their Chinese peers or staff during formal workshop time. This revealed that even the public language of *necesidades* still allowed for complicated cleavages among *Mujeres Unidas* members in terms of class and race politics.

It was cash benefits, referred to always in English as "welfare," that was the most contentious issue in these side discussions among *Mujeres Unidas* members. There seemed to be general agreement that the government had the responsibility to provide housing, healthcare, nutritional, and educational services to all people who needed these, without regard to income or personal industry. These types of supports, as opposed to cash, corresponded with the language of *necesidades* and seemed more congruent with Latin American governmental policy and popular claims for social citizenship benefits.

Among the Latina participants, Esperanza Solorzano had the least years of formal education, but was the only homeowner and proprietor of a small business. Now in her late 30s, she had emigrated more than 15 years earlier from Mexico City, and struggled with alcohol and violence in her family. Esperanza frequently expressed both her desire to leave her husband and her fear that she could not support her children on her own. She was highly critical of families who relied on cash benefits for economic subsistence and represented the most extreme position on economic independence and good citizenship of the women I interviewed.

Esperanza preferred to emphasize the inherent industriousness and worthiness of immigrant families based on their capacity for self-reliance and economic contributions to the US. She criticized immigrants for receiving government benefits, but reserved particular ire for African American and US-born Latinos whose unemployment she could not understand, since they had legal permission to work. In contrast, Alejandra Ocampo worked in an electronics manufacturing plant but had the most years of formal education in the group, having completed some college prior to emigrating from Colombia. She lived with her lover, Isabel Monreal, and their three children from previous relationships in public housing. She bristled at the implication that she or her mainly African American neighbors were somehow less worthy or contributed less to this country because they needed government subsidies to make ends meet.

When I interviewed Marta Rodríguez in September, she was excited about the workshops that she had just completed, and was animated and enthusiastic about her experiences in the project. At first I thought that her discussion of shared needs and problems seemed to gloss over all differences in a *sentimental* assertion of sameness.

> I learned a lot from them. I had never had anything to do with them before. They are really emotional, just like us. They have many problems. Although ours are such different cultures and such different countries, we are the same in our feelings and way of thinking. Like us, they suffer a lot from racism in this country.

Her first comments about the experience of *"convivencia"* (spending time together, literally, living with) with Chinese immigrant women in the workshops and subsequent efforts seemed straightforward. Marta's direct reference to racism, however, was a signal that hers was not a romantic, idealized view. Instead she rooted her sense of solidarity and identification with her Chinese coparticipants not only in the life experiences they shared and discussed in the workshop, but also in a sense of shared history that developed from learning more about immigration, race, and citizenship in the US.

The extent to which participants sought out commonalities of experience and other ways of learning more about each other was particularly clear in the importance they placed on what they had learned about US history in the workshops. Marta spoke with particular emotion about the session devoted to immigration history, in which a community organizer gave a down-to-earth summary of US conquest and expansion, slavery, and immigration. For most of the Latina participants, this was the first time they had heard a version of the US national story in which they could locate themselves or their experiences. When I asked Marta whether she had been particularly impressed by anything during the summer, she replied that yes, she had been really taken aback by some information.

> For example, the workshop that they gave on immigration . . . it was the one that I liked the most. Because I learned things that I never imagined could exist. For example, . . . these people th at they brought from Africa . . . the slaves . . . it seemed so inhuman to me, so unjust. In that moment, I got to thinking that today we are suffering from so much discrimination but we don't think about how back then they lived in such inhumane conditions, so unjustly were they treated . . . I began to reflect on why people are so, so bad that they treat other humans like animals.

Marta reported that prior to this workshop, she had never before heard of African slavery or the 19th-century xenophobia against European and Asian immigrants. It was the first time she had considered how she might write herself into this national citizenship story. Rather than eliding differences in the experiences of Chinese, Mexicans, and Africans in the US, in learning more about these distinct histories, Marta identified (but did not generalize) her own experiences of discrimination with those of other people of color, especially African Americans.

Despite her ambivalent attitude toward poor blacks and US-born Latinos, Esperanza also reported that the popular history education about immigration, race, and ethnicity in the US was one of the "best things" about the entire leadership training experience. Like Marta, she was moved personally and politically by the history of African American slavery in particular, as explained in the workshop by the popular educator and organizer "Maricarmen."

I learned about history. What disturbs me a lot and was always something I wondered about, was the history of black folks, of the laws that enslaved them, taking away even their names, that their children were not citizens. It was one of the classes which affected me the most and I had my hand in the air the whole time with more questions, until Rosa said to go read some book, I don't remember which . . . she even gave us the name of the book. The whole history's there. Because we were so enthusiastic learning about this subject that we kept getting more and more excited asking questions of Maricarmen.

Sometimes the language of *necesidades* referred not to instrumental needs, but to emotional bonds and relationships stressed by migration. Caridad Ríos had legalized her status under the 1986 Immigration Reform and Control Act (IRCA) amnesty provisions. After five years of residency, Caridad was eligible for naturalization; she even attended informational sessions on naturalization sponsored by a nonprofit legal services group. She reported having wanted to naturalize, and had the list of questions in English and Spanish to study, but feared both the content of the test and the language requirement. Several years later, she remained fearful of the legal process of naturalization, but feels quite settled in the US. At first she justified her plan to remain in the US permanently in terms of her children's *necesidades,* their need for their mother's physical proximity.

I don't believe I'll ever return to my country, because of them. Because how could I leave them? For better or worse they need their mother here, even if they're grown . . . (I'll leave) only if Clinton runs me out of the country! . . . I have now gotten used to living here. I'd like to go (to Mexico) for a week, at the most, two, because I'm such a clown (fool) now that I get sick to my stomach!

The summer leadership-training workshops helped her articulate a legitimate place for herself in the US. Caridad offered an expansive and inclusive, if somewhat primordialist, notion of American citizenship that contrasted with the exclusivity of classic formulations of who legally belongs in this country.

This country is made up of immigrants. From the earliest times, immigrants came . . . Since the very first people arrived, across the Bering Strait from Asia, starting in Alaska, they were immigrants. This country belongs to the whole world . . . I have worked, now I am receiving food stamps but who cares? I have worked, I have contributed here . . . Well, during the training, like I told you, everything was very good, because through drawings, talks, writing, cartoons and everything, they made us understand a lot of things that we didn't know . . . the rights that we all have, as human beings, as immigrants, as hard-working people, everything. I did not know a lot of that.

As Caridad's words made clear, this process of claiming a legitimate place for oneself, one's children, and one's community in an inhospitable nation-state can lead to conflicting or contradictory discursive strategies to define one's own status. Even though Caridad at first based her desire to remain in the US on her children's need for their mother, it is clear that she herself does not imagine returning to live permanently in Mexico. She was more than sheepish about this, calling herself a "clown" for embodying the outsider subject position in her hometown, symbolized by her physical inability to "stomach" life in Mexico anymore. Although she is now qualified to naturalize, she still referred to her own sense of insecurity with respect to the state—embodied by the then president Bill Clinton—which might try to run her out of the country. Caridad claimed her rightful place in the US by linking her own decades of contributions as a worker to the history of immigration and the invaluable contributions of other immigrants over time to the US.

PROBLEMAS: PRODUCTIVE PROBLEMS AND ENCOUNTERS WITH DIFFERENCE

Women's narratives specifically linked personal changes in their sense of self to the transformation of their ideas about their political identities, roles, and rights in the US. Intimate needs and problems were not only fodder for solidarity and identification with other women in the leadership-training workshops, but the quest for solutions to such problems motivated these women toward political engagement as well. For example, Adela remembered the moment during the training, after it had been under way for several weeks, when she finally felt herself personally engaged in the project and interested in the workshop at hand. This workshop dealt with the concept of self-esteem (*autoestima*), what the women thought it meant, and how it related to how they felt about themselves, individually and as immigrant women. Although Adela had heard this concept discussed in meetings with the Latina women's group, she cited the power of this experience for her as lying in what she learned about the Chinese women in this discussion.

The first time that I really got interested, I think was in the third session (of the workshop), when it was about self-esteem . . . that I began to notice, I said yes, they also feel bad, they also have problems. They also go through what I'm going through, so, Adela, what are you complaining about? . . . It was when I began to pay more attention to them. Because I said, I have to learn from them. I have to learn a lot from all my *compañeras,* but even more from them (the Chinese women). First of all, because they are another, they have another nationality, they have other customs, they have another language . . . And maybe the nicest thing they made me learn was just that, that I realized that there are people, of whatever origin or whatever nationality who will help you, will motivate you. And you know whose example I really learned from? From Lily, she's the one in the wheelchair, right? I said, 'She's here. Why, if she's here, doing things for her people, and I'm perfectly fine—Can't I do something for mine? Can't I also do something for myself?' So she helped me a lot.

Adela formulated self-esteem issues as collective ones that could be shared among women of very different backgrounds and whose solutions lay not in individual life changes but collective action for social transformation. Adela did not assert that she had to "get herself together" before she could help her community, but rather that both processes needed to occur together in mutually supportive ways.

Iris Marion Young asserts that the daily experience of diverse urban life reframes the very definition of citizenship, leading away from an insistence on a homogeneous, assimilating polity to a "politics of difference" that emphasizes social differentiation without exclusion (Young, 1990). It was, in part, through such engagement with difference in structured and sustained multiethnic and multilingual encounters that the women I interviewed reported coming to see themselves as occupying legitimate, significant social roles in the US as immigrants, mothers, workers, and political agents. For the women I interviewed, the most powerful discursive shift in their own sense of belonging in the US came with increased personal identification with US immigration and ethnic history, and with the legacy of African American struggle in particular. Women credited the history lessons they received as part of the workshop series, but also what they had learned in the course of life in the US and in fellowship with one another in their weekly *Mujeres Unidas* meetings.

Adela Aguirre seemed to consider life in San Francisco as well as these workshops as productive sites for encountering and working through issues of difference. She spoke of how, with the right mindset, just living in the US provided her with multiple opportunities to "open your mind" (*"te abre la mente"*) to different concerns, histories, and people who were different from herself. As an example, she cited her own feelings when she watched a television program about Martin Luther King Jr. and the March on Washington. "If they could do it, why can't we?" she remembered asking herself at the time, without resentment or anger, but rather with some surprise at her own identification with African Americans and a civil rights movement she had never before heard about.

This shift in mindset, however, entailed a whole new kind of resistance at the household level for Adela. She described a constant struggle to overcome the influence of her US-born Mexican American husband's racism on herself and her son, while also trying to understand how he could hold these attitudes despite having grown up in the diverse Bay Area rather than in "a little town in Mexico."

> I believe that most of all it was from him that I learned what the word 'racism' means . . . (In the US) you are more open-minded, you have more opportunities for everything, and you can learn about more things. So you can't have that mentality. You can't.

Adela repeatedly interrogated the contradictory nature of US pluralism and democracy. According to her thinking, the chance to interact with diverse peoples is one of many opportunities (including educational and economic opportunities) available to members of US society that should preclude the kind of derogatory attitudes her husband espoused. Yet even though she insists that "you can't" think these things, she knows her husband absolutely *does* have "that mentality." Then she shared stories of her own experiences of poor treatment at the hands of white Americans simply because she was Latina, and at the hands of some middle-class Latino service providers because she was a poor immigrant. In other words, Adela was not all that surprised at her husband's prejudices, because his attitudes are more normal than exceptional in the US.

Adela struggled with both the promise of equality and the reality of racism and discrimination that characterize US national experience. Like Marta in her interview, Adela rather gently and indirectly addressed my own subjectivity with respect to middle-class, nonimmigrant American racism. Marta did this by abstract references to third person "others" and Adela through the example of her own US-born husband. In general, I am sure that my own identity softened the language that women used in interviews to describe their experiences and critiques of American racism, though they still found these indirect third-person strategies to make their points while trying to avoid putting me personally in a defensive position.

Adela's narratives of her husband's *racismo* (racism) toward other groups were intertwined with stories of his abusive attitude toward her. This politicized her personal resistance to him in her stories, signaling that "private" arguments between husband and wife can also be part of women's process of claiming cultural citizenship. Adela explained that without any provocation, he would launch into a litany of stereotypes or generalizations about other groups, but always beginning with her as a point of departure. Since he considers her to be from Mexico City, he would begin by targeting her, saying "*Chilangos* are like this"[12] and then expand with more comments such as "*Los salvadoreños son así*"("Salvadorans are like this"). Adela did not dwell on the particularities of his comments, but on their overgeneralizing and dehumanizing nature. Resisting his prejudices with the strength garnered from information and experience thus became part of her resistance to the emotional abuse he directed against her as well.

She reported being surprised and impressed by how many people in the *Mujeres Unidas* group were from different countries, including Central and South American. "Since we all spoke Spanish, I thought we were all from Mexico!" she said, laughing a little. "I felt so good to be spending time with people from so many different places." Participating in the *Mujeres Unidas* women's group gave her a position of strength from which she could not only resist her husband's prejudices, but argue back at him with authority. Now, she says, when her husband starts insulting Salvadorans or Nicaraguans, "I tell him that the women in the group (from other countries) speak better Spanish than he does." She feels that sharing information and personal experiences with diverse women has provided her strength to resist her husband's hateful comments about her and others.

> But then I said, how strange that one says, why does this only happen to me? And why me? And one makes themselves the sufferer, and one makes oneself out to be the martyr, and one says, 'Oh, God, only me, only to me, only to me,' and 'This and that only happens to me' and 'Why does this only happen to me?' But that's not the truth. One always, like me in the group, I saw that, regardless of nationality, we are women and we all have the same problems. As much as in marriage as in society as sometimes spiritually as well. That's the truth.

Adela's stories of coming to identify with other Latinas and the experiences of people of color in the US were, of course, complex and multilayered, shaped by her own national identity, political views, and domestic life. In addition to addressing the gender solidarity and common experiences as women, she discussed the importance of recognizing the cultural differences that were invisible to her until she got to know other immigrant women better. Adela assumed no global or even ethnic sisterhood or solidarity, as she indicated in her discussions of class and cultural diversity among Latinas, as well as between Latinas and other immigrant women. However, her ability to appreciate differences without either trivializing or reifying them put her in a position to respond positively to the chance to participate in the leadership-training project with Chinese women.

Most of the women I interviewed subsequent to these training workshops either asserted directly or alluded to holding strong prejudices about Chinese people prior to this experience. In describing her own attitudes toward Asian people, Adela revealed a deep ambivalence about some of her own views, at one point seeming to ascribe them to a third party, and another time speculating about which attitudes she may have brought with her from Mexico, rather than learned in the US. This ambivalence may have been part of coming to terms with the US "model minority myth"—a set of attitudes that may seem complimentary on the surface but that signals underlying attitudes of distrust or hostility toward Asian Americans—or may have reflected a familiarity with the historic prejudices against Asians in Mexico that led to violent attacks on immigrants and a subsequent large-scale Chinese exodus from Mexico in the early 20th century.

The following passage from her interview conveys the struggle Adela faced trying to articulate her ideas on this topic. The fact that this otherwise eloquent woman's speech became disjointed reflected the genuine difficulty she had in articulating her conflicting feelings about Chinese people. She traced the logic and genealogy of her prejudices as she sought to reject them after the experience of *convivencia*, or sharing experiences, with actual Chinese women. She also linked these views to her own adjustment to the idea of national and other differences among Latinas, as well as between differently racialized immigrant communities.

> Another one of the things which really surprised me, because I tell you that in the beginning when I saw people here from Guatemala, from El Salvador, from Honduras, from Nicaragua, I said 'Oh! How can this be possible, no?' Imagine how nice it was for me to know that I could

work with Asian people, I never could have imagined that. I had never really had much of an impression, neither good nor bad, of them . . . for me they were simply another group, another class of people, that's about it, just with other customs, another language . . . But even on this I say, how can it be possible that I had the idea that, there's always someone saying that, 'No, if you pay attention, (you'll see that) the Chinese are really united.' They, if something happens to one of them, they are all there, and I had not ever seen that until now. I had never seen evidence, that it was true that they are so united, but I had observed living in Mexico was that they are so intelligent and that's why they do so well in all the businesses, and I always said that they were rich. Think of that! Or at least, if not rich, that they lacked nothing . . . And wouldn't you know, what a surprise to find out that that's not true. It is like with our races, there are people who struggle, who get ahead, who are united. But that's not to say that they all are . . . That was one thing that I really liked a lot.

Like Adela, Isabel Monreal also spoke of the unique opportunity the training provided in the US to speak across divides of race and language. Although she lived in a public housing project that she described as 75% African American and 25% Latino, she had not had such a chance to spend time with and communicate with non-Latinos in the way she was able to in the training workshops. When I asked what she liked best about the workshop experience, she returned to the notion of *convivencia*.

Number one, the experience of spending time with two different races, because in this country we Latinos are always separate, the Chinese are separate, the Black people are separate, and all the ethnic groups are separated, divided and what I liked is that for the first time we are, we took a training with different races, with different languages, even though it was really difficult because of the translations . . . but it still turned out nicely . . . because we know that Latinas just like any other race have the same problems, the same discrimination in this country and that is something that helps us, makes it possible to unite. And when the Chinese have a protest, we Latinos can go support it and when the African Americans protest, we can unite with them and say 'we are supporting them' and not because they are a different color or race that they must be protesting for another thing and that's what I learned the most from this group. That we all have the same problems in this country.

This strong sense of identification with Chinese and African Americans seemed remarkable in a woman who literally lives in a predominantly African American housing project, but reported being afraid to speak to any of her neighbors, black or Latino. Isabel explained that the hostile atmosphere of her public housing development undermined friendships among neighbors in general, but this has not affected her ability to politically identify with African American civil rights struggles and the racism she knows to be directed against all people of color in the US, also affecting relations between communities of color such as Latinos and blacks.

> I pretty much don't start friendships because I don't know them and am afraid, because I don't know how they might be. Because they are always tarred by the fact that people says that blacks are really bad-hearted, and that's really not true, there are many good people too, but because of this same fear, I try not to make friends there (in public housing).

Isabel regarded her African American neighbors with a mixture of fear and solidarity. She knew that Latinos and blacks are both "tarred" by negative stereotypes. At the same time, there was crime in the housing projects where she lived, her family was the only lesbian family and the only non–African American one she knew there, she did not speak English, and she did feel anxiety. She desired *convivencia*—the opportunity to spend time with and get to know other people of color in particular, but there seemed to be many obstacles to real *convivencia* with others in her daily experience of urban American life.

CHALLENGES TO *CONVIVENCIA*

These women's stories reflect how, even in the most diverse American cities, racial and ethnic groups can live alongside one another yet find very little opportunity to interact in meaningful ways or get to know one another well. What is striking in these interviews is this particular group of women's evident interest in bridging these parallel social worlds, and how few opportunities they have found to do so in day-to-day life. Many of the evaluative comments on the workshop experience used the term *convivencia* to describe both the unique opportunity they had to get to know the Chinese women and their issues and concerns, and also in terms of the real barriers to forging deeper personal and political connections that remained after the workshops concluded. Language stood in for the multiple barriers to sustained communication and personal connection that women faced in their work together. As Adela Aguirre put it, her enthusiasm about the workshops was diminished somewhat by the fact that the dialogue was mediated entirely through third parties.

> Yes, that was a really big problem, the languages, because I would have really liked to have been able to talk personally with a Chinese woman and tell her what I feel and how I would have expressed myself with her and it was something that I couldn't do because it's so different with translation, but that was something I wish it could change. . . . What I would like to improve is to give us the chance to spend more time together.

In the face of a project that emphasized speaking across the Chinese–Latino divide, the language of *convivencia* and its emphasis on getting to know one another on a more personal, individual level reflected participants' attempts to avoid reinscribing racial differences in ways that would potentially have been destructive to the fragile coalition the women were forging. One of the CPA participants in particular embodied the slippery nature of "ethnic" identity as a coalitional-mobilizing tool and category of social analysis. An outgoing and personable woman in her sixties, Wei-Ying "Alicia" Chu spoke both Spanish and Cantonese fluently, was retired, and lived alone. She was born in Panama and lived there continuously before returning to China at age 16 with her family. Alicia's personal social location was a clear marker of the flexibility and the social constructedness of ethnic and national boundaries.

The fact that Alicia's own capacity to move socially between the two groups did not actually lead to sustained relationships between her and *Mujeres Unidas* members revealed some of the internal contradictions of a project that promoted equality without sameness without addressing thornier issues of other obstacles to more egalitarian social relations. Racism and prejudice against immigrants were discussed only in the US context. It would have taken far longer to achieve the level of mutual trust necessary to consider other attitudes that might have originated in Asia or Latin America.

Convivencia was a positive ideal, but also a profoundly difficult one to achieve outside the structured setting. Even in the workshops, where interpretation was readily available, women rarely tried to engage someone from the other group in conversation during breaks or lunch times. In fact, as *Mujeres Unidas* members pointed out, it was difficult to make real connections through an interpreter (particularly a nonprofessional volunteer interpreter) at all.

The project succeeded marvelously when grassroots organizational members and staff could create the opportunity to make connections across and through difference. Women were able to develop new tools for understanding social divisions and potentials for solidarity outside the protected realm of the workshops as well. However, the moments of stress and disagreement among the Latina participants reflect some of the very real global, institutional challenges that exist to extending these ideas of belonging and citizenship from the community meeting space out into mainstream US political and social life.

MINDING THE GAPS IN CITIZENSHIP THEORY

In the US, the phrase "coalition-building" evokes images of understanding across boundaries defined by political interest, class, race, language, gender, dis/ability, and sexuality. These categories are among the most salient in defining categories of citizenship identities around which political subjectivity and collective agency emerge in contemporary liberal democratic politics (Hall and Held, 1990; Rosaldo, 1994). While the formulation of a "Chinese–Latina women's leadership training project" itself reinscribed US racial boundaries, the women also surfaced and discussed their own diversity along national lines, immigrant generation, level of education, family structure, physical disability, and sexual preference. While the constant trilingual translation continually marked certain kinds of difference, as the women I interviewed described, the content of the discussions and their own analysis of their structural location led them to focus on the commonalities of their needs and experiences across ethnic and racial lines.

The experience of working together as *Latinas,* rather than in groups defined by Latin American nationality, contributed to the women's analyses of their position and rights in the US. Yet the identity they articulated as *Latina* citizen-subjects was not a homogenized vision of a uniform community, politics, or experience. Their sense of place and rights was defined out of a new idea of historic relationships to non-*Latinas* and people of color, with their divergent experiences of struggle against racial, sexual, and national oppression. The workshops structured a multilingual and multiracial "contact zone" in which women could develop analyses of "how differences and hierarchies are produced *in and through contact* across such lines" (Pratt, 1993: 88).

These women offer a striking comparison to popular American notions of immigrants coming to feel a part of the US over time through an increasing identification with the state, dominant cultural practices, and social groups. Instead these women reported a greater sense of belonging in this society as they learned that their experiences of exclusion in fact related them to more insurgent versions of US citizenship. The emergent discourses of Latina immigrant citizenship in women's stories of comparison and contrast with *las chinas* are products of the specific process of dialogue and exchange they experienced with this particular group of women. In this urban landscape, whether or not they ever manage more sustained *convivencia* with one another, they remain related through public institutions like the public health care and education systems, and through a postindustrial service and manufacturing economy dependent on immigrant workers. They also refused to privilege home or family concerns over social or national ones in their understanding of what constituted interests that they shared with other immigrant women.

Mujeres Unidas members articulated their claims for belonging and entitlement in the US not only relative to codified rights and political institutions, but also in more expansive and processual terms that encompassed experiences of emotion, personal relationships, racial oppression, and social movements. In interviews and in the workshops, they shared stories of the intersections between their struggles to gain voice outside the domestic sphere and to gain influence and control over their personal lives as well. These narratives indicated that women acted to claim their rights and define their own subjectivity, sometimes alternately and at other times simultaneously, on individual, familial, community, and national levels. Herein lies the power of the new models of citizenship suggested in these encounters. As low-income, sometimes undocumented, often non-English-speaking women of color, these women occupy multiple positions and offer perspectives that have been excluded from normative definitions of US citizenship. Yet in discussing, defining, and asserting their common *necesidades* and *problemas* as mothers, immigrants, and women in ways that were politically and personally empowering for them, they revealed the resilient artifice of the public–private dichotomy embedded in Western ideas of citizenship.

Taken as vernacular expressions of citizenship, *problemas, necesidades,* and a more problematized understanding of *convivencia* constitute bases for coalitions among new citizen-subjects and link the discourses of both Latin American and North American popular movements, especially African American and Asian American liberation traditions. Grassroots social analysts like these women suggest that not only is a new, more multifaceted and inclusive citizenship theoretically possible, but that the processes of building upon and changing the terms of belonging and entitlement in the US are already well under way.

NOTES

1. In this essay, I use the term "Latina" (rather than "Latin American") because the women cited in this essay referred to themselves collectively as Latinas or individually in terms of their own nationality (Mexicana, Salvadoreña, Ecuatoriana).

2. The objective here is neither to evaluate the content or efficacy of the leadership-development project and the role of philanthropic foundations in funding it, nor to reflect comparatively on the Chinese and Latina participants' experiences. The larger ethnographic project of which this research is a part was based in the *Mujeres Unidas y Activas* organization (1996–1999). It was in the context of sustained relationships with and accountability to that organization that I developed my methods, priorities, and conclusions. A very rich analysis could result from a very different kind of comparative consideration of both groups of women's narratives, as well as from considering the Chinese participants' stories on their own terms.

3. The organization now also has a staffed office and women's group in Oakland's Fruitvale neighborhood.

4. The CPA later drew on the model of these workshops to develop a community leadership program for immigrant Chinese and Latino youth jointly organized with People Organizing to Demand Environmental and Economic Rights (PODER). The Common Roots youth leadership program is now in its sixth year (Gordon Mar, CPA executive director, personal communication, January 26, 2004).

5. Inda (2002) has analyzed the particular significance of Mexican immigrant women and their reproductive health in the xenophobic discourse of this period in California.

6. The sponsor of Proposition 209, University of California regent Ward Connerly, sponsored yet another initiative campaign in 2003, "The Racial Privacy Initiative," to eliminate all governmental data collection or monitoring based on race.

7. "Es una guerra psicológica en contra de los inmigrantes."

8. Since California's initiative passed, similar Unz-initiatives have passed in Arizona and Massachusetts, and one was defeated in Colorado.

9. All participants are referred to here by pseudonyms, but the organizations are referred to by their actual names.

10. All interview quotes are translated from the original transcriptions in Spanish.

11. See also Andreas, 1985; Alvarez, 1990; Massolo, 1991; Jelin, 1997.

12. "Chilangos son así." (Chilangos are people from Mexico City).

ACKNOWLEDGMENTS

I particularly thank Suzanne Oboler, participants in the 2003 Conference on Latino/a Citizenships at the University of Illinois, Chicago, and the anonymous reviewers of *Latino Studies* for their engaged and constructive comments on previous drafts. Kia Caldwell, Tracy Fisher, Renya Ramirez and Lok Siu (a.k.a. the Gender and Cultural Citizenship Working Group), Ann Holder, and David Sweet offered careful editing and nurturing critiques. My deepest gratitude is to the members of *Mujeres Unidas y Activas* and the Chinese Progressive Association.

REFERENCES

Alvarez, Sonia. 1990. Engendering Democracy *in Brazil: Women's Movements in Transitional Politics.* Princeton, NJ: Princeton University Press.

Andrade, Juan. 1998. Press Release from United States Hispanic Leadership Institute, Washington, DC, October 1. In Davis (2000).

Andreas, Carol. 1985. *Why Women Rebel: The Rise of Popular Feminism in Peru.* Westport, CT: Lawrence Hill.

Barbalet, J. M. 1988. *Citizenship: Rights, Struggle and Class Inequality.* Minneapolis: University of Minnesota Press.

Bell, David, and Jon Binnie. 2000. *The Sexual Citizen: Queer Politics and Beyond.* Cambridge, UK: Polity Press.

Benmayor, Rina, Rosa M. Torruellas, and Ana L. Juarbe. 1992. *Responses to Poverty among Puerto Rican Women: Identity, Community, and Cultural Citizenship.* New York: Centro de Estudios Puertorriqueños, Hunter College.

Berlant, Lauren. 1997. *The Queen of America Goes to Washington City: Essays on Sex and Citizenship.* Durham, NC: Duke University Press.

Bhabha, Jacqueline. 1998. "Get Back to Where You Once Belonged": Identity, Citizenship, and Exclusion in Europe. *Human Rights Quarterly* 20: 592–627.

Brubaker, William Rogers, ed. 1989. *Immigration and the Politics of Citizenship in Europe and the United States.* Lanham, MD: University Press of America.

Clarke, Paul Barry. 1996. *Deep Citizenship.* London: Pluto Press.

Dagnino, Evelina. 1994. On Becoming a Citizen: The Story of Dona Marlene. In *Migration and Identity*, ed. Rina Benmayor and Andor Skotnes, Vol. 3, 69–84. Oxford: Oxford University Press.

Davis, Mike. 2000. *Magical Urbanism: Latinos Reinvent the U.S. Big City.* London: Verso Press.

De Genova, Nicholas, and Ana Yolanda Ramos-Zayas, ed. 2003. *Latino Crossings: Racialization and Citizenship Between Mexicans and Puerto Ricans in Chicago.* New York: Routledge.

Díaz-Barriga, Miguel. 1996. Necesidad: Notes on the Discourses of Urban Politics in the Ajusco Foothills of Mexico City. *American Ethnologist* 23: 291–310.

Díaz-Barriga, Miguel. 2000. The Domestic/Public in Mexico City: Notes on Theory, Social Movements, and the Essentializations of Everyday Life. In *Gender Matters: Rereading Michelle Z. Rosaldo*, ed. Bill Maurer and Alejandro Lugo, 116–142. Ann Arbor: University of Michigan Press.

Flores, William, and Rina Benmayor. 1997. *Latino Cultural Citizenship*. Boston, MA: Beacon.

Goldring, Luin. 2001. The Gender and Geography of Citizenship in Mexico–US Transnational Spaces. *Identities* 7: 501–537.

Hall, Stuart, and David Held. 1990. Citizens and Citizenship. In *New Times: The Changing Face of Politics in the 1990s*, ed. Stuart Hall and Martin Jacque, 172–188. New York: Verso.

Hayes, Linda B. 1994. Letter to the Editor: California's Prop. 187. *New York Times*, October 15, A18.

Herrell, Richard K. 1996. Sin, Sickness, Crime: Queer Desire and the American State. *Identities: Global Studies in Culture and Power* 2: 273–300.

Inda, Jonathan Xavier. 2002. Biopower, Reproduction, and the Migrant Woman's Body. In *Decolonial Voices: Chicana and Chicano Cultural Studies*, ed. Arturo Aldama and Naomi Quiñones, 98–112. Bloomington: Indiana University Press.

Jelin, Elizabeth. 1997. Engendering Human Rights. In *Gender Politics in Latin America: Debates in Theory and Practice*, ed. Elizabeth Dore, 65–83. New York: Monthly Review Press.

Kymlicka, Will. 2001. *Politics in the Vernacular: Nationalism, Multiculturalism and Citizenship*. Oxford: Oxford University Press.

Lister, Ruth. 1997. Citizenship: Towards a Feminist Synthesis. *Feminist Review* 57: 28–48.

Lowe, Lisa. 1996. *Immigrant Acts*. Durham, NC: Duke University Press.

Marshall, T. H. 1950. Citizenship and Social Class. Cambridge: Cambridge University Press.

———. 1964. *Class, Citizenship and Social Development*. Westport, CT: Greenwood Press.

Massolo, Alejandra. 1991. *Por Amor y Coraje: Mujeres en movimientos urbanos de la ciudad de México*. Programa Interdisciplinario de Estudios de la Mujer, Universidad Nacional Autónoma de México.

Moore, Lisa. 1995. Gender, Immigration, and Political Participation: A Study of Community Involvement among Guatemalan Immigrant Women in Rhode Island. Undergraduate Honors Thesis in Women's Studies, Brown University.

Mouffe, Chantal. 1992. Feminism, Citizenship, and Radical Democratic Politics. In *Feminists Theorize the Political*, ed. Judith Butler and Joan W. Scott, 369–384. New York: Routledge.

Ong, Aihwa. 1996. Cultural Citizenship as Subject-Making. *Current Anthropology* 37: 737–762.

Orloff, Ann Shola. 1993. Gender and the Social Rights of Citizenship: The Comparative Analysis of Gender Relations and Welfare States. *American Sociological Review* 58: 303–328.

———. 1996. Gender in the Welfare State, *Annual Review of Sociology* 22: 51–78.

Pateman, Carole. 1989. *The Disorder of Women, Democracy, Feminism and Political Theory.* Stanford, CA: Stanford University Press.

Pratt, Mary Louise. 1993. Criticism in the Contact Zone: Decentering Community and Nation. In *Critical Theory, Cultural Politics and Latin American Narrative,* ed. Steven M. Bell, Albert LeMay, and Leonard Orr. Notre Dame, IN: University of Notre Dame Press.

Rosaldo, Renato. 1994. Cultural Citizenship in San José, California. POLAR 17: 57–63.

———. 1996. Foreword. *The Stanford Law Review* 48: 1037–1046.

Shklar, Judith. 1991. *American Citizenship: The Quest for Inclusion.* Cambridge, MA: Harvard University Press.

Somers, Margaret R. 1993. Citizenship and the Place of the Public Sphere: Law, Community, and Political Culture in the Transition to Democracy. *American Sociological Review* 58: 587–620.

Soysal, Yasemin Nuhoglu. 1994. *The Limits of Citizenship: Migrants and Postnational Membership in Europe.* Chicago, IL: University of Chicago Press.

Taylor, David. 1989. Citizenship and Social Power. *Critical Social Policy* 26: 19–31.

Turner, Bryan S. 1990. Outline of a Theory of Citizenship. *Sociology* 24: 189–217.

———. 1993. Contemporary Problems in the Theory of Citizenship. In *Citizenship and Social Theory,* ed. B. S. Turner, 1–18. London: Sage.

Walby, Sylvia. 1994. Is Citizenship Gendered? *Sociology* 28: 379–395.

Young, Iris Marion. 1990. *Justice and the Politics of Difference.* Princeton, NJ: Princeton University Press.

Yuval-Davis, Nira. 1999. The "Multi Layered Citizen": Citizenship in the Age of Globalization. *International Feminist Journal of Politics* 1: 119–136.

Yuval-Davis, Nira, and Floya Anthias, eds. 1969. Introduction to *Woman-Nation-State,* 6–11. London: Macmillan.

CHAPTER 9

"Getting out the Vote" in Los Angeles: The Mobilization of Undocumented Migrants in Electoral Politics

Monica W Varsanyi

The vast majority of us here are not documented, but once you're here, you're part of the community, you're working, you pay taxes, so you should have the ability to voice opinions, to put your candidates in . . ."

—*Blanca, undocumented resident of Los Angeles and "Get Out the Vote" drive volunteer*[1]

INTRODUCTION

This chapter illuminates a paradox in the contemporary political mobilization of new Americans. On the one hand, as in the past, organizations such as labor unions are taking an increasingly active role in the successful mobilization of foreign-born residents in formal campaign politics (see, e.g., Wong, 2001). As a result, many immigrants are becoming "active citizens" and making their voices heard in electoral politics. Immigrant participation in electoral politics is not a new phenomenon, per se: political parties and (more infamously) political machines are well known to have employed various tactics to get immigrants to the ballot box in, for instance, Chicago, New York, and Boston during the last "great wave" of immigration (Allswang, 1986; Erie, 1988; Sterne, 2001). While some claim that the era of machine politics and union political mobilization is over and that the contemporary "dearth of mobilization in immigrant ethnic communities has been well documented" (DeSipio, 2001: 90), this chapter demonstrates that a number of progressive labor unions are again coming to terms with both the growing immigrant workforce and the need to organize these new workers.

As Jamin Raskin (1993b) has compellingly written:

> We do not think of aliens, legal or illegal, as being 'disenfranchised,' because we assume that voting must be based on nation-state citizenship. We do not even think of aliens having politics. They are here mainly for their physical survival and our convenience: to work as janitors, domestics, nannies and drivers. They are here to scrape by, not govern. They inhabit Aristotle's realm of private necessity rather than the space of public deliberation. We don't pause to question the prevailing exclusion of aliens; they are meant to be ruled, not to share in ruling.

On the contrary, early work on this subject, most specifically Stephen Castles and Godula Kosack's book *Immigrant Workers and Class Structure in Western Europe* (1973) demonstrated that noncitizens— such as guest workers—were quite politically engaged. In the absence of the ability to vote and influence the political process directly, they utilized alternative pathways to political power, in this case, labor unions. As this chapter will demonstrate, it is not only legal residents or guest workers who find alternative routes to political participation. Indeed, with mobilization and organization, even undocumented migrants— who are otherwise radically excluded from American political life—are interested, able, and willing to participate in electoral politics.

On the other hand, however, while an increasing number of undocumented immigrants and residents are being politically mobilized, their legal status presents a serious challenge. While many are becoming involved in grassroots campaign politics, they will never be able to cast votes in formal elections.[2] At the same time as economic liberalization has created the conditions for substantial undocumented immigration flows between (for example) Mexico and the US, there has not been a concurrent liberalization of political structures that would incorporate undocumented immigrants into the polity. As Saskia Sassen writes:

> The production of new forms of legality and of a new transnationalized legal regime privilege the reconstitution of capital as an internationalized actor and the denationalized spaces necessary for its operation. At the same time there are no new legal forms and regimes to encompass another crucial element of this transnationalization . . .: the transnationalization of labor. (1996: 216)

The undocumented migration of low-wage workers and families across national borders has become a prominent characteristic of globalization over the past several decades. Their number is, by the nature of their legal status and official invisibility, difficult to estimate. However, several estimates based on Immigration and Naturalization Service (INS) and US census statistics have been attempted. By one estimate, there were approximately 3 million undocumented persons residing in the US in 1994. By 2000, this number had grown to approximately 7 million, an estimated 69% of whom are from Mexico (INS, 2003). As these numbers do not take into account the fact that undocumented migrants are often under- or miscounted in the US census, it is more likely that the actual number of undocumented people in the US is greater than 7 million, with a recent study led by the prominent demographer Frank Bean, estimating a high of 9.9 million in mid-2002 (Bean *et al.*, 2002; see also Lowell and Suro, 2002).

While there is much discussion in the popular press regarding the need to "fix the illegal immigrant problem" and, particularly in the post-9/11 era, to better fortify the borders against unauthorized crossings, I would argue that the unauthorized migration of a low-wage labor force is tacitly permitted and encouraged in the US (see also Nevins, 2002; Massey *et al.*, 2003). Rather than being an aberration, undocumented migration can be more accurately understood as a key feature of the increasingly fine-tuned logic of late capitalism. Indeed, migrant labor has always played a key role in capital accumulation in the US, but the increasing criminalization of unauthorized migration over the past decades creates an increasingly marginalized, disenfranchised, and exploitable labor force that is, in turn, a great benefit to capital.

What is developing in the US, therefore, is a two-tier membership regime, with citizen increasingly becoming an elite "insider" status, and noncitizen, most particularly in the case of undocumented residents, becoming the status of this exploitable, racially othered, and disenfranchised working class.[3] As William Rogers Brubaker has written, "The exclusion . . . of immigrants from formal citizenship leaves a significant fraction of the population, and a much higher fraction of the manual working class, without electoral voice; and the interests of disenfranchised groups do not count for much in the democratic political process" (1989a: 146). This constitutes a growing political crisis, or in the words of Joaquin Avila, former president and general counsel of the Mexican American Legal Defense and Educational Fund (MALDEF), an emerging "political apartheid" (2003). Twenty years ago, the political philosopher Michael Walzer contemplated the shifting migrant landscape in various European liberal democracies. To fill critical labor shortages, a number of nation-states began to import guest workers, who then lived for generations as a permanently disenfranchised, noncitizen working class in their host countries (the most prominent example was of Turkish guest workers in Germany). Walzer ultimately concluded that permitting permanent second-class membership was unjust: "Democratic citizens . . . have a choice: if they want to bring in new workers, they must be prepared to enlargé their own membership; if they are unwilling to accept new members, they must find ways within the limits of the domestic labor market to get socially necessary work done. And those are their only choices" (1983: 61). Undocumented migration to the US offers a parallel example. Welcome as labor, but unwelcome in other respects, the long-term presence of undocumented residents in the population presents a serious challenge to notions of popular sovereignty and democracy. As I discuss below, undocumented residents are subject to the laws of their communities and are impacted by the outcome of electoral contests, yet are unable to influence the constitution of these laws directly. As Walzer argues, if democracy in a liberal democratic state is restricted to a privileged class of citizens, then democracy cannot exist.[4]

In this chapter, I explore a case study that illustrates this paradox of contemporary immigration and immigrant political mobilization.[5] I first discuss the roots of this contemporary mobilization, specifically within the labor movement in Los Angeles. Los Angeles is an ideal city in which to explore the connection between noncitizen political participation and labor unions as it has evolved from being a longtime bastion of anti-union politics into being a prominent node in innovative, organized labor strategy and policy in the last decade (Milkman, 2000a). Furthermore, the greatest absolute number of undocumented migrants live in large cities such as Los Angeles and New York, making them focal points of immigrant disenfranchisement. According to 1990 census data on citizenship status, for instance, while on average 5.4% of US residents were noncitizens, 26% of adults in Los Angeles County were not citizens. In the two congressional districts, the 30th and 33rd, representing Latino neighborhoods in East Los Angeles during the 1990s, the adult populations were 53.5% and 58.6% noncitizen, respectively (Varsanyi, 2001, 2004).

Following an exploration of the roots of political mobilization, I detail several means by which noncitizens actively participate in campaign politics despite their inability to vote in elections. I conclude with some reflections on this current paradox. Robert Reich, former US secretary of labor, recently commented, "As California goes, so goes the nation" (2003). As undocumented migrants increasingly settle in "non-traditional" locations such as Dodge City, Kansas; Raleigh, North Carolina; and Atlanta, Georgia, the experience of Los Angeles will prove instructive.

THE ROOTS OF CONTEMPORARY NONCITIZEN POLITICAL MOBILIZATION

What are the roots of this novel and powerful form of political participation, one that was previously not available to noncitizens, especially undocumented residents, but has emerged in Los Angeles, particularly since the mid-1990s? How is it that thousands of noncitizen immigrants have become active in campaign politics over the past decade? There have been three main processes underlying this political mobilization: the political mobilization of Latinos, broadly speaking; labor's dramatic shift toward organizing the low-wage immigrant workforce; and labor's shifting political strategy over the past decade. These processes originated at the local and state scales, but have since been instrumental in influencing politics and policy shifts at the national scale.

A. The Emerging Latino Electorate

As evidenced by the sheer quantity of current news stories following politicians and their quest for the "Latino vote," Latinos have emerged, in the last decade, as an increasingly active and sought-after constituency across multiple political scales in the US.[6] In 2000, 5.8% of registered adults in the US were of Hispanic origin (US Census Bureau, 2002a), as compared with 4.6% in 1994 (US Census Bureau, 1996). This trend has been magnified in California: while Latinos constituted only 5% of the state electorate in the early 1990s (Block, 2002), they are now approximately 15–17% of the state's registered voters (US Census Bureau, 2002b and Gold, 2001, respectively). Furthermore, in urban areas with large Latino populations, such as Los Angeles, while 10% of the Latino population voted in the 1994 mayoral election, 22% voted in the 2001 election (Meyerson, 2001a).[7]

These rising rates of Latino political participation have been the result of several factors. On the national scale, Congress passed the Immigration Reform and Control Act (IRCA) in 1986, which offered amnesty to approximately 3 million undocumented residents, and by 1993, they were eligible for naturalization and registering to vote. In 1996, the passage of welfare reform legislation and Antiterrorism and Effective Death Penalty Act (AEDPA) provided further incentive for eligible legal residents to naturalize. The former excluded legal immigrants from eligibility for means-tested government benefits, such as food stamps and welfare assistance, and the latter specified that legal residents who committed crimes would be eligible for deportation and permanently barred from returning to the US.

Latino mobilization at the national scale was prompted and mirrored by mobilization at the state scale. During the mid- to late 1990s, a number of controversial ballot initiatives in California were instrumental in politically mobilizing Latinos in the state. Proposition 187, which passed with 59% of the vote in the November 1994 election (though was later overturned in court), was designed to deny publicly funded social services to illegal immigrants (Gibbs and Bankhead, 2001). Latino voters did not uniformly oppose Proposition 187, but most did, and the anti-187 fight leading up to election day had the overall effect of mobilizing citizen, legal resident, and undocumented Latinos. A series of controversial propositions followed Proposition 187, all of which further mobilized Latinos across the state. The "California Civil Rights Initiative" (Proposition 209) passed with 55% of the vote in 1996. It eliminated affirmative action policies in public employment and contracting and in state university admissions and hiring. In 1998, the "English for the Children Initiative" (Proposition 227) was approved by 61% of the electorate and eliminated bilingual education in California public schools. And finally, in that same 1998 election, the "Paycheck Protection" measure (Proposition 226) was narrowly defeated with 53% of the vote. Had it passed, Proposition 226 would have required labor unions to receive annual approval from individual union members to use a portion of their dues for political purposes. The proposition's narrow defeat was attributed by many to a labor-led campaign (Bailey, 1998) heavily staffed with rank-and-file volunteers, citizen and noncitizen.

Latino voter participation and political mobilization has also increased in California and Los Angeles over the past 15 years as a cohort of dynamic Latina/os have been running for office on pro-labor, pro-immigrant platforms. Many of these politicians, including Antonio Villaraigosa (current Los Angeles City Council member, former Speaker of the California State Assembly), Gil Cedillo (current California State Senator, former State Assembly member), and Fabian Núñez (current Speaker of California State Assembly, former political director of the Los Angeles County Federation of Labor (the LA County Fed)), are sons and daughters of immigrants themselves, were originally politicized in the Chicano civil rights movement, and have also emerged out of positions in the local labor movement (Pulido, 2001, 2002).

B. *Labor's Shifting Stance toward Immigrant Workers*

As organized labor has been instrumental in the political mobilization of undocumented workers, another factor leading to their mobilization has been labor's dramatic turnaround in its stance toward immigrant workers. In the decades leading to this shift, organized labor was openly hostile to immigrant workers, particularly undocumented workers. As Ruth Milkman recounts, as recently as the early 1990s, the leadership of one of Los Angeles' most currently progressive locals, Hotel Employees & Restaurant Employees International Union (HERE) Local 11, spent millions of dollars in a lawsuit to *prevent* executive board minutes from being translated into Spanish, although a large majority of the local's membership was composed of Mexican and Central American immigrants (Milkman, 2000a). In another example, Cristina Vásquez, national vice president of the Union of Needletrades, Industrial and Textile Employees (UNITE!), remembers the anti-immigrant stance of the LA County Fed during the 1980s:

> One time, we brought a group of Latino workers to an LA County membership meeting. The union people there were asking very racist questions like, "Where's your green card?" "You're not supposed to be here." "You're working for lower wages." That was the kind of "support" that we used to get from the LA County Federation. (quoted in Milkman and Wong, 2000: 8)

Though both of these are egregious examples, they represent the general anti-immigrant atmosphere that was pervasive in the vast majority of labor unions until very recently (see also Nissen and Grenier, 2001).

In a shift that started in a number of progressive locals during the late 1980s and early 1990s, a number of up-and-coming organizers and union leaders in Los Angeles and other cities realized that without embracing immigrants, the future of the labor movement in low wage, service industries was doomed. In the past decade, therefore, these locals have shifted from a servicing to organizing model, dedicating up to half of their resources and staff toward organizing new workers and decreasing the amount of resources they use on servicing the contracts of existing union members. The vast majority of these newly organized workers, especially in private service-sector jobs, are immigrants—some citizen, but more often, legal and undocumented residents. In Los Angeles, despite the common conception that undocumented immigrants would be impossible to organize, locals in the service industries have been at the helm of prominent organizing victories among low-wage immigrant workers (Delgado, 1993, 2000; Savage, 1998; Milkman, 2000a, 2000b; Milkman and Wong, 2000). At the same time, women and people of color, such as Maria Elena Durazo (president of HERE Local 11 and general vice president of HERE International) and Miguel Contreras (executive secretary/treasurer of the LA County Fed), rapidly increased their influence in the leadership of Los Angeles labor.

In 1995 these shifts impacted the national scale. Former Service Employees International Union (SEIU) president John Sweeney was elected president of the international AFL-CIO on a pro-immigrant worker organizing platform. And in 2000, he announced a drastic turnaround of the AFL-CIO's former policies by calling for a general amnesty for undocumented immigrant workers and their families. As the executive board statement made clear, "Undocumented workers and their families make enormous contributions to their communities and workplaces and should be provided permanent legal status through a new amnesty program" (AFL-CIO, 2000).

This commitment was put to the test in a labor-union-sponsored and operated amnesty program called the "Freedom Ride" campaign. Modeled after similar efforts during the 1960s civil rights movement and drawing upon similar discourses, the Freedom Ride campaign included a postcard drive, asking supporters to sign a statement calling for amnesty and progress on the "road to citizenship" for undocumented workers and their families. The campaign culminated in September and October 2003 in another attempt to draw attention to the injustices of undocumented status: buses of undocumented migrant workers and legal-resident and citizen supporters left from a number of major cities around the country, stopped in Washington, DC to draw further attention to the cause, and finished their two-week journeys at a mass rally in Queens, New York—according to census data, the county with the most ethnically diverse (immigrant and native) population in the US.

C. Labor's Shifting Political Strategy

A final factor that has contributed to the trend toward immigrant political and campaign involvement has been labor's shifting political strategy. This refers to two primary changes.

First, there has been a movement in Los Angeles' progressive locals away from a servicing model toward an organizing model. In the past decade, locals such as HERE 11 and SEIU 1877 have shifted their strategy dramatically and dedicated up to 50% of their resources and staff toward organizing new workers, decreasing the amount of resources they use on servicing the contracts of existing union members. The vast majority of these newly organized workers, especially in private service-sector jobs, are immigrant—some citizen, but more often, legal and undocumented residents. This movement has been mirrored at the national level, as President Sweeney has urged other locals to pursue an organizing model and shift resources toward increasing membership numbers.

Second, there has been a shift in labor's political strategy away from indirect means (i.e., television advertising) to direct means that rely on grassroots, member-to-member, "pound-the-sidewalk" efforts—efforts that require a willing army of volunteers. While candidates and political parties also rely upon door-to-door grassroots campaigning, labor unions have been particularly successful with this campaign strategy for a variety of reasons. Unlike party or candidate-led campaigns, which need to create or partially rebuild their structure at election time, labor unions have a preexisting organic structure, from the local to national level, which facilitates the parallel coordination of political campaign work. Additionally, locals with democratic decision-making structures have a ready and willing army of volunteers to staff grassroots campaign efforts.

This shift in national-level strategy has dovetailed nicely with, and in many respects, has grown out of, emerging immigrant "get out the vote" (GOTV) efforts in Los Angeles, which have relied heavily upon the volunteer efforts of immigrant workers, many of them noncitizens. For example, with Miguel Contreras at the helm, from 1996 to 2000 the LA County Fed's grassroots endorsement and campaign assistance played a decisive role in campaigns for 9 of the 15 LA City Council districts, as well as in those for 24 Los Angeles area state legislative districts (Meyerson, 2003). This success rate has led Los Angeles political commentators to refer to the LA County Fed, and Los Angeles labor in general, as the "800 pound gorilla" of local politics (Milkman et al., 2001). As one of the most prominent of these commentators, Harold Meyerson, has written about Contreras specifically, "I can think of no one in city politics today—and I don't mean just in Los Angeles, I mean anywhere in the United States—who commands quite the network of dedicated precinct walkers, financial resources and skilled consultants that Contreras does, year in, year out" (2003).

While grassroots political campaigning emerged initially out of various progressive locals, the AFL-CIO quickly recognized the power of member-to-member persuasion. After the Republican-dominated

1996 election, the AFL-CIO shifted its political strategy away from television advertising and toward "pound-the-sidewalks" efforts, which proved highly successful in subsequent elections. In the 2000 elections, for instance, the turnout of union households was higher than for nonunion households for the first time in years. As a Democratic Party campaign organizer told me in reference to his participation in the Gore campaign, if it was economical and feasible to do so, he would have focused all his campaign resources on face-to-face contact (knocking on doors, etc.) rather than on phone calls or mailings.

NONCITIZEN POLITICAL MOBILIZATION

Enabled by these intertwining roots, undocumented residents in Los Angeles have become increasingly involved in electoral politics over the past decade. In this section, I discuss specific ways in which noncitizen residentsparticipate in politics: through their local's candidate endorsement process, by attending campaign rallies, and particularly, via participation in "get out the vote"(GOTV) drives.

A. Endorsements

Political participation begins with the endorsement process. The degree to which union locals are democratic in their decision-making processes is central in this issue. There is a spectrum across which locals operate in this regard: at one end of the spectrum are locals that make political endorsements in a top–down manner, without consulting the rank –and file; and at the other end of the spectrum are locals that heavily involve their membership in the endorsement process and whose endorsement represents, more or less, the choice of the rank –and file.

While there are many cases of the former in Los Angeles, there are also several prominent examples of the latter—locals whose membership is almost entirely composed of immigrants and whose endorsement processes are highly democratic, if not still highly complex and political. As one of my labor informants explained, the endorsement process in her local, currently identified as one of the most progressive, begins in town hall meetings, in which candidates speak and are directly questioned by the rank –and file. The rank –and file then vote on their preferred candidate, who is normally the candidate endorsed by the leadership of the local and who is forwarded to the LA County Fed as part of its broader endorsement process. While there certainly are instances in which the rank –and file's candidate does not end up being endorsed by the local or LA County Fed, more often than not, the direct will of the union's membership is expressed in the endorsement process in these immigrant-dominated, democratic unions.

B. Rallies

Undocumented immigrants and residents are also participating in campaign rallies in increasing numbers. Once a local or the LA County Fed has endorsed a candidate, this endorsement is usually accompanied by a promise of volunteers who will attend rallies, participate in GOTV drives, and so on. When a rally is scheduled, each of a participating local's field managers will be asked to bring a certain number of volunteers to the event, a process that practically guarantees a healthy turnout. During the 2001 mayoral election in Los Angeles, for instance, hundreds of supporters could be found to attend rallies and campaign stops at the last minute (Meyerson, 2001b).

Especially in democratic locals, volunteers who have participated in the endorsement of a candidate are usually pleased to attend a rally and support their candidate, even if they will not be able to vote for the candidate on election day. Eduardo, one of the undocumented workers I interviewed, spoke glowingly about his participation in union-sponsored rallies and repeated that "if someone needs us, we go."

During the 2001 mayoral campaign in Los Angeles, this devotion was enhanced by the immensely popular candidacy of Antonio Villaraigosa, who, while ultimately narrowly defeated, was poised to become the city's first Latino mayor since the mid-1800s. In an article in Los Angeles' progressive free weekly newspaper, the *LA Weekly*, Harold Meyerson recounts a Villaraigosa campaign bus tour through the city:

> Besides the crowd downtown and the 100-plus supporters who rode along in the buses, scores of Villaraigosa supporters turned out at each of the stops, despite the short notice and the fact that these were midday, midweek events . . . By the time the buses rolled into a South-Central park, the Hahn campaign was able to turn out a smattering of troops to show its flag . . .[8] A dozen or so Latino young men, who seemed to have been hired for the occasion a few minutes previous, also brandished Hahn placards. But when the buses rolled to a stop and Riordan and Villaraigosa debarked, to the chant of "An-To-Nee-Oh! An-To-Nee-Oh!" from Villaraigosa's cheering section, the young men—who'd apparently not been prepped that An-To-Nee-Oh himself would be among them—joined in the chant and rushed over to shake An-To-Nee-Oh's hand, the Hahn signs held discreetly behind their backs. (Meyerson, 2001b)

Interestingly, for Eduardo and others with whom I spoke, this devotion to a candidate was intertwined and often inseparable from devotion to one's local. While ineffective for many years, Eduardo's local had recently become highly proactive in the workers' struggles. A number of long-standing problems, most specifically a conflict between full-time and temporary/part-time employees, had been solved through union efforts, so he was very supportive of not only his local but of organized labor in general. Therefore, when the union called on workers to attend rallies and become involved in the mayoral campaign, just as he would march in solidarity with workers from other unions over workplace struggles, he felt the desire to march for the union's candidate, Villaraigosa, who came out of a labor background and was a strong union supporter.

C. *"Get Out the Vote" Drives*

The third means by which undocumented residents are becoming directly involved in campaigns and the democratic process is via GOTV drives, which include precinct walking (walking door-to-door and talking with residents about the issue at hand), phone banking, hanging campaign literature ("door hangers") on potential voters' doors, providing polling locations to registered voters, and urging voters of the importance of voting on election day.

I attended a typical GOTV drive during the November 2002 election cycle, coordinated by a political mobilization organization composed of volunteers drawn from various Los Angeles union locals and community groups. This shift was run out of an empty office building in Southeast Los Angeles, an area of Los Angeles with a Spanish-speaking majority and including the heavily noncitizen congressional districts referred to in the introduction of this chapter. As such, only a handful of participants were *not* Spanish speakers and the shift was run almost entirely in Spanish. This particular organization runs a highly sophisticated GOTV campaign, and the activity of the weekend prior to the election represented the culmination of, in the longer term, several years of energy and experience that had been maintained and perpetuated through each election cycle since the organization was created in the late 1990s, and in the shorter term, by three weeks of work by 40 full-time staffers.

The activities of the day commenced at nine in the morning with a rally to psych up the approximately 400 people who had shown up to participate in the drive. Among the speakers were well-known local Spanish-language television and radio personalities who worked up the crowd with rousing encouragements such as, "We're going to count!" "Hispanos together!" "Watch out, here we come!" and "Why are we here? To get out the vote . . . To help the community!"

After the rally, participants broke into the groups with whom they would be working for the day. As a participant later mentioned to me, the organization carefully matches potential voters with particular precinct walkers, as Armenian and African American GOTV participants, for instance, are matched with potential voters of their ethnic group, nationality, or language group. While this could be perceived as divisive, this participant felt that this was the right strategy as ultimately, all the minority groups were working together for a common cause.

In subgroups, participants were briefed on the issues they would be discussing with potential voters. In this particular GOTV drive, precinct walkers were concerned with three issues:first, Los Angeles County Measure B, which if failed, would close five local trauma centers and hospital emergency rooms; second, a controversial referendum on the secession of the San Fernando Valley from the city of Los Angeles; and third, as is always the case, the date, time, and location of each voter's polling place, to ensure that the voter would not miss the opportunity to vote. Before heading out to walk the precincts, members of the group participated in role plays that not only provided them with the necessary knowledge to discuss the upcoming election with voters, but gave them the confidence and information to handle uncomfortable situations (i.e., unreceptive v oters and slamming doors) and to stay safe (i.e., avoiding dogs).

Armed with this knowledge, training, and the time to report back for lunch (a meal provided by the organization), participants set off for their assigned areas in smaller groups and spent the rest of the morning and the hours following lunch locating the households specified on their precinct list, knocking on doors, talking with potential voters about the issues (sometimes briefly, but often in depth), and leaving door hangers for everyone on their list. Volunteers finished their day of work at around five in the evening.

Volunteers working phone banks participate in a similar process, only they reach potential voters via telephone. When reporting for a shift, a volunteer is given a place at a computer terminal and telephone from which to work. As one of my labor informants mentioned, telephone banks have evolved into a technologically sophisticated means of political outreach. She likened political phone banking to sophisticated telemarketing. Volunteers sit in front of a monitor, on which a name, telephone number, and script appear. When they finish one call, the next name pops up and the process

repeats. As my informant chuckled, "Instead of selling people subscriptions to a magazine, they're selling subscriptions to the democratic process!"

VOTING WITHOUT THE VOTE, AND STRETCHING THE
BOUNDARIES OF CITIZENSHIP

Many of the individuals with whom I spoke at GOTV drives—by my
research assistant's and my estimation 80% undocumented—expressed
the importance of getting the Latino community out to vote. For
these GOTV drive participants, the Latino community was unified by
its ethnicity and it was their job to encourage Latinos who could vote
to support the interests of a broader community, which included
undocumented and legal residents as well as naturalized and native-
born citizens. For instance, as one man said, "There are a lot of people who don't have papers, but everyone who can vote needs to get
out and support the community. Many more Latinos are citizens now,
but they don't get out and vote. They need to get out and vote!"

While the long-established Chicano community in Los Angeles is
not consistently a supporter of undocumented migrants' rights, the
GOTV volunteers appealed to a broader sense of ethnic community
and solidarity. Indeed, as has often been the case with ethnic labels,
"Latinos" are more of a construct of the dominant culture of and the
desire of politicians to appeal to a bloc of voters who in some cases,
share more similarities with other "ethnic" voting blocs than they do
with one another. Nonetheless, the disenfranchised volunteers needed to find a common ground with which to appeal to potential
Spanish-speaking voters. A GOTV drive participant said:

> It's important that we fight for our rights. There are a lot of people
> who don't have papers, and everyone who can vote needs to get out
> and support the community—people without papers need the trauma
> centers—that's often the only place they can go for medical care, so,
> the whole community needs to get together to pass it.

And while there are undeniably divisions between long-term citizens
and undocumented migrants in the "Latino community," many families are composed of persons with the full range of legal status, which
supports the appeal for a unified Latino community: "I'm doing this
because it's important for Latinos to get out and vote—to support the
community. My three sisters are citizens and they are really active and
vote. I'm not a citizen but it's important to get the community out."

The T-shirts and posters printed for this GOTV drive drew upon this reality of multiple-status families:

> Mi família vota: 100%
> My family votes: 100%
> Por la Amnistía, Por Derechos
> For Amnesty, For Full Rights

While the majority of GOTV volunteers were calling for solidarity within the Latino community, for others, their "community" was class-based, and they said that they were out in solidarity with other working people and the working poor across the city: "No matter where we're from, what part of LA, what union, we come together, we're united, and our unity will lead us to win."

Importantly, the discourse used by volunteers—Latino solidarity versus worker solidarity—shifted according to which GOTV drive they were a part of. For instance, during campaigns, OLAW simultaneously runs GOTV drives in various locations throughout Los Angeles. The drives staged in locations outside union halls are dominated by the discourse of Latino community, while the drives staged within union halls, particularly in the progressive and militant locals, are perhaps not surprisingly dominated by a discourse of class solidarity. While the drives operating out of empty office buildings are heavily attended by members of labor unions and their families, they are also attended, as I discussed above, by members of various community groups. For this reason, the rallying cry of these GOTV drives emerge more from their location in a predominantly Spanish-speaking area of Los Angeles. On the other hand, the drives operating from within union halls are imbued with past worker struggles: in the case of one drive, walls were painted with vivid murals depicting worker struggle and solidarity. The woman quoted directly above, for instance, had been part of the highly militant and successful "Justice for Janitors" campaign, and she brought her sense of solidarity, energy, and militancy to the GOTV drive as well.

This is not to claim that different GOTV drives focused on either Latinos or workers, to the exclusion of the other category. In reality, both discourses were present, sometimes in competing ways. When I asked two men why they had come to participate in a GOTV drive, the following conversation ensued:

> Miguel: "We're all a part of this community."
> Rafael: "Yes, we want to support Latino communities."

> Miguel: "No, it's not about race, its about the community of working poor—it's about workers. It doesn't matter where we're from—Guatemala, Costa Rica, Mexico—we're all here together struggling, fighting for our rights."

These GOTV drives also represent a success in the mobilization and fostering of active "citizenship" of an otherwise politically marginal and disenfranchised population of undocumented residents. These volunteers' noncitizen status did not dissuade them from *performing* as citizens would, just short of casting a ballot on election day—going door-to-door, and talking with members of their community about ballot measures, the merits of candidates, and the simple importance of casting a vote if one were able to do so.

Importantly, the volunteers believed in the power of the vote and that this was a power that should not be taken for granted. As one of my interviewees exclaimed, "We need to get the people who have the power to vote to use it!" In this sense, they were almost exemplary "citizens" and very much *unlike* many formal members of the electorate, who do not participate in elections on a regular basis. Part of these volunteers' experience, therefore, was also in training eligible voters—in this case, predominantly naturalized voters who came from Mexico, Central and South America—that voting *did* count in the US. In the training session prior to precinct walking, the following role play took place:

> Potential voter: "Why should I vote? They're just going to go and put in whoever they want."
> GOTV volunteer: "It's not like that! Votes count here in the US."

So in an interesting twist on "citizenship," undocumented residents are instructing registered voters on the value of their participation, the fact that their votes count, and ways in which to "change laws in our favor."[9]

Just as they are "selling subscriptions to the democratic process," I would also add that the GOTV volunteers themselves are "buying" subscriptions to the democratic process via their direct and active involvement in these campaign efforts. While they are not able to cast a ballot themselves, their mobilization has the potential to influence the voting behavior of many individuals. One of the labor organizers put it this way:

> If a rich woman from Beverly Hills votes on election day, but doesn't talk to anyone about her vote, then she's only voted once. When an immigrant get involved in GOTV drives, the idea is: "No, I can't vote, but I can bring 38 other folks on board for a certain candidate. I have persuasion." After all, it's not who can vote, it's who actually votes.

And of course, these campaign experiences extend beyond the GOTV drive, as workers go home and talk with other coworkers, friends, and family about the importance of voting or about the merits of a certain candidate, thus persuading more people to accept their views.

Finally, the inspiration to become involved in these efforts arose from a number of immediate concerns, and further highlighted the importance of election outcomes in the lives of these residents. Many of the GOTV volunteers felt very much a part of their communities, yet were frustrated by their disenfranchisement—for many, a long-term status. A volunteer who has lived in the US for nearly two decades without legal status told me in a moment of exasperation, "It's ridiculous that becoming a citizen in US is a problem. I've been here for seventeen years! This is my home. You need to make a difference where you live!" This sentiment was shared by a number of GOTV participants. Many felt that Los Angeles and the US were their home and that despite their undocumented status, they should be able to make their voices heard in the formal electoral realm. To repeat Blanca's words from the beginning of the chapter, "The vast majority of us here are not documented, but once you're here, you're part of the community, you're working, you pay taxes, so you should have the ability to voice opinions, to put your candidates in." In essence, these undocumented migrants were calling for a citizenship and suffrage based on *presence* and *residency*, as opposed to formal and explicit admission to the polity (Varsanyi, 2004).

For a number of the GOTV participants, the desire to participate also came from a sense of desperation. As with the regressive ballot measures that had swept through California elections in the 1990s, the outcome of the vote on Measure B was of great importance to the undocumented residents of the region. If the measure had failed, five of the region's hospital trauma centers and emergency rooms would have closed. As these emergency rooms are often the only access that these residents have to health care, the closing of these centers would have dealt a disastrous blow to health care access in their communities. In essence, as undocumented migrants had the most to lose in this particular battle—as one man said to me in hesitant English, "If we don't have trauma centers, then we don't have no place to go."— they were particularly inspired and somewhat desperate to convince eligible voters in their communities to vote for the bond measure. Thankfully, Measure B passed with 73% of the vote, and the trauma centers remained open.

CONCLUSIONS

The 2001 mayoral election in Los Angeles was an example of this trend of growing Latino, immigrant, and labor clout, and an example in which many noncitizens "voted without the vote." It also represents the current crisis of citizenship and disenfranchisement, in which many of the city's residents are *formally* unable to have their voice heard. Antonio Villaraigosa narrowly lost the election with 46.5% of total votes (Rainey and Krikorian, 2001). He was heavily supported by many of the Latino residents of the city—citizens, legal residents, and undocumented residents alike. Though not widely discussed after the election, had the legal resident and undocumented immigrant populations been able to vote, Villaraigosa would almost certainly have won, ushering in an interesting new chapter in big-city politics in the US.

On the other hand, however, the GOTV are highly successful from a voter-mobilization perspective. According to a union researcher with whom I spoke after the 2001 mayoral election, precincts that had been the focus of GOTV campaigns had the highest voter turnout in the city of Los Angeles, measured as a proportion of registered voters. This is even more remarkable because these precincts were in East Los Angeles, an unincorporated region of the city with a majority Latino population, low rates of citizenship, and traditionally low voter turnout.

It is important to note that the interests of progressive labor unions and immigrants are not always congruent. While a number of progressive locals in Los Angeles are actively committed to organizing immigrant workers and advocating for a general amnesty for undocumented residents, and the AFL-CIO now has an openly pro-immigrant, pro-amnesty platform, organized labor will generally commit resources only to those political projects that will have a direct positive effect on it. Perhaps this can be expected, given limited resources, but it presents a slightly different picture than the "pro-immigrant" platforms imply. One of the labor organizers I interviewed complained of this disjuncture. His local, one of the more progressive and openly pro-immigrant in Los Angeles, had been heavily involved in gubernatorial and mayoral campaigns, and drew heavily upon its immigrant rank –and file to staff grassroots campaign efforts, but did not contribute financial or volunteer resources to the fight against Proposition 227, the antibilingual education, or "English for the Children" measure, which undoubtedly had substantial effects on the families of its rank –and file.

Nonetheless, the factors I have discussed above have intertwined in a virtuous circle in one segment of the undocumented Latino population in Los Angeles to the benefit of labor unions, many Democratic candidates, and many immigrant workers and families. An increasing number of progressive Latino candidates have entered the public realm at a time when those who have been long disenchanted with the political process are starting to view electoral politics as a potential force for positive change in the city. The successful strategies employed in organizing and membership drives in progressive labor unions have been transferred to political campaign work. The LA County Fed has endorsed many of these progressive candidates, and in doing so, has committed a great deal of resources and volunteer time to their election efforts. In the vast majority of these races, pro-immigrant, pro-labor candidates have won, which has, in turn, boosted the clout of organized labor in the city and county and furthered immigrant-worker concerns and struggles in Los Angeles.

However, while joining GOTV drives and participating in campaign rallies are important acts of political belonging and validation for many disenfranchised individuals, they are far from full and formal citizenship and suffrage, which would provide a fully legitimate floor from which to voice concerns. Of course, while liberal democratic citizenship and the right to vote are problematic institutions, even for those who are citizens and have the franchise, the importance of being a formal citizen and having the vote should not be underestimated. As this chapter has demonstrated, election outcomes can have a serious material impact on the lives of undocumented residents. Furthermore, legal status permits a person to remain in the country without fear of deportation and act as an empowered agent in society; and, as political theorist Judith Shklar has written, at a very basic level, citizenship and suffrage confer social standing and a "minimum of social dignity" (1991: 3). To be a noncitizen in American society today, particularly one with dark skin, implies otherness, difference, deficiency, a transient or illegal status, and even the possibility of being mistaken for a "terrorist."

In this light, while the political mobilization that I have discussed in this chapter does not propel undocumented migrants to full, formal membership, it does represent a deeper desire of marginalized populations to be legitimate, valid members of their communities in the US and to find strength in their solidarity. In contrast to the common notion that undocumented migrants "live in the shadows," this political participation placed the undocumented migrants with whom I spoke squarely in public space and the public sphere. I have no doubt that there are undocumented individuals who do not feel comfortable or safe participating in such a public activity as a campaign rally or GOTV drive, but none of the individuals with whom I spoke ever expressed any fear of being apprehended by the INS. The simple act of taking up space in the public and the polity was, in and of itself, an act of legitimacy and belonging, and as such, an important step toward demanding recognition as full members in society.

Finally, this chapter focuses specifically on the paradox of the political mobilization of a permanently disenfranchised population. While the ability to vote is not the only pathway to political participation, it is an important one—one that has been the focus of struggles for marginalized groups throughout the history of the US (Williamson, 1960; Keyssar, 2000). In this chapter, I have intentionally discussed citizenship and suffrage as if they were the same institution; in other words, as if, as is commonly assumed, the right to vote is an exclusive right attached to citizenship. However, while citizenship is bestowed at the scale of the nation-state, suffrage is still constitutionally situated at the scale of the state and locality. From the founding of the US until the 1920s, noncitizen immigrants and residents were eligible to vote in local, state, and national elections in 22 states and territories (Rosberg, 1977; Raskin, 1993a, 1993b; Harper-Ho, 2000; Brozovich, 2002). Suffrage was detached from citizenship as many citizens (particularly, African Americans and women) were not permitted to vote, and those who were able to vote included both citizens and noncitizens (primarily white, property-owning men). Beginning in World War I and into the xenophobic 1920s, however, suffrage became de facto the exclusive right of citizens. However, de jure, noncitizen suffrage is still constitutional. Given this history, the continued legality of "alien suffrage," and the contemporary migratory context, a national movement has recently emerged that argues for the reestablishment of noncitizen suffrage in various states and localities (see Raskin, 1993b; Hayduk, 2004).

This movement for "alien suffrage" and the political mobilization of undocumented residents discussed in this chapter represent a growing dissatisfaction within these communities with remaining on the margins of formal politics, while, at the same time, being active and long-term participants in the economic, social, and cultural life of their city. I argue that such struggles over political belonging in Los Angeles portend future struggles over the meaning and constitution of membership and citizenship in a world increasingly open to economic flows, but restricting the free flow of people. Migration, particularly undocumented, has become a distinguishing characteristic of this period of globalization and economic integration, and with it, a democratic crisis has emerged. If this crisis is to be resolved in a just manner, the boundaries of suffrage and of citizenship will have to be redrawn again to include all those residents who have a stake in their communities.

Notes

1. Names and identifying information have been changed or suppressed to protect the anonymity of all interviewees. Additionally, all direct quotations from the fieldwork have been translated into English from Spanish.

2. In 2001, President Bush and Mexican president Vicente Fox met to discuss the possibility of an amnesty similar to the IRCA of 1986, but the events of 9/11 put these plans on hold. In January 2004, Bush proposed a guest-worker program for undocumented workers, but rather than providing these residents with an opportunity for permanent residency, this plan creates a three-year work permit (also limiting the right to unionize), after which these workers are supposed to return to Mexico, but more likely, would return to "illegal" status within the US. In effect, therefore, Bush's plan further institutionalizes and formalizes this marginalized and disenfranchised working class.

3. In this chapter, I address the citizen/noncitizen divide, though it is important, and perhaps obvious, to note that many full citizens are still disenfranchised or are unable to partake of their full citizenship rights in the US.

4. For further theoretical discussions regarding the challenges of migration to the liberal democratic nation-state, see Brubaker, 1989b; Hammar, 1990; Layton-Henry, 1990; Bauböck, 1994, 1998; Kofman, 1995, 2002; Rubio-Marín, 2000; Castles and Davidson, 2000; Joppke and Morawska, 2003; Varsanyi, 2004. Additionally, legal scholar Linda Bosniak has contributed significantly to the theoretical literature regarding undocumented migration and citizenship in the US context (1988, 1994, 2000).

5. The fieldwork discussed in this chapter was completed in Los Angeles between October 2001 and November 2002. Utilizing a qualitative methodology and snowball sampling, it consisted of open-ended interviews with labor researchers, organizers, and rank-and-file members of several progressive Los Angeles locals. In addition, I attended GOTV drives and talked with individuals participating in these drives. Working with undocumented individuals is sensitive given their potential vulnerability, so I was not comfortable asking people's legal status directly. As a proxy, my research assistant and I asked the following question: "Are you planning to vote on Election Day?" If people responded that they were not planning to vote, this was a fairly clear indication that they were, at the very least, noncitizens. Furthermore, on the basis of discussions my

research assistant and I had with GOTV volunteers (for example, with individuals who were frustrated that they could not become citizens, though they had lived in the US for many years), anecdotal evidence provided by union organizers (speculating, for instance, that a large percentage of their membership was undocumented), and the particular neighborhoods in which these GOTV drives were being held, we estimated that the majority of the participants in these GOTV drives were undocumented.

6. While popularly referred to as a singular voting bloc, the "Latino vote" actually encompasses a broad and complex range of political opinions, from, for example, longtime Republican Cuban American voters in Miami to recently minted Democratic Mexican American naturalized citizens in Los Angeles. For more on this political complexity, see Schmidt *et al.,* 2000 and De la Isla, 2003. For more on the problematic construction of a "Latino" identity, more generally speaking, see Oboler, 1995 and Davis, 2000.

7. For discussions regarding the contemporary naturalization, political incorporation, and voting habits of first-generation immigrants, generally speaking, see Bass and Casper, 1999; DeSipio, 2001; Gerstle and Mollenkopf, 2001; Ramakrishnan and Espenshade, 2001 and Fix *et al.,* 2003. Regarding the Latino electorate and Latino politics, more specifically, see De la Garza *et al.,* 1994; DeSipio, 1996; Yáñez-Chávez, 1996; Jones-Correa, 1998, 2001; García, 2003 and Escobar, 2004.

8. In the nonpartisan municipal elections of Los Angeles, Antonio Villaraigosa (a progressive Democrat with radical roots in the Chicano civil rights movement) was running against James Hahn, a centrist democrat and son of revered city councilman, Kenny Hahn.

9. As William Flores writes, "Being a citizen guarantees neither full membership in society nor equal rights" (1997: 255), hence for marginalized groups in society, developing alternative pathways to dignified membership is essential. A number of authors have described this process as "Latino (cultural) citizenship," or "a broad range of activities of everyday life through which Latinos and other groups claim space in society, define their communities, and claim rights." (Flores, 1997: 262). The case study presented in this chapter both adds nuance to and offers a critique of the concept as it celebrates alternative and *informal* pathways to belonging, while at the same time underscoring the importance of *formal* citizenship and suffrage. For more on Latino (cultural) citizenship, see Rosaldo and Flores, 1993; and Flores and Benmayor, 1997; Rocco, 1999, 2004; Flores, 2003.

ACKNOWLEDGMENTS

I offer many thanks to my informants, who found time in their busy schedules to speak with me, and to my research assistant,

Juan Contreras, who was of great help during the fieldwork. This research was supported by dissertation-year fellowships from the University of California Institute for Labor and Employment (UC ILE) and the UCLA Department of Geography. An earlier draft was presented at an ILE-sponsored conference in January 2002. I wish to thank those attending my conference session, Stephanie Arellano, Edna Bonacich, Michael Burawoy, and Hinda Seif, among others, for their comments. An earlier version of this chapter also appeared in *Antipode: A Radical Journal of Geography* with the title "The Paradox of Contemporary Immigrant Political Mobilization: Organized Labor, Undocumented Migrants, and Electoral Participation in Los Angeles" (2005, 37: 775–795), and I wish to thank Blackwell Publishers for extending the copyright permissions for this chapter. Finally, I would like to thank John Agnew, Nick Entrikin, Joshua Muldavin, Laura Pulido, and Ray Rocco for their helpful suggestions.

REFERENCES

AFL-CIO Executive Council. 2000. *Statement on Immigration*. New Orleans, LA. www.afl-cio.org.

Allswang, John M. 1986. *Bosses, Machines, and Urban Voters*. 2nd ed. Baltimore: Johns Hopkins University Press.

Avila, Joaquin. 2003. Political Apartheid in California: Consequences of Excluding a Growing Noncitizen Population. *Latino Policy & Issues Brief*, No. 9. Los Angeles: UCLA Chicano Studies Research Center.

Bailey, E. 1998. Labor Upset Prop. 226 by Focusing on Backers: Aggressive Telephone and Door-to-Door Push, Media Blitz Helped Undercut Support for Initiative. *Los Angeles Times*, Monday, June 8, A1.

Bass, Loretta E., and Lynne M. Casper. 1999. Are There Differences in Registration and Voting Behavior between Naturalized and Native-Born Americans? US Bureau of the Census Population Division Working Papers, Number 28. Washington, DC. www.census.gov/population/ www/ documentation/twps0028/ twps0028.html.

Bauböck, Rainer, ed. 1994. *From Aliens to Citizens: Redefining the Status of Immigrants in Europe*. Brookfield, MA: Avebury.

———. 1998. The Crossing and Blurring of Boundaries in International Migration. Challenges for Social and Political Theory. In *Blurred Boundaries: Migration, Ethnicity, Citizenship*, ed. Rainer Baubock and John Rundell, 17–52. Vienna: Ashgate.

Bean, Frank D., Jennifer Van Hook, and Karen Woodrow-Lafield. 2002. Estimates of Numbers of Unauthorized Migrants Residing in the United States: The Total, Mexican, and Non-Mexican Central American Unauthorized Populations in Mid-2002. Pew Hispanic Center, Washington DC.

Block, A. G. 2002. The Legacy of Proposition 187 Cuts Two Ways: Democrats Can't Count on the Fear Tactic Forever. *Los Angeles Times,* Sunday, April 7, M2.

Bosniak, Linda. 1988. Exclusion and Membership: The Dual Identity of the Undocumented Worker Under the United States Law. *Wisconsin Law Review* 955: 998–1006, 1019–1135.

———. 1994. Membership, Equality, and the Difference that Alienage Makes. *New York University Law Review* 69: 1047–1091.

———. 2000. Universal Citizenship and the Problem of Alienage. *Northwestern University Law Review* 94: 963–982.

Brozovich, Elise. 2002. Prospects for Democratic Change: Non-Citizen Suffrage in America. *Hamline Journal of Public Law and Policy* 23: 403–453.

Brubaker, William Rogers. 1989a. Membership without Citizenship: The Economic and Social Rights of Noncitizens. In *Immigration and the Politics of Citizenship in Europe and North America,* ed. William Rogers Brubaker, 145–162. New York: German Marshall Fund of the United States and the University Press of America.

———, ed. 1989b. *Immigration and the Politics of Citizenship in Europe and North America.* New York: German Marshall Fund of the United States and the University Press of America.

Castles, Stephen, and Alistair Davidson. 2000. *Citizenship and Migration: Globalization and the Politics of Belonging.* New York: Routledge.

Castles, Stephen, and Godula Kosack. 1973. *Immigrant Workers and Class Structure in Western Europe.* London: Oxford University Press.

Davis, Mike. 2000. *Magical Urbanism: Latinos Reinvent the US City.* London: Verso.

De la Garza, Rodolfo O., Martha Menchaca, and Louis DeSipio. 1994. *Barrio Ballots: Latino Politics in the 1990 Elections.* Boulder, CO: Westview Press.

De la Isla, José. 2003. *The Rise of Hispanic Political Power.* Los Angeles: Archer Books.

Delgado, Héctor L. 1993. *New Immigrants, Old Unions: Organizing Undocumented Workers in Los Angeles.* Philadelphia, PA: Temple University Press.

———. 2000. Immigrant Nation: Organizing America's Newest Workers. *New Labor Forum,* Fall/Winter: 29–39.

DeSipio, Louis. 1996. *Counting on the Latino Vote: Latinos as a New Electorate.* Charlottesville: University of Virginia Press.

DeSipio, Louis. 2001. Building America, One Person at a Time: Naturalization and Political Behavior of the Naturalized in Contemporary American Politics. In *E Pluribus Unum? Contemporary and Historical Perspectives on Immigrant Political Incorporation,* ed. Gary Gerstle and John Mollenkopf, 67–106. New York: Russell Sage Foundation.

Erie, Steven P. 1988. *Rainbow's End: Irish-Americans and the Dilemmas of Urban Machine Politics, 1840–1985.* Berkeley: University of California Press.

Escobar, Cristina. 2004. Dual Citizenship and Political Participation: Migrants in the Interplay of United States and Colombian Politics. *Latino Studies* 2: 45–69.

Fix, Michael E., Jeffrey S. Passel, and Kenneth Sucher. 2003. *Trends in Naturalization,* Brief No. 3. Washington, DC: Urban Institute.

Flores, William V. 1997. Citizens vs. Citizenry: Undocumented Immigrants and Latino Cultural Citizenship. In *Latino Cultural Citizenship: Claiming Identity, Space, and Rights,* ed. William V. Flores and Rina Benmayor, 255–277. Boston: Beacon Press.

———. 2003. New Citizens, New Rights: Undocumented Immigrants and Latino Cultural Citizenship. *Latin American Perspectives* 30: 87–100.

Flores, William V., and Rina Benmayor, ed. 1997. *Latino Cultural Citizenship: Claiming Identity, Space, and Rights.* Boston, MA: Beacon Press.

Garcia, John A. 2003. *Latino Politics in America: Community, Culture, and Interests.* New York: Rowman and Littlefield.

Gerstle, Gary, and John Mollenkopf, ed. 2001. *E Pluribus Unum? Contemporary and Historical Perspectives on Immigrant Political Incorporation.* New York: Russell Sage Foundation.

Gibbs, Jewelle Taylor, and Teiahsha Bankhead. 2001. *Preserving Privilege: California Politics, Propositions, and People of Color.* Westport, CT: Praeger.

Gold, Matea. 2001. Wooing Latinos Tough for the GOP. *Los Angeles Times,* Monday, December 31, B7.

Hammar, Tomas. 1990. *Democracy and the Nation-State: Aliens, Denizens, and Citizens in a World of International Migration.* Brookfield, MA: Avebury.

Harper-Ho, Virginia. 2000. Noncitizen Voting Rights: The History, the Law and Current Prospects for Change. *Law and Inequality Journal* 18: 271–322.

Hayduk, Ronald. 2004. Democracy for All: Restoring Immigrant Voting Rights in the US. *New Political Science* 26: 499–523.

Immigration and Naturalization Service. 2003. Estimates of the Unauthorized Immigrant Population Residing in the United States: 1990 to 2000. Washington, DC: Office of Policy and Planning.

Jones-Correa, Michael. 1998. *Between Two Nations: The Political Predicament of Latinos in New York City.* Ithaca, NY: Cornell University Press.

———. 2001. Institutional and Contextual Factors in Immigrant Naturalization and Voting. *Citizenship Studies* 5: 41–56.

Joppke, Christian, and Ewa Morawska, (ed.). 2003. *Toward Assimilation and Citizenship: Immigrants in Liberal Nation-States.* New York: Palgrave.

Keyssar, Alexander. 2000. *The Right to Vote: The Contested History of Democracy in the United States.* New York: Basic Books.

Kofman, Eleonore. 1995. Citizenship for Some but Not for Others: Spaces of Citizenship in Contemporary Europe. *Political Geography* 14: 121–137.

———. 2002. Contemporary European Migrations, Civic Stratification and Citizenship. *Political Geography* 21: 1035–1054.

Layton-Henry, Zig, ed. 1990. *The Political Rights of Migrant Workers in Western Europe.* London: Sage.

Lowell, B. Lindsay, and Roberto Suro. 2002. How Many Undocumented: The Numbers Behind the U.S.-Mexico Migration Talks. Washington DC: Pew Hispanic Center.

Massey, Douglas S., Jorge Durand, and Nolan J. Malone. 2003. *Beyond Smoke and Mirrors: Mexican Immigration in an Era of Economic Integration.* New York: Russell Sage Foundation.

Meyerson, Harold. 2001a. L.A. Story. *The American Prospect,* July 2–16.

———. 2001b. Hope and Fear: A Week in the Mayor's Race, with Just Two More to Go. *LA Weekly,* May 25–31.

———. 2003. The Godfather: Miguel Contreras and the New Los Angeles. *LA Weekly,* May 30–June 5.

Milkman, Ruth. 2000a. Immigrant Organizing and the New Labor Movement in Los Angeles. *Critical Sociology* 26: 59–81.

———, ed. 2000b. *Organizing Immigrants: The Challenge for Unions in Contemporary California.* Ithaca, NY: ILR Press/Cornell University Press.

Milkman, Ruth, and Kent Wong. 2000. *Voices from the Front Lines: Organizing Immigrant Workers in Los Angeles.* Los Angeles: UCLA Center for Labor Research and Education.

Milkman, Ruth, Kent Wong, and Joseph Schwartz. 2001. Organizing Immigrant Workers: Los Angeles and the Future of the U.S. Labor Movement. *Democratic Left,* Fall/Winter: 7–9, 14.

Nevins, Joseph. 2002. *Operation Gatekeeper: The Rise of the "Illegal Alien" and the Making of the US–Mexico Boundary.* New York: Routledge.

Nissen, Bruce, and Guillermo Grenier. 2001. Union Responses to Mass Immigration: The Case of Miami, USA. *Antipode* 33: 567–592.

Oboler, Suzanne. 1995. *Ethnic Labels, Latino Lives: Identity and the Politics of (Re)Presentation in the United States.* Minneapolis: University of Minnesota Press.

Pulido, Laura. 2001. Personal communication with author.

———. 2002. Race, Class, and Political Activism: Black, Chicana/o, and Japanese-American Leftists in Southern California, 1968–1978. *Antipode* 34: 762–788.

Rainey, J., and G. Krikorian. 2001. "The Mayor's Race: Hahn Won on His Appeal to Moderates, Conservatives." Los Angeles Times, Thursday, June 7, A1.

Ramakrishnan, S. Karthick, and Espenshade Thomas J. 2001. Immigrant Incorporation and Political Participation in the United States. *International Migration Review* 35: 870–910.

Raskin, Jamin B. 1993a. Legal Aliens, Local Citizens: The Historical, Constitutional and Theoretical Meanings of Alien Suffrage. *University of Pennsylvania Law Review* 141: 1391–1470.

———. 1993b. Time to Give Aliens the Vote (Again); Green-Card Power. *The Nation* 256: 433–436.

Reich, Robert. 2003. Back jacket quotation. In *The State of California Labor (2003)*, ed. Ruth Milkman, Christopher Erickson, Michael Reich, and Margaret Weir. Los Angeles: University of California Institute for Labor and Employment.

Rocco, Raymond. 1999. The Formation of Latino Citizenship in Southeast Los Angeles. *Citizenship Studies* 3: 253–266.

———. 2004. Transforming Citizenship: Membership, Strategies of Containment, and the Public Sphere in Latino Communities. *Latino Studies* 2: 4–25.

Rosaldo, Renato, and William V. Flores. 1993. *Identity, Conflict, and Evolving Latino Communities: Cultural Citizenship in San Jose, California*. Research Report No.G5-90-5. Washington, DC: National Institute for Dispute Resolution.

Rosberg, Gerald M. 1977. Aliens and Equal Protection: Why Not the Right to Vote? *Michigan Law Review* 75: 1092–1136.

Rubio Marín, Ruth. 2000. *Immigration as a Democratic Challenge: Citizenship and Inclusion in Germany and the United States*. Cambridge: Cambridge University Press.

Sassen, Saskia. 1996. Whose City Is It? Globalization and the Formation of New Claims. *Public Culture* 8: 205–223.

Savage, Lydia A. 1998. Geographies of Organizing: Justice for Janitors in Los Angeles. In *Organizing the Landscape: Geographical Perspectives on Labor Unionism*, ed. Andrew Herod, 225–252. Minneapolis: University of Minnesota Press.

Schmidt, Ronald, Edwina Barvosa-Carter, and Rodolfo D. Torres. 2000. Latina/o Identities: Social Diversity and U.S. Politics. *PS: Political Science and Politics* 33: 563–567.

Shklar, Judith N. 1991. *American Citizenship: The Quest for Inclusion*. Cambridge, MA: Harvard University Press.

Sterne, Evelyn Savidge. 2001. Beyond the Boss. Immigration and American Political Culture from 1880 to 1940. In *E Pluribus Unum? Contemporary and Historical Perspectives on Immigrant Political Incorporation*, ed. Gary Gerstle and John Mollenkopf, 33–66. New York: Russell Sage Foundation.

US Census Bureau. 1996. Table 1. Characteristics of the Voting-Age Population Reported Having Registered or Voted: November 1994. Washington, DC.

———. 2002a. Table 2. Reported Voting and Registration, by Race, Hispanic Origin, Sex, and Age, for the United States: November 2000. Washington, DC.

———. 2002b. Table 4a. Reported Voting and Registration of the Total Voting-Age Population, by Sex, Race, and Hispanic Origin, for States: November 2000. Washington, DC.

Varsanyi, Monica W. 2001. Undocumented Immigrants and the Challenge to Formal Citizenship in Los Angeles. Paper presented at the Annual Meeting of the Association of American Geographers, New York, February.

————. 2004. Stretching the Boundaries of Citizenship in the City: Undocumented Migrants and Political Mobilization in Los Angeles. PhD dissertation, UCLA.

Walzer, Michael. 1983. *Spheres of Justice: A Defense of Pluralism and Equality.* New York: Basic Books.

Williamson, Chilton. 1960. *American Suffrage from Property to Democracy 1760–1860.* Princeton, NJ: Princeton University Press.

Wong, Janelle Staci. 2001. The New Dynamics of Immigrants' Political Incorporation: A Multi-Method Study of Political Participation and Mobilization among Asian and Latino Immigrants in the United States. PhD dissertation, Yale University.

Yáñez-Chávez, Anibal, ed. 1996. *Latino Politics in California.* San Diego: Center for US-Mexican Studies and University of California, San Diego.

CHAPTER 10

"Wise up!" Undocumented Latino Youth, Mexican-American Legislators, and the Struggle for Higher Education Access

Hinda Seif

AN UNDOCUMENTED YOUTH AT THE STATE LEGISLATURE

At a rally in front of the California capitol building on Immigrant Lobby Day in May 2001, my eyes were drawn to a T-shirt with the message, "Education is a Human Right." David,[1] the skinny teenager who wore the shirt, had a moustache spare with youth, and his gelled hair stood up in pointed tufts. David told me that he had come from Los Angeles on a bus full of activists to lobby for Assembly Bill (AB) 540, authored by his assembly member, Marco Antonio Firebaugh. The T-shirt came from a youth conference with the same theme run by a community-based coalition that joins Latinos and African Americans to develop leaders in South Los Angeles.[2]

By waiving out-of-state tuition for California's undocumented youth, AB 540 would make their education more affordable, hence increasing their access to public colleges and universities.[3] As a member of multiple nongovernmental organizations (NGOs), David mobilizes persons across immigration status on a variety of issues, including access to education, in his community in Southeast LA. "Sadly enough some people would say, 'I can't do anything—I'm just illegal.' And it's like—I disagree totally with that. 'Cause I mean—you still live here. You still have rights. So you have a voice—make it heard!'" With his comfort in English and a style that demands attention, I assumed that he was a second-generation youth lobbying in solidarity with undocumented peers. It was only later, while visiting him in his neighborhood, that I learned of his undocumented status. David organized for the bill as a member of Get Smart!, a youth group affiliated with an NGO in Los Angeles.[4] Two months later, he returned to Sacramento to testify at a legislative hearing. In October, he was invited by Governor Gray Davis to witness the historic signing of AB 540 into law and had his photo taken with him.[5]

Following the 2001 passage of the first laws designed to increase college access for the undocumented in Texas and California, similar bills were introduced in traditional and emerging states of immigrant settlement across the US.[6] The effort has reached the federal level, where legislation moves through Congress to help undocumented youth of "good moral character" who graduate from the nation's high schools to attend college and obtain lawful US status. The DREAM (Development, Relief, and Education for Alien Minors) Act, first introduced in the US Senate in 2001 and most recently reintroduced in 2006, places undocumented youth squarely in tropes of immigrant opportunity and the American Dream that lie at the heart of US national identity.

The successful struggle for AB 540 challenges assumptions that legislators only serve citizen voters and that legislative activists are adult citizens. Members of California's Latino Legislative Caucus and their staff made it a priority to fight for increased access to public higher education for undocumented youth who are long-term residents of the state.[7] Undocumented teens such as David are engaged in legislative struggle through NGOs despite their extreme marginality in relation to the US nation-state. These political developments are rooted in changing Latino demographics and politics. This includes the personal histories of educational struggle of Latinos from working-class and poor backgrounds who have achieved positions in the legislature.[8] The struggle for AB 540 points to the significance of youth in 20th-century Latino politics despite the fact that many are ineligible to vote owing to age or immigration status. Since the late 1960s, the historical trajectory of Chicano educational struggle has increasingly incorporated undocumented Latino youth as a result of the growing settlement of undocumented Mexican and Central American immigrants and the reactive political organizing that constructs the undocumented as "illegal" in the educational system.[9] I argue that the educational sphere has emerged as an important site of political struggle over US institutional belonging for Latino youth over time and across immigration statuses.[10] AB 540's successful passage depended on both the advocacy of Latino legislative professionals from working-class and poor backgrounds who are first-generation college graduates and the active participation of undocumented Latino youth.

The Latino Century in Politics: A Qualitative Approach

The political activities of Latino youth and their influence on politics are difficult to study through the standard methods of political science. The dawn of the "Latino Century" in California has generated great interest in Latino politics, including Latino's voting patterns and political beliefs (Rodríguez, 2000; Baldassare, 2002). While two out of three Californians in 1980 were European American and less than one in five was Latino, by 2001, California was a "majority minority" state. One-third of all Californians were Latino, and Latinos represented the largest group under the age of 30 (Johnson, 2003). Latinos have also had a growing impact on state politics. Their electoral participation surged following the 1994 approval of Proposition 187, an anti immigrant voter referendum. During the 1990s, approximately 1 million of California's 1.1 million newly registered voters were Latino (Baldassare, 2002: 161).

Political science scholarship, including work that illuminates the above trends, largely analyzes adult political beliefs and behaviors through electoral polls, public opinion surveys, and election and registration data analyses (de la Garza and DeSipio, 1999). These methods reveal some differences in political beliefs between Latino and European American voters, including the former's greater trust in government and support for government spending (Baldassare, 2002). While most political polls have historically been conducted in English, there is increasing recognition of the need for multilingual polls to capture the nuances of contemporary political life in the US.[11]

Yet political participation of adult citizens has historically been only one facet of politics in Latino communities, with low voting rates and large proportions of noncitizens and minors. For example, the activities of minors like David, who are disenfranchised by age, race, class, or immigration status, are the least likely to be captured through quantitative methods. Yet compared with their parents, some Latino youth have achieved higher levels of formal education and literacy and are more inclined to participate in US politics. As US citizens or English speakers, children of immigrants are accustomed to serving as intermediaries and translators for adults in the English-speaking public sphere. Some use these skills to engage in political action.

Many minors do not share their parents' expectations of returning to a "home" in Latin America—all these youth may have is an American Dream. Moreover, since they are socially rooted in US communities, some undocumented youth may claim rights and a political voice. Since political power and gains stem from the interaction between constituents and elected officials, we also need to understand why and how legislators advocate for the needs of Latino youth, including the undocumented ones.

Qualitative and historical scholarship has contributed to a growing understanding of Latino political practices. Cultural citizenship studies elucidate ways that Latinos "struggle to build communities, claim social rights, and become recognized as active agents" in a country where even those who trace their families to the US over generations "feel rejected as full and equal citizens" (Flores and Benmayor, 1997: 2). Latino scholars have revealed the activism of youth (Muñoz, 1989) and women (Zavella, 1987; Pardo, 1998) and the "walls and mirrors" that reflect the political relationships between immigrant and US-born Latino communities (Gutiérrez, 1995). Others have documented organizing among noncitizens who are ineligible to vote (Delgado, 1993; Hagan, 1994; Coutin, 2000). While undocumented Latino immigrants have largely been depicted as leading "shadowed lives" out of fear of the US state (Chavez, 1992), the research cited above examines their strategies in relation to US labor and government politics.

Such examinations of nontraditional political activities and actors are critical to understanding Latino politics in an era of large-scale Latin American immigration, including the emergence of the educational rights of the undocumented Latino youth as an important political battle. Since the politics of the undocumented are controversial, I employ an ethnographic approach supplemented by semi-structured interviews to elucidate them. By following the struggle for AB 540 at both state legislative offices and at grassroots activist organizations including Get Smart!, I trace the circuits of power that link Latino legislators and legislative staff to grassroots organizers and undocumented youth.[12] I argue that this contemporary struggle is rooted in a history of Chicano educational activism in which numerous legislators and other legislative professionals participated during their youth. As a result of Latino demographic and political change since the 1960s, the fight by undocumented youth for their place in US schools has become a part of this trajectory of educational struggle. For Latinos from working-class backgrounds, educational struggle and achievement was a key avenue to positions of influence in California legislative politics. Similarly, it emerges today as an important route for the political engagement of undocumented Latino youth and their claims for inclusion in the US public sphere. Youth such as David assert a political voice with the support of Latino legislative professionals, who in turn rely on these courageous teens to humanize the plight of undocumented immigrants and challenge popular stereotypes of the "illegal alien." The presence of David and his peers at press conferences and legislative hearings and visits compels elected officials and voters to look these California students in the eye as they make important decisions about their educational access and futures.

LATINO LEGISLATIVE PROFESSIONALS: THREE PHASES OF HIGHER EDUCATION STRUGGLE

In 2000, the California Latino Legislative Caucus voted unanimously to endorse AB 540. Why would 22 legislators from diverse regions of California and political perspectives support one of the most politically marginalized groups in the state? This vote reflected a demographic reconfiguration of California's Latino population and a political mandate from Latino communities that organized at unprecedented levels to challenge the state's anti-immigrant politics of the 1990s. Their willingness to lead this uphill battle also reflected the personal histories of Latino legislative activists. The similarities between the class backgrounds and educational struggles of these professionals and Latino youth of today—including the undocumented—helped motivate the former to fight for AB 540, despite the tremendous barriers to advocating politically for persons who lack lawful US status.

As discussed below, Latino Caucus members, their staff, and other legislative professionals participated in at least three phases of education struggle. One group, now in their 40s and 50s, was part of the early Chicano youth movement and among the first to claim a significant presence at colleges during the 1970s. A younger cohort comprising members in their 30s fought to consolidate the earlier gains of students of color and to defend them against political and economic backlash during the 1980s. A third group of legislative staffers, campaign workers, and lobbyists, now in their 20s, comprised people who as students during the 1990s had fought to retain a variety of programs that aided Latino citizen and immigrant students. Higher education has provided these Latino professionals with access to political power; today, as adults, they work at the capitol to provide similar opportunities to a new generation of Latino youth. As Gil Ojeda of the California Program on Access to Care observed, "In many cases, Latino legislators were the first of their families to become educated and move into power positions in society. . . So many say that public service comes easy to these politicians, because they remember" (Interview, February 5, 2001).

THE BLOWOUTS: THE CHICANO YOUTH MOVEMENT

Assembly Member Simón Salinas is one of the caucus members who voted for AB 540. His district, which includes the Salinas Valley and Watsonville, has a large Mexican farmworker population and is called "America's Salad Bowl" because of its huge and diverse fresh produce industry. During his childhood, Salinas was one of 12 children of Mexican-born farmworkers who migrated annually between Texas and California. He described the educational conditions of the 1960s that inspired him to become a bilingual education teacher and to run for public office as follows:

> Sometimes we'd go places for three weeks, and it wasn't even worth enrolling in school because we'd leave right away. In Texas, they didn't have any programs like bilingual ed.—it was either sink or swim. So a lot of the kids would drop out after fifth or sixth grade . . . If you spoke Spanish you would get punished. They would spank you . . . They didn't seem to mind if the child labor laws were broken. When the inspectors came . . . we could just go and hide . . .. There were children who were 14 . . . years old who were working full-time . . . With no insurance—no glasses, speaking Spanish—you would feel like an outsider. The odds were stacked against a lot of those kids—they weren't going to make it . . .. My father somehow managed to get clothes together for us. But other kids didn't have clothing, or their *tenis* [tennis shoes] were all torn—their sweaters were tattered. They were embarrassed . . .. And you're already so far behind your reading level . . .. They'd be in fifth or sixth grade. You *know* they didn't want to go to school. (Interview, August 24, 2001)

Salinas describes the destitute conditions and suppression of cultural heritage that migrant students faced in the public schools of South Texas. At the time, most migrant youth were constructed as "outsiders" in the social space of schools and relegated to a future of poverty. The fight for improved educational conditions and opportunities was central to the early Chicano movement in which the young Salinas participated. When students walked out of L.A. high schools in 1968, these "blowouts," which Carlos Muñoz Jr. called "the first loud cry for Chicano power and self-determination," spread to

10,000 students in 39 schools citywide (1989: 66). They reached schools in other states, including Texas.

Because he had migrated between two states, the young Salinas walked out of school in both Texas and Watsonville, California. The blowouts reflected growing resistance to the cultural, racial, and class subordination of students of Mexican ancestry. Recalling his reasons for joining the Texas protests, Simón Salinas explained: "We walked out of school because we said we wanted new policies. We wanted the history of the Mexican American taught in schools. We wanted more diversity in the faculty. We wanted the policy of getting punished for speaking Spanish terminated." The key role played by these junior high and high school students from working-class backgrounds challenges assumptions that student protests are led by affluent European American college students. Salinas explains that since people of Mexican ancestry were largely excluded from higher education until the late 1960s, high schools became key sites of educational resistance. "In high school you'd get . . . a critical mass . . . People to walk out . . . Parents to support them" (Interview, August 24, 2001).

With the expanding presence of Chicanos in higher education during the late 1960s, the secondary-school movements reached universities. In 1969, many student organizations, including MAYO (Mexican American Youth Organization), of which Salinas later became president at his Texas school, joined the umbrella network of El Movimiento Estudiantil Chicano de Aztlán (MEChA). While California's Latino elected officials have been politically targeted for their past MEChA membership, the organization provided a critical cultural environment for working-class Chicano students who sought to integrate higher education institutions (Sifuentes, 2003). MEChA continues to carve a space for Latino students, cultures, and histories in schools. As part of the Chicano movement, MEChA also encouraged students to take pride in their working-class, Mexican heritage; it contributed to a broader notion of community and increased solidarity with Mexican immigrants.

IMMIGRANT YOUTH AND EDUCATIONAL BELONGING THROUGH 1992

I come . . . to welcome you to your building, to your legislature . . . . Ten years ago when I first came to work in Sacramento . . . I was a recent graduate . . . a MEChista from Berkeley. . . I wanted to change the world. (California Immigrant Welfare Collaborative Training, March 6, 2001)

At a 2001 training workshop for immigrant advocates at the state legislature, the AB 540 author Assembly Member Firebaugh alluded to his prior participation in a second wave of educational activism in California as a member of MEChA.[13] The Tijuana-born student was one of many Chicanos who joined others across races to maintain and expand the foothold of working-class students and faculty of color in higher education. As an undergraduate at the University of California, Berkeley, during the 1980s, Firebaugh and other students took over the chancellor's office to demand greater opportunities for minorities (Rojas, 2002). His fight for racial diversity at Berkeley presaged his arrival at the capitol as an idealistic legislative staffer and creator of space for immigrants and their advocates at *their* legislature as an elected official. At the training, he discussed his working-class background and his road toward educational achievement and political power:

> I'm an immigrant from México and I came to the United States when I was four years old. I didn't speak a word of English. On the strength of a public school education, I get to make decisions that affect all of our lives. I'm tremendously proud of that. And I'm also grateful for the leadership of those who have come before me to give me the opportunity . . . I'm absolutely committed to making sure those opportunities are available to those who follow me . . . I went to high school and I wasn't a great student. I went to a community college and I was a better student. Then I went to Berkeley and graduated with honors—went to law school at UCLA. I'm a proud beneficiary of affirmative action . . . But as you know, those opportunities aren't there today in many ways. So that's going to be part of a fight. It's the same way with immigrant rights issues. There was a time . . . when . . . young people who graduated from high school could go to college in California . . . for modest . . . state tuition. That's not the case today. (California Immigrant Welfare Collaborative Training, March 6, 2001)

Firebaugh highlights the role of government programs in making higher education accessible for Latino youth such as himself and of public higher education itself as an avenue for Latino political power. He pays tribute to generations before him who fought for educational access, and he vows to restore educational opportunities for future generations of youth of color, including immigrants.

Firebaugh's personal history as a Mexican immigrant and his political engagement in struggles for the undocumented also suggest the changing demographics of the Latino population in California and the growing importance of immigrant youth in Latino educational struggle. Since the 1942 Bracero Program, Mexican migrant males have been constructed as lone, laboring arms detached from family and community (Flores, 2002).[14] Although the program was terminated in 1965, demand for low-paid immigrant labor has continued. Since the 1965 revision of US immigration laws that eased unification of family members from non–Western European countries, there has been an increase in documented and undocumented family immigration from Mexico and other parts of Latin America (Marcelli and Cornelius, 2001). This includes the settlement of immigrant youth.[15] Family settlement also accelerated after 3 million undocumented immigrants legalized their status through the Immigration Reform and Control Act (IRCA) of 1986. Enforcement of the US southern border intensified after IRCA was enacted, making unauthorized, circular labor migration increasingly hazardous and further stimulating settlement. Conditions in Mexico and Central America, including the impact of civil war, the North America Free Trade Agreement (NAFTA), and changing gender and family relations also accelerated the settlement rate. Both the educational spaces forged through struggle for US-born Latinos and the increasing presence of Latino immigrants in California public schools became the targets of political backlash.[16] These attacks were aimed at Latino youth across immigration statuses. Chicano educational activists increasingly expanded their struggle to include Latino immigrant students.

Undocumented Youth and Education

Since the 1970s, proponents of immigration restriction have attempted to use the unauthorized federal status of undocumented immigrants to deny their belonging at the state and local levels, where public schooling takes place. This lawful access to public education has been challenged at two levels: K (Kindergarten) to 12th grade and higher education. Since noncitizens have little power in the political arena, advocacy groups such as the Mexican American Legal Defense and Education Fund (MALDEF) responded initially by filing class action lawsuits. Judicial decisions have provided educational access that is subject to legal and political challenge; thus, until recently, California's undocumented students have relied upon a complex and often contradictory web of case law.

In 1975, the Texas legislature revised its laws to withhold state funds for the education of undocumented students from local school districts and authorized those districts to deny them school enrollment. When parents challenged the new law, the US Supreme Court fell short of declaring public education a fundamental right in its

Plyler v. Doe decision (*Plyler v. Doe,* 457 U.S. 202 [1982]: 80–1538). However, the Court denied states the ability to exclude undocumented minors from primary and secondary schools. In the Court's majority opinion, Justice William Brennan declared that "by denying these children a basic education, we deny them the ability to live within the structure of our civic institutions, and foreclose any realistic possibility that they will contribute in even the smallest way to the progress of our Nation" (*Plyler v. Doe,* 457 U.S. 202 [1982]). The Court found no compelling argument that the state would benefit in the long run by denying undocumented youth basic education and focused on their potential contributions to the nation-state as adults. Thus, it established a rudimentary form of social belonging for these minors.

While undocumented youth were granted lawful access to public K-12 education, this did not provide them with a route out of their parents' position as exploited laborers. Their legal fight to attend California's public colleges has largely revolved around the classification of state residency for purposes of calculating tuition and awarding state educational grants. Thus, it is a fight for financial access that lies at the intersection of immigration and class status. Furthermore, the decision to define those who grow up in California yet lack lawful immigration status as "residents" or "nonresidents" symbolically delimits the boundaries of the state by either incorporating or excluding these youth as Californians.

Until 1984, all who had lived in the state for over one year qualified to pay in-state fees at California's public universities.[17] That year, the chancellor of the California State University system declared undocumented students "nonresidents" of the state for tuition purposes. Guatemala-born Mario Muralles, who graduated from high school in the 1980s, describes the impact of this decision on students:

> Even before I was a senior, I knew that I was not going to college. . . . There's nobody holding you from going to college—admission is open. It's the nonresident fee that kills all of us immigrants. For me to ask my parents for $10,000 for one year . . . there was no way I could expect my parents to be able to afford me going to college. You don't know the kind of depression an undocumented senior goes. . . through. I know, and I lived it . . . Everybody saying . . . I'm gonna go to Cal State LA, or I'm going to go to East LA College. The only thing you can say is, I'm going nowhere. It's very depressing—very frustrating to not reach out for those things. Also, having counselors that didn't think I was college material . . . guiding me towards vocational . . . courses in high school . . . The path was already painted for me so I could not steer away from it. (Interview, June 28, 2001)

Like other motivated students, Muralles' vocational tracking as a working-class Latino combined with the financial inaccessibility of college made him despair. He also suggests that undocumented Latino youth have a different relationship to the public sphere than their parents do, although both live under the constant threat of deportation. Most undocumented working adults labor daily at one or more poorly paid jobs from which they are barred by federal immigration law yet obtain through the use of false papers or intermediary labor contractors. This primary relationship to the public sphere is constructed through illegality and subterfuge yet is necessary to support family in the US and abroad. Undocumented youth, on the other hand, interact primarily with public schools. While Latino and immigrant students have for the most part attended substandard schools, throughout most of California's history, their ability to attend public schools was not dependent on federal immigration status. Thus, undocumented youth have a direct, daily relationship with a government entity that is not structured as illegal. Many undocumented seniors used metaphors of closed doors and jail cells to describe their transition from their relatively protected status as 12 graders to a future of illegal, low-wage labor.

MALDEF filed a lawsuit on behalf of undocumented students (*Leticia A. v Board of Regents,* 588982-4: Superior Court, County of Alameda, May 7, 1985), and concerned educators and community activists founded the Leticia A. Network to support these California youth.[18] Muralles described his own early participation in the Leticia A. Network, when he attended press conferences and court hearings and observed the environment of fear that faced undocumented youth activists during the 1980s. However, the lawsuit could not move forward without the active participation of undocumented students as plaintiffs. They also needed to speak out to raise public awareness and support:

> One of the concerns of the network and we were all new to this—was really the protection of the students. We did not have politicians involved in our inception . . . I did a press conference with MALDEF, and my face was hidden from the camera because . . . we didn't want to hurt students. We wanted to help students. One of the last things the network wanted . . . was to have Immigration come knocking on our doors. (Interview, June 28, 2001)

While the courts ruled in favor of the students in 1985, this was appealed and overturned in 1991. Yet his activism later inspired Muralles to pursue Chicano Studies to further develop his political consciousness and pride as a Guatemalan American and Latino: "The issues that they were talking about were my issues."[19] After legalizing his status through IRCA, Muralles continued his political activity as Citizenship Director of the National Coalition of Latino Elected and Appointed Officials (NALEO).[20]

Richard Polanco, a young Chicano assembly member from Los Angeles and the leader of a small Latino caucus, shifted the struggle to the political arena in 1991.[21] Polanco introduced a bill (AB 592) to assist students who were at the mercy of conflicting court decisions. With the assistance of his young legislative aide, Marco Firebaugh, this bill restoring the definition of state residency to include California's undocumented students passed both legislative houses, only to be vetoed by Governor Pete Wilson. This early legislative failure reflected the extreme disenfranchisement of undocumented youth and the inability of a small but growing Latino caucus to overcome political opposition. However, Muralles sees the growing support of Latino elected officials and attorneys as providing a space for the increased political activism of undocumented students: "Now, you have Assembly Member Firebaugh and Senator Polanco. So . . . we have some political pull. . . . Strong friends make you a little bit braver." (Interview, June 28, 2001)

VOTING WITH THEIR FEET: PROPOSITION 187 AND ITS AFTERMATH

Governor Wilson also supported Proposition 187, a voter referendum that was placed on the 1994 California ballot. Although most of it was overturned by the courts in 1998, Proposition 187 represented a broad attack on California's immigrants. Its provisions included ending undocumented women's access to state-funded prenatal care and barring undocumented youth from all public education institutions. By requiring teachers and other state-funded professionals to report suspected "illegal aliens," Proposition 187 effectively aimed to transform them into extensions of immigration enforcement, with repercussions for all Latinos and persons of color perceived to be undocumented. Other controversial measures having an impact on the educational access of Latino youth across legal statuses soon followed. Proposition 209 (1996) prohibited affirmative action, restricting college access of Latino youth from low-performing schools with de facto segregation. Proposition 227 (1998) severely limited bilingual instruction for immigrant children, curtailing their ability to become bilingual and biliterate leaders in a global economy.

The three propositions had the effect of revitalizing Latino youth protest and educational organizing. After over 1,000 students walked out of Oakland schools in April 1993, mobilizations against Proposition 187 spread through the Bay Area and the state's agricultural center (Martínez, 1998). In 1994, approximately 15,000 students walked out of more than 40 junior high and high schools throughout Southern California (Kadetsky, 1994), recalling the blowouts that had occurred almost 25 years before. "Walkouts were so widespread that the L.A.P.D. [Los Angeles Police Department] was placed on tactical alert, and police in riot gear swarmed the streets in several neighborhoods and aimed pepper spray and stingball grenades at students on at least two campuses" (Kadetsky, 1994). Adalberto, whose family's status had been legalized through IRCA, described his participation in walkouts in Salinas:

> Propositions 187, 209, and 227 . . . really inspired me to get involved—education and immigrant policy for Latinos. I was in high school during Prop. 187. There was discussion and a lot of jokes around high school. People would say, "'You guys are going back to Mexico". There was so much passion involved—a sense of frustration and stabbing in the back. Because here are my parents working in the fields—picking the crops—and here's this legislation being written. Even though we weren't undocumented anymore, we felt threatened. So when I was sitting in a classroom and half is Caucasian and the other half is Mexican, if you don't walk out what are you doing in the classroom? You didn't even have to think twice.

Proposition 187 affected all Latino students in Adalberto's school, for regardless of their immigration status, some European American classmates told them that they would have to "go home." Adalberto affirms his solidarity with undocumented youth and claims space in California schools for the children of farmworkers who contribute to the state. Like the children of Simón Salinas' generation, the youth who voted with their feet in the 1994 walkouts, were not able to register a formal vote at the polls. All three propositions were approved by a majority European American electorate. Yet through the protests, many students were swept into political engagement. Six years later, for example, Adalberto became a naturalized citizen and registered to vote the very day he turned 21. Part of a third wave of Latino educational activists who engaged in California legislative politics, he enrolled in public college. After his assembly member voted against Firebaugh's bill to aid undocumented youth, Adalberto participated in the campaign to elect Simón Salinas to the state assembly.

Salinas brought his dedication to Latino immigrant students to the capitol as a member of the Assembly Education Committee.

As a result of these kinds of reactive mobilizations, California's Latino Legislative Caucus grew to 22 members. Marco Firebaugh, who, as mentioned earlier, had fought for immigrant access to higher education as one of Assembly Member Polanco's legislative staffers, has represented Assembly District 50 (AD 50) in Southeast Los Angeles since 1998. He quickly placed this issue at the center of his legislative platform. A look at demographic and political-economic restructuring in this district where David lives elucidates the significance of the issue to the Latino community both there and across the state.

REDEFINING CONSTITUENCY: SOUTHEAST LA IN 2000

In 2000, AD 50 was a mixed residential and industrial community that included the cities of Bell Gardens, Bell, Commerce, Cudahy, Huntington Park, Maywood, South Gate, and Vernon. This working-class region had ready freeway access to shipping at Long Beach Harbor. It bordered Latino East LA and African American South Central LA, and was largely racially segregated and dominated by European Americans through the 1960s. For example, the City Charter of South Gate confined its residents to Caucasians, and property deeds included race-restrictive covenants through the 1940s (Nicolaides, 2002). Most of its inhabitants had moved away in the 1970s and 1980s after the large unionized plants that dominated the area's economy, including Firestone and General Motors, relocated to the southern US and abroad, and residents of South Central LA demanded entrance into the region's schools (Nicolaides, 2002). From the 1980s, empty factory buildings were filled with a sweatshop economy of minimum wage needle trades, furniture makers, food distributors, and toxic waste disposal, all of which were largely fueled by Mexican immigrant labor.

Homes were rented and purchased by these workers, such that by 2000, the district was over 93% Latino (Institute of Governmental Studies Statewide Database, 2001). Seven to ten percent of its population was of Central American ancestry, with smaller numbers from South America, Cuba, and Puerto Rico (Thornton, 2003). AD 50 had the second-lowest number of registered voters of state assembly districts (Institute of Governmental Studies Statewide Database, 2000). In addition to facing formal disenfranchisement, many also faced educational and economic barriers to state-level political participation. In all, 57% of the population in David's hometown, Maywood, were US citizens, including minors; more than 57% of adults had been born abroad (US Census Bureau, 2002). Seventy-seven percent of the immigrants were noncitizens and thus unable to vote in US elections. Almost half of the adults in Maywood (over age 25) had less than a 9th grade education, and 70% did not have a high school diploma (US Census Bureau, 2002). Over 90% of the people who were over age 5 spoke a language other than English at home, and 60% spoke English less than "very well" (US Census Bureau, 2002). A large proportion of its citizens, English speakers, and high-school-educated residents—characteristics that facilitate legislative activism—were youth. The district had a history of undocumented high school valedictorians, and it was a source of community pain and debate to see its best students unable to attend college. Undocumented teens such as David and his peers, who participated in the struggle for AB 540 as members of Get Smart!, have the idealism and lack of resignation to a world that "sucks." This has placed youth at the forefront of political struggle throughout history.

GET SMART! LATINO YOUTH ACTIVISM IN CONTEMPORARY LA

David symbolizes the new leadership in LA. He's an immigrant—he's from the area. He's taking the initiative to go out and talk with the community. He has the drive, and he believes he can make the difference. (Angelo, community organizer)

As Angelo asserts, David's age and immigrant experience equip him to represent contemporary LA, with its large population of youth and immigrants. I joined David with Chris and Angel, two other student activists from Southeast LA, at Get Smart! meetings. Angel explained the group's name, which student members decided by consensus. "It means that people should know what's going on. But not [just] knowing—it means taking action. Like—get smart! Wise up! . . . There are problems . . . and you should try to do something about it." Members organized to pass AB 540 with the support of educators, community activists, legislators, and parents. In 2001, 34 youth were active members in Get Smart! , and up to 20 attended biweekly meetings.

The youth spoke to the press, petitioned, educated others by "tabling" at community events, and sent letters to elected officials with their personal stories. In 2001, David and three other group members testified in favor of AB 540 in legislative hearings at the state capitol. While Latino professionals and undocumented youth did not always agree on tactics, the active participation of both was critical to the bill's passage. Youth participation was facilitated by the mentorship and support of Latino adults in NGOs.[22] The presence of powerful Latino allies at the legislature helped them feel safer as activists. The youth's visible engagement was a significant challenge to negative, popular stereotypes of "illegal aliens" and began to redefine them as promising Californians. It made palpable the frustration and tragedy of growing up undocumented. In the words of Steve Zimmer, an LA high school teacher and activist: "These kids are our future. If we are going to rehumanize the issue of immigration, this is the legislation" (Interview, June 25, 2001).

On one visit, when I entered the room, I noticed that Emilio, a Salvadoran youth who was waiting for his green card, had dyed the top of his brown hair fuchsia. Some of the youth were wearing T-shirts with political inscriptions—"Mujerista" stood out in red on the matching black T-shirts of Angel and Chris. Margarita, who had been legalized through IRCA and was a member of the UCLA group Raza Womyn, sported a crimson shirt with the word FIERCE in bold black lettering. Agustín wore a rainbow necklace with baby blocks that spelled QUEEN. David's gray shirt, with a drawing of a gas mask, announced the new campaign of an environmental NGO against a proposed power plant in South Los Angeles. These bold sartorial statements reminded me that public school access is only one of many struggles that engage group members through participation in multiple NGOs. Members also fight against sexism, heterosexism, and environmental racism. The group included both undocumented youth and their peers, who have seen the oppression of undocumented immigrants tearing their schools and communities apart. Margarita explained that she is inspired by the teens although she is no longer undocumented. "The youth are beautiful. They are such organizers. They are artists—poets—excellent public speakers . . . They have so much energy—so much rage."

As the group members sat in a circle, David told us about participating in a press conference and joining the caravan to Immigrant Lobby Day. He related his identification and pride as an immigrant:

> We had this media conference, and that's where I . . . talked to people about [being] an immigrant. In front of a lot of people, I talked about my situation and others' . . . I actually did not mind saying that I am quote illegal. Because, I mean, I am not ashamed of being an immigrant . . . but I also do not go sharing it with everybody either. After that I went up to Sacramento. That's where I talked to some of the legislators—to tell them what I thought about the bill.

David's parents did not go to the capitol; unlike their son, who has time for activism as a student, his parents could not afford to travel by bus to Sacramento and miss even one or two days of work in the garment industry, because they had to keep up with mortgage payments on their condominium. Armed with the minimal protection of his California high school ID card, raised in California, and able to pass for a US-born Latino, he also felt safer traveling across the state than his parents did. Despite his fears, David publicly revealed his "illegal" status, yet by using quotation marks, refuses to internalize it. " I fear life itself. But because of that fear, it makes me want to live more. That's something I like about myself. If I fear something, I go for it."

THE EDUCATIONAL TRAJECTORIES OF THREE FRIENDS

As members of Get Smart! from Southeast LA, David, Angel, and Chris organized and socialized together yet faced distinct barriers to college. They each managed to excel in severely overcrowded, under-performing schools where far more students drop out than go on to college. They also feared for their educational futures. David worked steadily at school and never gave up hope of obtaining a higher education. Angel, the son of janitors, first saw a stoplight and a backpack when he moved to California from a small town in southern Mexico at age nine. He pushed himself to learn English with the help of his cousin by reading children's books and watching television with a dictionary by his side, looking up words that he did not understand. Like Muralles a generation before him, Angel became very depressed and his grades plummeted when he found out he would not be able to attend college owing to the high cost of out-of-state tuition. He started to study again after David brought him to Get Smart! and he learned about the legislative struggle for AB 540. Angel's grade point average was still low after two years of poor grades, and he feared that he would not get into a four year college.

Although Chris's and Angel's matching T-shirts reflect their closeness, Chris is the only one who went on a tour of California universities with a local NGO and was applying to the state's top public universities. As the US-born daughter of Mexican immigrants, she will be able to attend college and pay nominal in-state fees with student loans. Chris worried about being the first one in her family to graduate from high school or enroll in college. Her parents and schools had not prepared her academically to compete with California's best students. Her mother has a 6th grade education, and her father attended school for only a few months. "Sometimes he doesn't like to do his signature because it's a little off." Chris, Margarita, and other young women organized in solidarity with their undocumented peers. "There are many things that I feel aren't right, and I want to contribute. I have friends who are affected and I want to do something about it. [Being undocumented is] a big issue at school. People are either embarrassed or afraid to talk about it—to seek help or ask for information. But I know the person next to me may be in that situation." The organizer discussed an upcoming legislative hearing in Sacramento for AB 540; NGOs raised funds to fly two students to testify. The group decided that David and another student named Lisa would attend the hearing.

Multiple Layers of Belonging

At the hearing, a wall of advocates from educational institutions, NGOs, and labor unions stood protectively behind David and Lisa. Sitting beside them were Senator Polanco and Assembly Members Firebaugh and Abel Maldonado, the latter a freshman Republican who coauthored the bill in a show of bipartisan support.[23] After years of advocacy and electoral mobilization, Latino legislators and others who struggled for their own college education created a protective space in the hearing room for a new generation of Latino students. First, Assembly Member Firebaugh addressed the legislative committee:

> This bill is about . . . California kids . . . We have a number of immigrant students who, despite being the very best and brightest kids of their own communities, are effectively precluded from a college education . . . On average these kids have spent ten years of their lives in California . . . They are kids who . . . didn't come of their own volition—they were brought by their parents. They are kids who have achieved despite tremendous obstacles—who had to overcome language obstacles, . . . poverty. They . . . attend our worst schools . . . Eighty percent of them have a parent or a sibling . . . who . . . is either a citizen or permanent resident . . They are kids who have grown up in California and will remain in California. And so the challenge before us is, what policy direction do we take? Do we give them the tools to be the most productive citizens of our society? To achieve—to better their communities? Or do we effectively preclude them that opportunity? They will live here. They'll be our neighbors. They'll be our friends. (Senate Education Committee, July 7, 2000)

Firebaugh referred to the youth as "California kids" who cannot be separated from the state's Latino families and communities. By repeating that they are "kids," he stressed their innocence in an attempt to separate them from negative judgments about their parents. Overcoming the obstacles of poverty, language, and substandard education has placed the youth in a trajectory of Latino educational struggles and has linked them to the assembly member's own educational achievements. Firebaugh argued for educational opportunities in order to create the "most productive citizens," highlighting the dreams and potential of exceptional youth rather than their laboring parents, who did not speak at the hearing.

Next, Lisa began her testimony. A star student and community volunteer who arrived in the US a year after her birth, she is usually very articulate and poised. But that day, Lisa could hardly speak. She was unable to clearly recount her accomplishments and goals through her deep sobs of years of pain and frustration. The legislators and advocates around her held her shoulders, gave her tissues, and told her to take a deep breath. Her youthful promise and emotional testimony challenged images of an "illegal immigrant" threat. Many in the hearing room appeared to be moved, including some of the staunchest advocates for immigration restriction.

That day, David had replaced his activist T-shirts with a suit. This distinguished him from stereotypes of the poor and laboring "illegal alien" and the militant Latino activist, and suggested an American Dream of professional upward mobility. When the assembly member introduced him, David began with a quivering voice:

> Growing up in the United States has been a difficult transition for me . . . I would like to acknowledge here today . . . the sacrifices that both my parents made by choosing to bring me to the United States . . . in order to have better opportunities . . . My parents have worked hard in this country. I too have worked hard. Like them, I would like to contribute to this society . . . I always knew that education was important. In school I am enrolled in advanced placement courses, extracurricular activities, and I hold a 4.0 GPA. I'm a volunteer with a community-based organization in my neighborhood, and I am involved in working toward bettering our communities . . . . The day I was told by my counselor about college tuition costs . . . I was overwhelmed with fear. I have become lost. I cannot comprehend that, after I have worked so hard, after my parents have sacrificed so much, after I believed I could be someone, I now face . . . tremendous fear . . . I believe that I and the students that could not be here today have earned a piece of the American pie. Education is and should be a human right for everyone . . . Without your support, my goals will be in vain . . . On behalf of my parents . . . please do the right thing and vote yes on . . . AB 540.

David described the shock of transitioning from institutional inclusion in high school to the legal exclusion he now faces as an undocumented adult. His arguments for educational access both overlap and challenge those offered by his assembly member. They suggest the differences in perspective and tactics between the citizen legislators and youth activists. While both focus on communal rather than individual arguments, David asserted belonging at the levels of family, community, nation, and humanity and made rights claims from each of these arenas. As a budding activist, he opposed "ageism" and resisted calling students "kids." Instead, David challenged the separation of "innocent" undocumented youth from their laboring parents and focused on family and neighborhood obligations. Although David asserted national belonging with the claim that the undocumented have "earned a piece of the American pie," he did not frame his struggle in citizenship terms, which he saw as exclusionary. His declaration that education is a human right echoed the slogan on his T-shirt and the messages he received from the NGOs serving communities with large noncitizen populations.

FIGHTING FOR YOUTH ON THE BORDERLANDS OF THE NATION-STATE

The fight for AB 540 is not the political anomaly that it appears to be. It belongs to a history of Latino educational struggle, in which Latinos who walk the hallways of the California State Legislature participated. Through these efforts, Latino youth across generations and ancestries have been introduced to political action and participation as policymakers, community leaders, and elected officials.

The importance of AB 540 to Latino politics suggests that in an era of large-scale Latin American labor migration, we must look beyond polls and voting statistics to understand the political engagements of youth and the undocumented. The construction of some immigrant youth as "illegal" produces a crisis for Latino politics and citizenship. Significant portions of contemporary Latino communities are growing up as formal outsiders to the nation-state. The cause of these youth is upheld by Latino legislative activists who represent these communities. As the children and grandchildren of immigrants, many Latino professionals have overcome their own educational barriers and believe in education as a pathway to personal and community empowerment. The struggle for educational belonging is also an important site of political initiation for undocumented youth; it underscores the need to examine the particular experience of being undocumented from the position of minors. As English speakers whose daily participation in public schools is protected by law, these youth's relationship to government and the public sphere in the US is different from their parents'.

Latino legislators and undocumented youth struggle together despite differences in power and perspective. The legislators rely on courageous teens to humanize the plight of immigrants in the communities they represent. These youth become political actors through NGOs with the mentorship of Chicano and Latino activists and educators. They gain a place at the legislative table through the active support of Latino citizen legislators. While these students may be formally excluded from the nation-state, legislators and the youth themselves argue for their belonging as members of Latino families and communities, as Californians, and as human beings.

The victory of AB 540 is a tribute to the bravery of undocumented youth and their peers, who believe that everyone in their high schools should have educational opportunities. The active participation of high achievers who were once undocumented and have attained lawful status challenges the essentialization of the "illegal alien." It confirms the great potential of these immigrants to contribute to society when they are given a chance. The work of Latino activists across immigration statuses suggests channels through which to confront the global tragedy of undocumented children raised on the borderlands of the nation-state and to assert their belonging wherever they reside. Latino community members have demonstrated the necessary dedication and persistence to emerge as leaders in this global struggle.

DEDICATION

This chapter is dedicated to the memory of Marco Antonio Firebaugh (1966–2006), who graciously welcomed me to conduct research out of his state assembly offices in 2001. His passionate persistence was critical to the passage of AB 540.

NOTES

1. When persons are identified by one name, I use a pseudonym to protect the confidentiality of group members; their stories are a composite.
2. While this article focuses on Latinos and AB 540, the bill had an impact on immigrants from throughout the world. Activists of all races supported it.

3. During academic year 2000–2001, nonresidents of California paid tuition that was over two to ten times higher than the resident fees to attend California state colleges and universities (Mitchell, 2001).
4. This organizational name is a pseudonym to protect the confidentiality of its members.
5. Section 68130.5, California Education Code.
6. As of April 2006, similar bills had been enacted in an additional eight states (KS, IL, NB, NM, NY, OK, UT, and WA). They were introduced or pending in 15 more states. Bills to restrict access to higher education had been introduced in at least four states (National Immigration Law Center, 2006).
7. The California Chicano Caucus first formed at the California Legislature with five members in 1973. In 1991, it changed its name to the Latino Legislative Caucus to include a more diverse membership (Latino Legislative Caucus, 2003). Although Latino Republicans have been elected to the legislature since 1996, the Latino Caucus is affiliated with the Democratic Party and does not include Republicans.
8. My use of the term "Latino" primarily refers to persons of Mexican and Central American ancestry, who predominate in California.
9. I use the term "persons of Mexican ancestry" rather than "Mexican American" or "Chicano" because of the political nuances of the latter terms. I use "Chicano" for persons that identify with the Chicano movement. For a discussion of the use of identity categories by persons of Mexican ancestry in California, see Zavella, 1996.
10. This analysis is based on ethnographic research conducted over 12 months between 1999 and 2001 at three sites, namely, the California State Legislature and the offices of two assembly districts (AD) with large Mexican immigrant populations. AD 50 in suburban Southeast Los Angeles was represented by Assembly Member Firebaugh. In 2000, AD 28 in Central California's agricultural Salinas Valley elected Assembly Member Simón Salinas as its first Latino legislator in over 100 years. By observing activities related to AB 540 at legislative offices and an LA-based youth group called Get Smart!, I traced the circuits of power that link Latino legislators to grassroots immigrant activists. Fieldwork was supplemented by 40 semistructured interviews with legislative staff, legislators, and activists. In addition, I analyzed legislative files, hearings, historical and organizing materials, and Spanish and English media coverage.
11. Recent bilingual polls shed light on the political beliefs of Latino adults who are not fluent in English or are noncitizens (Hajnal and Baldassare, 2001; DeSipio *et al.*, 2003).
12. Thanks to Ralph Cintron for helping me with this insight.
13. Assembly Member Firebaugh was unanimously elected chair of the Latino Legislative Caucus in 2002.
14. During World War II in 1942, the US entered into an agreement with the Mexican government to bring temporary agricultural laborers across

the border through the Bracero Program. With pressure from labor unions and Chicano organizations, the program ended in 1964.

15. Jeffrey Passel (2006) estimates that there are 1.8 million undocumented persons under age 18 who live in the US, constituting 16% of all residing in the US without authorization (7). Passel (2003) also estimates that 40% of these youth live in California (2).

16. For a discussion of the broader political and economic context of the New Right and the forces that challenged educational programs that served Latinos, including conservative think tanks and foundations, see Acuña (2004).

17. For a brief historical overview of undocumented immigrants and access to higher education in California, see Guillen (2003).

18. Network leaders included Hilda Solis and educators Alfred Herrera and Arnulfo Casillas. Solis served in the state assembly from 1992 to 1994 and as state senator from 1994 to 2000. That year, she was elected to the U.S. House of Representatives. The daughter of Mexican and Nicaraguan immigrants, she is a first-generation college graduate.

19. When Muralles enrolled in Chicano Studies courses, there was no university program geared toward the experience of Central Americans in the US The first Central American Studies minor was established at California State University, Northridge, in 2000.

20. Muralles held this position from 1993 to 1998, a crucial time for Latino naturalization campaigns.

21. Richard Polanco served as assembly member from 1986 to 1994 and as state senator from 1994 to 2002. For ten years, he was the chair of the Latino Legislative Caucus.

22. In Los Angeles, these organizations included CARECEN, the Coalition for Humane Immigrant Rights of LA, MALDEF, and Public Advocates, Inc.

23. Richard Polanco served as assembly member from 1986 to 1994, and as senator from 1994 until 2002. He was unable to run for reelection owing to term limits.

ACKNOWLEDGMENTS

This research was conducted with the support of the University of California Pacific Rim Research Program, UC Mexus, UC San Diego's Center for US-Mexican Studies, and the UC Institute for Labor and Employment. While all who helped me to understand and relate the struggle for AB 540 are too numerous to mention, I especially thank the offices of Assembly Members Firebaugh and Salinas, Roger Rouse, Wayne Cornelius, Liz Guillen, Bianet Castellaños, and UC ACCORD. Thanks to Suzanne Oboler and the anonymous reviewers of *Latino Studies*. I am solely responsible for this article's imperfections. Although the youth activists of Get Smart! changed

California history, many cannot be named here owing to their continued legal vulnerability. They are a great inspiration and give me hope for the future of California and my country.

REFERENCES

Acuña, Rodolfo. 2004. *Occupied America: A History of Chicanos.* 5th ed. New York: Pearson Longman.

Baldassare, Mark. 2002. *A California State of Mind: The Conflicted Voter in a Changing World.* Berkeley: University of California Press.

California Immigrant Welfare Collaborative. 2001. Immigrant Legislation Training, California State Legislature, Sacramento, CA, March 8.

Chávez, Leo R. 1992. *Shadowed Lives: Undocumented Immigrants in American Society.* Fort Worth, TX: Harcourt Brace Jovanovich.

Coutin Bibler, Susan. 2000. *Legalizing Moves: Salvadoran Immigrants' Struggle for U.S. Residency.* Ann Arbor: University of Michigan Press.

Delgado, Hector L. 1993. *New Immigrants. Old Unions: Organizing Undocumented Workers in Los Angeles.* Philadelphia, PA: Temple University Press.

de la Garza, Rodolfo, and Louis DeSipio, eds. 1999. *Awash in the Mainstream: Latino Politics in the 1996 Elections.* Boulder, CO: Westview Press.

DeSipio, Louis, Harry Pachon, Rodolfo de la Garza, and Jongho Lee. 2003. *Immigrant Politics at Home and Abroad.* Los Angeles: Tomás Rivera Policy Institute.

Flores, Richard. 2002. It Ain't That Free, Honey!: Prosthetic Mexicans and the Phantom Democracy. Paper presented at the American Anthropological Association Annual Meeting, New Orleans, LA, November 20.

Flores, William V., and Rina Benmayor. 1997. Introduction: Constructing Cultural Citizenship. In *Latino Cultural Citizenship,* ed. William V. Flores and Rina Benmayor, 1–23. Boston, MA: Beacon Press.

Guillen, Liz. 2003. Undocumented Immigrant Students: A Very Brief Overview of Access to Higher Education in California. In *Teaching to Change LA's School Report Card 3,* ed. J. Rogers. Los Angeles: UCLA's Institute for Democracy, Education, & Access.

Gutiérrez, David. 1995. *Walls and Mirrors: Mexican Americans, Mexican Immigrants, and the Politics of Ethnicity.* Berkeley: University of California Press.

Hagan, Jacqueline. 1994. *Deciding to Be Legal: A Maya Community in Houston.* Philadelphia, PA: Temple University Press.

Hajnal, Zoltan, and Mark Baldassare. 2001. *Finding Common Ground: Racial and Ethnic Attitudes in California.* San Francisco: Public Policy Institute of California.

Institute of Governmental Studies Statewide Database. 2000. Report on Minority Registration from the 2000 General Election. University of California, Berkeley.

————. 2001. (Latino/Non-Latino) Race Variables by 1991 Districts. University of California, Berkeley.

Johnson, Hans P. 2003. *California's Demographic Future.* Rancho Mirage, CA: Public Policy Institute of California.

Kadetsky, Elizabeth. 1994. School's Out. *Nation.* November 21, 601.

Latino Legislative Caucus. 2003. History and Purpose. http://democrats. assembly.ca.gov/latinoCaucus/history.htm.

Marcelli, Enrico, and Wayne Cornelius. 2001. The Changing Profile of Mexican Migrants to the United States: New Evidence from California and Mexico. *Latin American Research Review* 36(3): 105–131.

Martínez, Elizabeth. 1998. *De Colores Means All of Us: Latina Views for a Multi-Colored Century.* Cambridge, MA: South End Press.

Mitchell, Paul. 2001. AB 540 Assembly Floor Analysis. Sacramento, California State Assembly, September 18.

Muñoz , Carlos, Jr. 1989. *Youth, Identity, Power: the Chicano Movement.* London and New York: Verso.

Muralles, Mario. 2001. Interview by author, Los Angeles, CA, June 28.

National Immigration Law Center. 2004. State Proposed or Enacted Legislation Regarding Immigrant Access to Higher Education. Los Angeles, CA, January 22.

————. 2006. Basic Facts about In-State Tuition for Undocumented Immigrant Students. Los Angeles, CA, April.

Nicolaides, Becky. 2002. *My Blue Heaven: Life and Politics in the Working-Class Suburbs of Los Angeles, 1920–1965.* Chicago, IL: University of Chicago Press.

Ojeda, Gil. 2001. Interview by author. Sacramento, CA, February 5.

Pardo, Mary. 1998. *Mexican American Women Activists: Identity and Resistance in Two Los Angeles Communities.* Philadelphia, PA: Temple University Press.

Passel, Jeffrey. 2003. Further Demographic Information Relating to the DREAM Act. Washington, DC: The Urban Institute, October.

————. 2006. The Size and Characteristics of the Unauthorized Migrant Population in the US: Estimates Based on the March 2005 Current Population Survey. Washington, DC: Pew Hispanic Center.

Rodríguez, Gregory. 2000. The Latino Century. *California Journal* 31(January 1): 8–15.

Rojas, Aurelio. 2002. Latinos go from protests to ballots. *Sacramento Bee,* September 28, A1.

Salinas, Simón. 2001. Interview by author, Salinas, CA, August 24.

Senate Education Committee. 2000. AB 1197. California State Senate, Sacramento, July 7.

Sifuentes, Edward. 2003. Local Chicanos Defend MEChA from Bustamente Critics. *North County Times,* September 5.

Thornton, Gary, ed. 2003. Hispanic or Latino Population by City Los Angeles County, 2000 Census. In *Los Angeles Almanac.* Montebello, CA: Given Place Publishing Co.

U.S. Census Bureau. 2002. Profile of General Demographic Characteristics: 2000 Geographic Area, Maywood City, CA. Washington, DC: United States Department of Commerce.

Zavella, Patricia. 1987. *Women's Work and Chicano Families: Cannery Workers of the Santa Clara Valley.* Ithaca, NY: Cornell University Press.

———. 1996. Feminist Insider Dilemmas: Constructing Identity with 'Chicana' Informants. In *Feminist Dilemmas in Fieldwork,* ed. Diane Wolf, 138–159. Boulder, CO: Westview Press.

Zimmer, Steve. 2001. Interview by author, Los Angeles, CA, June 25.

PART V

Redefining Citizenship—The Present Conundrum

Delinquent Citizenship, National Performances: Racialization, Surveillance, and the Politics of "Worthiness" in Puerto Rican Chicago

Ana Y. Ramos-Zayas

Alma Juncos,[1] an outgoing and energetic parent-volunteer whom I met in the corridors of the Roberto Clemente High School in the Puerto Rican barrio of Chicago, once commented: *"Los nacionalistas son los únicos que se preocupan por los suyos. Si hay una comunidad aquí, es por ellos"* ("The nationalists are the only ones who care for their own people. If there's a community here, it's because of them"). Alma was one of many Puerto Ricans who professed that Chicago was the "Mecca of Puerto Rican nationalism." On the basis of Alma's characterization of the nationalists, one would never imagine that these Chicago barrio residents would be the same people implicated in front-page newspaper scandals and deemed terrorists in the media throughout the late 1980s and 1990s (Blanchard, 1988; Cruz, 1995). The Chicago mainstream media and legal authorities accused the Puerto Rican "nationalists" of influencing the Roberto Clemente High School parents' council to spend funds in activities aimed at "indoctrinating" students into radical, anti-American politics that deserved FBI investigation (Cruz, 1995; Committee for Clemente Community Hearings, 1998). Why would a Latino barrio in the postindustrial US, otherwise marginalized from public discourse and politics, occupy center stage in accusations of terrorism and anti-Americanism? Moreover, how are these media- and state-generated characterizations of the barrio as "terrorist" and "crime-ridden" related to contemporary nation-state configurations of so-called homeland security and the current state of civil rights and citizenship? More importantly, how are the performance of Puerto Rican nationalism and everyday experiences of US citizenship reflected in the development of grassroots educational initiatives in the barrio?

Drawing from ethnographic research in Chicago in the mid-1990s, as well as from more current domestic and international developments,[2] I examine the processes by which Puerto Rican spaces become racialized in ways that effectively render Puerto Rican US citizenship delinquent.[3] My main goal is to deconstruct the everyday processes by which the state targets Puerto Rican spaces, educational programs, and national performances in Chicago such that Puerto Rican citizenship increasingly approaches a status of illegality equivalent to that produced by the state in relation to other Latino (and Asian) groups during the "war on terrorism."

In his brilliant examination of the conflictive views of citizenship in US history entitled *Civic Ideals* (1997), the legal scholar Rogers Smith demonstrates that constitutional analyses of citizenship should not construe the US nation-state's "egalitarian strand" as its most authentic form. Instead, they must give full weight to the US's pervasive ideologies of ascriptive inequality—along with liberalism and democratic republicanism—and explain that each has been a centrally constitutive, fundamental, and ideological component of American life (Smith, 1997: 30). Until recently, illegality and deportability were central to a Latino experience that Puerto Ricans—as US citizens— were not a part of. Nevertheless, the ascriptive white supremacist core of civic identity in the US has effectively reduced the marginal value of Puerto Rican US citizenship (and the US citizenship of other racialized US-born populations) almost to a vanishing point compared with "resident alien" status. Many of the community-initiated educational programs are considered bastions of "terrorism" and "anti-Americanism" in Chicago's Humboldt Park and are likewise subjected to the global penalties of clearly discriminatory measures that violate the civil rights of teacher-activists and youth alike.

I first examine the history of radical politics and state surveillance in the neighborhoods comprising "Puerto Rican Chicago." Humboldt Park has historically been targeted by surveillance units that have policed grassroots radicalism since the formation of a geographically concentrated Puerto Rican area in Chicago in the 1960s. I next examine the concept of national performances—that is, the anticolonial strategies of self-assertion for advancing civil rights demands and community formation—in relation to state productions of Puerto Rican "terrorists." In particular, I consider how neighborhood-based educational programs, oftentimes ensconced in discourses critical of the US nation-state's colonialist and imperialist foundation, are in fact produced as "terrorist" spaces. Moreover, I consider the US military recruitment of Puerto Rican poor and working-class youth in Chicago in connection to the deployment of a politics of "worthiness," according to which Puerto Ricans are continuously asked to prove that they are worthy of US citizenship. Finally, I analyze the production of a delinquent citizenship through which Puerto Ricans, despite being nominal US citizens, actually approach the condition of illegality imposed on immigrant "aliens," and are ultimately implicated in white supremacist constructions of homeland security.

State Surveillance and Community Formation in Puerto Rican Chicago

Only a few subway stops northwest of downtown Chicago, the intersection of the two adjacent neighborhoods of West Town and Humboldt Park—with a third, Logan Square, further north along the same mass-transit line—came to serve as a point of convergence and as the principal "port of entry" for Puerto Ricans migrating to Chicago in the 1960s. The stark white–black racial segregation of residential patterns in much of the city was clearly one of the decisive motivations for Puerto Ricans to establish their own distinct racialized enclave on the North Side. As early as 1965, police brutality in this growing barrio served as a flashpoint for community organizing when two Puerto Ricans were arrested after police broke into their Division Street home and were then repeatedly subjected to group beatings in police custody. Then, in June 1966, immediately following the first annual Puerto Rican Day Parade, police brutality touched off what has been called "the first Puerto Rican riot in the history of the United States" (Padilla, 1985: 46–50; 1987: 123–125, 144–155).[4] The events, which lasted three days and nights, began when a white police officer shot and wounded a 20-year-old Puerto Rican man, Aracelis Cruz. This young man was alleged to be a gang member, and the police claimed that they suspected him of having been armed. The outrage of the community was inflamed when the police unleashed trained dogs to disperse angry onlookers and a Puerto Rican bystander was bitten. Chicago mayor Richard J. Daley publicly blamed the unrest on "unthinking and irresponsible individuals and gangs . . . seeking a climate of violence and uncertainty" (Padilla, 1987: 150).

The Puerto Rican riots were a local expression of the more general climate of radical politics and racial militancy in Chicago during the 1960s. Chicago was the focus of national attention during the summer of 1966, when the city became the scene of civil rights marches against racial segregation in housing. The demonstrations culminated with the summit meeting of Martin Luther King Jr. and the Chicago Freedom Movement and were met with organized white hostility and violence and subsequent confrontations between African Americans and police in black neighborhoods (Anderson and Pickering, 1986). The Puerto Rican community in West Town and Humboldt Park was still in its formative stages at the time, however, and thus, the 1966 events shaped the barrio's destiny in significant ways. The 1966 riots were the first widely publicized collective action attributed to Puerto Ricans in Chicago. The racist stereotypes of criminality and violence had already been extended to the Chicago Puerto Rican community in 1960, when the *Saturday Evening Post,* a prominent national publication, ran a piece entitled "Crime without Reason" (November 5, 1960), with a yellow tag attached to newsstand copies that read: "Racial Violence in Chicago." The article told the story of two Puerto Ricans who allegedly murdered a man they had never met for the simple reason that he was Italian, thus identifying the source of "racial violence" in the irrational criminality attributed to Puerto Ricans. The same article depicted Chicago's Puerto Ricans as "noisy" and "nervous," living on the streets and sidewalks during the warm weather season, and having no social organizations or civic institutions other than taverns (Padilla, 1987: 61).

Regardless of whether or not most barrio residents had approved of, participated in, or condemned the riots, Humboldt Park immediately became an urban space definitively associated with Puerto Ricans, as both the people and the neighborhood became synonymous with civil rights unrest and conflict, and so were effectively criminalized. These events galvanized not only the creation of specifically Puerto Rican-identified organizations but also the consolidation of a geographically based notion of Puerto Rican community that had been deferred for over 20 years by the group's prior history of dispersal throughout the city. Already in the 1970s, within less than a decade, the West Town–Humboldt Park barrio had come to be marked as the distinctively Puerto Rican section of Chicago and boasted the largest Puerto Rican community in the Midwest.

Chicago's Puerto Rican community is exceptionally distinguished for the historical prominence of its proindependence and nationalist political radicalism.[5] The recognition of Puerto Rico's colonial reality and its manifestation in an incomplete and unequal citizenship whose parameters have been determined historically by white supremacy provided the ideological template on which anticolonial nationalist politics developed in Puerto Rican Chicago. One manifestation of political insurgency in Chicago's Puerto Rican community took the form of independent electoral campaigns that challenged the hegemony of Mayor Richard J. Daley's Democratic Party machine.[6] The Young Lords Organization in the 1960s and 1970s,[7] and the Fuerzas Armadas para la Liberación Nacional (FALN) in the 1980s—both among the most nationally renowned and better documented embodiments of Puerto Rican political militancy in the US—were each first organized and remained centrally based in Chicago, and shaped much of the militant grassroots politics in the Puerto Rican barrio. The salience of this history of political radicalism and concomitant state repression, then, has been a particularly distinctive feature of community formation for Puerto Ricans in Chicago. This was especially true for the West Town–Humboldt Park neighborhood, which came to be criminalized not only as a result of its reputation of riots in the 1960s and 1970s but also because of allegations of "terrorism" thereafter.

Grassroots organizations in the Puerto Rican barrios since the late 1960s frequently articulated a level of political militancy that resulted in the intensive monitoring of Puerto Rican activists in Chicago by FBI, CIA, and Defense Department surveillance units (Anderson and Pickering, 1986; Padilla, 1987: 168–179). The late 1960s and the 1970s marked a period of intense counterinsurgency in Chicago that sowed confusion and suspicion within the community. Like black militant organizations and some segments of the predominantly white New Left, many Chicago Puerto Rican activists—particularly those advocating Puerto Rico's independence—have been beleaguered by the harassment and surveillance of federal agents and infiltrators from the 1970s to the present. Police files were maintained to record individual Puerto Rican barrio residents' activism and "communist" or "un-American" tendencies in the most meticulous ways (Padilla, 1987: 171–173; Fernández, 1994).

The early 1980s found the Chicago Puerto Rican community at the center of political controversy on a national scale in the US as well as in Puerto Rico. The FALN, a clandestine group advocating political independence for Puerto Rico, claimed responsibility for a series of bombings in US military facilities. A total of 15 Puerto Rican members of the group, 13 of whom were Chicago barrio residents, were eventually caught and given lengthy sentences in the mid-1980s on charges of "seditious conspiracy to overthrow the US government." Owing to the fact that the FALN political prisoners, prior to their incarceration, had participated in grassroots programs serving the Puerto Rican poor, many barrio residents and activists continued to associate grassroots activism with militant nationalism.[8] At the peak of FALN military actions and FBI persecution (when most group members had already gone "underground"), Puerto Rican residents of Humboldt Park–West Town appeared divided. "Signs of 'FALN Welcomed Here' appeared on people's houses and cars," commented Ileana Díaz, a Puerto Rican woman in her 30s, who is the niece of one of the political prisoners and the ex-girlfriend of another. Other community members had agreed with the FBI and other government agents that the FALN members were "terrorists" that "gave all Puerto Ricans a bad name," as Jaime García, an active statehood advocate, remarked.

Throughout the 1980s and 1990s, instances of FBI infiltration and surveillance in Humboldt Park contributed to the criminalization of the area most prominently racialized as "Puerto Rican." During the period of my fieldwork, at least three cases involving FBI intervention were documented in the media and supplied a recurring theme in many of the informal conversations I had with Puerto Rican barrio residents. In one of these instances, a teacher at one of the Puerto Rican alternative high schools where I volunteered was eventually revealed to be an FBI infiltrator who left the school unexpectedly and later testified against nationalist activists who were alleged to be "terrorists" involved in the local high school's school council (Oclander, 1995: 1). Likewise, the Humboldt Park Infant Mortality Reduction Initiative (HIMRI), a community health center, was shut down for several weeks while the FBI subpoenaed the agency's files for no publicly stated reason (Espinosa, 1995: 4). Finally, in the summer of 1995, Roberto Clemente High School was also labeled a hotbed of "terrorist" activity in the mainstream news media, as teachers and administrators were required to hand over their records to FBI investigators (Oclander, 1995: 1). These instances exemplify some of the ways in which Humboldt Park has continued to be targeted by the FBI and other government surveillance units, contributing to its stigmatization not only as a "criminal" space of street gangs and drugs, but also, and not entirely unrelatedly, as one of "anti-Americanism" and "terrorist" conspiracies.

RACIALIZED SPACES, NATIONAL PERFORMANCES

In Chicago, one of the most racially segregated cities in the US,[9] ubiquitous distinctions about neighborhoods are virtually inseparable from their overt or submerged racial and also class-inflected meanings, and so have a pronounced importance for struggles over identity formation (Bowden and Kreinberg, 1981). The politics of space is necessarily implicated in racialization processes, and likewise, the politics of race plays out in remarkably spatialized terms in Chicago. Space has been conventionally presupposed as a naturalized and self-evident "context" for social relations. Rather than being a mere background, however, space can be usefully understood as a social relation in itself (Williams and Smith, 1983). As Lefebvre points out with specific regard to the city and the urban sphere, space may be "the setting of struggle," but it is not only this; it is also "the stakes of that struggle" (Lefebvre, 1991[1974]: 386). Indeed, struggles over social space and the differences they produce are inseparable from more general conflicts over inequalities of power and wealth (De Genova and Ramos-Zayas, 2003). Far from being a neutral frame of reference for points on the map, the mere mention of Humboldt Park signaled to Chicagoans of any racialized group a particularly stigmatized image of Puerto Ricanness, associated with criminality, poverty, and welfare dependency—even though by the year 2000, Puerto Ricans had become a minority within that geographical area.[10]

As the symbolic and physical boundaries of the historically segregated Puerto Rican neighborhood are blurred by urban displacement and a growing number of Mexicans, Central Americans, African Americans, and whites reinscribing sections of Humboldt Park, West Town, and Logan Square with distinctive meanings, official symbols, and narratives of the Puerto Rican nation are evoked to reappropriate or, at least, mark physical and social spaces (Ramos-Zayas, 2001). Thus, paradoxically, as Puerto Ricans move out of the area traditionally regarded as "the Puerto Rican community," increasing attention is drawn to the two Puerto Rican flags of steel that mark the commercial section of Division Street. The Paseo Boricua, as the commercial strip of Puerto Rican Chicago is popularly called, becomes analogous to the national territory, the Puerto Rican nation, the area where the "real" Puerto Ricans live.

The negotiations involved in the processes of creating marked urban spaces suggest ways in which nationalism becomes performative. I deliberately emphasize the aspect of *performance* to foreground the existence of various rehearsals—strategies that are tried and rejected or embraced—in the constructions of the nation in so-called diasporic communities, while understanding that these rehearsals are taking place in the public eye, in front of an audience (Ramos-Zayas, 2003). Puerto Rican nationalism in Chicago was a performance in progress;

not a final product, but a relational and consistently reconfigured exposé of the politics of race, class, space, and citizenship on a population frequently represented as apathetic, pathological, crime-ridden, and anti-American. In this sense, an understanding of nationalism developed in the act of performing it, since the act of "doing" a social category is what constitutes it as real (Butler, 1999).

These national performances were particularly prominent in the production of critical pedagogy programs in *el barrio*. Educational programs such as Roberto Clemente High School's parents' council referenced in the introduction to this essay and the Puerto Rican–centric Pedro Albizu Campos Alternative High School (PACHS) served as vehicles to mark and reassert Puerto Ricanness. Through the formulation of a grassroots historiography premised on a critical understanding of the political and economic contexts of the barrio in relation to broader systems of state power and surveillance, barrio residents and activists attempted to exert a degree of agency and claimed a social space. These processes of self-affirmation are evocative of what Renato Rosaldo has termed "cultural citizenship;" that is, the creation of a range of social practices designated to attend to subordinate aspirations for and definitions of enfranchisement (Rosaldo, 1997).[11] Notwithstanding these instances of self-assertion and resistance among subordinate and marginalized populations in Humboldt Park, however, the power of state surveillance remained an everyday feature of life in Puerto Rican Chicago.

The Pedro Albizu Campos High School (PACHS), a high school conceived and developed by nationalist activists in Humboldt Park and West Town, is an example of the critical pedagogy on which nationalism was performed (Ramos- Zayas, 1997, 1998). In May 1995, sitting informally with students on the floor of the high school's main area, Amarilis Martínez, a teacher-activist, explained how in the mid-1980s the Council for American Private Education and the US Department of Education had selected PACHS as one of the exemplary schools of the year. Shortly after the school was notified that it had been selected for the award, a local TV newscast ran a three-day series interspersing shots of the high school with images of the trials of FALN members, suggesting that the school was a poor choice for the award because of its controversial politics. When the series aired, the award was temporarily withheld. Eventually, the award was reinstituted only to be rescinded again a few hours before the graduation ceremony where it was going to be celebrated. Believing that they did deserve an award for educational excellence, PACHS teachers and students inscribed their own plaque and placed it at the entrance to the high school.

During the 17 months of my fieldwork, the PACHS staff and students frequently discussed the high school's turbulent history, including the time when the FBI raided the high school building while its founders were being apprehended. As an interviewee recalled, "In 1983 the FBI raided the building. They caused a lot of damage. We thought we'd have to close down, but the community helped out in rebuilding the place. In the first day alone, we collected $3,000 through fundraising. Eventually, we raised $15,000 among the people of West Town." The school and the cultural center that housed the school were listed as sites to be searched for terrorist activity. Long after, this description colored the community's perception of the building, even though area residents continued to participate in formal and informal pedagogical spaces such as the high school, adult literacy programs, and HIV-prevention health clinics. The Excellence in Teaching Award incident and the FBI raid served as metahistories. These narratives and the numerous public demonstrations in which students, parents, and teachers engaged, created unique pedagogical spaces connected to processes of community formation that relied on the performance of Puerto Rican nationalism. Indeed, for Humboldt Park residents, PACHS and the cultural center acted as leading examples of how nationalism was performed and continuously rearticulated in the context of popular education programs.[12]

Puerto Rican nationalism must be understood as a series of highly contested performative processes in which both Chicago Puerto Ricans and the state are implicated, and which formulate and recast ideas of inclusion and exclusion based on racial formations resulting from normative, white supremacist definitions of belonging in the US nation-state.[13] These nationalist performances rely on highlighting Puerto Ricans' status as "US citizens" while racializing Latinos of other nationalities—particularly the large Mexican and Central American populations—as "illegal," irrespective of actual legal status (De Geneva and Ramos-Zayas, 2003). Hence, Puerto Rican national performances in Chicago rely on the deployment of a "citizenship identity" in contradistinction to a presupposed Mexican "illegality." Moreover, these national performances serve as defensive self-racializations in response to the state's historical criminalization of Puerto Ricans and "Puerto Rican" spaces in Chicago (Ramos-Zayas, 2003). More significantly, in the context of the current "war on terror," Puerto Rican US citizenship has been further devalued to a status that approaches the "illegality" of Mexicans in Chicago and other Latino undocumented migrants in the US. As the state continues to construct Chicago Puerto Ricans as "terrorists" and "criminals"—slippery terms that are oftentimes deployed interchangeably in reference to the social space of Chicago's Humboldt Park—the most vulnerable sectors of Puerto Rican Chicago further insist on proving their "worthiness" of being US citizens by performing a Puerto Rican nationalism. These national performances are both consistent with and actually *dependent on* emphasizing one's role in the increasing militarization of the US nation-state. Joining the military or having served in the military are examples of the *politics of worthiness* among Chicago Puerto Ricans.[14]

US MILITARY IDENTITIES AND THE POLITICS OF "WORTHINESS"

A principal hesitation to granting citizenship to Puerto Ricans in the years following the US invasion of Puerto Rico in 1898 was the objectionable "racial composition" of the population in the newly acquired territory. Although the Jones Act granting US citizenship to Puerto Ricans was ultimately enacted in 1917, it was never intended to be a grant of *full* citizenship as other non–Puerto Rican US citizens know it. When Senator Foraker first introduced the possibility of granting Puerto Ricans citizenship in the early 1900s, he described such federal citizenship not as an acknowledgement of the individual rights Puerto Ricans might have but rather as recognition "that Puerto Rico belonged to the United States of America" (Perea, 2001: 161).[15] These congressional discussions in the early 1900s eventually rendered the US citizenship of Puerto Ricans born on the island as "legislative" and that of US-born Puerto Ricans as "constitutional." Nevertheless, even if the citizenship of US-born Puerto Ricans is "constitutional," and hence not as easily revocable as the "legislative" citizenship of islanders could be, the translocal nexus on which all Puerto Ricans are implicated and the perpetual racialization of Puerto Ricans as "nonwhite" in a white supremacist nation-state, contribute to a more problematic inclusion of US-born Puerto Ricans into US citizenship.[16]

The racialization of Puerto Ricans by the institution of US citizenship has been a historical process of constructing Chicago Puerto Ricans as the "enemies of the state," as "anti-American," and, more significantly, as "terrorists." In fact, the US citizenship of Puerto Ricans has become a *delinquent* citizenship, characterized as illegal and marginal. References ranging from the civil disobedience of the Chicago-born Young Lords in the 1970s to the FALN incarcerations of the 1980s and the media hype about anti–American student "indoctrination" at the Clemente High School throughout the 1990s are deployed and disseminated to locate securely these nominal US citizens in culturally and politically bounded rubrics, outside the parameters of the imagined "American nation."

Various state surveillance practices—from COINTELPRO in the 1970s and 1980s to the FBI referenced in this chapter's introduction—have characterized life in Puerto Rican Chicago as the legitimized subordination of a racialized population to a heavy-handed state.[17] Public media representations become powerful disciplining strategies of the state, as they aim to compartmentalize Puerto Ricans into those who are "deserving" American citizens—namely, those invested in proving their worthiness with their upward mobility, aspirations, and accomplishments—and those who are "criminals" and deemed "undeserving" of claiming full citizenship rights (Ramos-Zayas, 1997; 2003).

Perhaps one of the most poignant results of the devaluation of Puerto Ricans' US citizenship on the island and mainland alike is what I refer to in this chapter as the "politics of worthiness;" that is, the tacit and explicit insistence that Puerto Ricans in general, and the Puerto Rican poor in particular, must *prove their deservingness of US citizenship* to be legitimately entitled to civil rights and social benefits that other—particularly white male—populations can assume as inalienable. Puerto Ricans are certainly not the only ones drawn into these politics of worthiness, as the cases of previous migrants from Europe (and Asia) and contemporary migrants from Latin America suggest.[18]

Puerto Ricans do not engage in these politics of worthiness as a way of *seeking* US citizenship, which they nominally have, but rather as a way of circumventing their own racialization and even deploying a self-defensive reracialization. By painfully demonstrating their deservingness of the benefits of full –citizenship, otherwise only enjoyed, constitutionally, by whites, Puerto Ricans also challenge facile associations between their US citizenship and "unearned" welfare benefits.

Proving one's worthiness consists of first accepting the very racialization of all Puerto Ricans as lazy, welfare-dependent, apathetic, and crime-prone and then making sure one positions oneself, as an individual, outside these "culture-of-poverty" arguments by following prescriptive rules of patriotism, social mobility, and national acceptability. Hence, Puerto Ricans are called to demonstrate how one is not "like other Puerto Ricans." Dominant racialization of Puerto Ricans and the production of Puerto Rican illegality and criminality can never be effectively or radically challenged if one's individual intent is to secure a place within the parameters of "citizenship." Indeed, this politics of worthiness castigates critical pedagogical projects directed at uncovering the white supremacist processes by which Puerto Ricans are racially marked by the US nation-state, which was a central component of educational programs such as the Clemente High School's local council or the PACHS. In fact, the fundamental rejection of radical politics simultaneously validates liberal, "self-help" processes that exalt individual values, hard work, and moral character.

In the conversations I have had with Chicago Puerto Ricans in the months following September 11 and the US invasion of Iraq, the politics of worthiness has surfaced prominently in narratives of decisions concerning educational and employment opportunities and involvement in the US military among Puerto Rican youth, their parents, and their teachers. In March of 2003, I spoke with Carmen Rivera, a former parent-volunteer at Clemente High School and resident of Humboldt Park. Carmen's 19-year-old son, Eladio, was about to graduate from Clemente High School and was trying to decide between attending culinary school to become a chef and going into the military. Carmen described Eladio's quandary:

> Eladio cooks really good. He tells me "Mami, you know that I can cook better than you!" And it's true [she laughed]. He could have his own restaurant or catering business someday. But, his grandfather tells him "Join the army, join the army. You need to become a man and take on responsibility. I'm a proud army veteran. I haven't been given anything for free." His grandfather always talks about being in the army, you know? The army recruiter has called Eladio at home many times . . . They [the recruiters] go to the school, you know, and tell them that they pay for their education and they can do both, go to school and be in the military, at the same time. Or that's what they say, you know. And [Eladio] tells me "Mami, I'm not gonna end up like those losers at school who get killed in gang [activities] or go on welfare. I'm gonna make something out of myself!" But I'm very scared about letting him go . . . because now it's not like they go to training and that's it. Now they really get sent to war right away.

The masculinist discourse of being "toughened up" by the military, perhaps also a homophobic reaction against men in traditionally "female" fields such as cooking, is evident in the grandfather's remark. However, what is specifically noteworthy is Carmen's emphasis on her son's insistence that he would not end up "killed in gang [activities]" or "on welfare." In Carmen's quote, joining the military is viewed not only as a way of "becoming a man," as the grandfather allegedly stated, but also as a way of demonstrating one's true "worthiness" by avoiding presumably the only other options for Puerto Rican youth, namely, street crime and violence or being welfare dependent.

Carmen's narrative is particularly telling of the ways in which allegations of criminality and welfare abuse directed against Puerto Ricans in Chicago become a disciplining mechanism of the state. The poor and working-class residents of Humboldt Park are used by the state to discipline one against the other, always at pains to demonstrate to the "real Americans"—namely, those "real" citizens enjoying the real benefits of their whiteness—that they are hardworking, not lazy; that they are, indeed, deserving of membership in the nation; and that their citizenship has not come for free. Carmen's interpretation of Eladio's words demonstrates the paradox of the poor and working-class residents of Humboldt Park: these residents' attempt to separate themselves from the stereotype of the criminal is achieved by using the same strategies against one's neighbors that have been used against oneself. As a consequence, the category of the criminal and its repertoire of prejudices and derogations are rarely contested, but are rather continuously legitimated, and prejudices and stereotypes against poor people are reenacted on a daily basis. This differentiation was not only a matter of citizenship status but also of belonging to the "proper" social space or to the improper space of crime (Caldeira, 2000).

It is imperative to note that serving in the US military and other symbols of US nationalism are not always explicit attempts at securing one's inclusion in the US nation-state. Many, if not most, of the Puerto Rican poor and working-class men and women who enroll in the military admit to having been seduced by the employment and educational offers of persistent recruitment personnel, who presented the army as their only likely road to financial security, higher education, or more structured lives (G. Pérez, 2002). As Pérez argues, many of the young Puerto Rican women who enter JROTC programs are motivated by economic hardship as well as by parents who see the military as a way for their daughters to gain independence and gender equality and even avoid abusive relationships or unwanted pregnancies. Indeed, precisely by targeting the most disenfranchised neighborhoods, the US military recruitment offices first contribute to the criminalization of the social spaces in which they are located, and then act as paternalistic "saviors" of these very communities. In the case of working-class Puerto Rican youth such as Eladio, the military legitimizes citizenship not as service to the nation-state in an international context, but as a route to deracialize oneself—to prove that one is disciplined, not lazy; productive, not a parasite of the system; law-abiding, not criminal. Military service symbolizes the ultimate willingness to die for one's country as well as to strive continuously to reposition oneself within the acceptable parameters of whiteness in the domestic political economy of the US nation-state—that is, indeed, to be "An Army of One."[19]

The US military becomes a de facto substitute for weeding out the "unworthy" US citizens in a way that the effectively dismantled and purportedly "abused" welfare system was presumably unable to do.[20] A major problem with this condition is that the top–down dispensation of "worthiness" for the poor increasingly means that joining the military is the only route to securing citizenship rights and social benefits. Even more problematic is the fact that the US army investment in targeted recruitment of poor and working-class populations unfolds largely at the expense of severe budget cuts in areas that have traditionally been considered "mobility roads" for some, such as higher education. Nowhere have these tendencies of increased military investment coupled with significant educational budget cuts been more severe than in racialized neighborhoods like Humboldt Park. It is not a coincidence that Chicago public schools lead the nation in the number of public school military programs, with close to 10,000 students participating in either full-time military academies or military programs within regular high schools, such as the JROTC, mostly targeting the poorest populations in the city (G. Pérez, 2002). The Pentagon's strategy of increasing the military recruitment of young men and women, particularly in racialized populations, from very early on in their educational careers is evidenced by the expected increase in funding, aimed to expand the JROTC program, from its current $215 million in 2001 to a projected $326 million by 2004 (G. Pérez, 2002).

Puerto Ricans challenge the "parasites of the system" stereotype often imposed on them by the dominant culture and other Latinos alike, by emphasizing duties that, as citizens, they have historically paid to the American nation, thus proving to the state and to fellow Latinos their degree of worthiness. The talk of crime in reference to the Humboldt Park area deals not with detailed descriptions of criminals, but with a set of simplistic categories: a few essentialist images oftentimes involving youth, particularly young men, and opportunism, especially in images of the "welfare mother," that eliminate the ambiguities and categorical mixtures of everyday life and gain currency at moments of social change.

In Chicago, state surveillance units, along with increasing military recruitment programs, continue to engage in punitive measures against the incorporation of nationalist activists into political citizenship through pedagogical projects such as the PACHS and the Clemente High School's parents' council of the late 1990s. Such pedagogical projects have historically assumed radical postures that are critical of US policies. They illuminate the invariable ways in which US patriotism is unequivocally and unmarkedly white under the ideological guise of its capacity to "assimilate" racialized groups into an elastic and easily tractable workforce consisting of people with "good immigrant values." Ironically, the "good immigrant values" attributed to other Latinos, and which are a euphemism for docility and subordination, actually render these "illegal" Latinos better citizen-subjects than Puerto Ricans themselves are.

The Puerto Rican Taliban: Delinquent Citizenship and "Homeland Security"

The USA Patriot Act of 2002 and the Domestic Security Enhancement Act (DSEA) under consideration by the Supreme Court are clear examples of the ways in which Puerto Ricans—and particularly the localized, pedagogical expressions of citizenship rights and national performances, such as those noted among Chicago nationalist activists and teachers—have rapidly approached the status of "alien" not too different from that of illegal immigrants. Puerto Rican US citizenship effectively becomes a delinquent citizenship, a citizenship that approaches the purported "illegality" of other undocumented Latino "aliens." Whereas the Patriot Act renders traitor anyone who challenges its sweeping new powers of surveillance, detention, and prosecution, the DSEA provides that any citizen, even native-born, who supports even the lawful activities of an organization that the executive branch deems "terrorist" is presumptively stripped of his or her citizenship (Cole, 2003). As David Cole notes, "To date, the 'war on terrorism' has largely been directed at non-citizens . . . but the DSEA would actually turn citizens associated with 'terrorist' groups into aliens." These targeted citizens would be subject to deportation, and the attorney general would possess the authority to deport any noncitizen whose presence is deemed a threat to the US "national defense, foreign policy or economic interests" (quoted in Cole, 2003). One federal court of appeals has already ruled that this standard is not susceptible to judicial review. Hence, the provision would give the attorney general unreviewable authority to deport any noncitizen without having to prove that the person has engaged in any criminal or harmful conduct. Other provisions are similarly designed to further insulate the "war on terrorism" from public and judicial scrutiny.[21]

Not unlike the so-called illegal aliens, Puerto Ricans are susceptible to accusations of illegality that oftentimes span the gray area
between media-produced (and officially sanctioned) images of barrio-
grown criminality and the US imperialist investment in configuring
racist understandings of international terrorism. These accusations
further incite many Puerto Ricans, particularly the Puerto Rican poor,
to prove retroactively their deservingness of a US citizenship imposed
on them in 1917.

The Puerto Rican case may perhaps serve as a blueprint for other
Latinos who "successfully" navigate the "legalization" process in the
US only to gain access to a lesser form of social and legal existence.

In May 2002, a reporter from a nationally renowned US news magazine asked me about José Padilla, otherwise known as Abdullah
al-Muhajir, the so-called Puerto Rican Taliban. A 31-year-old US
citizen, Padilla had been arrested at O'Hare Airport in Chicago for
allegedly plotting a bomb attack and having links to the Al Qaeda
terrorist network. The reporter had read a few articles I had written
about a popular education program directed by Puerto Rican nationalist activists in Chicago and she wanted to know if I thought the
reason why José Padilla was "so angry at the United States" had to do
with his experience as "the son of a single mother, growing up in
Chicago's Logan Square and being influenced by the barrio's nationalist activism and gang involvement." In this well-intentioned
reporter's view, Padilla's involvement with the Taliban was almost
explained away by his Puerto Ricanness, in general, and his *Chicago*
Puerto Ricanness in particular. More significantly, however, was the
reporter's view of Padilla's involvement with the Taliban as a natural
progression stemming from his "un-American" citizenship and from
growing up in a social space that does not quite "exist" within the
boundaries of how the US is imagined as perpetually prosperous and
white. This, of course, is in stark contrast to how John Walker, the so-
called American Taliban, was portrayed: as an unexplainable aberration, an exception to the otherwise normative whiteness emphatically
represented in images of his upper-middle-class professional suburban
upbringing. In drawing these distinctions, not only is citizenship naturalized to mean whiteness but also citizenship rights are dispensed
accordingly so that John Walker's judicial and human rights take
precedence over the rights of José Padilla, who has remained untried
and, for many months following his arrest, almost invisible from mainstream US political discourse. Not long after his fateful flight from
Pakistan to O'Hare, Padilla basically disappeared from public view. A
few weeks after his arrest, the federal government transferred Padilla

to a military prison off the coast of South Carolina, precluding him from having any form of contact with either his family or his lawyer.

Distinctions to determine degrees of "Americanness" and of entitlement within US society reinstate whiteness as the definition of the "real American" and as the dominant reference against which racialized "others" are securely kept outside the purview of US culture and citizenship. The criminalization of Puerto Rican spaces in Chicago is part of a fundamental logic by which US citizenship serves as a racializing institution that promotes a moral economy of inequality on which concepts such as homeland security and the USA Patriot Act[22]—and the gradations of belonging implicated in them—are legitimately deployed to establish that only subjects who conform to normative racial privilege (e.g., whiteness) are truly part of the nation. The everyday educational programs of Puerto Rican nationalist activists and the poor barrio residents and youth involved in these programs are truncated as un-American terrorist activities and used as evidence to legitimate the very criminalization to which Puerto Rican citizenship is subjected. Rather than a unifying US citizenship, we must consider the existence of multiple and inherently unequal citizenships. Unequal citizenships are produced in discursive and substantive practices that legitimize the subordination of Chicago Puerto Ricans by criminalizing the social space of *el barrio* as well as any critical pedagogical initiative aimed at challenging the US foundational mythologies of equality, mobility, and the American Dream. Contemporary policy around homeland security and antiterrorism are nation-state projects that not only unfold on an international arena but also configure domestic educational policies and discourses of criminality that invariably produce unequal citizen-subjects in everyday life. With regard to Puerto Ricans and other "native minorities," US citizenship serves as a white supremacist institution that renders the rights of some citizen-subjects as birthrights, while requiring others to prove their worthiness. As demonstrated in the production of the Puerto Rican "terrorists" in the critical educational programs in Humboldt Park, the politics of worthiness condemns any form of engagement in radical programs that are critical of the US nation-state.

The performance of Puerto Rican nationalism in Chicago is complicated in the construction of a politics of worthiness and the assumption that people are only entitled to full citizenship rights provided they disavow radical political demands that challenge the US foundational mythologies of meritocracy and equal opportunity. The universe of crime not only reveals a widespread disrespect for rights and lives but also directly delegitimizes citizenship. The circulation of discourses of fear and the proliferation of practices of segregation invariably intertwine with other processes of social transformation, including conceptions of homeland security, in ways that invariably configure educational and community developments at the most fundamental, everyday levels.

NOTES

1. The names used throughout the text are pseudonyms, which have been changed even from those used in previous manuscripts and publications to further protect peoples' identities. Only when the name of the person or place has already appeared in local publications or in the media is the real name used (e.g., those of authors of locally published poems, names of community landmarks).

2. For a comprehensive methodological discussion of this ethnographic project, see Ramos-Zayas (2003).

3. The analytic framework of racialization emphasizes the ways that race or racial difference cannot be presumed to be based upon the natural characteristics of identifiable groups or the biological effects of ancestry, but rather comes to be actively produced as such, and continually reproduced and transformed. Race is always entangled in social relations and conflicts and retains an enduring (seemingly intractable) significance precisely because its forms and substantive meanings are always eminently historical and mutable (Omi and Winant, 1986: 64–66; Winant, 1994: 58–68; De Genova and Ramos-Zayas, 2003). With reference to Puerto Ricans, the concept of culture has been persistently deployed, historically, to account for poverty, marginality, and other "deficiencies" that might otherwise have been depicted in terms of shared blood (Lewis, 1965). Thus, the idea of culture has never been coherently or consistently separable from racialized notions of groups defined by their putative "biology." By treating "Hispanic" as an "ethnic" designation, the US census has encouraged Latinos to identify "racially" as white, or black, or Native American—in short, as anything but Latino, while reserving "Hispanic" as an officially non-"racial" category. Nevertheless, this hegemonic "ethnic" distinction instituted by the US state, which has also relied upon biological or phenotypic notions of racial categories, has been particularly instrumental for the allocation of affirmative action entitlements, deliberately constructing "Hispanics" as an effectively homogenized minority population analogous to African Americans. Thus, the "Hispanic" status of Latinos is widely treated as a racial condition all the same.

4. Only days before the riot, the Chicago police superintendent Orlando Wilson had ordered a special report on racial tensions in both the Puerto Rican and Mexican communities and the investigation had shown no signs whatsoever of unrest in either community (Padilla, 1987: 149).

5. I am in no way suggesting that only Chicago Puerto Ricans have been subjected to state surveillance or have engaged in political radicalism. Puerto Ricans in other US cities—including Philadelphia and New York—and on the island have also been targeted by state surveillance units (see, for instance, Fernández, 1987, 1994). However, in the Chicago Puerto Rican barrio, radical politics have been deployed in efforts that transcend the initial militant logic of these politics, to also address issues of urban neglect affecting a heavily segregated neighborhood (see Massey and Denton, 1989). In this sense, and perhaps to a greater extent than in other largely Puerto Rican areas in the US that are less racially segregated or even on the island of Puerto Rico, the everyday lives of barrio residents have been affected, to various degrees of intensity, by the initiatives of an openly nationalist faction that has deployed the 1950s discourse of Puerto Rican nationalism to engage in issues of housing, education, commercial development, and other urban projects otherwise only tangentially related to radical politics.

6. In 1971, Graciano López became the first Puerto Rican to run for elected public office in Chicago when he made a bid for alderman of the city's 26th Ward in the heart of the West Town–Humboldt Park barrio (Padilla, 1987: 250 n3). By 1975, three Puerto Rican independent Democrats ran against the Daley Democratic machine in a concerted campaign for the aldermanic seats for the 26th and 31st Wards (encompassing most of the Division Street barrio) as well as the 46th Ward in the Lakeview neighborhood, where the candidate was José "Cha-Cha" Jiménez. Jiménez had been one of the founders and a former leader of the Young Lords (Padilla, 1987: 196).

7. The Young Lords had begun as a street gang based in Chicago's Lincoln Park neighborhood that transformed itself in 1967 into a Puerto Rican youth organization comprising second-generation Puerto Ricans who had been inspired by the Black Panthers (Browning, 1973: 25; Padilla, 1987: 120–123).

8. Since these individuals had been renowned community activists prior to their arrests, various sectors of the community—not only those self-identified as *nacionalistas* or advocates of Puerto Rican independence—devoted considerable energy and resources to their release. In September 1999, most of these prisoners were given presidential pardon. In Chicago, nationalist activists recognized the prisoners' release as a bittersweet victory after 15 years of amnesty campaigns. The victory was bittersweet, not only because the release had not been unconditional (the release was criminalized, rather than a recognition of the purely political character of the charges), but also because two of the most revered prisoners were not considered for presidential pardon. The two prisoners who remained in jail, considered the "masterminds" of the FALN, were the brothers of a renowned Chicago activist and the sons of the reverend of a local church.

For various accounts of the individual or collective motivations that led to the creation of the FALN, see Fernández (1994) and Zwerman (1995).

9. Chicago ranked 1st for Latino/Asian segregation, tied for 1st for black/Asian segregation, 3rd for black/Latino segregation, 5th for white/black segregation, 6th for white/Latino segregation, and 18th for white/Asian segregation, according to measures of residential dissimilarity scores in US cities, calculated from the 2000 census by researchers at the Lewis Mumford Center for Comparative Urban and Regional Research at the State University of New York at Albany (Hirsch, 1983; Squires, 1987; Harrigan and Vogel, 2000).

10. For a more elaborate discussion of the racialization of space in Humboldt Park, as well as an examination of the relationship between Puerto Rican residential "displacement" and a correspondent increase in Puerto Rican national symbols, see Ramos-Zayas (2003).

11. The concept of "cultural citizenship" incites scholars to anchor their studies in the subjectivities and aspirations of subordinate agents, rather than focusing on systems of domination alone. Thus, notions of "cultural citizenship" formulate an equivalency between cultural production designed to seek respect among Latinos and a demand for full citizenship rights that Latino populations emphasize through a discourse of the "right to have rights" in the US. For an ethnographic examination of "cultural citizenship" and popular education, see the remarkable work of Benmayor, Torruellas, and Juarbe (1997). For more elaborate analyses of the subjectivities and discursive strategies of subaltern groups, see also Hall and Held (1990) and Scott (1985).

12. Nationalist narratives, educational projects, and iconography, including the multivalent representations of Nationalist leader Pedro Albizu Campos, which most literature on nationalism consider as attempts to mute divisions within the nation, have a more mediated effect in Chicago: they are oftentimes responsible for generating spaces of contention and denunciations of internal subordination along race, class, and gender lines, as well as issues of cultural "purity" and "authenticity," between "nationals" on the island and "migrants" in the US and between the Puerto Rican poor in *el barrio* and the "professionals" in the suburbs. This paradigmatic proposition is critical to understanding the intricacies and areas of contention underlying the performance of nationalism in Chicago. For a more comprehensive discussion, see Ramos-Zayas (2003).

13. It is important to note that the problem of who does or does not deserve citizenship and of who belongs in the hegemony of whiteness dates back to the origins of the US and is not specific to the case of Puerto Ricans. The specific issues raised here, or racialized national "substance" enacted in trouble-making, surfaced in the mid-1800s. Hence, the criminalization that is attributed to Puerto Ricans was also projected onto the Irish, Italians, Jews, and other European immigrants in previous centuries. However, what makes the Puerto Rican case unique is, of course, the fact that Puerto Ricans had US citizenship imposed upon them.

14. Another example of this politics of worthiness includes the multiple instances of civic engagement in volunteer organizations among Puerto Rican barrio residents in Chicago, particularly those residents who were unemployed. Even when unemployed barrio residents did not get monetary compensation for their volunteer work at not-for-profit agencies, for instance, they were able to construct a self-image as productive citizens, rather than subscribing to negative stereotypes of welfare-dependent or lazy Puerto Ricans that were imposed on them (see also Benmayor et al. (1997) for a comparable discussion of El Barrio Educational Project in New York's Spanish Harlem).

15. In the so-called *Insular Cases* of the 1900s, the Supreme Court held that Puerto Rico and the other new insular territories were not "foreign territory," but it also held that they were not "a part of the United States" for all constitutional purposes (Cabranes, 1979, 2001: 43). In fact, as M. Pérez (2002) demonstrates in an analysis of the US congressional hearings in the 1990s surrounding the issues of Puerto Rico's political self-determination, the question of whether Puerto Ricans (born in Puerto Rico) are protected, like Americans born within the 50 states, under the 14th Amendment of the Constitution has brought forth the distinction between a citizenship resulting from legislation versus a citizenship conferred constitutionally. A memo from the Congressional Research Services (Killian, 1989) states that the US citizenship of Puerto Ricans (born in Puerto Rico) was not granted under the 14th Amendment, but rather was given legislatively under the Jones Act of 1917 and that therefore, the US Congress has the power to revoke these Puerto Ricans' US citizenship. In a personal conversation, Pérez mentioned, anecdotally, that many Puerto Ricans attending the hearings, upon becoming aware of their "lesser" form of US citizenship, had inquired about the possibility of seeking naturalization.

16. Throughout this chapter, the concept of whiteness signals a combined system of privilege that retains its power by appearing as an unspoken racial "norm," an unmarked set of dominant assumptions that persist despite official "diversity" and "multiculturalist" rhetoric in the US. The privilege of whiteness is sustained precisely through its invisibility, as reflected in mainstream notions of order, duty, submission to the nation-state, and ideologies of class mobility, and further transmitted by the public education system, for instance. Because these are key elements that, ideologically speaking, anyone can acquire if they try hard enough, white supremacy in the late 20th century and early 21st century places a burden on the individual to make an effort to belonging that was not required a century ago. As Lipsitz (1998) has argued, the "possessive investment in whiteness," or what white people gain from their whiteness, is not a simple matter of black and white; all racialized minority groups have suffered from it, albeit to different degrees and in different ways. Moreover, the power of whiteness depends not only on white hegemony over separate racialized groups but also on manipulating racial

outsiders to fight against one another, to compete with one another for white approval and the benefits of whiteness. For a more extended discussion of "whiteness," see the seminal works of bell hooks, Ruth Frankenberg, Noel Ignatiev, George Lipsitz, Toni Morrison, and David Roediger.

17. An extensive discussion of the numerous interventions by the FBI, CIA, and other domestic surveillance units (e.g., COINTELPRO) into Puerto Rican political groups in the US and on the island is beyond the scope of this chapter. For a historical account of such surveillance, see Fernández's works on "*los macheteros*" (literally, "the cane-cutters"; a nationalist paramilitary organization in Puerto Rico) (1987) and the FALN prisoners (1994), as well as Cruz's (1998) volume on Puerto Rican politics in the US.

18. Particularly instructive here is Coutin's (2003) examination of the legal transcripts of suspension of deportation hearings and how Salvadoran detainees are asked to prove their "Americanness" to avoid deportation. Coutin shows how the Salvadorans perceived to be eligible for amnesty tended to be portrayed as hardworking, church-going individuals, often with families, whereas those deemed ineligible were portrayed as problematic and possible troublemakers See also Haney López (1996) and Ong (1999).

19. The most current recruitment campaign of "An Army of One"—not unlike the previous one of "Be All That You Can Be"—cannot be more blatantly invested in the reinsertion of the US military as the only acceptable venue toward whiteness available for the "deserving" members of otherwise pathologized communities (US Army, 2002). The evident suggestion is that in order to avoid the criminality, welfare "abuse," single motherhood, and other forms of "illegality" viewed as endemic to their corrupt neighborhood, young men and women from poor and working-class backgrounds would need to be redeemed (and "reprogrammed," to use the word of an army recruiter in Newark) by the US military.

20. More recently, the US military has also become involved in dispensing citizenship status, previously the realm of the INS, to young migrants from Latin American countries who have been casualties of the war on Iraq. The notorious case of Guatemalan José Gutiérrez, who was granted US citizenship posthumously after being a casualty of the US invasion of Iraq, is the most renowned case (see, for instance, Keane [2003]). As Arturo Souza, a Brazilian high school student in Newark, told me in the weeks following the dispensation of Gutiérrez's citizenship: "Sometimes I think of joining the army so I can get the U.S. citizenship faster and be able to bring my mom from Minas [Gerais]. But I don't now think they give it [the citizenship] by just joining. I think you have to be sent to war . . . or do you have to actually die in war? I'm not sure."

21. As David Cole (2003) notes, "A US citizen stripped of his citizenship and ordered deported would presumably have nowhere to go. But another provision authorizes the attorney general to deport persons 'to any country or region regardless of whether the country or region has a government.' And failing such deportation plans, the Justice Department has issued a regulation empowering authorities to detain indefinitely suspected terrorists who are ordered deported but cannot be removed because they are stateless or their country of origin refuses to take them back." This bill would authorize secret arrests, allow secret government wiretaps and searches without even a warrant from the supersecret Foreign Intelligence Surveillance Court when Congress has authorized the use of force, and terminate court orders barring illegal police spying. Likewise, the government is granted access to credit reports as private companies, without judicial supervision.

22. As stated in an ACLU report, the USA Patriot Act expands terrorism laws to include "domestic terrorism" that could subject political organizations to surveillance, wiretapping, harassment, and criminal action for political advocacy. With the DSEA, the administration seeks to transgress both the alien-citizen line, by turning citizens into aliens for their political ties, and the domestic-international line, giving to wholly domestic criminal law- enforcement agencies tools that were previously reserved for international terrorism investigations. Likewise, the act expands the ability of law enforcement to conduct secret searches, giving them wide powers of phone and internet surveillance and access to highly personal medical, financial, mental health, and student records with minimal judicial oversight. Moreover, the USA Patriot Act allows FBI agents to investigate US citizens for criminal matters without probable cause of crime if they say it is for "intelligence purposes." Finally, the act permits noncitizens to be jailed on the basis of mere suspicion and to be denied readmission to the US for engaging in free speech. Suspects convicted of no crime may be detained indefinitely in six-month instalments without meaningful judicial review (ACLU, 2003; Cole, 2003). Ironically, many of these forms of government intervention have characterized life in Humboldt Park since the 1960s.

ACKNOWLEDGMENTS

I want to thank Suzanne Oboler for organizing a stimulating conference and workshop on "Latinos and Citizenship" at the University of Illinois in Chicago, and the insightful feedback from the colleagues who participated in the conference. I am also grateful for the comments of this journal's anonymous readers.

REFERENCES

American Civil Liberties Union. 2003. *The USA PATRIOT Act and Government Actions that Threaten Our Civil Liberties*. New York: ACLU. http://www.aclu.org/safeandfree.

Anderson, Alan B., and George W. Pickering. 1986. *Confronting the Color Line: The Broken Promise of the Civil Rights Movement in Chicago*. Athens, GA: University of Georgia Press.

Benmayor, Rina, Rosa M. Torruellas, and Ana L. Juarbe. 1997. Claiming Cultural Citizenship in East Harlem: "Si Esto Puede Ayudar a la Comunidad Mía . . .". In *Latino Cultural Citizenship: Claiming Identity, Space, and Rights*, ed. William V. Flores and Rina Benmayor, 152–209. Boston, MA: Beacon.

Blanchard, Elizabeth. 1988. Three Teachers Talking. *The Reader* (newspaper), January 22.

Bowden, Charles, and Lew Kreinberg. 1981. *Street Signs Chicago: Neighbor and Other Illusions of Big-City Life*. Chicago, IL: Chicago Review Press.

Browning, Frank. 1973. From Rumble to Revolution: The Young Lords. In *The Puerto Rican Experience: A Sociological Sourcebook*, ed. Francesco Cordasco and Eugene Bucchioni, 231–245. New Jersey: Littlefield, Adams & Co.

Butler, Judith. 1999. Performativity's Social Magic. In *Bourdieu: A Critical Reader*, ed. Richard Shusterman, Oxford: Critical Readers and Maiden, MA: Blackwell.

Cabranes, José A. 1979. *Citizenship and the American Empire*. New Haven, CT: Yale University Press.

———. 2001. Some Common Ground. In *Foreign in a Domestic Sense: Puerto Rico, American Expansion, and the Constitution*, ed. Christina Duffy Burnett and Burke Marshal, 39–47. Durham, NC: Duke University Press.

Caldeira, Teresa. 2000. *City of Walls: Crime, Segregation, and Citizenship in São Paulo*. Berkeley: University of California Press.

Cole, David. 2003. Patriot Act's Big Brother. *The Nation*, February 27.

Committee for Clemente Community Hearings, ad hoc. 1998. Community Hearings: Determining the Truth Behind the Clemente Story. Panel held at Malcolm X City College, September.

Coutin, Susan Bibler. 2003. Suspension of Deportation Hearing and Measures of "Americanness." *Journal of Latin American Anthropology* 8(2): 58–95.

Cruz, José E. 1998. *Identity and Power: Puerto Rican Politics and the Challenge of Ethnicity*. Philadelphia, PA: Temple University Press.

Cruz, Wilfredo. 1995. Witch Hunt at Clemente High: Puerto Rican Nationalism and Chicago Politics. *Crítica: A Journal of Puerto Rican Policy & Politics* (34–35): 1, 8–9.

De Genova, Nicholas, and Ana Y. Ramos-Zayas. 2003. *Latino Crossings: Mexicans, Puerto Ricans, and the Politics of Race and Citizenship*. New York and London: Routledge.

Espinosa, Leticia. 1995. El cierre de HIMRI. *La Raza*, July 27–August 2: 4–6.

Fernández, Ronald. 1987. *Los Macheteros: The Wells Fargo Robbery and the Violent Struggle for Puerto Rican Independence.* New York: Prentice-Hall.

———. 1994. *Prisoners of Colonialism: The Struggle for Justice in Puerto Rico.* Monroe, ME: Common Courage Press.

Hall, Stuart, and David Held. 1990. Citizens and Citizenship. In *New Times: The Changing Face of Politics in the 1990s,* ed. Stuart Hall and Martin Jacques, 173–188. London: Verso.

Haney López, Ian F. 1996. *White By Law: The Legal Construction of Race.* New York: New York University Press.

Harrigan, J., and R. Vogel. 2000. *Political Change in the Metropolis.* 6th ed. New York: Longman.

Hirsch, Arnold R. 1983. *Making the Second Ghetto: Race and Housing in Chicago, 1940–1960.* New York: Cambridge University Press.

Keane, Fergal. 2003. Guatemalan Orphan to War Hero. British Broadcasting Network News, UK Edition, April 7.

Killian, Johnny. 1989. Discretion of Congress Regarding Citizenship of Puerto Ricans'. Congressional Research Service Memo.

Lefebvre, Henri. 1991[1974]. *The Production of Space.* New York: Blackwell.

Lewis, Oscar. 1965. *La Vida: A Puerto Rican Family in the Culture of Poverty—San Juan and New York.* New York: Vintage Books.

Lipsitz, George. 1998. *The Possessive Investment in Whiteness: How White People Profit from Identity Politics.* Philadelphia, PA: Temple University Press.

Massey, Douglas, and Nancy Denton. 1989. Residential Segregation of Mexicans, Puerto Ricans, and Cubans in Selected US Metropolitan Areas. *Sociology and Social Research* 73: 73–83.

Oclander, Jorge. 1995. Public School's "Pathetic" Use of Poverty Funds. *Chicago Sun-Times,* June 15.

Omi, Michael, and Howard Winant. 1986. *Racial Formation in the United States: From the 1960's to the 1980's.* New York: Routledge.

Ong, Aihwa. 1999. *Flexible Citizenship: The Cultural Logics of Transnationality.* Durham and London: Duke University Press.

Padilla, Felix M. 1985. *Latino Ethnic Consciousness: The Case of Mexican Americans and Puerto Ricans in Chicago.* Notre Dame, IN: University of Notre Dame Press.

Padilla, Felix M. 1987. *Puerto Rican Chicago.* Notre Dame, IN: University of Notre Dame Press.

Perea, Juan. 2001. Fulfilling Manifest Destiny: Conquest, Race, and the Insular Cases. In *Foreign in a Domestic Sense: Puerto Rico, American Expansion, and the Constitution,* ed. Christina Duffy Burnett and Burke Marshal, 140–166. Durham, NC: Duke University Press.

Pérez, Gina. 2002. How a Scholarship Girl Becomes a Soldier: US Military Recruitment in a Chicago High School, Post-September 11th. Paper presented at the American Anthropological Association Meetings, November 20–24, New Orleans, Louisiana.

Pérez, Marvette. 2002. The Political "Flying Bus:" Nationalism, Identity, Status, Citizenship and Puerto Ricans. *Critique of Anthropology* 22: 305–322.

Ramos-Zayas, Ana Y. 1997. "La patria es valor y sacrificio:" Nationalist Ideologies, Cultural Authenticity, and Community Building among Puerto Ricans in Chicago. PhD diss., Columbia University.

———. 1998. Nationalist Ideologies, Neighborhood-Based Activism, and Educational Spaces in Puerto Rican Chicago. *Harvard Educational Review* 68: 164–192.

———. 2001. Racializing the "Invisible" Race: Latino Constructions of "White Culture" and Whiteness in Chicago. *Urban Anthropology* 30: 341–380.

———. 2003. *National Performances: The Politics of Class, Race and Space in Puerto Rican Chicago*. Chicago, IL: University of Chicago Press.

Rosaldo, Renato. 1997. Cultural Citizenship, Inequality, and Multiculturalism. In *Latino Cultural Citizenship: Claiming Identity, Space, and Rights*, ed. William V. Flores and Rina Benmayor, 27–38. Boston, MA: Beacon.

Scott, James. 1985. *Weapons of the Weak: Everyday Forms of Peasant Resistance*. New Haven, CT: Yale University Press.

Squires, Gregory D. 1987. *Chicago: Race, Class and the Response to Urban Decline*. Philadelphia, PA: Temple University Press.

Smith, Rogers. 1997. *Civic Ideals: Conflicting Visions of Citizenship in U.S. History*. New Haven and London: Yale University Press.

US Army. 2002. "The Making of a Soldier" pamphlet. January.

Williams, C., and A. Smith. 1983. The National Construction of Social Space. *Progress in Human Geography* 7: 502–518.

Winant, Howard. 1994. *Racial Conditions: Politics, Theory, Comparisons*. Minneapolis: University of Minnesota Press.

Zwerman, Gilda. 1995. The Identity-Vulnerable Activist and the Emergence of Post–New Left Armed, Underground Organizations in the U.S. Center for Studies of Social Change. New School for Social Research. The Working Papers Series. Working Paper no. 218, September.

CHAPTER 12

Transforming Citizenship: Membership, Strategies of Containment, and the Public Sphere in Latino Communities

Raymond Rocco

It's great now that they're calling José Antonio a hero. But when he was up crossing the border they called him a wetback . . .In my mind, he was a hero when he chose to leave the streets. The rest is just politics and window dressing.

—Bruce Harris, Director of Casa Alianza

Whatever their legal citizenship status, and however many genera-tions of American citizens they can trace in their ancestry, Hispanics/Latinos in the United States are liable to be treated as foreigners.

—Iris Young (2000b: 158)

On Wednesday, April 2, 2003, the US Bureau of Citizenship and Immigration Services "awarded" citizenship to two young Latino immigrants, José Garibay and José Gutiérrez, who were serving in the Marines and were killed during the first few days of the US invasion of Iraq. The official reason given for bestowing citizenship was that it was meant to reward them for losing their lives.[1] However, given the rise in anti-immigrant sentiment during the last few years, the charges that Latino/a immigrants in particular have undermined the "American way of life," and drained our resources, and that the 37,000 noncitizens in the military pose a problem of "dual loyalty," the Bush administration is in a somewhat awkward position. Is it possible that the granting of citizenship was intended to reconcile the tension inherent in the fact that noncitizens were performing duties normally associated with the highest loyalties of citizenship? Clearly, citizenship has no meaning for these two Latinos now, so granting it to them posthumously is a symbolic act meant to appeal to a national audience. Immigrants do not enjoy, to use T. H. Marshall's notion, "full membership in the community" (Marshall, 1950) but making Garibay and Gutiérrez citizens posthumously is a way to rectify what may seem to some as an unfair, perhaps even unjust situation, that is, that these two were willing to risk their lives for a country that limited their ability to participate fully in its major institutions.[2] At the very least, the action highlights the complex question of how the relationship between citizenship, identity, and the meaning of "belonging" to a political community applies to Latino/as in the US.

This relationship takes on added significance in the contemporary period because of the rapid and extensive growth of Latino/a communities during the last three decades. The results of the 2000 census released recently confirm what most researchers on Latino/a communities have argued for some time. However, even they underestimated the growth of this population, both in terms of numbers and of location.[3] Not only did this last decade witness a dramatic increase in the size of the Latino/a population, significant Latino/a communities grew in states that had virtually no Latino/a presence a short time ago. Latino/a restaurants, stores, churches, soccer leagues, home associations, and celebrations of holidays such as Cinco de Mayo are now a basic part of life in small towns in Georgia, North Carolina, Iowa, and Kentucky. In Ames, Iowa, the Mexican Independence Day parades of the 16th of September are as visible and significant as those on the 4th of July.

These dramatic increases in the Latino/a populations' size and rate of growth have played a fundamental role in transforming the configuration of political, cultural, spatial, and economic characteristics and relations of many of the most important urban regions in the country. These are both cause and effect of a complex set of processes of societal restructuring embodied in a broad variety of institutional strategies, policies, and practices at both the regional and international levels, which have been documented extensively in the literature on restructuring, globalization, and transnationalization (Rocco, 1996; Bonilla *et al.*, 1998; Sassen, 1998; Short and Kim, 1999; Cohen, 2001). As these developments have unfolded, the specific issues around which political and social divisions and conflicts revolve have shifted considerably.

Prominent among these is the reemergence of citizenship as a major focus of political and cultural relations, discourse, and policy agendas. This is in large measure a direct consequence of the massive and rapid increases in the level of transnational migrations from Latin America, Africa, Asia, and the Caribbean to the major urban regions of the US and Europe (Castles and Miller, 1993; Papastergiadis, 2000). Unlike immigrants of the late 19th and early 20th century, these "new" or more recent arrivals come from cultural backgrounds and contexts dramatically different from those of the country where they have settled. This disjunction or "difference" has generated a qualitatively different set of political issues and alignments, including the contestation of established notions of rights, responsibilities, obligations, entitlements, which in turn has led to a broader debate about the meaning of and criteria for societal membership and national "belonging" (Castles and Davidson, 2000).

The debate has found expression in a wide-ranging scholarly literature that focuses on the need to retheorize the issue of citizenship within the context of the consequences of the new social formations, including the increased levels of interdependence brought about by globalization (Zolberg and Norman, 1997). However, despite the obvious relevance of these issues for Latino/a communities in the US, relatively little of this scholarly work attempts to conceptualize the articulation between the transformation these communities have experienced and the issue of citizenship and societal membership.[4] The following advances a particular formulation of this relationship that I believe is the most useful for understanding and explaining the current positionality of the various and diverse sectors of Latino/a communities. It incorporates three essential dimensions: (1) the historical experience of exclusion; (2) the forms of colonization of that marginalization; and (3) situating Latino/a communities within the context of the changing parameters of the nation-state.

CITIZENSHIP, LATINO/A COMMUNITIES, AND DIFFERENCE

A number of scholars have commented on the recent reemergence of citizenship as the subject of widespread analysis and have indicated that it is one of the most contested theoretical terrains across the political spectrum in the contemporary period (Holston, 1999; Isin, 2000; Kymlicka and Norman, 2000; McKinnon and Hampsher-Monk, 2000; Vandenberg, 2000). Not only are the substantive differences considerable, the manner in which the problematic of citizenship is framed varies widely.[5] The argument here is that the most productive approach to rethinking citizenship in a way that is most salient for Latino/a communities is to focus on the particular factors that have characterized their experiences and that have been most fundamental in affecting the level and nature of the articulation between these communities and the major institutions of power in the US.[6] The literature on this subject is characterized by very different theoretical and disciplinary approaches and models that ascribe the condition of Latino/a communities in the US to various elements and processes. Nevertheless, it is widely recognized that one of the defining factors throughout the complex and changing history of these relations is the racial and cultural disjunction inscribed in and affecting class relations, political access, participation in the economic sectors, and, more generally, the complex dynamics of exclusionary processes that have maintained a level of marginalization and systematic disempowerment for significant sectors of Latino/a populations.

This is not to imply, however, that these processes have been or are the same for all Latino/as. Latino/a populations in the US are far from homogenous, and each of the groups normally referred to as Latino/as has a very different history and mode of articulation with the major institutional spheres of life in the US.[7] Thus, for example, the particulars of the transnational dimension are quite different for Dominican communities than they are for Mexicans. And clearly, the process of Cuban incorporation, based on the logic of the Cold War, has been completely different from that of Puerto Ricans, whose status and modes of access cannot be understood without situating these in the context of the continuing legacy of the colonial relation with the US. Despite these important differences, however, cultural disjunctions have nevertheless played a fundamental role in shaping the particular configuration of institutional relations and social locations affecting all Latino/a communities. This includes the particular articulation between Latino/as and the institutional practices of citizenship.[8] Although this cultural friction has been a constant feature of the relations between Latino/as and the Anglo- and Eurocentric groups in the US, it has taken on a different set of manifestations as a result of the demographic changes of the last 30 years. Hence, it has to be understood within the broader and more significant role of the diversity that has redefined the public sphere.

A range of theoretical approaches have emerged in the last decade or so that attempt to assess the significance and implications of this extensive degree of cultural diversity for the theory and practice of citizenship in liberal democracies.[9] Those that are most relevant to the Latino/a experience in the US are the postnationalist, transnational, dual citizenship, and postliberal reconceptualizations of citizenship. Each of these focuses on and highlights a different dimension or configuration of elements. While the first three offer important insights for understanding the political status of Latino/as, because of limitations of space, I want to focus here only on the fourth category, that is, recent attempts within the field of political and social theory to modify and extend the liberal model of citizenship that has been the normative foundation for conceptualizing the relationship between membership, culture, and political community in the US for the last 150 years.[10] More specifically, I will address two particularly influential approaches within this broader project. One revolves around developing a model of multicultural citizenship, and the other focuses on elaborating the notion of differentiated citizenship. Both approaches place diversity at the center of their considerations. The most well-known theorist within the first perspective is Will Kymlicka, who developed it as part of his effort to modify the basic tenets of the liberal principles that have been at the core of the traditional conceptions of citizenship in Western democracies for the last two centuries (Kymlicka, 1995a,b). Retaining the emphasis on the notion of the individual as the bearer of specific rights that guarantee freedom, Kymlicka attempts to incorporate the role of culture into the liberal paradigm by arguing that the latter can only be meaningful if there are choices available to the individual. But the meaning and significance of choices are provided by the particular culture, which Kymlicka refers to as a "societal culture," within which the individual functions. Hence, the diversity in cultures must be incorporated in the assessment and justification of the rights claims that are fundamental to liberal citizenship. While this might appear to have significant relevance for the study of Latino/as in the US, Kymlicka has very little to say about the latter. It is true that he recognizes the heterogenous nature of Latino/a populations and refers to a number of districting cases that relate to Latino/a populations. Nevertheless, he makes no sustained, detailed analysis of these groups and the most he offers is an argument that the voluntary status of "Hispanic" immigrants puts them on a different footing than "national" minorities who have a legitimate claim to cultural rights.[11]

There are several variations of Kymlicka's approach to reconcile liberal principles with some level of recognition of group cultural rights. One of the more fully developed is found in the work of Joseph Raz, who agrees with Kymlicka that the value of cultural membership is a function of the contribution it makes to the promotion of individual well-being, prosperity, and autonomy (Raz, 1994).

The major difference is that while Kymlicka's model is based on the assumption that a form and level of political reconciliation of diverse cultures within a given state can be achieved through institutional arrangements, Raz holds that even if group rights are granted and policies to protect minority cultures are developed in these types of societies, conflict between cultural groups is inevitable. This is because cultures are fundamentally about deeply held beliefs and values, and thus it is unrealistic to expect that these can be in some way reconciled without remainders. The most effective path to prosperity and greater access to institutions, Raz suggests, is to take advantage of group rights and protective policies to incorporate the basic principles of liberalism, particularly individual autonomy. This, of course, appears to contradict the notion that cultural tensions are resolved and instead offers what is ultimately a politics of assimilationism.

While there are a number of other arguments advanced to reconcile multiculturalism with the liberal principles of autonomy and individual rights, I want to focus on what I believe to be the most helpful approach provided by the notion of differentiated citizenship, most fully developed in several works by Iris Young (1990, 2000a). The main argument here revolves around the concept of equality. Young builds her notion of citizenship on the premise that sameness and equality are not equivalent in the context of societal relations. The universalist notions of liberal citizenship assume that all "citizens" are equal and therefore require equal treatment. But Young observes that this formulation ignores the particularity that defines the actual condition of various groups in a society, such as the reality of the differences in power, status, and resources that characterize institutional location in capitalist democracies. In this context, the principle of equality requires that individuals or groups who occupy different social, political, or economic locations must be treated differently, that is, policies and practices must differentiate between the social locations of the different groups. Unlike Kymlicka's notion of multicultural citizenship, differentiated citizenship foregrounds the issue of power and privilege and thus is much more resonant with the Latino/a experience of political marginalization in the US.

Young has recently addressed the Latino/a experience in a much more detailed way (Young, 2000b). Her primary argument is that Latino/a claims to justice are concerned with issues of structural inequality. Extending her notion of structural social group to Latino/as, Young examines three axes of justice claims: (1) citizenship and belonging; (2) language support; and (3) racism, stereotyping, and discrimination. Here, I focus on and build upon the analysis of the first of these (Young, 2000b: 148). As indicated in the quote at the beginning of this chapter, Young suggests that the particular mode of alterity experienced by Latino/as is that of difference as "foreigners." This is an argument I have made in other works. I concur with Young's assertion that Latino/as "are liable to be treated as not belonging to their communities and societies in a full sense, and they often do not feel that they belong . . . Hispanics/Latinos are uniquely positioned as permanently foreign immigrants in the imagination of Anglo Americans" (Young, 2000b: 159). This notion of foreignness is the thread of continuity between the contemporary positions of Latino/as and the initial engagement between Anglo society and Mexicanos in the early 19th century. It is the political imaginary that has defined the issue of citizenship as it applies to Latino/as. What is at issue here is nothing less than the nature and extent of societal membership and access to and participation in the major institutions of society.[12] As such, Latino/as' efforts to contest their exclusion question the parameters of political community as defined by the dominant institutions.

MODES OF EXCLUSION, RACIALIZATION, AND SOCIETAL MEMBERSHIP

It is my contention that the current pattern of politics of contestation over citizenship in Latino/a communities has been framed and shaped by the modes of exclusion that were established during the period when the new Anglo political elites and settlers established political, economic, and cultural dominance over the Southwest, structuring a particular mode of incorporation that set a framework for future relationships and societal location. In particular, I want to argue that the initial cultural and ideological construction of the Mexican population in the region as racialized "foreigners" has been a continuous thread in the historical relationship between Mexicans and the political and legal apparatus, as well as with the general Anglo population that became the majority and dominant sector in the Southwest shortly after the Mexican– American War.[13] This initial racialized construction has served as the lens through which later-arriving Latino/a immigrants have been conceptualized.[14] This is not to imply or ignore Latino/a communities' heterogenous nature and their very different histories of articulation with and modes of incorporation into the US, each of which requires its own specific and detailed analysis. My claim is that despite these differences, most Latino/a groups have been categorized within a preexisting, racialized, cultural imaginary produced, limited, and modified by the dominant cultural institutional apparatus in spheres such as the media, law, and education.[15]

This racialized conception of Latino/as runs counter to much of the more traditional social science literature that categorizes Latino/a populations as ethnic groups, and thus frames the study of Latino/as as an extension of the conceptualization of European immigrants to the US.[16] Yet the pattern of relations that established the initial set of parameters that defined the "place" of Mexicans in the transformed landscape of the Southwest was clearly racially as well as class-encoded. It was obviously a different mode of racialization from that of African Americans that structured the institutional basis of the social order in the southern and northern states. Recent works on the transformation that the Mexican population underwent in the 19th-century Southwest provide strong support for this claim. Although acknowledging that the particular mode of Mexicans' racialization varied by region and that Mexicans were legally defined as "white" at the conclusion of the Mexican–American War, Almaguer's study of the "origins of white supremacy" in California clearly shows the foregrounding of racial imaging in the process by which the modes of access and incorporation of the majority of Mexicans were established (Almaguer, 1994). It is important to note as well that Anglo settlers made a clear class distinction between the small Mexican elite who had controlled virtually all of the land-based form of capital and who were considered "acceptable" in terms of status and interaction, even intermarriage, and the rest of the working-class, mestizo population. Although this issue is not the central concern of his study, Vélez-Ibáñez (1996) also documents some of the prevailing cultural constructions of Mexicans, particularly in the latter half of the 19th century. He quotes Henry Lewis Morgan, who greatly influenced the early development of anthropology in the US, to the effect that the racial mixing of European and Indian evident in the majority of Mexicans produces a racially inferior "breed." While there were variations of the racial stereotype in Texas, Arizona, California, and New Mexico, there was a convergence on the basic premise of Mexican racial inferiority. David Weber's study of the US frontier also highlights the centrality of this theme, stating that most Anglo-Americans considered the racial mixture that characterized most Mexicans as "violations of the laws of nature" (Weber, 1992: 337). In an earlier study, Barrera demonstrated the significance of the role of the ideology of white supremacy in establishing a racialized labor force during the latter half of the 19th century (Barrera, 1979). But the most comprehensive study of this racialization process is the recently published work by Menchaca in which she demonstrates, through detailed historical analysis and documentation, the centrality of race in establishing the forms of hierarchies that led to the political and economic marginalization of Mexicanos in the Southwest (Menchaca, 2001). These studies make clear that the subordination of the Mexican population was achieved through legal and political strategies. Moreover, the sites of civil society were major spaces for regulating the nature and level of Mexican access and incorporation into the emerging social order on a racialized basis. The combination of formal state policies with social restrictions in effect became the mode by which the nature of societal membership was contained and defined. This justifies the need for a concept of citizenship that is capable of accomodating the relationship between Latino/as and the state as well as their status within the institutions of civil society.

In his analysis of the dynamics of inclusion and exclusion in the relationship between nation and membership, Nieguth provides a useful way of conceptualizing the role of civil society in these processes of marginalization:

> Membership is a condition for individuals to gain access to societal goods and power. As such, it is a multidimensional phenomenon: the organizing principle guiding processes of boundary construction in a given society manifests itself not only in who is admitted physically from a spatial outside, but also in the relative societal status enjoyed by members of different social groups within a state—in other words, admission. Hence, no measurement of the distribution of membership in a specific nation can rely on legal definitions of membership alone, such as political citizenship. Instead, it will have to take into account the distribution of political, economic, social, and cultural status among individuals. (1999: 157)

The differential and unequal access of Mexicans in the US to the major forms of resources, particularly institutionalized resources that determined the type and level of societal membership, then, was clearly not simply a by-product of the process of social transformation in the Southwest. It was, instead, the result of the combined forces of legal and political isolation and the social mechanisms of marginalization operative in the sphere of civil society, both of which converged around the imaginary of the perennial "foreigner." And while the particular factors that have had the greatest effect have varied over the last 150 years, I would argue that the societal positionality of significant sectors of the Latino/a population continues to be primarily determined by these twin processes, albeit in a different form and register.

However, the works on Mexicans in the US referred to above, as well as others, document that at the same time that the sphere of civil society functioned to limit their membership status in the larger society, Mexicans also developed a range of strategies rooted in the institutional sites of their internal civil society to confront these restrictions. Among the most important social mechanisms that individuals, households, and communities developed to survive and generally function in the new environment were relations and networks based on social trust. Drawing on common but limited resources, providing services on an exchange basis, developing mutual aid associations, and improvising informal market relations were common ways in which these relations manifested themselves. Although some of these included and emerged from relations of reciprocity, there were other forms of mutuality for the development of forms of social trust and cooperation that were the basis of community collective institutions.

While these practices were consolidated and incorporated within the networks of civil society in the 19th and early 20th centuries, these kinds of relations have not disappeared as some might have expected. Quite the contrary, results from several studies, including my own field work in several working-class urban Latino/a communities in Los Angeles over the last ten years, reveal that these networks of interaction and cooperation, based on forms of mutuality, continue to be one of the major mechanisms of group adaptation, survival, and advancement not only in Mexican-origin communities but also among Central Americans, Dominicans, Colombians, Peruvians, and Ecuadorans. Through these relations of mutuality, individuals and households in these communities have found ways to accommodate, resist, circumvent, and engage the restrictive barriers that continue to affect them.

CONTESTING THE BOUNDARIES OF POLITICAL COMMUNITY

As indicated above, a concept of citizenship that adequately accounts for the historical trajectory of Latino/as in the US must focus not only on the level and nature of their incorporation into the state but must also construe this dimension in relation to the qualitative nature of associational practices within the institutional sites of civil society. Expanding the scope of citizenship would thus require a strategy that David Held has discussed as a process of "double democratization" (Held, 1991). In a sense, then, I am arguing for "inverting" the traditional "location" of citizenship within the state. I am not arguing that the legal and juridical constructions of citizenship are unimportant or that they are mechanistically derivative from these associational practices. Rather, I am arguing that a one-dimensional conception of citizenship fundamentally obscures its real political nature because it is incapable of capturing the contextual figurations that enable its essentially regulative function of controlling and containing societal membership.[17] Thus "citizenship" is interpreted here as primarily a political strategy whose meaning changes over time as it is contested by a variety of claims. Certainly the history of the changes in the meaning of citizenship in the history of the US supports this interpretation. While I disagree with the particular interpretation offered in Rogers Smith's *Civic Ideals* (1997), Smith's research traces clearly traces in meticulous detail the ways in which the meaning of citizenship has shifted in response to specific political interests and goals. The recent work by Evelyn Nakano Glenn, *Unequal Freedom: How Race and Gender Shaped American Citizenship and Labor* (2002), documents how changing formulations and interpretations of citizenship have played a basic role in legitimating and sustaining unequal and oppressive race and gender relations in the US.

What works like these make clear is the need to understand the regulative political function of citizenship in the US as it was applied to Latino/as as part of the strategy of establishing the nation-state as the primary form of political community. The assumption of the isomorphic relationship between the nation, territory, state, and cultural identity has been the basis of this form of political community in the West since the Treaty of Westphalia established the basic parameters of international relations in 1648. But it is precisely this conception of political community that has been challenged in the last few decades by the various consequences of processes of globalization, particularly the very significant growth in the immigrant, or "foreign," populations in traditionally Euro- and Anglocentric societies.

In a recent essay on the effects of globalization on conceptions of political community, David Held argues that most contemporary notions of democracy rest on an incorrect assumption of the coincidence between political community and the territorially bounded nation-state, or, as he puts it, the "uncritically appropriated concept of the territorial political community" (Held, 1999: 91). In fact, he claims, political communities have rarely coincided in this way with a given territorial or geographical space. Instead, political communities emerge on the basis of a complex set of interactions between social practices, economic linkages, political power, cultural and ethnic loyalties, and military conquest. The modernist notion that territorial boundaries should coincide with the right of rule and governance developed as a specific element of the processes of nation-building in Europe during the period between the 17th and 19th centuries. This is a view that has been advanced with increasing frequency in the literature on the challenges that globalization poses for democracy. One of the clearest articulations of this position is provided by R. B. J. Walker, who states:

> It has been abundantly clear to many observers that the principle of state sovereignty is increasingly problematic. As a formalization of configurations of power and authority that emerged in a specific historical context, it has been criticized as an inappropriate guide to both theory and practice in an age of rapid transformation. It has come to seem particularly inappropriate in view of the current internationalization or globalization of economic, technological, cultural, and political processes. (Walker, 1990: 161–162)

Thus, the way in which the relationship between power, governance, territory, identity, and membership was construed as part of what was a specific historical process of political and economic development in a limited region of the world at a particular time has been transformed into universalistic claims that equate the dimension of explicit authority with the boundaries of territorial space (Camilleri, 1990).

It should be recalled that this formulation and figuration of these elements were the product of a specific set of political conflicts in 17th-century Europe that focused on rival claims precisely about the right to control and govern contested areas. The Treaty of Westphalia of 1648 was promoted and accepted as the basis for ending the Thirty Years' War and established the central principles of the nation-state—territoriality, sovereignty, autonomy, and legality—that continue to be the basis of political relations 350 years later (McGrew, 1997: 3–60). The nation-state thus provided a particular answer to fundamental political questions such as: How should we understand the meaning of political community? Where are power and authority to be located? And how is such power and authority to be legitimized? Despite the fact that this was an answer that corresponded to a specific, bounded historical set of circumstances, this model of political community and organization became the modality that was imposed on societies and nations characterized by entirely different conditions, cultures, values, and societal practices.

The effects of the processes that constitute globalization, economic restructuring, and transnationalization have given rise to a debate about the extent to which this particular construction of the principles on which the nation-state continues to function can accommodate the new patterns of relationships and linkages that have resulted from the flows of people, technologies, capital, images, and ideas that increasingly define the global map (Habermas, 1995). A variety of theoretical positions have emerged that challenge the forms of political discourse that have either ignored or been insensitive to these flows and the transformations they have initiated. The critiques focus on attempting to demonstrate "how the questions to which the principle of state sovereignty has seemed to provide an uncontestable answer for so long—questions about who "we" are, where "we" have come from, and where "we" might be going—might be answered differently" (Walker, 1990: 160).

It is precisely the constitution of the "we" that is assumed by the nation-state form that has been contested by the particular pattern of migration from non-European regions to the Euro-US center. The fact that the predominant political unit is designated by the combined terms of nation and state is often overlooked. But it is clear that a foundational element of this framework was the attempt to link the dimension of identity and jurisdictional elements. The form of state nationalism in the particular context of nation-state building in Europe was essentially developed as a strategy for promoting cultural homogenization, while citizenship was the means for regulating the level and type of societal membership in a given nation-state. Territoriality was key in articulating these two dimensions and incorporating them into the institutional basis of governance and control. The exclusivist "we" that was privileged and granted membership in the initial formulations has been consistently contested since then by the political coalescence of a series of different types of groups, such as labor, women, racial and ethnic groups, and now, immigrants. It is clear that an essential element in the history of the development of the nation-state and its corresponding form of citizenship is the story of the various mechanisms, devices, laws, and regulations that have been created and relied on to contain the tension between independent logics of nation and state. The goal was to make the forms of social and cultural bonding and solidarity that characterize nations of peoples coincide with the jurisdictional prerogatives that established the right to govern through the control of the political institutions, including the control of the organized means of violence. This is why the issue of membership has been such a crucial element in defining the parameters of the nation-state. The definition of the "we" is created and maintained by the nation-state's sovereignty over controlling membership, and although the means for doing so are varied, citizenship has played a particularly important role in this area.

However, there have been few instances in which this control has been completely effective. In fact, the popular notion of citizenship as a rather clear-cut status is mostly fictional. Citizenship is not singular, discrete, or unchanging. Instead, we need to understand the theories and practices of citizenship as developed by nation-states as primarily a set of political mechanisms intended to control and regulate the level, type, and range of societal membership. Along with the dispersion of economic elements vital to the domestic system, wide-scale changes such as those in the racial and ethnic makeup of the US that have resulted from the processes of globalization present nation-states with a challenge to their ability to exercise effective control over who the "we" are that constitute its normatively privileged "citizens." From this perspective, citizenship is not solely nor even primarily a legal status, but rather a political mechanism for the control and containment of access to institutions of power and of the distribution of rights, benefits, privileges, entitlements, and resources to different sectors of the populations that reside within the territorial, sovereign boundaries of the nation-state.[18]

In response to these issues, a growing body of work has been devoted to the analysis of alternative forms of determining societal membership in a global context. Drawing on these discussions, my view is that the nation-state continues to play a fundamental role in determining the configurations of power in the sphere of global politics, but the particular ways in which this occurs have changed. The question of whether the power of the nation-state has been eroded by the processes of globalization should be reframed to ask in what ways the character of the modern nation-state has changed in response to these processes. The issue is not whether the state is withering away but rather its "transformation under specific historical circumstances" (Walker, 1990: 167). One result of this transformation is that political authority is no longer solely exercised within clearly demarcated territorial boundaries. New regimes for the regulation, control, and regulation of economic relations have been created by treaties, contracts, and agreements that nation-states have entered into during the last 30 years. While most of these have been driven by economic concerns, the fact is that there is an inevitable political dimension to them. Policies and institutions such as NAFTA, the WTO, MERCURSUR, and the European Union (EU) have all proposed that member nation- states agree to share some aspects of political authority, of their national sovereignty. The protestations or denials of some of the member states notwithstanding, all of these efforts have created spheres of political and economic coauthority that are simply inconsistent with the claims of exclusive sovereignty that have characterized the conception of the nation-state for so long now. The very existence of these new institutional arrangements is an indication of the growing disjunction between traditional forms of political authority tied to the nation-state and the most recent forms of global economic organization. In effect, the strategies developed to promote the viability of the global capitalist system have implicitly established the principle of shared sovereignty.

These practices and perspectives reflect the recognition that the processes of globalization and the impact they have had on the structure of societal relations require new institutional forms of governance and present a series of challenges to principles fundamental to democracy such as representation, accountability, and responsiveness. As indicated above, nation-states have been forced to address the economic dimensions and, with the participation of transnational capital, have established an extensive set of instruments that in effect creates a regime of economic and political rights for transnational capital. The logic and form of these regimes are driven by the need to respond to transnational networks, relationships, and practices that define regional communities of common economic interest. However, as I have stressed several times, these economic relationships do not and cannot exist or function in a vacuum. As the quote cited from Held indicates, political communities are defined by "social practices, economic linkages, political power, cultural and ethnic loyalties." In order to be viable over time, the structures of governance, including the particular form of citizenship and the scope of rights that are its foundation, must correspond, articulate with, and reflect these patterns of society. While the interests of the networks and practices of transnational capital are finding expression in sectors of the apparatus of governance, those specific forms of social relations, economic transactions, and cultural loyalties that constitute the lived reality of the majority of the population have not yet been incorporated in any systematic way into the institutions that define the official parameters of political community. As a result, there is a disjunction between the forms of governance still based exclusively on territorially defined notions of sovereignty and the actual social space created by the organic sets of relationships that define the real boundaries of a particular community. Societal relations evolve as a result of the interaction between individuals and groups with particular sets of values and beliefs, seeking to realize their goals and promote their interests within a specific institutional context. What often occurs, however, is that the latter becomes a barrier to the kinds of strategies that individuals, families, households, and groups develop to meet changing circumstances. This, I believe, is the case in the current period. Institutional change has occurred to facilitate the operations of transnational corporations, but not in response to the changes in the broader sectors of society. What is at issue then, is precisely the conception of who the specific "we" are who should be considered full members of society. While there are literally millions of Latino/a households that have been and continue to be a vital part of the economic, social, and cultural fabric of the US, legal and political parameters that emerged as part of a very different societal configuration prevent them from having equal standing and membership in the very society, the community of common linked fate, that they have helped to create.[19]

LATINO/A COMMUNITIES, REGIONALIZATION, AND DEMOCRATIZING CITIZENSHIP

How are these considerations relevant for Latino/as' political situation in the US? While the particular situation of each national group is quite different, there are nevertheless some common elements that come into play here. Over half of Latino/as are either immigrants or children of immigrants, a large proportion of whom maintain relatively strong ties with their respective countries of origin. These linkages include the very substantial level of remittances sent home, the existence of hundreds of hometown associations, forms of networks within the institutions of civil society in Latino/a communities, the existence of Spanish-language media that emphasize and reinforce cultural identification with the home country, and, more recently, a number of instances of candidates for political office in Latin America campaigning or otherwise seeking support in the US. In addition, a review of some of the effects of globalization on Latino/a communities indicates that a large proportion of Latino/as work in sectors of the economy that are highly interdependent with other countries so that their opportunities are clearly tied to the economic viability of these internation networks.

Given these conditions and characteristics, I would argue that the existing modes of governance in the US cannot promote the effective inclusion of Latino/as in the polity nor the achievement of full and equal societal membership. We have reached a point where the level of democracy in the US will continue to decline unless the institutional framework for political participation and representation is modified in response to the reality of social relations that are no longer contained within the territorially defined boundaries of the nation-state. Just as the latter has made adjustments and created new regional-level instruments and regimes to accommodate the interests of economic actors, so too must there be parallel regionalization of the principles and institutions of governance for democracy to be effective. The consideration and development of regional forms of governance and citizenship are already a reality in Europe, which recognized early on that the process of economic regionalization was not viable without similar structural changes in the institutions and instruments of political governance.[20]

Let me illustrate the argument with the example of Southern California. If the flow of goods, people, culture, capital, images, values, and so forth, that occurs in the region and the networks to which these give rise were to be traced on a map, the territorial boundaries within which the majority of these flows occur would be clearly demarcated. In other words, these networks of interdependence are what in fact determine a community of common fate despite political or legal barriers that might exist. In the case of Southern California, this region of interdependence stretches from the northernmost area of Los Angeles County at the border with Ventura, all the way to the Mexican seaport of Ensenada, some 75 miles south of the international border. This argument, and the supporting evidence, has already been advanced by James Wilkie in a recent volume on regional integration in North America (Wilkie, 1998). Far from being unique, Southern California is but one of several emerging sub- and transnational regions that are the basic units of political and economic reality on the continent. The Pacific Northwest region of the US known as Cascadia, consisting of the Canadian province of British Columbia, Washington, and the northern part of Oregon, is another region where there has been significant integration of the industrial base, including forms of unionization, as well as a high level of cross-settlement and the emergence of a common regional culture. These developed from what initially was an effort by urban areas on both sides of the international border to confront common challenges of environmental degradation. The common linkages and challenges of the tristate region consisting of New York, New Jersey, and Connecticut, although not crossing international borders, nevertheless illustrate that traditional structures of governance, in this case state governments, are no longer capable of responding effectively to what are in effect regionwide issues and challenges. Efforts to address this level of regional integration have even been undertaken within large-scale areas within one country. Toronto, for example, created a regionwide governing structure, the Regional Municipality of

Metropolitan Toronto, which shares responsibility for policy-making with the various municipalities of the area.

Each of these regions constitutes a community of common linked fate based on economic, cultural, and social linkages that function within a common environment. These are what, I would argue, define the boundaries of an organic political community that should be the basis of democratic governance and a regional form of citizenship. This is not to say that there are no common ties with other parts of the country, nor does it address the difficult question of the relationship between these regional political communities and the nation-state as a whole, although the principle of shared governance has already been incorporated in the US in the form of federalism. What these do demonstrate, however, is that legally established borders and boundaries that define the jurisdictional powers of governance as well as establish the criteria for citizenship in these regions no longer correspond with nor facilitate the development of democratic principles. This in effect has resulted in the dedemocratization of regions such as Southern California, where millions of members of the regionally defined society have no opportunity to influence the decisions that affect them directly through the political process. Recent work in regional political economy on governance and scale is now routinely based on the assumption that regions are the basic units of the international system. The development of the EU is but another example of attempts to create new structures of governance that can more effectively address the forms of interdependence across national boundaries that already exists in the region.

CONCLUSIONS IN STRATEGIC CONTEXT

I am proposing that the development of regional forms of democratic governance and corresponding types of citizenship should be seen as a political strategy whose potential *effectiveness* must be assessed in terms of the context within which it would be used and the social and political positioning of the groups advancing it. From my perspective, the goal of strategic political analysis is to identify those aspects within the overall institutional framework of the society that provide structurally based openings or opportunities for reform, that is, conditions or characteristics that are vital to the effective functioning of major institutional spheres, such as the economy, state, and cultural apparatus.

What I am suggesting here is that the very logic and practice of the adjustments in the notion of sovereignty adopted by nation-states, and the US in particular, in response to the processes of globalization have themselves provided the rationale for the argument for transnational, regionally grounded rights for Latino/a communities, which would in effect establish the basis for a form of transnational or regional citizenship. While these communities have played an integral part in the development of those regions in the US most affected by globalization and that are most internationally interdependent, only a small percentage of Latino/as have benefited from their role in that process. From a strategic perspective, the argument for the extension of rights and the development of expanded conceptions and practices of governance and citizenship is rooted in this approach in the fact that the structure of governance has already incorporated the principle of shared sovereignty by establishing a regime of rights for transnational capital. To avoid moving in the direction of parallel rights for Latino/a communities, given the vital role they play in that very transnational economy, would be to risk undermining and eroding the legitimacy of democratic governance. While it is clear that the principles of democratic governance are not supported by transnational corporations on the basis of principle, they do, however, see these as one of the ways of securing the stability required for their effective functioning. I want to make clear that I am not endorsing the interests pursued by transnational firms, but rather arguing that empowerment strategies should be developed that can take advantage of the structures and practices set up to advance those interests and use these to promote the well-being of Latino/a communities. Far from being a utopian vision, this approach can be promoted by educating and urging Latino/a communities, advocates, and organizations to focus on pressuring governments and firms to make the extension of the kinds of rights argued for here a part of the various treaties, conventions, laws, etc., that are developed to promote the transnational sector of the economy and oppose any measures that do not provide for this form of inclusion. Given the demographic shift in the workforce and the interest of corporate actors in having a well-educated labor market, they can ill afford to ignore the fact that Latino/as will be a major component of that workforce.

If the notion of political community I am arguing for is accepted, this would then create a space where the regime of regional rights and their institutional embodiment can play a role in helping to ground and legitimate strategies of empowerment on the part of Latino/a communities. The latter are clearly an integral, although restricted, element of various regional political communities without, however, being fully incorporated into their governing processes. This configuration clearly challenges the notion that rights are the sole province of the nation-state. While the notions of transnational and dual citizenship are progressive advances, they apply only to the status of immigrants and do not really address the limitations imposed by the forms of citizenship on second and older generations of Latino/as. In some ways, these reinforce the notion of the nation-state as the appropriate political community since they only have meaning in terms of the relation between at least two nation-states. Regional citizenship, on the other hand, focuses on the forms of linkages and practices that constitute the basis of a linked fate but are not limited to or defined primarily by the parameters of the nation-state.

The essence of democracy is self-governance within the context of the rule of law. It requires effective participation by all members of the community who share a common, linked fate, which is what defines the effective boundaries of political community. When these boundaries of community are altered as they have been by the processes of globalization, realignments in the political structures of governance, including the nature and scope of rights and citizenship, are required to maintain the legitimacy and long-term viability of a democratic polity. And it is only within this context that principles of social justice can be achieved. While there is no one form that would be appropriate to all areas, in the context of the types of regional integration discussed here, what must begin to emerge are "regional" forms of citizenship based on a regime of regional rights that reflect the basic principles of effective democratic inclusion. And in the current configuration of economic and social relations, these would serve as vital resources that Latino/a members of these political communities would have available to them not only to achieve security and advancements in the economic marketplace but to also be able to create the types of inclusive structures of governance on which an effective democracy must be based.

NOTES

1. Their deaths and issues these raised for the status of citizenship were covered extensively across the country. There were a number of events honoring Gutiérrez and Garibay in their hometowns and elsewhere. For example, see the stories in the *Los Angeles Times,* Tuesday, April 1, 2003, A1; and Thursday, April 3, B2.
2. The troubling aspects that the deaths of Gutierrez and Garibay pose for the status of immigrants vis-à-vis citizenship were addressed in a letter sent by Cardinal Roger Mahoney to President Bush, in which he stated that "there is something terribly wrong with our immigration policies if it takes death on the battlefield to earn citizenship." See the online

version of the letter at http:// press.la-archdiocese.org/2003/030407_LETTER.html.

3. A useful summary of data on the changes in Latino/a communities nationwide can be found in the discussions in a special section on the 2000 census reports in the *Los Angeles Times*, March 30, 2001.

4. Fortunately, a small but important number of works either directly on Latino/as and citizenship or on issues that are related to that relationship have begun to appear. On the former, see, for example, Flores and Benmayor (1997), Rocco (1997, 1999, 2000, 2002a, b), Schuck (1998), and Jones- Correa (2002) . See also the essays in Gracia and De Greiff (2000), which discuss a range of issues that impinge on the question of citizenship.

5. See the range of approaches that are discussed in detail in Isin and Wood (1999).

6. This grounded approach is similar to the kind of framework advanced by Carens (2000) in his contextual study of the political theory of citizenship.

7. While there are a number of works that reflect the diversity among Latino/a groups, see Oboler's *Ethnic Labels, Latino Lives* (1995) for the most thorough, nuanced, and sustained analysis of the political significance of these differences. Also see Hardy-Fanta (1993), Jones-Correa (1998), Trueba (1999), and Hamilton and Stoltz Chinchilla (2001).

8. Although limited to the case of Mexicans, see Rosaldo (1989) and Velez-Ibáñez (1996) for examples of the structural and institutional significance of the cultural dimension.

9. For a useful overview of this literature, see Deveaux (2000).

10. I want to emphasize that my specific focus in this chapter is on a particular literature that addresses the issue of cultural difference and citizenship. This is in no way a claim that the cultural dimension is the most important determinant of power, nor that the economic forms of marginalization within a capitalist system are not a key element in the varied histories and experiences of different Latino/a groups. Instead, my goal here is to suggest the limitations of the current discourse specific to political theory precisely for not addressing the regulative function of citizenship vis-à-vis economic and political institutional relations. This is ironic since the seminal work acknowledged (but seldom addressed) in the contemporary analysis of citizenship is Marshall's *Citizenship and Social Class* (1950), which clearly is concerned with citizenship in relation to the phases of capitalist development in Britain. However, for exceptions that do make the economic realm and capitalist relations central to the study of citizenship, see Sassen's (1996a) "Whose City is It?" and especially chapter 2, "Economic Citizenship," in *Losing Control* (Sassen 1996b). For another approach, see the excellent collection of essays in Crouch *et al.* (2001).

11. This is not to say that Kymlicka's formulation cannot be useful in addressing the situation of Latino/a communities in the US, but because of limitations of length, I will not explore this here.

12. This extended notion of citizenship has been developed in a considerable body of works, particularly some feminist analyses of citizenship. See Lister (1997), Shachar (2001), and in particular Yuval-Davis (1999) and Yuval-Davis and Werbner (1999).

13. For a provocative and innovative analysis of the political and cultural role that the category of "foreigner" has played throughout the history of the US, see the recent study by Honig (2001). Also see the essay by Behdad (1997) for a discussion of the relationship between immigration policies and beliefs and the notion of the "foreigner" in the context of the US. For a discussion of this theme as related to Mexicanos, see Weber (1973).

14. Although they do not discuss Latino/as as a racialized group, Klinkner and Smith (1999) provide a useful discussion of the role of race in each period of US history. And Smith (1997) shows in great detail the connection between racial categories and citizenship in the US, providing convincing evidence of how the latter has been a fundamental mechanism for controlling the nature and extent of membership for over 200 years.

15. Although the processes by which Latino/as have been racialized is not yet a major theme in the social science literature on Latino/as, it is one of the primary foci of the work being carried out by primarily legal scholars in Latino/a critical race theory. See the online volumes Latcrit Primer: A Selection of Articles from the Annual Latcrit Symposia and Related Material at http://www.personal.law.miami.edu/~fvaldes/latcrit/pdf/latcrit_primer_vol1.pdf

16. For a unique and important analysis of the political process and significance of how Latino/as have been labeled, including racially, see the work of Suzanne Oboler (1995, 2002).

17. For studies of citizenship that incorporate a contextual approach, see the essays in Bauböck and Rundell (1998) and Statham and Koopmans (1999).

18. One of the most useful analyses of this relationship between the nation-state, citizenship, and membership is provided by Brubaker (1989).

19. I am adapting the concept of "linked fate" developed by Michael Dawson in his analysis of racial politics in the US (1994).

20. Studies of regionalization are so extensive that it has become virtually a subfield of study. For representative works that focus on the issue of the scale of governance in regional context, see Keating and Loughlin (1997), Keating (1998), MacLeod and Goodwin (1999a,b), Deas and Ward (2000), and Jones (2001).

References

Almaguer, Tomás. 1994. *Racial Fault Lines: The Historical Origins of White Supremacy in California*. Berkeley: University of California Press.

Barrera, Mario. 1979. *Race and Class in the Southwest: A Theory of Racial Inequality*. Notre Dame, IN: University of Notre Dame Press.

Bauböck, Rainer, and John Rundell, eds. 1998. *Blurred Boundaries: Migration, Ethnicity, Citizenship*. Brookfield, VT: Ashgate Publishing.

Behdad, Ali. 1997. Nationalism and Immigration in the United States. *Diaspora* 6:155–178.

Bonilla, Frank, Edwin Meléndez, Rebecca Morales, and María de los Angeles Torres, eds. 1998. *Borderless Borders: U.S. Latinos, Latin Americans, and the Paradox of Interdependence*. Philadelphia, PA: Temple University Press.

Brubaker, Rogers, ed. 1989. *Immigration and the Politics of Citizenship in Europe and North America*. Lanham, MD: University Press of America.

Camilleri, Joseph A. 1990. Rethinking Sovereignty in a Shrinking, Fragmented World. In *Contending Sovereignties: Redefining Political Community*, ed. R. B. J. Walker and Saul H. Mendlovitz, 13–44. Boulder, CO: Lynne Rienner.

Carens, Joseph H. 2000. *Culture, Citizenship, and Community: A Contextual Exploration of Justice as Evenhandedness*. New York: Oxford University Press.

Castles, Stephen, and Alastair Davidson. 2000. *Citizenship and Migration: Globalization and the Politics of Belonging*. New York: Routledge.

Castles, Stephen, and Mark J. Miller. 1993. *The Age of Migration: International Population Movements in the Modern World*. New York: The Guilford Press.

Cohen, Edward S. 2001. *The Politics of Globalization in the United States*. Washington, DC: Georgetown University Press.

Crouch, Colin, Klaus Eder, and Damian Tambini, eds. 2001. *Citizenship. Markets, and the State*. New York: Oxford University Press.

Dawson, Michael C. 1994. *Behind the Mule: Race and Class in African-American Politics*. Princeton, NJ: Princeton University Press.

Deas, Iain, and Kevin G. Ward. 2000. From the "New Localism" to the "New Regionalism:" The Implications of Regional Development Agencies for City-Regional Relations. *Political Geography* 19:273–292.

Deveaux, Monique. 2000. *Cultural Pluralism and Dilemmas of Justice*. Ithaca, NY: Cornell University Press.

Flores, William V., and Rina Benmayor. 1997. *Latino Cultural Citizenship: Claiming Identity, Space, and Rights*. Boston, MA: Beacon Press.

Glenn, Evelyn Nakano. 2002. *Unequal Freedom: How Race and Gender Shaped American Citizenship and Labor*. Cambridge, MA: Harvard University Press.

Gracia, Jorge J. E., and Pablo DeGreiff, eds. 2000. *Hispanics/Latinos in the United States: Ethnicity, Race, and Rights*. New York: Routledge.

Habermas, Jurgen. 1995. Citizenship and National Identity: Some Reflections on the Future of Europe. In *Theorizing Citizenship*, ed. Ronald Beiner. Albany: State University of New York Press.

Hamilton, Nora, and Norma Stoltz Chinchilla. 2001. *Seeking Community in a Global City: Guatemalans and Salvadorans in Los Angeles*. Philadelphia, PA: Temple University Press.

Hardy-Fanta, Carol. 1993. *Latina Politics, Latino Politics: Gender, Culture, and Political Participation in Boston.* Philadelphia, PA: Temple University Press.

Harris, Bruce. 2003. From Illegal Immigrant to Marines, Soldier's Death Spotlights Immigrants. From *Hispanic Online.* http://www.hispaniconline.com/lstyles/article.html?SMContentIndex=8&SMContentSet=0, March 27.

Held, David. 1991. Between State and Civil Society: Citizenship. In *Citizenship,* ed. Geoff Andrews, London: Lawrence and Wishart.

———. 1999. The Transformation of Political Community: Rethinking Democracy in the Context of Globalization. In *Democracy's Edges,* ed. Ian Shapiro and Casiano Hacker-Cordón, 84–111. Cambridge: Cambridge University Press.

Holston, James, ed. 1999. *Cities and Citizenship.* Durham, NC: Duke University Press.

Honig, Bonnie. 2001. *Democracy and the Foreigner.* Princeton, NJ: Princeton University Press.

Isin, Engin F., ed. 2000. *Democracy, Citizenship and the Global City.* New York: Routledge.

Isin, Engin F., and Patricia K. Wood. 1999. *Citizenship and Identity.* Thousand Oaks, CA: Sage.

Jones, Martin. 2001. The Rise of the Regional State in Economic Governance: "Partnerships for Prosperity" or New Scales of State Power? *Environment and Planning A* 33: 1185–1211.

Jones-Correa, Michael. 1998. *Between Two Nations: the Political Predicament of Latinos in New York City.* Ithaca, NY: Cornell University Press.

———. 2002. Seeking Shelter: Citizenship and the Divergence of Social Rights and Citizenship in the U.S. In *Dual Nationality, Social Rights and Federal Citizenship in the U.S and Europe: The Reinvention of Citizenship,* ed. Randall Hansen and Patrick Weil, 233–63. New York: Berhahn Books.

Keating, Michael. 1998. *The New Regionalism in Western Europe: Territorial Restructuring and Political Change.* Northhampton, MA: Edgar Elgar Publishers.

Keating, Michael, and John Loughlin. 1997. *The Political Economy of Regionalism.* London: Frank Cass.

Klinkner, Philip A., and Rogers M. Smith. 1999. *The Unsteady March: The Rise and Decline of Racial Equality in America.* Chicago: University of Chicago Press.

Kymlicka, Will. 1995a. *Multicultural Citizenship: A Liberal Theory of Minority Rights.* Oxford: Clarendon Press.

———, ed. 1995b. *The Rights of Minority Cultures.* Oxford: Oxford University Press.

Kymlicka, Will, and Wayne Norman. 1995. Return of the Citizen: A Survey of Recent Work on Citizenship Theory. In *Theorizing Citizenship,* ed. Ronald Beiner, 283–322. Albany: State University of New York Press.

————, eds. 2000. *Citizenship in Diverse Societies.* New York: Oxford University Press.

Lister, Ruth. 1997. *Citizenship: Feminist Perspectives.* New York: New York University Press.

MacLeod, Gordon and Mark Goodwin. 1999a. Reconstructing an Urban and Regional Political Economy: On the State, Politics, Scale, and Explanation. *Political Geography* 18:697–730.

————. 1999b. Space, Scale and State Strategy: Rethinking Urban and Regional Governance. *Progress in Human Geography* 23: 503–527.

Marshall, T. H. 1950. *Citizenship and Social Class.* Cambridge: Cambridge University Press.

McGrew, Anthony. 1997. Globalization and Territorial Democracy: An Introduction. In *The Transformation of Democracy? Globalization and Territorial Democracy,* ed. Anthony McGrew, 1–24. Cambridge: Polity Press.

McKinnon, Catriona, and Iain Hampsher-Monk, eds. 2000. *The Demands of Citizenship.* New York: Continuum.

Menchaca, Martha. 2001. *Recovering History, Constructing Race: The Indian, Black, and White Roots of Mexican Americans.* Austin: University of Texas Press.

Nieguth, Tim. 1999. Beyond Dichotomy: Concepts of the Nation and the Distribution of Membership. *Nations and Nationalism* 5:155–173.

Oboler, Suzanne. 1995. *Ethnic Labels, Latino Lives: Identity and the Politics of (Re)Presentation in the United States.* Minneapolis: University of Minnesota Press.

————. 2002. The Politics of Labeling: Latino/a Cultural Identities of Self and Others. In *Transnational Latina/o Communities: Politics, Processes, and Cultures,* ed. Carlos G. Vélez-Ibàñez and Anna Sampaio. New York: Rowman and Littlefield.

Papastergiadis, Nikos. 2000. *The Turbulence of Migration: Globalization, Deterritorialization and Hybridity.* Maiden, MA: Polity Press.

Raz, Joseph. 1994. *Essays in the Morality of Law and Politics.* Oxford: Clarendon Press.

Rocco, Raymond. 1996. Latino Los Angeles: Reframing Boundaries/Borders. In *The City: Los Angeles and Urban Theory at the End of the Twentieth Century,* ed., Edward Soja and Allen J. Scott. Berkeley: University of California Press.

————. 1997. Citizenship, Culture, and Community: Restructuring in Southeast Los Angeles. *In Latino Cultural Citizenship: Claiming Identity, Space, and Rights,* ed. Bill Flores and Rina Benmayor. Boston, MA: Beacon Press.

————. 1999. The Formation of Latino Citizenship in Southeast Los Angeles. *Citizenship Studies* 3:253–266.

————. 2000. Associational Rights Claims, Civil Society and Place. In *Democracy, Citizenship and the Global City,* ed. Engin F. Isin. London: Routledge.

————. 2002a. Refraining Postmodernist Constructions of Difference: Subaltern Spaces, Power and Citizenship. In *Transnational Latina/o Communities: Politics, Processes, and Cultures*, ed. Carlos G. Vélez-Ibàñez and Anna Sampaio. New York: Rowman and Littlefield.

————. 2002b. Citizenship, Civil Society, and the Latino City: Claiming Subaltern Spaces, Reframing the Public Sphere. In *Transnational Latina/o Communities: Politics, Processes, and Cultures*, eds. Carlos G. Vélez-Ibàñez and Anna Sampaio. New York: Rowman and Littlefield.

————. 2006. Democracy, Education, and Human Rights in the U.S.: Strategies of Latino/a Empowerment. In *Latino education: An Agenda for Community Action Research*, eds. Pedro Pedraza and Melissa Rivera. Mahwah, NJ: Lawrence Erlbaum.

Rosaldo, Renato. 1989. *Culture and Truth: The Remaking of Social Analysis*. Boston, MA: Beacon Press.

Sassen, Saskia. 1996a. Whose City Is It? Globalization and the Formation of New Claims. *Public Culture* 8:205–223

————. 1996b. *Losing Control?: Sovereignty in an Age of Globalization*. New York: Columbia University Press.

————. 1998. *Globalization and Its Discontents: Essays on the New Mobility of People and Money*. New York: The New Press.

Schuck, Peter H. 1998. Plural Citizenships. In *Immigration and Citizenship in the 21st Century*, ed. Noah M. J. Pickus, 149–191. New York: Rowman and Littlefield.

Shachar, Ayelet. 2001. *Multicultural Jurisdictions: Cultural Differences and Women's Rights*. New York: Cambridge University Press.

Short, John Rennie and Yeong-Hyun Kim. 1999. *Globalization and the City*. New York: Addison Wesley Longman.

Smith, Rogers M. 1997. *Civic Ideals: Conflicting Visions of Citizenship in U.S. History*. New Haven, CT: Yale University Press.

Statham, Paul, and Ruud Koopmans. 1999. Challenging the Liberal Nation-State: Postnationalism, Multiculturalism, and the Collective Claims Making of Migrants and Ethnic Minorities in Britain and Germany. *American Journal of Sociology* 105:652–696.

Trueba, Enrique (Henry) T. 1999. *Latinos Unidos: From Cultural Diversity to the Politics of Solidarity*. Boston, MA: Rowman and Littlefield.

Vandenberg, Andrew, ed. 2000. *Citizenship and Democracy in a Global Era*. New York: St. Martin's Press.

Vélez-Ibáñez, Carlos G. 1996. *Border Visions: Mexican Cultures of the Southwest United States*. Tucson: The University of Arizona Press.

Walker, R. B. J. 1990. Sovereignty, Identity, Community: Reflections on the Horizons of Contemporary Political Practice. In *Contending Sovereignties: Redefining Political Community*, ed. R. B. J. Walker and Saul H. Mendlovitz, 159–185. Boulder, CO: Lynne Rienner.

Weber, J. David. 1973. *Foreigners in Their Native Land: Historical Roots of the Mexican Americans*. Albuquerque: University of New Mexico Press.

———. 1992. *The Spanish Frontier in North America.* New Haven, CT: Yale University Press.

Wilkie, James W. 1998. Afterword: On Studying Cities and Regions: Real and Virtual. In *Integrating Cities and Regions: North America Faces Globalization,* ed. James W. Wilkie and Clint E. Smith, 525–544. Joint publication of Universidad de Guadalajara, UCLA Program on Mexico, and El Centre Intemacional Lucas Alamán Para El Crecimiento Económico, AC.

Young, Iris Marion. 1990. *Justice and the Politics of Difference.* Princeton, NJ: Princeton University Press.

———. 2000a. *Inclusion and Democracy.* Oxford: Oxford University Press.

———. 2000b. Structure, Difference, and Hispanic/Latino Claims of Justice. In *Hispanics/Latinos in the United States: Ethnicity, Race, and Rights,* ed. Jorge J. E. Gracia and Pablo De Greiff. New York: Routledge.

Yuval-Davis, Nira. 1999. The "Multi-Layered Citizen:" Citizenship in the Age of "Globalization." *International Feminist Journal of Politics* 1:119–136.

Yuval-Davis, Nira and Pnina Werbner, eds. 1999. *Women, Citizenship and Difference.* London: Zed Books.

Notes on Contributors

Alejandra Castañeda is currently a postdoctoral fellow at the Universidad Iberoamericana in México City, where she is conducting research on the U.S.-México Border, Water, and Law. She was a researcher at the Instituto Nacional de Antropología e Historia from 2003 to 2005. Her research interests include citizenship, migration, the border, and Mexican migrants' political activities, legal battles, participation, and political rights. Her publications include *The Politics of Citizenship of Mexican Migrants* (NY: LFB Scholarly Publishing, 2006) and "Ciudadanía y Transnacionalismo: el desafío de los Mexicanos en Estados Unidos" in *Mexicanos en el Estados Unidos: la nación, la política y el voto sin fronteras,*ed. Arturo Santamaría (Universidad Autónoma de Sinaloa, 2001).

Kathleen Coll is a cultural anthropologist and lecturer in Feminist Studies at Stanford University. Her research focuses on issues of immigration, gender, and cultural citizenship in the US. Her book in progress is "Remaking Citizenship: Latina Immigrants and New American Politics." She previously taught Women, Gender and Sexuality Studies at Harvard University, Anthropology and Women's Studies at City College of San Francisco, and also coordinated a Central America solidarity organization based in the San Francisco Bay Area. Her research has received support from the Radcliffe Institute for Advanced Study and the Social Science Research Council.

Nicholas De Genova is Assistant Professor of Anthropology and Latina/o Studies at Columbia University. He is the author of *Working the Boundaries: Race, Space, and "Illegality" in Mexican Chicago* (Duke University Press, 2005), co-author (with Ana Y. Ramos-Zayas) of *Latino Crossings: Mexicans, Puerto Ricans, and the Politics of Race and Citizenship* (Routledge, 2003), and editor of *Racial Transformations: Latinos and Asians Remaking the United States* (Duke University Press, 2006). He has previously published articles in the *Annual Review of Anthropology, the Journal of Latin American Anthropology, Latin American Perspectives, Estudios Migratorios Latinoamericanos, Anthropology and Humanism, Public Culture, Transition, and Social Text.*

Cristina Escobar received her PhD. in 1998 from the Department of Sociology at the University of California, San Diego. She was a post-doctoral fellow at Princeton University (Sawyer Seminar on Migration and Citizenship) from 1999 to 2000 and a Social Science Research Council Fellow on International Migration from 2000 to 2001. She has taught at Rutgers University-Camden and Temple University, and is currently a visiting assistant professor at Franklin and Marshall College. Since 2004, she has worked as a research associate at the Center for Migration and Development at Princeton University in a comparative research project on transnational organizations of Latin American immigrants in the United States (Comparative Immigrant Organization Project [CIOP]).

Greta A. Gilbertson is Associate Professor in the Department of Sociology and Anthropology at Fordham University. Her interests include immigration, citizenship, and gender. Her most recent publication (with Audrey Singer) is "The Emergence of Protective Citizenship in the USA: Naturalization Among Dominican Immigrants in the Post-1996 Welfare Reform Era," *Ethnic and Racial Studies* (26)1: 25–51 (2003).

Suzanne Oboler is Associate Professor of Latin American and Latino Studies at the University of Illinois at Chicago. Her current research focuses on race, citizenship, and national belonging in the Americas, and on the transnational experience of first- and second-generation South Americans in the US. She is the founding editor of the international academic journal *Latino Studies* (published by Palgrave Press, UK) and co-editor in chief of the 4-volume *Oxford Encyclopedia of Latinos and Latinas in the United States* (Oxford University Press, 2005). Her publications include: *Ethnic Labels, Latino Lives: Identity and the Politics of Representation* (University of Minnesota Press, 1995) and *Neither Enemies nor Friends: Latinos, Blacks, Afro-Latinos* (co-edited with Anani Dzidzienyo; Palgrave, 2005).

Ana Y. Ramos-Zayas is Assistant Professor of anthropology and Latino & Hispanic Caribbean Studies at Rutgers University. She is the author of *National Performances: Class, Race, and Space in Puerto Rican Chicago* (University of Chicago Press, 2003) and co-author of *Latino Crossings: Mexicans, Puerto Ricans, and the Politics of Race and Citizenship* (Routledge, 2003). Her current work examines spatialized conceptions of race and citizenship among Puerto Rican and Brazilian youth in Newark, New Jersey.

Raymond Rocco is Associate Professor of Political Science at the University of California at Los Angeles. His work focuses on the relationships between globalization, democracy, citizenship, human rights and marginalized communities, with an emphasis on Latin American communities in the US. Recent publications include "Reframing Postmodernist Constructions of Difference: Subaltern Spaces, Power and Citizenship" (in Carlos G. Velez-Ibañez, Anna Sampaio, and Manolo Gonzalez-Estay, eds. *Transnational Latina/o Communities: Politics, Processes and Cultures.* Rowman & Littlefield, 2002) and "Democracy, Education, and Human Rights in the U.S.: Strategies of Latino Empowerment" (in P. Pedraza and M. Rivera, eds. *Latino Education: An Agenda for Community Action Research.* Mahwah, NJ: Lawrence Erlbaum Associates, 2006).

Hinda Seif is Visiting Assistant Professor of Labor Studies and Employment Relations at Rutgers University, New Brunswick, and Research Associate with the Center for Comparative Immigration Studies at the University of California, San Diego. Trained as a cultural anthropologist, Seif studies the transformation of US democracy and citizenship under conditions of large-scale undocumented Latin American migration.

Lorrin Thomas is Assistant Professor of History at Rutgers University-Camden. She is working on a book titled *Juan Q. Citizen: Puerto Rican Migrants and the Politics of Citizenship in New York City, 1917–1970* (forthcoming, University of Chicago Press) that explores the meaning—and limits—of liberal citizenship for a group marked by its colonial relationship to the US.

Bonnie Urciuoli is Professor of Anthropology at Hamilton College. Her research interests focus on linguistic and cultural anthropology, specializing in race, class, and language ideology in U.S. culture. Her book *Exposing Prejudice: Puerto Rican Experiences of Language, Race, and Class* was published in 1996; it was awarded the 1997 Gustavus Myers Center Award for the study of human rights in North America.

Monica Varsanyi earned her PhD in Geography at the University of California at Los Angeles in 2004, and is currently a postdoctoral fellow at the Centers for Comparative Immigration Studies and U.S. - Mexican Studies at the University of California, San Diego. Her work addresses the growing gap between territorial and popular sovereignty in the United States, with particular reference to unauthorized migration. She is currently working on a book that explores local (city, county, state) policy initiatives re: unauthorized residents (i.e., debates over driver licenses, in-state college tuition, and the growing acceptance of the *matriculas consulares*), and how these local policies are in tension with the federal government's role in regulating borders, immigration, and citizenship policy.

Index